Tired of "quick-fix" diets that don't work?

- Do you want more energy to enjoy your life?

- Do you regularly try and fail at dieting?

- Do you have a weight problem?

- Do you regularly consume *diet* foods?

- Do you believe that *healthy* equals *low fat?*

- Do you rely on restaurants for most of your meals?

- Do you want to feed your family healthier food?

- Do you want scientific tests to determine your diet?

If you answered "yes" to any of these questions, you need to read this book! We'll explain how eating according to your individual *Diet Type* is the real secret to better health.

The Hauser Diet™:
A Fresh Look at Healthy Living
reveals that each of us need to follow an individualized diet. If you've tried and failed at other diets, we will explain the reason why! With over 15 years of clinical experience, we have developed an advanced form of *Diet Typing* to help start you on the road to wellness now. Learn how serum blood pH and glucose tolerance testing can scientifically determine which diet is best for you!

The Hauser Diet will show you how to choose healthy, great tasting foods and cook according to your Diet Type.

The Hauser Diet focuses on *real food* and *real answers* to the age old question: What diet is best for me?

The Hauser Diet™—A Fresh Look at Healthy Living

ISBN 0-9661010-7-3

Published by
BEULAH LAND PRESS
715 LAKE STREET, SUITE 600
OAK PARK, ILLINOIS 60301

For more information on Beulah Land Press: 708-848-5011 • www.beulahlandpress.com

Printed in the United States of America.

Recipe consultation, food styling and photography by Steven Chiappetti, Chef, Dreamworld Productions. www.chiappetti.com.

Food and portrait photography and styling by Alan Klehr • Churchill & Klehr Photography • www.aklehr.com.

Other food photography by Marion A. Hauser. Food styling also by Marion A. Hauser and Nicole M. Baird.

Cover design by Travis Mitchell • www.id3ntitycrisis.com.

Design, illustrations and charts by M. Hurley • Teknigrammaton Graphics • www.teknigram.com • 773-973-1614.

Select photostock © Dreamstime Agency.

to Mom & Dad:

Your influence in my life is immeasurable.

I cannot thank you enough for all you have taught me—

strong work ethic, being kind to people, and having heart...

You poured your life into your children—and for that I am thankful.

You can't help but succeed with parents like the two of you!

Mom—thanks for all the fun times cooking together, teaching me to love food, cooking, entertaining, planning, and trying new things. I'll never forget trying our first meal in the wok, Italian meat balls, or cake and cookie decorating! Many of the recipes you have shared with me over the years are contained in this book! Thanks! The only reason I can cook like I can is because of your patience and guidance in the early years!

Dad—thanks for teaching me about never giving up, hard work, learning to change a tire and the oil on my car, loving baseball (and going to all those Cubs games), running track (and watching all my meets), and what it means to serve others. You're more of a servant than I'll ever be!

Marion

Disclaimer

The information presented in this book is based on the experiences of the authors, publishers and editors, and is intended for informational and educational purposes only. In no way should this book be used as a substitute for your own physician's advice.

Because medicine is an ever-changing science, readers are encouraged to confirm the information contained herein with other sources. The authors, publishers, and editors of this work have used sources they believe to be reliable to substantiate the information provided. However, in view of the possibility of human error or changes in medical sciences, neither the authors, publishers, or editors, nor any other party who has been involved in the preparation of publication of this work warrants that the information contained herein is in every respect accurate or complete, and they are not responsible for errors or omissions or for the results obtained from the use of such information. This is especially true, in particular, when a person follows one of the diets in this book and a bad result occurs. The authors, publishers, and editors of this book do not warrant that *The Hauser Diet*™ or any diets described in this book, including The Lion Diet, The Otter Diet, The Bear Diet, The Monkey Diet, or The Giraffe Diet, is going to be effective in any medical condition and cannot guarantee or endorse any certain type of diet or other practitioner. It is the responsibility of the individual person who follows the guidelines in this book to thoroughly research the topic and pick a particular practitioner that they feel is qualified to provide medical nutritional advice.

Medical personnel should use and apply the principles of *The Hauser Diet*™ or any related diets described in this book, including the Lion Diet Type™, Otter Diet Type™, Bear Diet Type™, Monkey Diet Type™, and/or Giraffe Diet Type™, only after they have received extensive training and demonstrated the ability to properly educate the clients. The authors, publisher, or editors or any other person involved in this work, are not responsible if unqualified practitioners or any other person attempt to utilize the principles described in this book and a bad result occurs.

If *The Hauser Diet*™ or any diet plan described in this book, including the Lion Diet Type™, Otter Diet Type™, Bear Diet Type™, Monkey Diet Type™, or Giraffe Diet Type™, or any other treatment regime appears to apply to your condition, the authors, publisher, and editors recommend that a formal evaluation be performed by a physician who is competent in utilizing the techniques related to *The Hauser Diet*™. Those desiring an evaluation should make medical decisions with the aid of a personal physician. No medical decisions should be made solely on the contents or recommendations made in this book.

———

Table of Contents

ABOUT
THE
AUTHORS

about the authors

*We are passionate about **The Hauser Diet**! We feel that we have found the answer to the age-old question "What should I eat?" Most people do not know how to eat. We want to tell you how **The Hauser Diet** can teach you how to eat right for your Diet Type, as well as teach you how to get back into the kitchen and prepare real food that is not only healthy, but fast and easy. Our combined areas of expertise, education, and experience provide a unique approach to diet that may help you obtain the health you have always wanted.*

Marion A. Hauser, M.S., R.D.

As a "food enthusiast" Marion's career path lead her to the field of Nutrition and Dietetics, having completed her M.S. in Nutrition and Dietetic Internship from Eastern Illinois University and her B.S. in Nutrition from the University of Illinois at Urbana-Champaign. As a licensed and registered dietitian, Marion worked in the hospital setting for 10 years. While working at two major university-affiliated hospitals, Marion's duties ranged from teaching resident physicians, conducting nutritional research studies, and precepting dietetic interns, to working with pediatric, transplant, and I.V. nutrition support for critical care patients.

She now works as the Chief Executive Officer of Caring Medical and Rehabilitation Services, in conjunction with her physician-husband, Ross. Together they have written eight books on natural health including *Prolo Your Pain Away!* and *Prolo Your Sports Injuries Away!* Marion is a well-known speaker and writer on a variety of topics related to Natural Medicine and Nutrition.

After years of research and work with clients at Caring Medical, Marion and Ross Hauser developed an objective testing procedure called *Diet Typing* to determine which diet is best for each individual person. As an avid athlete, having completed numerous marathons, Olympic Distance Duathlons, century cycles, and a wide array of other races, Marion put *Diet Typing* to the test by using it to maximize her race performances, optimize her energy and normalize her weight. Having a passion for food, cooking, and educating, Marion embarked on writing *The Hauser Diet™: A Fresh Look at Healthy Living* so that she could share the power of *Diet Typing, The Hauser Diet way!*

Nicole M. Baird, C.H.F.P.

Ross A. Hauser, M.D.

Nicole M. Baird is a NESTA Certified Holistic Fitness Practitioner and Certified Personal Trainer. Her path crossed the Hausers in 1999 when she began working at Caring Medical and Rehabilitation Services, SC. and saw the power of Natural Medicine change her life. Being a triathlete and involved in various athletics, Nicole had some injuries and health issues. She utilized many of the techniques, including Prolotherapy, to cure her chronic pain. In 2003, Nicole began an apprenticeship in patient nutrition education with Ross and Marion Hauser.

She later headed up the Caring Medical Nutrition Center as the Nutrition and Lifestyle coach. Much of the work involved translating the science of **The Hauser Diet** to realistic everyday food and activity. Nicole coached clients on ways to incorporate healthy, practical foods into their recommended diets. Through this experience she saw how food alone can have profound effects on people's overall health. Having a love for food, food shopping, and cooking, she tried almost every one-diet-fits-all approach for herself, from low fat "diet" foods to vegetarianism to high protein, but only found real solutions in **The Hauser Diet**. Nicole is currently the manager of Beulah Land Nutritionals, a natural high-quality supplement resource, and the administrative team leader for Caring Medical and Rehabilitation Services. Along with her experience at Caring Medical, her passion for writing and research brought her on the journey of co-authoring *The Hauser Diet: A Fresh Look at Healthy Living!*

Dr. Hauser received his medical degree from the University of Illinois. He went on to do his residency in Physical Medicine and Rehabilitation at Loyola-Hines-Marianjoy. He subsequently joined the practice of Gustav Hemwall, M.D., one of the founders and experts in Prolotherapy. Dr. Hauser teamed up with his wife Marion to form one of the most comprehensive Natural Medicine centers in the country, Caring Medical and Rehabilitation Services in Oak Park, Illinois. Together they have written eight books on natural health including *Prolo Your Pain Away!* and *Prolo Your Sports Injuries Away!* Through their work, they came up with an objective testing procedure called *Diet Typing* to figure out which diet is best for individuals. Ross took the information to heart and went from 180 pounds and 30% body fat to 148 pounds and 7% body fat. While eating according to his Diet Type, Dr. Hauser found the energy to exercise, and was able to run several marathons and ultramarathons and to complete numerous Ironman Triathlons.

We have poured a lot of ourselves and our experiences into this book. We hope that it is as much a joy for you to read as it was for us to write—for you!

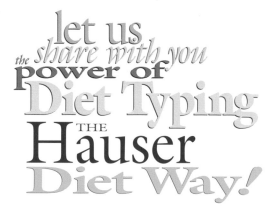

let us the *share with you* **power of** Diet Typing THE Hauser Diet Way!

WHAT WILL YOU GET FROM THIS BOOK?

what will you get *from this* book?

Having worked in the field of nutrition for many years, both in the hospital setting, as well as the clinic setting, I know how frustrating it is to try to help people lose weight or to change their eating habits due to a newly diagnosed disease or medical condition. Having never had a weight problem, I really couldn't relate to my patients that much. Then I turned 35! I now know what my mother and mother-in-law were talking about! It is much more difficult—especially for women—to continue to eat the same way you used to eat and to stay the same weight. Something in your body has drastically changed. How do we deal with that?

The Hauser Diet is a diet for life! It is not a "diet" per say, but a way of life. It teaches you concepts that you should utilize for yourself, as well as everyone in your family. There are so many different diets out there, and nobody knows where to turn. Having gone from working in the "traditional" nutrition arena, to a more "alternative" approach, I know that there is no one perfect diet for everyone. Everyone's body is different and responds differently to different foods. This is why some people do best on a carnivorous diet (meat-based), where others feel best on a vegetarian based diet (plant-based). Even patients with the same medical condition might need to eat differently, depending on their individual Diet Types. For example, some people with heart disease may actually need to eat more meat and eggs and less carbohydrates! It's true!

It is our goal to help explain what we at Caring Medical and Rehabilitation Services in Oak Park, Illinois, have discovered about diet, nutrition, wellness, and exercise. The Hauser Diet will teach you the following:

1. How you can make and follow an individualized lifestyle plan that is built only for you, utilizing simple tests, including finding out your Diet Type.

2. How to eat for your particular Diet Type. You will discover that the percentage of protein, carbohydrates, and fats that you require for your individualized lifestyle plan is probably different from your friends and spouse.

3. How certain circumstances like weather changes, moving to a different location, or day of the menstrual cycle can affect how you should be eating.

4. How always feeling cold or hot is an indicator that your body chemistry is not in balance and how to reverse it by eating differently, before it leads to chronic disease.

5. How eating according to your Diet Type can optimize your health and sports performance.

6. How eating according to your Diet Type will help to increase your energy and help you reach your weight goals.

7. How to really read a food label. What information should you be looking for? You may be surprised!

8. How to understand the basics of healthy shopping, including where to find the healthiest foods in the grocery store. You might not believe it yet, but you don't have to live in the pre-made diet food aisles!

9. How to prepare healthy recipes with great taste! We have included some of our favorite recipes. These will help you get started on your new eating plan for life, including ways to add soy to your diet, interesting salads, tasty smoothies, ways to make vegetables taste good, and how to dress up that chicken breast!

10. How to put it all together and make it work for you! Enhance your enjoyment of life by taking charge of your health!

Life is a journey . . . a good one. As a very good friend of ours, Tim Kenny, always says, "enjoy the journey."

Marion A. Hauser, MS, RD

the **Hauser** ...is not a "diet," **Diet** *but a* *way of life*

WHAT'S THE
HYPE ABOUT
DIET TYPE?

what's the hype *about* diet type?

What is Diet Type?

Did you ever wonder why some people appear to have really fast metabolisms enabling them to eat everything and never gain weight, where others' metabolisms are such that it seems like if they just look at food, they gain weight? Or why do some people wake up ravenous in the morning, and others grab a cup of coffee and do not feel hungry until the afternoon? These are all good questions. At Caring Medical, our natural medicine clinic in Oak Park, IL, we receive questions everyday from our patients regarding what type of diet they should eat.

We hear questions such as:

- Are high protein diets dangerous?
- Won't I lose weight if I just eat a balanced diet?
- What diet is best for an athlete?

- Should I go on a vegetarian diet?
- Do you recommend sugar-free, fat-free foods?
- How often should I eat?

The answers to these individual questions are different for each person reading this book and they lie in the manner in which a person extracts energy from his or her food. Our basic answer is always the same: Know your Diet Type! Knowing your Diet Type allows you to determine the foods that give you the maximum amount of energy, as well as which foods help you attain optimal health. We call this the *Hauser Diet—a fresh look at healthy living!*

In my (Marion's) personal experience, after graduating with my Masters in Nutrition, I worked as a registered dietitian in the hospital setting for 10 years prior to working at Caring Medical and Rehabilitation Services. I became quickly frustrated with the concept that everyone should be on the same diet—the low fat, high carbohydrate diet that was promoted by the American Dietetic Association, the American Diabetes Association, and the U.S. government. It just doesn't work for everyone. To be honest with you, it didn't work for most people! At first I just thought that I was a poor motivator and that I couldn't help my patients change their eating habits. But you can't say that for everyone. Some people are very diligent in following what you tell them to do. I remember one man who was not improving telling me, "I swear I am just eating that little chicken breast and all those diet products that you told me to get." That really hit me. I knew he was telling the truth. Yet, this "diet" did not work for him.

Each person is an individual. Therefore, each person requires an individualized nutritional, as well as a medical plan. Not all patients are the same. Medicine is not a "cookbook." I quickly moved out of nutritional counseling into critical care medicine because at least this way, I felt like I was making a difference. Our nutrition support team worked with the physicians of patients who were unable to consume food by mouth. They were therefore being fed by an alternate route, either via a tube down their nose or via an IV in their vein. This field of nutrition is called *enteral* and *parenteral nutrition*. We could figure out based on the patients' height, weight, laboratory tests, vital signs, oxygenation status, ventilator settings, overall medical status, and many other monitors, exactly what we needed to "feed" them. There are some exciting things happening in this arena. This is what really sparked my interest in figuring out what is best for each individual person, as far as their diets are concerned.

After leaving the hospital setting, and embarking on a whole new adventure at Caring Medical and Rehabilitation Services, Dr. Ross Hauser, my husband, and I were able to do some research for a number of years to come up with what we call the **Hauser Diet**—an individualized approach to your diet and health. We were both trained "traditionally" and thought that we would be able to offer people things that could help improve their lives. As a physician, Dr. Hauser found that he was very limited in treatment options, if he just continued down the same path from residency training. Thankfully for our patients, he was, and still is, very interested, almost obsessed, to find out the best approach to treating human disease. He is currently one of the most respected Natural Medicine and Prolotherapy specialists in the world! Check out the website **www.caringmedical.com** for more information about Dr. Hauser and Prolotherapy.

After years of analyzing our patients' nutritional needs and dietary requirements, we determined that people fit into one of five Hauser Diet Types: Hauser Diet #1, Hauser Diet #2, Hauser Diet #3, Hauser Diet #4, and Hauser Diet #5. The five Hauser Diets vary in their amounts of protein, carbohydrates, and fats. Hauser Diets #1 and #2 are highest in protein and fat, while being lower in carbohydrates. Hauser Diet #3 is a more balanced diet. Lastly, the Hauser Diets #4 and #5 lean more toward the vegetarian side of the diet spectrum. When recommending these various diets for our clients

based on Diet Typing results, we found ourselves using animal terms to describe the diets. For instance, when we had to tell someone to eat a high protein diet, we would say "Think of how a lion eats. A lion eats a lot of meat." Instantly, you could see the light bulb go on and the client would get the picture that he had to start eating a lot of meat because he had the physiology of a lion. Think about it. You would not picture a lion nibbling on a corn cob would you? We all understand that in the animal kingdom, a lion has to eat meat and a giraffe has to eat leaves to be vibrant and healthy. Well, humans are the same way. Some humans have a similar physiology to a lion and need to eat a lot of meat, whereas others have the physiology similar to a giraffe and need to eat vegetarian foods.

This "animal" idea stuck with us and we asked Zoo Nutritionist Kerri Slifka (Brookfield Zoo, near Chicago) if she could help us elaborate on it. She graciously provided the macronutrient breakdown of various animal diets. Based on this information, we were able to pair the five Hauser Diets to an animal with similar nutrition needs. These animals have now become the names of the five diets: The Lion Diet, The Otter Diet, The Bear Diet, The Monkey Diet, and The Giraffe Diet. *(See Figure 1-1.)*

Brookfield Zoo Nutritionist Kerri Slifka, working with one of her animals.

FIGURE 1-1 The Hauser Diet Lets You Eat Like an Animal!

The five Hauser Diets vary in the amount of protein, fat, and carbohydrates allowed. The Lion Diet allows the most protein and fat; the Giraffe Diet allows the most carbohydrates.

Lion Diet Type™
60% protein
25% fat
15% carbohydrates

Otter Diet Type™
50% protein
25% fat
25% carbohydrates

Bear Diet Type™
30% protein
20% fat
50% carbohydrates

Monkey Diet Type™
20% protein
15% fat
65% carbohydrates

Giraffe Diet Type™
10% protein
10% fat
80% carbohydrates

In the animal kingdom, it is important for animals to eat according to their "Diet Types."

When asked what would happen if an animal were to eat the wrong type of diet, Kerri answered, "Basically, the animal will get sick. For instance, in horses (this would apply to captive zoo equids as well), excess starch (grain compared to hay) can decrease the pH of the GI tract, which can lead to gas which can lead to lactate absorption and metabolic acidosis. This can cause colic, diarrhea, and laminitis. In domestic cats, high carbohydrate (cereal) diets increase blood glucose and insulin. It can predispose cats to obesity and diabetes. In domestic dogs (and I would apply this to some bear species) high fat diets are associated with pancreatitis.

Nutrition can also affect reproduction as well. Weight issues for the females can lead to difficulties in getting pregnant, giving birth or laying eggs. In males, if they are too chubby to mount the female, weight is an issue too. Beyond the physical, imbalanced nutrients (low vitamin E, carotenoids, fatty acids, for example) can reduce fertility. Viability of eggs can be affected by any number of nutrients."

Isn't it interesting that we see examples of these same issues in humans everyday? To us, it is obvious that many people are not eating according to their Diet Types. To optimize health, it is important for us to find the foods that give us a maximum amount of energy!

Cyclist Study

To further explain the concept that different Diet Types extract energy differently from foods let's take a look at this study on cyclists. This study examined the changes and type of substrate (energy source or food) utilization both at rest and during exercise in 61 trained cyclists. The object of the study was to determine the type of macronutrients that elite athletes used during exercise. In other words, did they utilize fat, protein, and/or carbohydrates equally as an energy source (substrate) and what variables accounted for the difference? To determine this, the athletes' respiratory exchange ratio (RER) was measured both in the fasting and at different exercise intensities. The RER correlates with the ability to break down fat for energy. This is called *fat oxidation*. Those who are able to break down fat for energy will have high fat oxidation rates. Those who cannot break down fat for energy will have low fat oxidation rates (low RER).

The results revealed that some cyclists could completely break down fat for energy (high percent fat oxidation rate), where others broke down fat very poorly (low percent fat oxidation). This occurred both at the resting state, and at various levels of exercise intensity. Therefore, the study concluded that the cyclists who

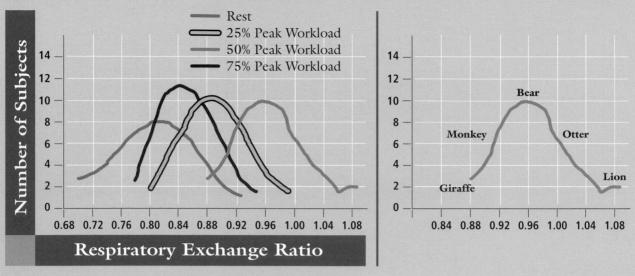

FIGURE 1-2 Ability to Oxidize Fat Remains Constant in Cyclists

Notice that the bell shape curve is reproduced, no matter if RER is measured at rest, 25, 50, or 75% peak workload. In other words, most people have the physiology of Bears, then Monkeys and Otters, and lastly, Lions and Giraffes. The higher the RER, the better the cyclist is at breaking down fat; conversely, the lower the RER, the better the cyclist is at breaking down carbohydrates. Their RER remained constant at all intensities of the workout, which means, once a Lion, always a Lion; and conversely, once a Giraffe, always a Giraffe, when it comes to the breakdown of fat for energy.

could break down fat efficiently should eat a more carnivorous (meat) diet, where those who could not break down fat would be better suited to consume a more vegetarian-type diet.[1] *(See Figure 1-2.)*

The large variability in RER at rest and during exercise at different intensities in endurance-trained athletes turned out to be a major finding in this study. The relative rate of fat oxidation at rest ranged from 23 to 93%, which is nearly a fourfold difference in fat oxidation in these athletes with above-average performance ability. Another important finding of this study was the normal distribution of RER at rest was maintained during exercise of increasing intensity. The normal distribution was found even at the relatively high exercise intensity of 70% maximum work. **This means "once a lion always a lion," even while exercising intensely.** Many athletes feel that they need to carbohydrate-load before and during a race in order to provide quick energy. This study reveals that if you are a lion-type person, you are able to mobilize your fat into energy so you don't need to be as concerned with eating simple carbohydrates for athletic events.

Why can't we all just eat the same diet?

The various factors that determine substrate (energy, or food) utilization were also analyzed in this cyclist study. Though the answers to this question are not completely known, this study and others give us some insight. Animals, including people, have muscle fibers that are slow-twitch or type I fibers. These types of muscle fibers more frequently use fatty acids as a fuel source because they have a high oxidative capacity due to a high mitochondrial and capillary density. The other type of muscle fiber is fast-twitch or type II muscle fibers which utilize carbohydrates for a substrate or energy source. Carnivorous Diet Types possess more enzymes in their body system (cells, muscle fibers, blood stream) that are needed for fat metabolism. The vegetarian Diet Types, on the other hand, have a higher percentage of enzymes that are needed to break down carbohydrates.

Other factors that have correlated with substrate utilization for energy include body type, various blood levels of substrates, and the sex of the individual. Men typically have a more efficient ability to utilize fat as an energy source than women.[3] *(See Figure 1-3.)*

Meat versus Vegetables: Energy Utilization Trends

	Carnivore (Meat-based)	Vegetarian (Plant-based)
Muscle Fiber	Type I (Slow-twitch)	Type II (Fast-twitch)
Enzyme Source	Lipase	Carbohydrase
Gender	Male	Female
Substrate (energy source)	Fat	Carbohydrate

FIGURE 1-3 Carnivores or meat eaters, tend to have more slow twitch muscle fibers, use fat as a substrate, use lipase as a primary enzyme to breakdown the fat, and are commonly male. Vegetarians have an increased number of fast twitch muscle fibers, use carbohydrates as a substrate, use carbohydrase as a primary enzyme to breakdown carbs, and are typically female.

What does all this mean?

For some reason, animals know what to eat.

The lion eats meat and the giraffe eats leaves from a tree. Other animals, such as bears, eat a combination of plant and animal-based foods. Humans, on the other hand, are not so sure about what they should eat. Many people just eat and eat until they are fat. Don't get us wrong, we love to eat and eat, but in order to maintain a healthy weight, we have to be sure to eat according to our Diet Type. Weight gain starts when you eat a significant proportion of foods outside of what you should eat for your Diet Type. Subsequently, many people find themselves scheduling an appointment with a nutritionist, physician, or the latest weight loss center, where they are put on a low calorie or even a very low calorie diet. This slows their metabolism further, contributing to their obesity. (See Figure 1-4.)

When you eat carbohydrates, proteins, and fats in the wrong proportions for your Diet Type—your metabolism slows. Following a very low calorie diet for rapid weight loss, popular with many people who want to lose weight quickly for a particular event, will slow your metabolism even further. The long term results will be terrible. You may look better initially, but your energy will eventually decline because the food you are eating is not giving you enough energy. The end result is an even slower metabolism that causes fatigue, lethargy, and "brain fog." When you return to eating regular food, the weight comes right back because of your slowed metabolism. Providing your body with just the right amounts of food or the substrates in the proper proportions is key to supplying the energy needs to the cells, blood, and body tissues.

A better approach to achieving optimal health and weight is to understand what substrate, or food, your body most efficiently utilizes. In other words, what is your Diet Type? Your Diet Type should consist of the breakdown of protein, fat, and carbohydrates that gives you the maximum amount of energy. Let's take

Gains weight.
Slows metabolism.
No energy.
Decreases exercise.
Person eats wrong diet for their Diet Type...
Produces obesity.
Cycle Continues
Continues to eat the wrong diet.
Slows metabolism further.
Metabolism slows further.

FIGURE 1-4 The Consequences of Ignoring Diet Type
Eating the wrong diet slows the metabolism, causing a downward spiral of events leading to obesity and further decline in health.

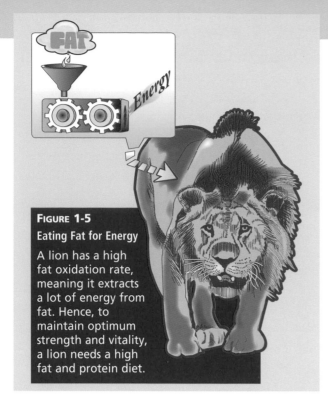

FIGURE 1-5

Eating Fat for Energy

A lion has a high fat oxidation rate, meaning it extracts a lot of energy from fat. Hence, to maintain optimum strength and vitality, a lion needs a high fat and protein diet.

a look at "low fat" diets. Many people are obsessed with counting fat grams and buying low fat foods. But how do you know if you need a low fat diet? If you are able to utilize fat efficiently, fat is actually a healthy fuel for your body. *(See Figure 1-5.)* However, if you are unable to convert the fat into energy, guess what your body will do with it? You got it! Store it as fat! In other words, the individual whose fat oxidation rate is low will get fatter and more lethargic by eating a diet high in fat. But the benefits of eating according to your Diet Type are not just weight loss. Diet Typing is used to help balance the body chemistry which can help in the overall management of many conditions, including weight problems, chronic fatigue, allergies, chronic pain, diabetes, heart disease, cancer, rheumatologic diseases, and autoimmune disorders, just to name a few.

> **For some,**
> Eating more fat = getting fat.
>
> **And for others,**
> Eating more fat = getting more energy!

So how do I find out which animal I am?

Caring Medical and Rehabilitation Services utilizes two specific tests—and frequently a third and fourth—to determine Diet Type: venous Blood pH, Oxidative Rate, and often Food Allergy testing and Insulin levels.

Once the results of these variables are determined, your true Diet Type is known. We discuss these five Diet Types and the Hauser Diet principles in greater detail in the next few chapters. But first, let's take a look at each one of these variables and their role in determining your Diet Type.

1. Venous Blood pH: Am I Acid or Alkaline?

One of the key variables related to the Hauser Diet is blood pH. You may recall talking about pH in chemistry class in high school. The pH is the level of acidity or alkalinity. Many practitioners have never heard of looking at a person's blood pH as it relates to their patients' overall wellness. We have done a lot of research on this topic at Caring Medical, and have observed a multitude of patients over the years. Our physicians utilize venous blood pH as a means of testing basic metabolic physiology in our patients. Interestingly enough, we have found that subtle changes in blood pH can have profound effects on your overall health, feeling of wellness, level of fatigue, pain, weight, and a myriad of other conditions.

Why Blood pH Is So Important!

Energy is required for a human being to function optimally. The production and management of sustainable biological energy resources is of vital concern for everyone. In its most basic terms, energy comes from the breakdown of the oxygen we breathe and the food that we eat.

Energy production takes place inside each cell of our bodies. All cells must produce energy to survive. The energy factories in our bodies are called mitochondria.

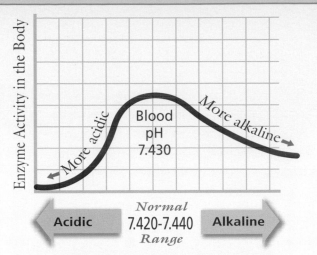

FIGURE 1-6 The Relationship Between Blood pH and Enzyme Activity

Keeping your blood pH in balance will help to boost your cellular energy output by optimizing enzyme efficiency.

Each one is like its own power plant. The primary function of these tiny organelles (each cell contains between 500 and 2,000 mitochondria) is to convert energy found in nutrient molecules (carbohydrates, fats, proteins, and oxygen) and store it in the form of adenosine triphosphate (ATP). ATP is the universal energy-yielding molecule used by enzymes to perform a wide range of cellular functions. Humans cannot survive, even for a second, without a constant supply of ATP.

The main process by which the mitochondria and cells produce energy is called oxidative phosphorylation. The chemical reactions that occur to produce energy are sped up by catalysts called enzymes. Without enzymes the energy required to run these reactions is much greater. Thus, enzymes increase the efficiency of our energy production and in the end, more energy is produced. (See Figure 1-6.)

Each enzyme has an optimal temperature and pH range for its activity. In the human body, the enzymes that have to do with energy production function best when human body temperature is 98.2-98.6 degrees Fahrenheit with a venous blood pH of 7.420-7.440. (See Figure 1-7.) When the body temperature or blood pH moves out of this range, enzyme activity declines. When the enzyme activity is inhibited, so is energy production both inside the cells and in the body as a whole.

You can easily imagine the consequences of this for the human body. Without optimal energy, fatigue starts to set in. For many who do not eat according to their Diet Types, fatigue is most often the first symptom of ill health a person experiences. If eating habits do not change, chronic fatigue results. Eventually mental fatigue also develops. With the fatigue comes a slowed metabolism, which is the body's response to decreased energy. Because the person cannot do as much as he/she used to do, feelings of being stressed or overwhelmed often result. Many people will then start overeating due to the stress. Soon weight gain appears. If the person is an athlete, of course, sports performance plummets. Because the body has reduced energy, it develops an impaired immune and healing response. Illnesses can start to develop like upper respiratory and sinus infections. Often muscle, ligament, and tendon injuries do not heal and the person develops various body aches. Because the body does not have enough energy, detoxification processes are hampered. The person can develop whole body aches and feel fluish (usually consistent with a "fibromyalgia" diagnosis from their primary care doctor.) The bowels

pH Ranges

Acidic				Normal			Alkaline			
7.380	7.390	7.400	7.410	7.420	7.430	7.440	7.450	7.460	7.470	7.480

FIGURE 1-7 The Range of Blood pH

The blood pH figures are based on the testing equipment and protocols used at Caring Medical and Rehabilitation Services in Oak Park, Illinois. For the purposes in this book, a venous blood pH below 7.420 is considered "acidic" and a venous blood pH greater than 7.440 is considered "alkaline." Normal venous blood pH is between 7.420 and 7.440.

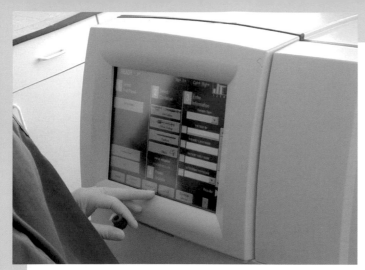

can become leaky and then various allergies appear. Do you see how this vicious cycle continues? It does not take a genius to see that the body requires optimum energy to function. Optimum energy can only occur if the enzyme systems of the body are functioning at peak capacity. The enzymes cannot function at peak capacity if the body's temperature and pH levels are not within the normal range. This is why blood pH is so vital!

What Is Normal Blood pH?

Our pH meter at Caring Medical shows a normal serum blood pH level at about 7.420-7.440. Caring Medical uses a CLIA approved blood pH measuring system. The 7.420-7.440 range is our normal based on testing we have done and by using our specific pH meter at the temperature of our lab. The normal range will vary depending on the pH meter. The pH of the body, as you can see, has a very narrow range for normal levels. Small fluctuations of 0.01 increments can produce profound changes in the body.

As discussed above, the enzymes in the cells and blood, as well as digestive enzymes, are easily affected by the pH of the blood. In the stomach, trypsin and chymotrypsin require the pH to be acidic or low, whereas enzymes in the small intestine such as sucrase and maltase require an alkaline pH. Enzymes in the blood that run most of the the chemical reactions of the body (for instance, the enzymes of the Kreb's cycle) need a neutral blood pH or 7.420-7.440. A pH level

outside of that range will cause them to work a lot slower or not at all.

Many factors can change pH and affect how you should eat. When the blood pH is acidic (low), you should be eating a Lion or Otter Diet because protein and fat contained in these diets raise the blood pH, moving the blood pH into the normal range.

When your blood pH is alkaline (high), you should be eating more vegetarian, like the Monkey or Giraffe Diets because the carbohydrates contained in these diets lower the blood pH, making it more normal.

A normal pH means that you should be eating more of a balanced diet, such as a Bear Diet, which is a balance of protein, carbohydrates, and fat.

The following are examples of the effects of pH that we have observed at Caring Medical through our many years of clinical experience in this area.

How Hormones Effect Blood pH
Menstrual Cycle/Pregnancy

We have seen a number of women at Caring Medical who get horrible migraines on day 20 to 23 of their menstrual cycles. What happens at this time of the month? Progesterone levels increase. Increased progesterone levels raise the venous blood pH and make the body more alkaline. This is easy to remember because Progesterone levels are elevated in pregnancy (hence the name, Progesterone, meaning "pro-gestation"). Think about it—most pregnant women usually complain of being too warm during their pregnancy. Thus, to cure a person of "menstrual migraines," a woman would have to get her blood pH lower. A woman with high pH levels on day 20 of the cycle should switch her eating to include more carbohydrates such as fruits and whole grains in order to lower her pH down to more normal. *(See Figure 1-8.)*

We have also seen women who become pregnant and all of a sudden become a totally different person. Completely "normal" women can become seriously

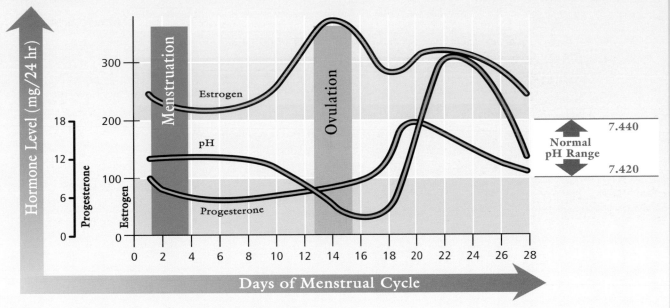

FIGURE 1-8 The Blood pH and Menstrual Cycle Relationship

This graph shows how blood pH changes in relationship to the menstrual cycle. From days 18-24 in the menstrual cycle, blood pH rises as progesterone levels rise, producing PMS symptoms. Eating more carbohydrates just before, and during, this time will reduce pH and lessen these symptoms. From days 10-16, pH levels decline as estrogen levels increase, producing cramping and irritability. Eating more protein and fat, just before, and during, this time will increase blood pH and lessen these symptoms.

anxious and fearful. Typically all they have to do to feel better is eat according to the Monkey or Giraffe Diet to increase the percent of nutrients coming from carbohydrates, which will balance (by lowering) the blood pH levels, thus, stabilizing their emotions and physical symptoms.

Maria: Was she becoming mad? Here is an example of blood pH and pregnancy: Maria, already a Caring Medical patient, saw Dr. Hauser because she was having a hard time with her first pregnancy and was feeling very anxious, when normally she was a very "together" person. Maria's blood pH was tested and it was 7.480 which was one of the higher levels we have seen at the office. Maria reported that since becoming pregnant, these were her symptoms (directly quoted from our patient):

1. **"*Nausea and vomiting are very bad.* If I eat breakfast in the morning, the nausea and vomiting is twice as bad. It is best that I vomit first, then wait about an hour and then eat something. I feel better if I eat something for breakfast like bananas, a bagel, or some toast with jam.

2. *Heat:* Since becoming pregnant, I can't seem to cool down. I always feel hot. The only time I feel at a comfortable temperature is as soon as I wake up in the morning.

3. *Fatigue:* I am always tired and feel like I could sleep all day. In fact on the weekends, I wake up at about 8:30 am. Go back to bed at about 1:00 pm and sleep until 7:00 pm or so. Then I go to bed at about 11:00 pm. My legs always feel tired and it is an effort to make it through the day.

4. *Irritability:* I am much more irritable. I lose my temper a lot more easily than before. I could cry at the drop of a hat. I have become much more sensitive to people's comments. I cannot stand to be touched. I am too hot and uncomfortable and would prefer it if people did not touch me."

To lower her blood pH into normal range, a high carbohydrate diet was prescribed for Maria, yet she had the battle of making sure she got enough protein for her growing baby. She visited with our Nutrition and Lifestyle Coach for Giraffe Diet instructions. She began incorporating more vegetarian forms of protein into her diet. After about two weeks of following the diet, many of her symptoms abated.

Testosterone and Estrogen: Men have much higher testosterone levels than women. When testosterone is given to a woman, this hormone can induce a hot flash if she is given too much. Testosterone makes the body hotter, so it raises the blood pH. When a woman has hot flashes what hormone is she usually given? Correct—she is usually given estrogen. Estrogen, therefore, helps cool off the body, therefore lowering the blood pH. Estrogen causes the blood pH to drop on days 10-16 in the menstrual cycle. *(Refer back to Figure 1-8.)* If a woman experiences symptoms such as cramping, irritability, or other symptoms during that time of the month, then eating more protein and fat would be recommended.

Thyroid hormone is known for its effects to raise the metabolism. When the metabolism is raised, the body temperature goes up. Thyroid hormone raises body temperature. If this is true, what effect would it have on blood pH? Yes, it would raise the blood pH! You're getting this! So people who are hypothyroid are typically cold, and therefore would tend to have low (acidic) blood pH levels. The blood pH can be raised by the Lion or Otter Diet. You are on now your way to understanding Diet Typing!

Cortisol and DHEA: DHEA is a precursor to testosterone, so yes, it raises blood pH. Similarly, people who have too much Cortisol tend to gain weight. When you gain weight, you are typically warm (with all that added insulation from the fat). So both Cortisol and DHEA tend to raise the blood pH levels.

How does this information help you?
People everywhere are learning about the amazing benefits of natural hormone replacement. At our office,

we have many years of experience prescribing these when a patient's blood hormone levels are low. Natural (bio-identical) hormones include estriol, progesterone, DHEA, testosterone, cortisol, thyroid, and others. Understanding the effects these hormones have on blood pH can assist in the care of a patient. Lisa is a good example of this.

Lisa came to Caring Medical after being prescribed natural hormone replacement at another physician's office. She was on estrogen, testosterone, DHEA, and thyroid. She felt better on these hormones, including having more energy and a better sex drive. However, after starting on the hormone therapy, she began complaining of sleeplessness and anxiety. Her other doctor checked her hormone levels and stated they were fine, so what was the problem? You're right—her blood pH was too high. When Lisa's doctor didn't find anything wrong with her hormones, she came to us for another opinion. We checked her blood pH to confirm our suspicion and found that though the hormones were correcting some problems, they were creating others. The problem of sleeplessness and anxiety caused from alkaline blood pH could be fixed by lowering her blood pH with food. Lisa followed the Monkey Diet, which is high in carbohydrates, and her symptoms vanished. This is just one small example of how the Hauser Diet takes into account multiple aspects of a person's health in order to have the best effect.

Other Factors that Effect Blood pH
Stress
During times of stress our bodies actually become more acidic. We often turn to comfort foods such as chips, cookies, candy, popcorn, and soda during these times, which will actually worsen the stress because these foods enhance the acidity. This can then lead to problems with hypoglycemia and fatigue. This may explain, however, why some people feel better when they are under stress. They may be the alkaline pH people whose stress is lowering the pH into the normal range.

Personality Type

In our experience, we have observed tendencies in personality types. The "Type A-Go-Getters" tend to have alkaline, or high, blood pH levels. We have found that supplementing with magnesium and potassium tends to relax them, as well as lower their pH levels. The "Type B-More Relaxed" people tend to be on the acidic side, and require higher protein diets. Adding more salt to the diet, along with supplementing with calcium will help balance their pH levels.

Age

It is important to realize that your pH can change for a variety of reasons. The aging process, of course, can also have an effect on pH (just like everything else!). You may have been eating a Monkey Diet for most of your adult life feeling great on it. Then all of a sudden, you no longer feel good. Fatigue, weight gain, and allergies may set in. Typically as people age, they start feeling colder, right? Go to any nursing home and you'll find the temperatures in the rooms are set at near boiling. You'll start peeling off your extra layers of clothing if you stay there for any length of time! In other words, the blood typically becomes more acidic as we age, To balance this, protein and fat usually need to be increased in the diet. Here's a case of a man with the exact same thing happening to him!

Jim is a 49 year old male who ate a high carbohydrate diet for most of his life. All of a sudden, he developed allergies which he never had before. We tested his pH and ran an allergy test on him. His blood pH was 7.405 and the allergy test revealed that he was allergic to gluten. His pH became acidic and he became allergic to gluten—which is contained in wheat and other grain products. Guess what? Jim needed to change his eating to the opposite end of the Hauser Diet spectrum. He had changed from a Monkey to a Lion! He needed a diet that was higher in protein and lower in carbohydrates. Some of his allergy problem could be related to a break down in the gut wall, leading to a leaky gut type syndrome. Jim changed his diet

accordingly, as well as started a supplement program to help nourish the gut. Within a month he was feeling like his old self again. Was it difficult for him to change? Of course! Change is always difficult! But he likes how he feels, so he sticks with it! We retest Jim's pH every six months just to be sure he's in balance.

The right diet was wrong for you!

We wanted to share an example of a patient named Pat. Pat saw a Natural Medicine doctor for vague GI complaints and fatigue. He put her on a zero grain Candida diet. This diet involves complete elimination of sugar and grains. In other words, it is a high protein, low carbohydrate diet similar to the Lion Diet. Pat is a very compliant patient, so she followed the diet strictly. She felt great for three years on the high protein diet.

After this time, however, she found herself losing that great feeling, and actually felt worse and worse. She couldn't sleep. She was extremely anxious. She

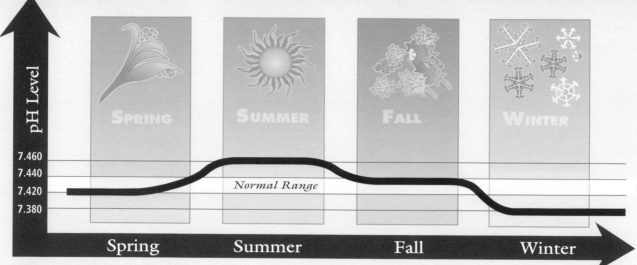

FIGURE 1-9 Blood pH and Seasons

Moderate temperatures during the spring and fall seasons cause blood pH levels to stay the same. In the extreme heat of the summer, blood pH's rise. In the cold of the winter, pH's can plummet below normal range. This is why symptoms can be revealed during summer or winter months.

became very depressed, and even suicidal. She came in to Caring Medical describing this scenario. Dr. Hauser surmised that the high protein diet initially balanced her acidic blood pH, but then over time raised it too much to the point where she had become too alkaline. We checked her pH level and it was 7.492. We have since seen this phenomena in many other patients. High anxiety = High pH. Treatment? Pat was given a high-dose Vitamin C IV. After that IV, her pH went down to 7.440. She was told to eat more carbohydrates everyday. Amazingly enough, her symptoms started abating and she began to feel much better. She was on our "wall of fame" in the hallway of our office—completely back to normal and feeling great again! She now follows the Bear Diet to stay in balance. She comes in to get her pH level checked every six to eight months.

Seasons/Weather

A case that really sticks out in our minds is a 48 year old woman who struggled with weight and fatigue for years. She told us that she will gain about 10 pounds in the winter and lose six pounds in the summer. She says that she usually feels good on a Lion or Otter Diet, but sometimes feels more fatigued in the summer, which

she found to be strange. She was tested in the summer and her blood pH at that time was 7.467. Interesting, isn't it? This patient is very compliant with following the Lion Diet. She is typically a carnivore who feels good on a high protein diet during the cooler months. Her pH increases too much, even above normal, (i.e., she becomes more alkaline) in the summer (due to the heat). At this time, we prescribed the Bear Diet which included more carbohydrates than the Lion or Otter Diets. So during the summer, she can actually eat a few more carbohydrates like fruits and whole grains. (See Figure 1-9.)

In the winter, when her blood pH lowers, (i.e., she becomes too acidic), she requires more alkalinizing foods such as protein. We prescribed the Lion Diet in the winter which is much higher in protein and lower in carbohydrates. When she made these changes in her diet, her blood pH levels stabilized and she felt good all year round.

Marion's Story

As a runner, you really hate it when something stops you from doing what you love to do—run! My running was getting better and better. I completed three marathons and a host of other races, including duathlons. But the

> Good health has allowed me to achieve physical feats beyond my wildest dreams, including finishing a number of 26.2 mile marathons.

start of "running season" (March/April) was starting to become something I dreaded, instead of anticipate. I was repeatedly getting "heat headaches" when running during the summer, (or really, in any temperature over 60 degrees). I had no problem running during the winter. Having alkaline pH tendencies, I started to figure out what the problem was. Running heats up your body, which in and of itself makes it more alkaline. Cold weather decreases pH, therefore, it only made sense that I would feel better in the cold. As an alkaline person, this meant that the cold weather lowered my high blood pH into the normal range.

What do I do now? During the warm summer months, I make sure to consume acidifying foods such as fruits, fruit juices, and Emer'gen C powdered Vitamin C from **www.beulahlandnutritionals.com** in order to acidify my blood. During the summer, I have to strictly follow the Monkey Diet. By doing so, I have been able

to greatly reduce the problem of headaches during exercise. I still prefer running in cooler weather, but now I am not completely shut down by the heat. If I do feel overheated after a run, I take an ice pack and put it on my neck and head or jump in a cold shower or swimming pool if they are available.

More On the pH-Weather Connection

We feel that this is a very important point, so we want to make sure you understand it. Let's say a group of us went skiing in the mountains of Colorado. The temperature that day was hovering below 32 degrees Fahrenheit. We are all cold, but had a great time skiing all day. At the end of the day, we are looking for a place to relax and have something to eat. Would we want to get a light salad and a fruit drink, or would we want a heavier food like a steak? The majority of us, if we are in tune with what our bodies are craving at the time, would vote for the steak house.

Likewise, if we were on the beaches of Florida all day, roasting in the 100 degree heat, would we want something light like a salad and fruit or something heavy like a steak after our day of fun in the sun? Yes, we would be more inclined to want something light like a salad, fruit, and/or fish. Most of us have not thought about the reasons for this. The answer lies in how weather (temperature) affects the blood pH. *(See Figure 1-10.)*

The warmer the temperature gets, the more pH increases (gets higher). It is this elevated venous blood pH that causes some of the symptoms associated with heat, including headaches, nausea, and extreme fatigue. To lower the blood pH down into the normal range the body will crave foods that help acidify the blood. These are foods that are high in carbohydrates, most commonly breads, pasta, salads, fruit, and sugary items. When we are thirsty in the heat of the summer we prefer lemonade to milk, correct? The milk would raise our blood pH because of the fat and the protein, whereas the lemonade would lower our blood pH because of the acidic lemon and sugar. Colder weather

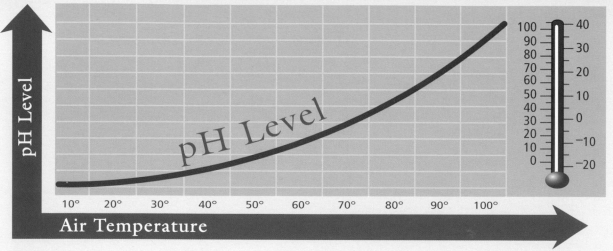

FIGURE 1-10 Temperature and Blood pH
The effect of temperature on blood pH: The higher the temperature, the higher the blood pH. Likewise, the colder the temperature, the lower the blood pH.

lowers the pH (becomes more acidic.) To raise the blood pH back into the normal range, the body will crave foods that raise the blood pH, such as protein and fat. Thus, we crave steaks and other meats.

Take this one step further! Do you feel best in hot weather or cold weather? If you feel better in hot weather, it is probable that you have a low blood pH (acidic) and thus need to be on the Lion or Otter Diet, or a diet containing more fat and protein to get your blood pH back into the normal range. The person who tends to feel best in cold weather will have alkaline blood compared to normal and needs foods that will lower blood pH. Eating according to the Monkey or Giraffe Diet would be best because these provide the carbohydrates that will help balance alkaline blood.

Weather can change how you feel. If you live in New York City and have a condition such as knee arthritis but it doesn't bother you when you travel to Florida, we have an answer to why that is. It is likely that your blood pH is too acidic when you are in New York. Since New York is a colder climate, your symptoms are worsened because the weather is acidifying your blood even more. But in Florida, the warm weather normalizes your blood pH, causing your symptoms to decrease. Your symptoms will be better while in New York if you eat to alkalinize your blood (just as the

warm weather has done for you in the example.) You do this by eating a diet that is higher in protein and fat such as the Lion and Otter Diets. This is why we recommend athletes·regularly get Diet Typing. It allows the athlete to properly plan their nutrition for their events and optimize their sports performances.

The athlete who tried to bulk up on protein during the summer: A young athlete named Jacob who was entering his senior year in high school came to see us at Caring Medical. His parents brought him to the office because he had terrible migraine headaches during warm weather. He also noted that his overall athletic performance was sub-optimal in hot weather. He was a very good football player hoping to earn a college scholarship. He reported to us that his headaches were less frequent and his performance on the football field was much better during the colder weather. Jacob is 6'3" and still growing and currently weighs 280 pounds.

Dr. Hauser told Jacob that he suspected that his blood pH was alkaline (above normal) and that he needed to eat more vegetables and fruits to lower his blood pH back to normal. With that, Jacob gave Dr. Hauser the "you've got to be kidding!" look. Interestingly enough, delving into Jacob's history a little more, we found out that Jacob wanted to "bulk up" to get ready for the football season, so he had been consuming an inordinate amount of protein during the summer to accomplish this, which Dr. Hauser suspected had alkalinized his blood too much. His blood pH was 7.478 on initial testing, which is alkaline. Jacob was instructed to add more carbohydrates and to take extra vitamin C (to acidify the blood).

What happened after Jacob started doing this? His headaches abated and his athletic performance quickly improved, despite the heat of the summer and early fall.

Listen to your body! Think about this! If you are an acidic person with a low pH, you really need to follow your Lion or Otter Diet most closely during the colder months. Because the cold makes you more acidic, you must avoid acidifying foods such as coffee, breads, pasta, rice, potatoes, fruit, fruit juice, and sugar. When the temperature is warmer, you are able to liberalize your diet a little more and include a few more carbohydrates.

A practical example of this is the people who get sick around the holidays. They are most likely people with acidic blood who cave in and eat a lot of sweets and alcohol during the holidays. As we said above, these people need to eat more protein-containing foods in the cooler months such as November, December, and January. The ones who get really sick are most likely filling up on carbs, carbs, and more carbs! They have one cookie, then a piece of pecan pie, then before you know it they are consuming candy, cakes, cookies, eggnog and all sorts of sinful goodies all day long. The blood pH all the while becomes more and more acidic. The end result is being stuck sick in bed with a bunch of pillows and a box of tissues!

The Ultimate Test of Rising Temperatures and Blood pH

The reason that outside temperature raises blood pH is because it raises body temperature. To prove this point, we put five Ironman triathletes into the hyperthermia chamber that we have in our office at Caring Medical. We tested their body temperature and

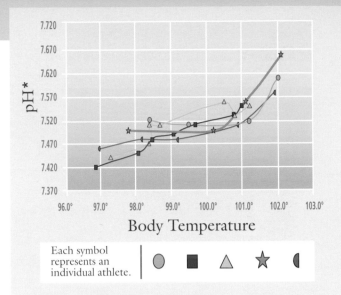

FIGURE 1-11 Rises in Body Temperature Correlates to Rises in Blood pH

A direct correlation between a rise in the five athletes' blood pH levels was observed with a concurrent rise in body temperatures.

This study was conducted at Caring Medical using a blood pH meter which had a "normal" venous blood pH range of 7.500-7.520.

blood pH every 15 minutes, as well as monitored their symptoms, vital signs, hydration, and electrolyte status. A direct correlation between a rise in the five athletes' blood pH levels was observed with a concurrent rise in their body temperature. *(See Figure 1-11.)*

This data was collected as part of a study to prove this point. All five of these athletes completed a recent grueling Ironman Triathlon race in very hot conditions. For those of you who may not know, the Ironman race is a marathon in three sports—a 2.4 mile swim, 112 mile bike ride, and a 26.2 mile marathon run— all in one day. All five athletes were in tremendous shape and are great runners. However, all five had suboptimal races, due to the heat of the race which peaked during the last event—the run. All of the athletes experienced nausea, lack of appetite, cramping, and exhaustion during the run. With the rising outside temperatures came a corresponding rise in body temperature. Of all the blood parameters that we checked during this study, only blood pH changed significantly. The longer they remained in the hyperthermia chamber, the hotter they got; their body temperatures rose to 102 degrees Fahrenheit.

Along with the rise in temperature came basically all of their symptoms that they felt in the Ironman race—nausea, lack of appetite, cramping, and exhaustion. The athletes were taken out of the chamber when they could no longer take it!

The goal for these and other athletes who have difficulty in the heat or cold is to get your blood pH in the right range before the start of competition. If heat is the issue, an athlete must strive for acidic blood pH (7.380-7.410) prior to the competition. The heat of the race will cause the blood pH to move into the normal range (7.420-7.440) during the competition. Remember, heat raises blood pH. If the blood pH is within normal range during the event, performance will be enhanced because the blood enzyme systems start producing more and more energy, as we discussed earlier in the chapter.

Conversely, the person who has issues with the cold weather should strive for alkaline blood pH (7.450-7.480) prior to their cold weather competition. Competing in the cold weather will cause the blood pH to move into the normal range if the athlete started out alkaline, because cold temperatures acidify the blood pH, and will consequently enhance athletic performance. Many cold weather events take place in our area of the country (Chicago) every year—from skiing to long distance running. I clearly remember one specific event where we experienced this cold weather phenomenon. We attempted to run "The Huff Ultramarathon"—the frosty, frigid Huff. I was going to run one 10-mile loop (having never run more than six miles in my life) and Ross was going to attempt the entire 30-mile run. At this time, we did not fully understand the role of pH, weather, and nutrition. The air temperature that day was 9 degrees Fahrenheit with a wind chill of well below zero. Needless to say, we bonked on this race because, although we were dressed warmly, we did not eat nearly enough food, let alone protein and fats, in order to keep our blood pHs balanced. The other factor working against us was the large pasta dinner we ate the night before because we

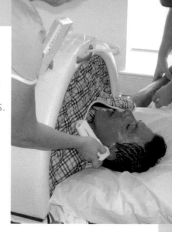

thought we had to carb-load. After finishing the race, we piled every blanket we had on top of us and fell asleep for four hours. Good thing we were able to wake up or we would not be here to talk to you about the Hauser Diet. We raced over to the local restaurant and devoured ribs and chicken! I can still remember that meal. Obviously, our race performances were suboptimal that day. But we learned an important lesson.

Summary of the blood pH and temperature relationship: Understanding the relationship of temperature to blood pH is key to understanding the basic tenants of the Hauser Diet. Knowing whether you feel better in hot or cold weather can give tremendous clues into what diet is best for you. Listen to your body! It's trying to tell you something important! *(See Figure 1-12.)*

The Effect of pH on Real People!

Here are a couple more cases of patients whose pH levels were changed by diet which in turn produced significant improvement in their overall health and well-being.

The Case of Heidi
Changing pH produces profound results for this athlete: Heidi came to Caring Medical because her ankle and knee were giving her trouble during long distance running, actually causing her to stop running altogether. Heidi heard about Caring Medical's success with Prolotherapy, an injection technique to repair ligaments and tendons, and thought she was a good candidate for it.*

Heidi received Prolotherapy treatments to the weak areas, particularly her ankle and knee. After a few weeks, her injuries were healed and she was excited

---

* Note: *For more information on Prolotherapy, see www.prolonews.com or www.prolotherapy.org.*

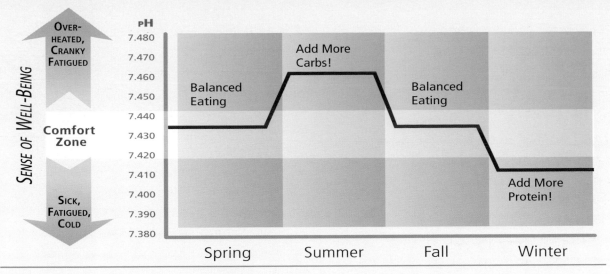

FIGURE 1-12
Summary of the Blood pH and Temperature Relationship
Effect of temperature on blood pH: The higher the temperature, the higher the blood pH, thus the need to increase carbohydrates in the diet. Likewise, the colder the temperature, the lower the blood pH, requiring more protein and fat in the diet.

to be back to running. The fascinating aspect of this case is that Heidi revealed in her history that she hated running in the cold and was always getting sports-related injuries more frequently in the cold weather. She tried everything she could to become a better athlete, reading all sorts of sports medicine and training literature. She was eating six to eight servings of grains and pasta per day and not over-training. She received comprehensive Natural Medicine testing to determine reasons for her time plateaus and increased injury rate.

She was shocked to find out that her blood pH was 7.385 (normal is 7.420-7.440 per our blood pH meter) and that she was a fast oxidizer of food. She met with our Nutrition and Lifestyle Coach and found that she had a carnivorous physiology. She needed to follow the Lion Diet, but she was eating like the Monkey Diet. She was feeding her Lion physiology the food of a Monkey! If we were lions, we know that we wouldn't like getting veggies and carbs for every meal! Lions need protein and fat!

What happened? Heidi changed the way she ate. She increased her protein and fat intake two to three times the amount she was previously eating. Race morning was a particularly important time for Heidi. She was just eating carbohydrates prior to her races. She needed to consume an adequate amount of fat and protein in order to sustain herself throughout the race. She seemed hesitant at first to do this, as most athletes do not like to make changes to their regimens! But Heidi was willing to give it a try. Within the next year her improved results were amazing. *(See Figure 1-13.)*

Exercise Endurance and Intensity Improved with Appropriate Hauser Diet

Another patient of ours, Karen, came to see us for Prolotherapy to her foot for a running injury. In taking her history, we were talking to her about her training (she's a marathoner and duathlete). She told us that

FIGURE 1-13

An Appropriate Hauser Diet Improves Running Times:

	TIMES BEFORE HAUSER DIET	TIMES AFTER HAUSER DIET
5K Time:	22:30	20:16
10K Time:	46:46	42:14
½ Marathon Time:	1:45.12	1:35.49
Marathon Time:	3:53.28	3:29.22

she noticed that if she exercised for over four hours, it became increasingly difficult for her to do well.

She found this to be particularly problematic when she was running in hot weather, stating that she felt much better during the cooler times of year like fall and winter. We explained to her that her body temperature increases the longer she exercises in the heat. In conjunction with the rise in body temperature comes a rise in blood pH. If she does not do anything to lower her pH, she will not be able to stop the cycle.

Her blood pH level tested 7.480 which is alkaline. We recommended the Monkey Diet which is a higher carbohydrate and vegetable diet in order to get her into balance. We also helped her figure out some foods that she can ingest before and during her runs that will lower her pH. This is one time where easily digestible carbohydrates, like sugar, can come in handy. It is needed to lower the blood pH as well as give you energy. We suggested she try natural fruit leathers, jelly beans, and various sports drinks to help balance her blood pH during the competitions. After trying this for her last few long runs, she has felt much better about running in the heat. She was able to get her blood pH back into the normal range (she re-tested at 7.430), therefore allowing her body to handle the heat better, ultimately leading to improvement in her running performance.

Take the Acid-Alkaline Quiz below! Try to figure out if you have acid, alkaline, or normal blood pH tendencies. The more circles per area, the more likely you are to be

in that pH range. It's not an exact test, but it may help you become more in tune with your body. Some people say that they never even thought about these things before. Try it! *(See Figure 1-14.)*

2. Oxidative Rate: How fast do I metabolize food?

Oxidative rate tells us how quickly or slowly we metabolize (or oxidize) food. In other words, how long it takes your body to breakdown, absorb, and then utilize the food you ate. This is your oxidative rate. We feel that this is crucial information in determining a diet because to feel your best, you must have a stable blood sugar level. Your cells live on two primary fuels: oxygen and sugar. If your blood sugar levels go too high or too low, energy production within the cell is compromised.

Remember the goal of Diet Typing is to figure out which Diet Type you need to follow for maximum energy. Hopefully, you are convinced that one variable that needs to be tested is blood pH. The second most important variable is figuring out whether you can maintain stable blood sugar after a carbohydrate load. The test used to determine this is called a Glucose Tolerance Test.

We perform a modified glucose tolerance test in our laboratory. After fasting for 12-15 hours, we will first take your fasting blood sugar level. After that is done, you are given 50 grams of carbohydrates in the form of a fruit drink. Your blood sugars are then taken with a fingerstick test every half-hour for 90 minutes.

FIGURE 1-14 Take the Acid-Alkaline Quiz! (Circle what best describes you.)

ACIDIC	NORMAL	ALKALINE
1. Cold intolerant	Feel good always	Heat intolerant
2. Love the hot weather	Like both hot/cold	Love cold weather
3. Sports worse in cold	Sports same in cold as heat	Sports worse in heat
4. Sports better in heat	Sports same in heat as cold	Sports better in cold
5. Feel cold most times	Feel just right most times	Feel warm most times

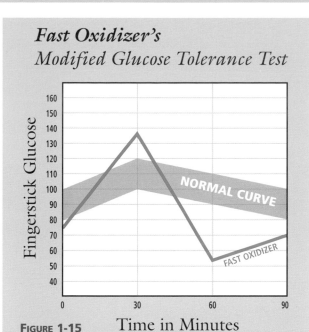

Fast Oxidizer's Modified Glucose Tolerance Test

FIGURE 1-15
Fast Oxidizer

This graph shows the glucose curve of a fast oxidizer who needs to eat a high protein/fat diet such as the Lion or Otter Diet.

We will plot your blood sugar levels on a graph so that you can see how your body responds to a carbohydrate load, compared to the normal range. The extremes of oxidative rates are seen in hypoglycemia (*fast oxidizer Figure 1-15*) and diabetes (*slow oxidizer with high insulin levels, Figure 1-17*).

Fasting Blood Sugar

Your fasting blood sugar level alone can tell us a lot about your biochemistry. The fasting blood sugar sample is taken after you have gone without food for 12 to 15 hours. Normal fasting blood sugar levels are between 80-100 mg/dL. This, in conjunction with your overall response to a glucose load over time, will tell us whether you are a fast, balanced, or slow oxidizer.

Fast Oxidizer

A person with a low fasting blood sugar level might show a blood sugar level of 60 in the morning. Think about how this could affect you if you had this problem. If you are always in a rush in the morning and don't take the time to eat breakfast, by 10:00 am, you will

feel terrible. This type of person needs to be especially careful to "break the fast" in the morning. If you do not eat breakfast, you may complain of things like difficulty getting up in the morning, fatigue, unable to get going in the morning, mental fog, and decreased ability to concentrate. As you may know, these are also symptoms of hypoglycemia (low blood sugar). People with hypoglycemia cannot go long periods of time without eating. They need to eat at least every three to four hours, but often even more frequently. (*See Figure 1-15.*)

The glucose curve of the fast oxidizer is usually one that starts out low and increases rapidly, but also decreases rapidly. In other words, ingesting sugar produces a quick rise in blood sugar, with a resultant increase in insulin levels in response to the high level of glucose in the blood. Insulin is secreted by the pancreas to remove glucose from the blood. The body responds to this increase in insulin very rapidly, hence, a fast oxidizer. These type of people will use up the glucose ingested very quickly and will find blood sugar levels plummeting again. In other words, these people oxidize or break down food too quickly, so they need to eat foods that are broken down slowly. Proteins and fats are the foods that are broken down (oxidized) the slowest.

So unless you consume frequent meals emphasizing protein and fat, your blood sugar will be bouncing all over the place, trying to get back to normal. This type of reaction is called *reactive hypoglycemia*. People with this condition generally feel highs and lows throughout the day. One minute they have a lot of energy, the next minute, they are so tired they can hardly lift their heads off the desk!

Insulin, as you recall, is secreted by the pancreas in response to high levels of sugar in the blood. At Caring Medical, we often monitor blood insulin levels along with glucose levels to obtain a little clearer metabolic picture. We like to see fasting insulin levels below 15uU/ml and one hour postprandial (after eating) below 40 uU/ml. If you get extremely fatigued after lunch, you are most likely a fast oxidizer.

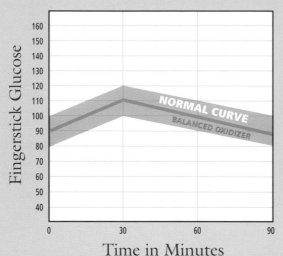

Balanced Oxidizer's Modified Glucose Tolerance Test

NORMAL CURVE

BALANCED OXIDIZER

Fingerstick Glucose

Time in Minutes

FIGURE 1-16
Balanced Oxidizer

This graph shows a normal glucose tolerance test or a balanced oxidizer who should follow a Bear Diet.

A person who is a fast oxidizer usually requires protein and fat with every meal instead of a meal made up solely of carbohydrates. These people typically do not do well with caffeinated products or sugary products. So a trip to your favorite coffee shop for that grande café mocha with a shot of vanilla and extra whipped cream is not a good idea for a hypoglycemic person! We'll discuss this more later on in the book. Don't get too depressed.

Balanced Oxidizer

A person with a normal fasting blood sugar level will have a blood sugar level between 80-100 mg/dL. *(See Figure 1-16.)* This type of person will usually feel good when rising in the morning. The balanced oxidizer does not typically experience highs and lows during the day related to blood sugar swings. Blood sugar levels rise and fall at the normal expected rate. They can usually tolerate carbohydrates, fats, and proteins equally well, and do best on a diet balanced between the three. The goal is to become more balanced—in more ways than one!

The balanced oxidizers break down food at a normal rate. In other words, they can keep blood sugar levels stable whether they eat protein, fat, or carbohydrates. Food does not affect how a balanced oxidizer feels, unless they significantly over or under eat.

Slow Oxidizer

The slow oxidizer's glucose curve typically starts out high and slowly rises over time, never coming down like it should.

A person with a high fasting blood sugar level will usually have a fasting blood sugar level above 100 mg/dL. People with high blood sugar levels are typically pre-diabetic or actually diabetic and have a problem processing carbohydrates. This is usually termed *Adult Onset Diabetes Mellitus* or *Type II Diabetes*. An amazing rise in the numbers of people being diagnosed with Type II Diabetes has been observed over the last decade. The sad part about this is the fact that it is a totally preventable disease.[4]

Slow Oxidizer—Normal Fasting Insulin Level

There are two types of slow oxidizers. The first type is the person who is a slow oxidizer and has a normal fasting insulin level (below 15). The normal insulin level means that the person's cells are responding to insulin normally. This type of person metabolizes food too slowly, so they need to eat foods that are metabolized quickly. Carbohydrates are the foods that are metabolized the quickest. A person who is a slow oxidizer and has a normal insulin level would then be prescribed the Monkey or Giraffe Diets as these are more vegetarian, carbohydrate-based diets.

Slow Oxidizer—High Fasting Insulin Level

A person with a fasting insulin level above 15 or a one-hour postprandial insulin level greater than 40 is a slow oxidizer (blood sugars are high is prediabetic or diabetic). As was explained earlier, when a person's blood sugar rises, the pancreas secretes insulin which is supposed to lower the blood sugar levels. With insulin resistance, Syndrome X, or adult-onset diabetes, the

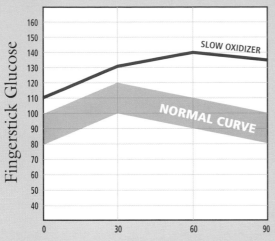

Slow Oxidizer's
Modified Glucose Tolerance Test

FIGURE 1-17
Slow Oxidizer
A slow oxidizer of food has high blood sugar levels on a glucose tolerance test. This is where the insulin levels are especially important. If a person has a low fasting insulin level (below 15 uU/ml), the person is a true slow oxidizer and will need to eat more carbohydrates, as in a Monkey or Giraffe Diet. However, if the person has a high fasting insulin level like in this graph, the blood sugar levels are being artificially raised because the cells have lost sensitivity to insulin's effect of lowering the blood sugar. Hence, this is someone who needs to follow a Lion or Otter Diet in order to help restore insulin sensitivity.

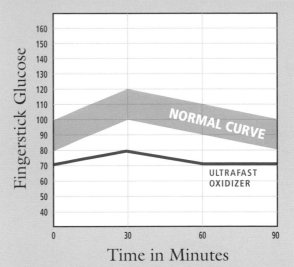

Ultrafast Oxidizer's "Flat Liner"
Modified Glucose Tolerance Test

FIGURE 1-18
Ultrafast Oxidizer "Flat Liner"
We call this glucose tolerance test a "flat line" because the blood sugar never moves much even after the glucose load. This person needs to follow a high protein/fat diet, the Lion or Otter Diet, as well as be tested for adrenal insufficiency.

blood sugar rises, the body makes insulin (thus the high insulin levels), but the blood sugar stays high because the cells are no longer responding normally to the insulin. They are resistant to it. The only way for the cells to become sensitive to the insulin again is to lower the insulin levels by eating a diet that is high in protein and low in carbohydrates. Thus, people who are slow oxidizers **and** have high insulin levels need to eat according to the Lion or Otter Diets.[5,6] *(See Figure 1-17.)*

Ultrafast Oxidizer (Flat Liner)

A common "atypical" response to this test is a "flat line." This person will typically exhibit a low fasting blood sugar. Upon ingestion of the glucose drink, the blood sugar barely rises, if at all. The curve is basically flat and low. This type of curve is an example of an ultrafast oxidizer. The 50 grams of carbohydrates ingested from the glucose tolerance test are used up within 30 minutes. *(See Figure 1-18.)*

"What is wrong with these people?" you ask. These people are often those who are totally stressed out to the point that their *adrenal gland* (stress gland) has started to shut down. They could not mount a response to a lion attacking them, let alone some glucose ingested! The underlying cause of this person's problem is most likely adrenal exhaustion. When underactive adrenal glands produce insufficient amounts of cortisol (corticosteroids), the result is adrenal insufficiency, also known as *subclinical hypocortisolism*. Males and females are equally affected, and it can occur at any age.

According to Natural Medicine specialists, adrenal insufficiency is most often due to a person undergoing stress for long periods of time, which eventually causes the adrenal gland to give out. Conventional medical treatments may help relieve the symptoms of an adrenal insufficiency, but they do not address *the root cause of the problem.* By addressing imbalances in the body, as Natural Medicine treatments do, an adrenal insufficiency may be alleviated permanently.

In addition to measuring adrenal gland blood hormone levels, Natural Medicine practitioners also perform a salivary hormone panel to check cortisol levels. This additional test will reveal the level of free hormones available to work and act in the body. To increase the sensitivity of this test, salivary hormone levels are often checked at various times during the day to get a complete assessment of adrenal gland function. If levels are low and adrenal insufficiency is diagnosed, nutraceuticals and natural hormone supplements such as DHEA and/or cortisol are started.

In those cases where stress plays a key role in the condition, counseling and lifestyle adjustments are explored and encouraged. Blood sugar levels and allergies are also checked to evaluate the patient's diet. A hypoallergenic diet as well as one high in protein and low in carbohydrates, such as the Lion and Otter Diets, are recommended. Adrenal gland hormone production is also dependent on various vitamins and minerals, including vitamin C, pantothenic acid, and thiamine, all of which would be supplemented in high doses. Adaptagenic herbs, such as ashwaganda, are also used to help the body cope with stress. For these types of situations, we like to use products from **www.beulahlandnutritionals.com**.

If left untreated, adrenal insufficiency can lead to *Syndrome H,* a condition characterized by hypoglycemia, hypocortisolism, and hypoimmunity and, eventually, chronic fatigue syndrome. However, using comprehensive testing including Diet Typing, as well as appropriate treatment options in order to treat concomitant conditions of adrenal insufficiency, the Natural Medicine approach can often resolve adrenal insufficiency.[7]

There surely are people who will read this information and say *"so what?"* This response indicates that they are not realizing their future health and mortality can be at stake. We would even go on to say that three out of four of you reading this right now have an abnormal glucose tolerance test. If you don't correct it, you will eventually end up with a condition that you will not like! In our experience there is a definite correlation between disease and the glucose tolerance test. *(See Figure 1-19.)*

3. Food Allergies

Not only do we take all of the aforementioned into consideration when assessing your nutritional needs, but we also look into the presence of other underlying conditions that might be contributing to your overall health or lack of health. One of those areas involves food allergies. Approximately 50 million Americans, or one in four, suffer from some form of allergic disease, and the incidence is increasing. When most people think of allergies, they think of sneezing, a runny nose, or watery eyes. While those are symptoms of some types of allergic disease, an allergic reaction is actually a product of several events occurring within the immune system.

How do allergies develop?

The immune system serves as the body's defense mechanism against the countless different substances present in the air we breathe, the foods we eat, and the things we touch. The term *"allergen"* refers to any substance that can trigger an allergic response.

Food allergies can produce a multitude of symptoms and conditions, which result from an allergen and an antibody interacting and irritating the affected tissue. If the tissue is in the intestines then irritable bowel syndrome with its alternating constipation/diarrhea will result. If the affected tissue is the swelling of the nasal lining, then runny nose and sinusitis can result.

FIGURE 1-19

Disease Correlation to the Glucose Tolerance

Many disorders are correlated with abnormal oxidative rates.

	FAST OXIDIZER	SLOW OXIDIZER
Arthritis	Yes	No
Attention Deficit Disorder	Yes	No
Autoimmune	None	Most
Cancer	Yes	Yes
Developmental Delay	Yes	No
Diabetes	No	Yes
Fatigue	Yes	Yes
Fibromyalgia	Yes	No
Heart Disease	Yes	Yes
High Blood Pressure	Yes	Yes
Irritable Bowel Syndrome	Yes	No
Mental Condition	Manic/Anxious	Depression
Migraine Headaches	Yes	No
Obesity	Yes	Yes

Although there is often an immediate cause-and-effect relationship with food allergies, people can experience delayed reactions, up to several days after the offending food is eaten. In such cases, diagnostic testing must be done. The most common is an IgG RAST test which measures specific IgG antibodies against various foods. A more sensitive blood test is the ALCAT, which combines the patient's white blood cells with a food antigen, and the reaction of the white blood cells is studied.

When a person eats a food that he or she is sensitized against, the body starts producing antibodies that act as little torpedoes against the food. If the allergenic food happens to be wheat, every time a person eats wheat cereal, pasta, or bread, these foods will actually take away energy, rather than give the person energy. If the person then eats these allergenic foods day after day, you can understand how fatigue can start to set in. We frequently recommend that our patients have food

allergy testing done, in addition to the other Diet Typing tests, to determine an optimal diet and to eliminate any foods that might actually be hurting you more than helping you. *(See Figure 1-20.)*

The most common food allergies seen at Caring Medical are to gluten, casein, and eggs. Gluten is a protein found in wheat products, including wheat, rye, barley, and their end products including wheat flour, cereal, and pastas. Casein is a protein found in milk products including cheese and yogurt. Eggs are found in obvious foods such as omelets and quiche, however are also used for many sweet and baked foods. As you can probably surmise, the typical American eats these foods on a daily basis. In fact, we have seen many people who practically live on dairy and wheat products.

Here is a very typical menu of many people we know and see at the clinic:

Breakfast: Bowl of cereal with milk or egg white and cheese omelet

Lunch: Turkey and cheese sandwich

Snack: String cheese or a yogurt

Dinner: Pizza or macaroni and cheese

If this looks similar to your diet and you suffer from poor health, get your food allergies checked!

Jason: Developmental Delay Halted

Jason was the second born of Jay and Andrea. He was progressing much slower than his brother and the doctors had even mentioned autism to the parents as a possible diagnosis. They were frantic and decided to try any and all alternatives, shopping around at various medical practitioners. They eventually came to Caring Medical. We explained to the parents that Jason was required to eat according to his Diet Type. We also discussed how food allergies can affect brain chemistry and development. They agreed to a food allergy blood test for Jason. As with most children with childhood illnesses, Jason was severely allergic to casein which is a component of milk. He was placed on the Otter Diet but was told to avoid anything with casein, including cow's milk, goat's milk, cheese, yogurt, cottage cheese—basically all dairy. He could have almond, rice, or soy milk. Within six months he was almost caught up at school for his age. Within one year he became completely normal. One wonders what would have happened to Jason if his parents didn't go doctor shopping?

How do we put this all together?

We know that this seems like a lot of information, but that is why we want you to read the book and then come and see us! The information in this chapter details the science behind the Hauser Diet, the trends we have seen in our years of recommending it, and case studies that illustrate its application. Ultimately, what we hope this chapter demonstrates to you is that determining your Diet Type may be the wisest health

FIGURE 1-20 Food Allergy Profile

RESULT		ALLERGEN	Reference Range Insignificant	Moderate	Significant
		DAIRY			
Pending	838	American Cheese	<186	186-580	>580
Equivocal	301	Bleu Cheese	<101	101-297	>297
Equivocal	298	Casein	<105	105-324	>324
Significant	1199	Cow's Milk	<117	117-358	>358
Significant	306	Mozzarella Cheese	<138	138-430	>431
Significant	223	Parmesan	<111	111-328	>328
Equivocal	447	Yogurt	<127	127-399	>399
		FISH			
Negative	0	Cod	<156	156-485	>485
Negative	0	Halibut	<105	105-332	>332
Negative	0	Salmon	<130	130-402	>402
Negative	0	Tuna	<85	85-266	>266
		FRUIT			
Pending	0	Avocados	<57	57-257	>257
Pending	18	Bananas	<36	362-1104	>1104
Pending	37	Blackberry	<155	155-479	>479
Equivocal	15	Cantaloupe	<122	122-378	>378
Equivocal	0	Cherries	<144	144-466	>466
Negative	20	Grapes (Red)	<113	113-345	>345
Negative	0	Limes	<104	104-320	>320
Negative	0	Peaches	<125	125-391	>391
Significant	0	Pears	<64	64-194	>194
Negative	2	Orange	<169	169-527	>527
Significant	986	Pineapples	<136	136-422	>422
Negative	176	Raspberries	<146	146-444	>444
Negative	0	Tangerines	<104	104-318	>318
Equivocal	27	Watermelons	<167	167-519	>519
		GRAINS			
Significant	4	Buckwheat	<211	122-374	>374
Negative	0	Corn	<113	113-337	>337
Pending	636	Gluten	<115	115-363	>363
Negative	94	Malt	<101	101-500	>500
Negative	0	Oat	<143	143-447	>447
Pending	196	Rye	<136	136-421	>421
Negative	506	Wheat	<171	171-528	>528
		MEATS			
Equivocal	12	Beef	<141	141-440	>440
Equivocal	2	Chicken	<226	226-697	>697
Negative	1608	Egg White	<111	111-345	>345
Negative	952	Egg Yolk	<196	196-608	>608
Significant	0	Pork	<253	253-782	>782
Significant	0	Turkey	<129	129-402	>402
		NUTS			
Negative	591	Almonds	<138	138-413	>413
Negative	0	Cashew	<116	116-356	>356
Equivocal	0	Peanuts	<206	206-638	>638
Pending	1	Sesame	<129	129-391	>391
Negative	0	Walnut	<116	116-356	>358
		SPICES			
Pending	0	Basil	<389	389-1166	>1166
Negative	73	Chili Powder	<181	181-562	>562
Negative	4	Cilantro	<344	344-1065	>1065
Negative	0	Cinnamon	<156	156-481	>481
Pending	145	Ginger	<117	117-357	>357
Negative	0	Vanilla	<104	104-317	>317
		VEGETABLES			
Pending	0	Artichokes	<141	141-417	>417
Negative	0	Asparagus	<126	126-390	>390
Equivocal	38	Brussels Sprouts	<154	154-479	>479
Negative	26	Carrots	<170	170-539	>539
Negative	5	Cauliflower	<176	176-544	>544
Equivocal	1	Garbanzo Beans	<122	122-366	>366
Negative	357	Garlic	<301	301-926	>926
Negative	135	Green Beans	<127	127-395	>395
Negative	1277	Kidney Beans	<258	258-793	>793
Equivocal	1218	Navy Beans	<124	124-362	>362
Negative	0	Lettuce	<187	187-581	>581
Pending	0	Olives	<90	90-270	>270
Pending	0	Peas	<259	259-804	>804
Pending	809	Pinto Beans	<102	102-310	>310
Negative	72	Red Peppers	<106	106-315	>315
Negative	705	Soybeans	<273	273-849	>849
Negative	1	Spinach	<178	178-553	>553
Negative	0	Squash (Winter)	<208	208-645	>645
Negative	46	Tomatoes	<156	156-482	>482
Negative	0	Yams	<91	91-298	>298
Significant	33	Zucchini	<153	153-475	>475

Sample of a Food Allergy Panel Conducted at Caring Medical
This panel shows a variety of reactions in the blood to specific food allergens.

decision you can make. At least, our clinical experience has proven that to us and thousands of our patients!

Don't wait until you are suffering from a chronic disease to get tested. Don't you want to optimize your health now?

Following the principles of the Hauser Diet could completely change your life. Your energy, stamina, and overall sense of well-being can be greatly enhanced, just by knowing how to eat for your specific Diet Type. Remember, if you eat great, you'll feel great.

What's the Hype About Diet Type?
Here are the take-home points:

- Always feeling hot or always feeling cold is an indication that your blood pH is not in the normal range.

- Hot weather alkalinizes the blood which means you need to eat more carbohydrates, like a Monkey/Giraffe.

- Cold weather acidifies the blood which means you need to eat more protein and fat, like a Lion/Otter.

- A woman's menstrual cycle will effect how she should eat. On days 10-16, the rise in estrogen acidifies the blood, meaning she may need to eat more protein and fat, like a Lion/Otter would eat. Later in the cycle, the progesterone alkalinizes the blood pH requiring her to consume more carbohydrates, like a Monkey/Giraffe would eat. No wonder we crave chocolates at this time!

- If you break down carbohydrates too fast (fast oxidizer), your diet may need to have more protein and fat than carbohydrates so you have optimal energy throughout the day. This means that you are likely a Lion/Otter instead of a Monkey/Giraffe.

- If you are a balanced oxidizer, you will likely feel great on a well-balanced diet, such as the Bear Diet.

- If you break down carbohydrates more slowly (slow oxidizer), this can mean one of two things. You may need to consume more carbohydrates such as in the Monkey/Giraffe Diets or if you have elevated insulin levels, you may need to consume more protein and fat such as in the Lion/Otter Diets.

- As you age, dietary needs may change. Food allergies may develop and blood pH levels may change.

- Not all athletes need to carbo-load the night before the race. Normalizing your blood pH can help improve how you perform during your event.

- Underlying food allergies can contribute to a decline in your health, so we recommend you determine if you have any!

Footnotes

1. Goedecke S., et. al., Determinants of the variability in respiratory exchange ratio at rest and during exercise in trained athletes. *The American Physiological Society*, 2000. PE 1325-E1334.

2. Ibid.

3. Ibid.

4. Dilman, V., Dean, W. *The Neuroendocrine Theory of Aging and Degenerative Disease.* Pensacola, FL: The Center for Bio-Gerontology, 1992.

5. DeFronzo, R., Insulin Resistance—a multifaceted syndrome responsible for NIDDM, obesity, hypertension, dyslipidemia, and atherosclerotic cardiovascular disease, *Diabetes Care.* 1991; 4(3):173-94.

6. Raven, G. Role of insulin resistance in human disease. *Diabetes.* 1988; 37, 1595-1607.

7. Reaven, G. Syndrome X. *Clinical Diabetes.* 1994; 3(4), 32-52.

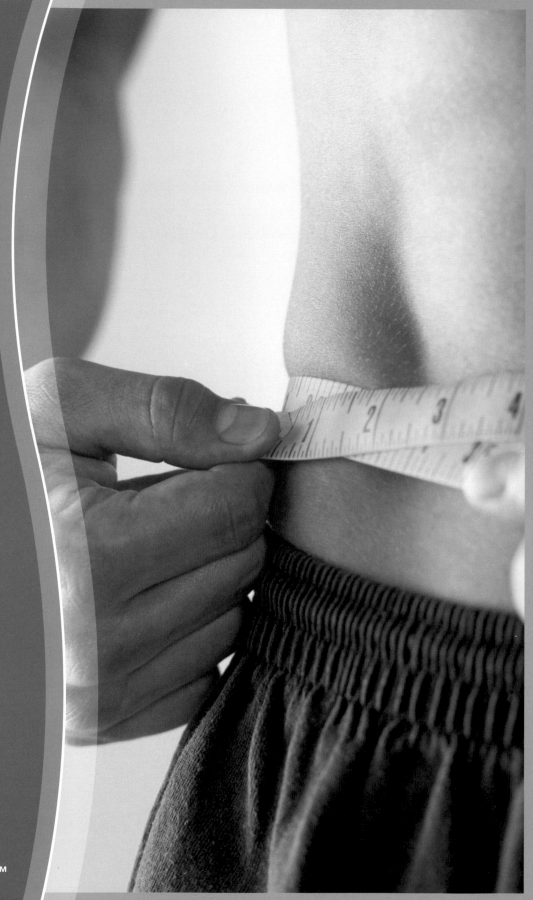

succeeding
on the
Hauser Diet™

As you have just read in *Chapter 1*, the principles of the Hauser Diet are backed by sound scientific principles, along with years of clinical experience. The principles of this book are not just theory, they work, as evidenced by the number of Caring Medical clients whose lives have been changed—just by altering their eating habits to better coincide with what their bodies need.

The Hauser Diet is not just a "diet." It is a way of life, a lifestyle. Obviously, a large part of the diet is food. But diet in this society is more than just the food itself. Food is involved in many aspects of people's lives. It is used to provide comfort, to entertain, to show gratitude, and to keep you alive. We want to show you how to select the foods that will help keep you alive and well for a long time. Whether you believe it or not, what you put into your mouth can have profound effects on your health—now, as well as later on in your life. You saw in *Chapter 1* how alterations in pH can dramatically change the way you feel on a day to day basis, as well as how eating the wrong foods can not only cause you to gain weight, but may produce all sorts of symptoms such as fatigue, lethargy, depression, anxiety, gastrointestinal problems, and even pain.

The Hauser Diet is not just one diet for everyone. The Hauser Diet is five different animal Diet Types that differ in the amounts of carbohydrate, protein, and fat based on the Diet Typing results of the individual. However, the Hauser Diet begins with certain "nuts and bolts" principles which should be followed by everyone, which we will discuss in the following pages. Some people notice significant improvement in their overall feeling of well-being, just by implementing these basic principles into their lifestyles. On top of that, determining their actual animal Diet Type then enables them to maximize their energy even further.

Unfortunately in today's society, fast food makes up about 40% of the food intake and is nearly completely devoid of fresh foods. The "fresh" foods that are readily available to us in the grocery stores are usually picked from the fields before they are ripe and contain pesticides or other chemical additives. The foods' enzymatic action has been halted in order to preserve shelf life. Processing foods disrupts the natural makeup of the food and adds chemicals and other artificial substances that add toxicity to the food itself. Learning to go back to the basics and consume fresh, real foods is one of the key principles of the Hauser Diet.

The Five Principles for Achieving Success on the Hauser Diet

1. Make your meals yourself instead of eating out.
2. Learn to cook.
3. Choose fresh, organic foods.
4. Drink water—purified clean water.
5. Exercise everyday.

You may be thinking that we are crazy and that you cannot do these things. Well, that's why we are writing this book. We want to help you figure out how you can make that happen. Remember, nobody cares about your health as much as you! It's up to you to make that choice. Is it worth sacrificing your long term health? We all think we are invincible and that we will not be the ones getting some terminal disease. Considering 70% of us will be diagnosed with cancer or heart disease with the current statistics, we all need to sit up and take notice. It's time to make a change—for life! It's now or never.

1. **Make your meals yourself instead of eating out:** Learn how to make meals from fresh foods that are not only healthier for you, but easy-to-make and wonderfully delicious! Once you can do this, it is very hard to go back to eating processed food or even go out to restaurants because you know that you could make something just as good, and more often than not, much better!

2. **Learn to cook:** Anyone who can read can cook. We have helped many-a-non-cook learn how to whip up easy meals in no time. All you need is a positive attitude and the desire to do it!

    Cooking takes time, we realize that. But there are many short cuts and time-savers that we will show you to help develop that chef within yourself! We know he/she is dying to come out! What better way to use your creative side than to prepare culinary masterpieces?

3. **Choose fresh, organic foods:** Why? It is common sense! Fresh, organic food is good food. Good to eat, good for your body, and good for the environment. Organic food purchasing practices are sky-rocketing. People are realizing the importance of putting good foods into their bodies versus those loaded with chemicals, hormones, antibiotics, additives, dyes, and all sorts of other toxins. Most consumers site concern with quality, taste, and freshness as their reasons for purchasing organic. More information on this topic is provided in *Chapter 8*.

    Choose whole, fresh, organic vegetables, meats, and fruits. Add more vegetables, especially dark colored ones, fish, and soy-based meals to your eating plans. Most people do not get enough of these in their diets. You'll definitely get more bang for your nutrient buck with consumption of these vitamin-packed foods!

4. **Drink water—purified, clean water:** Most people are walking around dehydrated. The best beverage by far is plain ol' water. Try to drink at least 40 ounces of purified water per day. All functions within the body require water. A well hydrated body enables these functions to occur quickly and efficiently. All chemical processes involve energy metabolism and drinking plenty of water will make you feel more energetic and boost your metabolic rate. Water makes your metabolism burn calories 3% faster.

    Drinking water is important if you are trying to lose weight, as some studies have shown that thirst and hunger sensations are triggered together. A slight dehydration may cause the thirst mechanism to be mistaken for hunger. Therefore you may eat, when in reality, your body is actually craving fluid. Drinking more water can help to prevent overeating and enhance weight loss. Water also helps lubricate the joints, improve skin tone, and reduce headaches and pain.

5. **Exercise everyday:** Physical activity has been associated with health for many years. Science has now confirmed the link, with overwhelming evidence, that people who lead active lifestyles are less likely to die early, or to experience major illnesses such as heart disease, diabetes, and cancer. Many people find it very difficult to change exercise habits. Evidence shows that regular exercise can increase HDL or "good" cholesterol levels, lower high blood pressure, help improve body composition by burning fat, promote healthy blood sugar levels, promote bone density, boost the immune system, improve mood, and reduce the chance of depression.

Despite the strong case for staying active, many people find it difficult to adapt their daily lives to incorporate physical activity. With cars in most driveways and the decline in the number of physically active jobs, much of the American population is sufficiently inactive enough to be classified as "sedentary." Being sedentary increases the risk of a heart attack or stroke by the same amount as smoking. Here's your chance to make a difference—in your own life! More to come on exercise in *Chapter 10.*

Clean House: It's Time for a Pantry Overhaul

Okay, now you know where we're going with this plan. We want to get fresh with you—fresh foods that is! What does that mean? It means that you need to do a little house cleaning. Yup, that means getting rid of some of your tried and true favorites and replacing them with fresher, more nutrient-dense, less toxic foods. It's like a bad relationship. We all have a relationship to food. Some are positive and build you up—like eating fresh organic veggies. Some relationships are toxic and bring you down—they are abusive and take away from your health, like fast food, instant noodle dishes, and frozen pot pies served with the latest diet beverage. We are going to teach you how to dump your toxic food like a bad date!

10 Tips for Dumping:

1. **Processed foods:** We mean pre-made foods in the freezer or pantry that contain long lists of chemicals and additives, such as pot pies, frozen dinners, and boxed entrees! It's time—to dump!

2. **Food with artificial colors or flavors:** Look for products with the words "dyes" or "artificial" on the labels, in the ingredient list. If you find them, throw them away. Why should your body have to process all of these chemicals?

3. **Artificial sweeteners:** You can read more about this in *Chapter 8*, but suffice it to say, consumption of artificially sweetened products does not help you lose weight—they actually help you gain weight. So get rid of all of those diet, low carb, sugar-free products that are on your shelves.

4. **Sugary products:** If you find that your shelves contain a large amount of sugar-laden products, then you have a problem with sugar. We can't tell you how many times we have gone to people's homes to find cookies, cake, ice cream, soda, candy, pastries, donuts, coffee cakes, and ice cream bars, all in the same household. Keeping one item for the occasional dessert is definitely okay, but your cabinets or refrigerator should not be lined with them!

5. **Fake fat or hydrogenated fats:** Most fat-free food is also food-free food. In other words, they contain additives that are often non-digestible, poor tasting, and down right disgusting. The real thing is much better for you in the appropriate portions.

   We have all heard of trans-fats and hydrogenated fats nowadays. That is the new marketing tool for the fat-crazed marketplace. Again, avoiding hydrogenated fats is a good idea, but it is certainly not the crux of eating a healthy lifestyle. More to come on this topic!

6. **Alcohol:** Does your refrigerator contain more beer, wine, and mixers than it does food? If this describes you, then start pouring those down the drain. A glass of red wine with dinner is one thing. Regularly consuming three or four beers or mixed drinks every night is another.

7. **Nutrient-poor foods:** Do you find that you regularly purchase things like soft white bread, iceberg lettuce, rice dishes, noodle packets, gravy mixes, canned spaghetti meals, and boxed mac n' cheese? This is not fresh food. Dump!

8. **Fake beverages:** Remember that water is the best beverage around. It's time to dump the hot cocoa mixes, lemonade mixes, iced tea mixes, and fruit drink mixes, which all provide empty calories, toxic chemicals, and no nutrition. Water with fresh lemon/lime or homemade tea are much better options.

8. **Margarine:** Butter and margarine contain equal amount of calories, however, butter has many nutritional benefits. Butter tastes much better than margarine and it can enhance the flavors of other foods. Most margarines are very high in trans fatty acids. Eating margarine can increase heart disease in women by 53% compared to eating the same amount of butter, according to a Harvard Medical Study. Studies have shown it to triple the risk of heart disease, increase total cholesterol and LDL (bad cholesterol), and lower HDL cholesterol, (good cholesterol). Margarine, interestingly enough, is but one molecule away from being plastic. This fact alone was enough for us to avoid margarine for life. If you leave margarine out in a cool place for a long time, you'll find that nothing will happen to it. It won't rot, smell, or attract flies. Why? Because it is nearly plastic! We figure that says enough. If you have margarine or bread spreads or any such thing in your refrigerator, it's time to dump them!

10. **Bottled salad dressings:** Most of us grew up on bottled salad dressings. Those bright orange dressings that tasted somewhat chemical and overly sweet? Or what about those dressing packets where you just add your own oil and vinegar? Have you ever taken a look at the ingredients? Sugar, sweeteners, dyes, chemicals, MSG—they are loaded! Make your own dressings! They will be fresh, flavored the way you want, in manageable sizes so you can use them up, and utterly delish! Start simply with a basic vinegar and oil dressing. *Chapter 9* will give you some of our favorite tried and true homemade dressings. Once you throw away all of those sticky bottles from the door of your refrigerator and experience the delightful flavors of homemade salad dressings, you'll have a hard time going back to bottled!

You may be thinking, "hum, if I dump all of those 10 things, I won't have anything left in my kitchen." Well, that's exactly the point. The rest of this book is going to help you determine what foods should be lining the shelves of your pantry and refrigerator. We'll give you real examples and lists to help you do it.

Portion Distortion

Once you rid your shelves of the bad foods and stock up on fresh foods, you are nearly there. Realize that even though you eat good food, you cannot consume more calories than your body needs. Fueling the body with good food is part one, but part two is consuming foods in the proper portion sizes. We all know about "biggie," "super sizing," and the like. Eating out in restaurants and fast food places contributes to over-eating. Most of us do not want to waste food, thus we clean our plates, even though we know that we are eating too much. One of the down sides of making delicious fresh foods is learning to control your portions. You may want to eat the entire dish of food because it tastes so great!

When reading food labels, you'll notice things like "2 servings" and "serves 4." What constitutes a serving size? What one person considers a serving may be very different from another person. Although the Hauser Diet is not a "calorie counting" diet, you do need to consider how much you are eating. Many of our clients have asked for meal plans and daily serving equivalents in order to help them gauge proper portion control. We recommend a consultation with a nutritionist or dietitian, such as our Caring Medical Nutrition and Lifestyle Coach. He/she can calculate your specific calorie requirements. We would love to see you at our office.

To get a general idea of your daily calorie requirements, here is a general formula that you can use to estimate your calorie needs:

1. **Determine your weight in kilograms:**
   Divide your weight in pounds by 2.2. For example, 150 pounds divided by 2.2 equals 68.2 kilograms.

2. **Multiply your weight in kilograms by the amount of calories needed for your daily activity level.**
   This is your estimated daily calorie need.

For example, a person weighing 68.2 kg with an "average" activity level will need an estimated 1,700 calories per day (or 68.2 kg x 25 calories/kg.) *See Figure 2-1* to find calories per kilogram body weight based on activity level.

FIGURE 2-1
Activity Levels to Gauge Daily Calorie Expenditure

This figure provides you with general guidelines for determining calorie needs. Each person's body composition and calorie needs will vary. If you desire to know your specific calorie needs, we recommend you seek the advice of a dietitian or physician.

Sedentary	Average Activity	Moderate Exerciser	Athletic	Super Athlete
No exercise, with minimal walking	Mobile, with some exercise: less than 30 minutes, 3 days per week	Moderate exercise, 30-60 minutes 3 days per week	Daily exercise, 30-60 minutes	More than 60 minutes of vigorous daily exercise
20 Calories per kilogram	25 Calories per kilogram	30 Calories per kilogram	35 Calories per kilogram	40 Calories per kilogram

To become a diligent calorie counter, we recommend you look into an online software that can calculate exactly what you ate, recognize various brands of food, and factor in daily activities. For the rest of us, the general concepts of the diet will work fine if we follow some general principles.

- **Eat the right portion sizes for your daily needs.** Most people eat too much food, period. Our bodies are not meant to take in so much food. This excessive food intake is stored as fat.

- **Adjust either food or exercise in order to lose weight.** Something has to give. You can either increase your activity and burn more calories, or decrease your food intake and consume fewer calories.

- **Only eat when you are hungry.** This should go without saying. But it is necessary to get a grip on your eating habits and break the habit of eating because of stress, boredom, or taste.

- **Chew your food completely.** This will help your digestion because your stomach will not have to work so hard to break down the food. This will also slow your rate of food consumption and you will begin to feel full after eating less food.

- **Stop eating when you just start to feel full.** If you eat past the point of just feeling full, you will overeat. If you overeat, even if you are eating the right kinds of food, you will not lose weight. This is typically the most difficult in the beginning of your new dietary plan. After a couple of weeks, your body will become adjusted to this style of eating, helping you decrease your overall appetite.

How to Break Down Your Food

We are not going to start talking about digestion here, but we want to help you understand the basic tenants of the Hauser Diet by looking at the basic macronutrient breakdown of food. There are three types of nutrients used as energy sources by the body—protein, carbohydrate, and fat. If you are going to count calories and watch your portion sizes, we need to first help you understand the three different types of nutrients. The five animal Diet Types are composed of different percentages of protein, carbohydrates, and fat. Proteins and carbohydrates each provide four calories of energy per gram, while fats produce nine calories per gram. In other words, fats have more than double the calories of protein and carbohydrates per gram of weight.

Protein:

Proteins are large molecules composed of one or more chains of amino acids in a specific order. Proteins are required for the structure, function, and regulation of the body's cells, tissues, and organs. Each protein has unique functions. Proteins are essential components of muscles, skin, bones, and the body as a whole. Proteins are fundamental components of all living cells and include many substances, such as enzymes, hormones, and antibodies that are necessary for the proper functioning of an organism. They are essential in the human diet for the growth and repair of tissue and can be obtained from foods such as beef, veal, pork, chicken, turkey, fish, eggs, and tofu. Foods such as milk or other dairy products contain some protein, in addition to carbohydrates and fat.

Carbohydrates:

Carbohydrates come in simple forms such as sugars and in complex forms such as starches and fiber. Complex carbohydrates are derived from plants. Dietary intake of complex carbohydrates can lower blood cholesterol and have been shown to prevent colon cancer.

Carbohydrates are easily converted to energy by the body. There are basically two main classes of carbohydrates: simple and complex carbohydrates. *Simple carbs* are sugars, like glucose, fructose, and lactose. Common sources include table sugar (sucrose), sweets, syrups, and honey. *Complex carbs* are either starches, or indigestible dietary fiber. Common sources include breads, pastas, rice, beans, and vegetables. Common sources of dietary fiber are fruits, vegetables, beans, and the indigestible parts of whole grains like wheat bran and oat bran.

Carbohydrates and Glucose: To understand the importance of carbohydrates in our diet, and how carbohydrates differ from protein and fats, remember two things:

1. The human body runs on glucose. Therefore all foods need to be converted into glucose before they can provide energy.

2. Carbohydrates are more readily converted into glucose than protein or fat, and may be considered the body's "preferred" source of energy. This is why different Diet Types require different amounts of carbohydrates, i.e., the Lion requires less carbohydrates than the Giraffe. The Lion is more prone to hypoglycemia, therefore he needs to consume fewer carbohydrates, and more protein.

Carbohydrates may be a very efficient source of energy, but they are not more important than fats or protein. Both fat and protein are absolutely vital for good health, and without a diet of all three, the human body quickly becomes malnourished. The Hauser Diet takes this one step further and states that human beings fit into one of five different Diet Types, requiring one of five breakdowns of protein, carbohydrates, and fat.

Simple carbs and complex carbs affect the body in different ways. Simple carbs (with the exception of fructose, fruit sugar) are basically sugars (glucose) so they are immediately absorbed into the bloodstream, causing a rise in blood sugar levels. Because blood sugar levels must be kept within a certain range, the body responds by telling the pancreas to secrete insulin into the blood stream, because insulin helps to gather up excess blood sugar and bring it into the cell where it can be turned into energy. Unfortunately, if exposed to repeated rapid increases in blood sugar, the pancreas starts to overreact to this sudden rise in blood sugar and secretes too much insulin. Within an hour or so, the insulin has cleared out too much blood sugar, so levels drop too far and

this triggers hunger and hypoglycemia symptoms. This rapid rise and fall in blood sugar levels caused by excess production of insulin is not good for our health or our eating habits. Over time, these sugar spikes can lead to impaired glucose tolerance, insulin resistance, and Type II Diabetes.

Complex carbs, on the other hand, need more time to be broken down into glucose. They, therefore, do not raise blood sugar levels as fast as simple carbs. This is why we recommend restricting our consumption of simple carbohydrates and eating complex carbohydrates instead, especially for the Lions and Otters, but really for all of the five Hauser Diets.

Dietary fiber's chemical structure is such that the human body cannot metabolize it, so it passes through the body mostly undigested. Thus, it helps with good, normal, daily bowel movements. Fiber is, however, very important for both health and weight control because it helps the body process waste efficiently and helps us to feel fuller for longer. Fiber also helps protect us against some serious diseases, including various cancers.

Fats:

Fat is the third of the three main classes of foods and a source of energy in the body. Fats help the body use some vitamins, keep the skin and nervous system healthy, are necessary for proper hormone production, help the body absorb the fat-soluble vitamins A, D, E, and K, and are the storage from of energy for the body.

Dietary fat provides flavor and makes you feel full, containing nine calories per gram, compared to four calories per gram in carbohydrates and protein. Food contains two types of fats: saturated and unsaturated. Saturated fat is found mainly in foods from animals. Major sources of saturated fats are cheese, beef, and milk. Trans fat results when manufacturers add hydrogen to vegetable oil to increase the food's shelf life and flavor. Trans fat can be found in vegetable shortenings, most margarines, crackers, cookies, and other snack foods. Cholesterol is a fat-like substance in foods from animal sources such as meat, poultry, egg yolks, milk, and milk products. Unsaturated fats come primarily from plant products, containing polyunsaturated and monounsaturated fatty acids, such as those that occur in fish, avocados, nuts, soybean, corn, canola, olive, and other vegetable oils.

The Lion and Otter Diets should consume more fat in their diets because fats are metabolized more slowly. The Lion and Otters are typically the fast oxidizers,

therefore requiring foods that take longer to break down in the body. Even if they consume saturated fats, their cholesterol levels do not become elevated. A perfect example of this is Dr. Hauser who is an Otter who consumes a very large amount of eggs and meat every week and his cholesterol level is below 140.

Food Equivalent Counting

Now that you understand the three different macronutrient types, let's talk about portion size

---

FIGURE 2-2

Hauser Diet Food Equivalent Chart

Use this chart to understand how to develop your own meal plans in the upcoming "animal" chapters.

Protein Equivalents
(Approximately 60 calories per 1 equivalent)

1 equals:
1 ounce beef, pork, or lamb
1 ounce fish
1 ounce poultry
1 egg
1 ounce tofu
½ scoop protein powder

Fat Equivalents
(Approximately 40 calories per 1 equivalent)

1 equals:
1 tsp butter or oil
1 slice bacon
⅙ avocado
½ Tbsp nut butter
1 tsp nuts
6 small olives
1 Tbsp cream cheese
1 Tbsp sour cream
1 tsp mayonnaise
1 Tbsp cream

Complex Carbohydrate Equivalents
(Approximately 80 calories per 1 equivalent)

1 equals:
½ cup cooked whole grain rice
1 regular corn tortilla
2 "La Tortilla Factory" high-fiber tortillas
1 slice whole grain bread
½ cup cooked oatmeal
¾ cup high fiber cereal
½ cup legumes (beans)
½ cup grits
½ cup whole grain pasta
1 medium potato with skin
5 whole wheat crackers
10 tortilla chips
½ cup couscous

Vegetable Equivalents
(Approximately 25 calories per 1 equivalent)

1 equals:
½ cup cooked vegetables
1 cup raw vegetables
1 cup vegetable juice

Simple Carbohydrate Equivalents
(Approximately 80 calories per 1 equivalent)

1 equals:
1 slice white bread
½ cup cooked white pasta
½ cup cooked white rice
1 small dessert
1 medium cookie
1 Tbsp jam
2 Tbsp 100% maple syrup
2 Tbsp sugar/honey

Fruit Equivalents
(Approximately 60 calories per 1 equivalent)

1 equals:
1 medium piece fruit
½ cup cooked or canned fruit
1 cup melon
½ cup berries
½ banana
¾ cup juice
2 Tbsp dried fruit
½ grapefruit

Dairy Equivalents
(Approximately 120 calories per 1 equivalent)

1 equals: (assuming 2% fat)
1 cup milk
1 cup soy milk
1 ounce cheese (1-inch cube)
1 cup yogurt (plain)
½ cup cottage cheese

Free Equivalents
(Approximately 0 calories per 1 equivalent)

1 equals:
1 cup lettuce
¼ cucumber
2 radishes
¼ cup sprouts
Water
Unsweetened herbal tea

references as they apply to the five different Hauser Diets. We want to help you figure out what to eat and in what quantities. Since many of our patients asked us to give them a way to count portions, we devised a process we call "food equivalent counting." *(See Figure 2-2.)* In *Chapters 3 to 7,* each of the individual Hauser animal diets will be explained in detail. We will tell you how much you can eat, assuming you are following approximately 2000 calories per day. If your calorie requirements are more or less than 2000 calories, you can make that adjustment yourself. As you know, this is only going to give you approximations due to variations from brand to brand, sizes of food pieces, etc.

Please note that you can divide an equivalent up into partial equivalents that you can use throughout the day's meals and not necessarily eat one entire equivalent at an entire meal. For example, 1 simple carbohydrate equivalent = 2 Tbsp sugar or 6 tsp of sugar. If you were allowed one simple carbohydrate equivalent for the day, you could divide that into 2 tsp sugar in morning coffee, 2 tsp sugar on your fruit salad at lunch, and 2 tsp of sugar in your meat sauce at dinner. *Figure 2-3* will help you determine

> ### Figure 2-3
> ## Food Measurement Conversions
>
> **Use this chart for a quick reference when dividing up food equivalents throughout the day.**
>
> | | |
> |---|---|
> | 3 tsp = 1 Tbsp | ½ cup = 4 ounces |
> | 1 Tbsp = ½ ounce | 1 cup = 8 ounces |
> | 2 Tbsp = 1 ounce | 2 pints = 1 quart |
> | 16 Tbsp = 1 cup | 4 quarts = 1 gallon |

how to divide a food equivalent using common household conversions.

How to put it all together?

Throughout this chapter, we have been talking about protein, carbohydrates, and fats and the fact that the five Hauser Diets each contain different amounts of these nutrients. *Figure 2-4* shows the breakdown for each of the Diet Types. The Lion contains the highest percentage of protein and fat, where the Giraffe contains the highest amount of carbohydrates. To put these percentages into real food for you, here are five breakfasts—one for each of the Hauser Diets. *(See Figure 2-5.)*

Figure 2-4
The Five Hauser Diet Types: Which Animal Are You?

Lion Diet Type™	**Otter Diet Type™**	**Bear Diet Type™**	**Monkey Diet Type™**	**Giraffe Diet Type™**
60% protein	50% protein	30% protein	20% protein	10% protein
25% fat	25% fat	20% fat	15% fat	10% fat
15% carbohydrates	25% carbohydrates	50% carbohydrates	65% carbohydrates	80% carbohydrates

the lion breakfast

This breakfast contains 3 eggs cooked in 1 tsp of butter, 2 slices of bacon, and an 8-ounce glass of milk. (3 protein, 3 fat, and 1 dairy equivalent.)

This protein-packed breakfast is just what Lions need to jump start their day. Protein foods such as eggs, and fats such as bacon are broken down slowly, providing sustained energy until lunch time.

This 3-egg Otter breakfast is a delicious way for Otters to get the protein they need to start their mornings. Sop up those egg yolks with a buttery piece of whole grain toast. Wash it down with a protein-packed glass of cold whole milk.

the otter breakfast

This breakfast contains three eggs cooked in 1 tsp of butter, 1 slice of whole grain toast with 1 tsp butter, and an 8-ounce glass of milk. (3 protein, 2 fat, 1 complex carbohydrate, and 1 dairy equivalent.)

the bear breakfast

This contains a 3-egg/veggie omelet cooked in 1 tsp butter, 1 slice of whole grain toast with 1 tsp butter, and hot tea. (3 protein, 1 vegetable, 2 fat, and 1 complex carbohydrate equivalent.)

This breakfast focuses on balance! The omelette provides the protein and sneaks in those necessary veggies. A piece of buttery whole grain toast, gives complex carbohydrates and fat. Herbal tea gets you going without the caffeine rush.

the monkey breakfast

Contains 1 egg cooked in 1 tsp butter, 1 whole wheat English muffin, 1 Tbsp jam, celery sticks, and 1 cup of tomato juice. (1 protein, 1 fat, 1 complex carbohydrate, 1 simple carbohydrate, and 2 vegetable equivalents.)

This mostly-vegetarian breakfast contains a high amount of carbs coming from the whole grain muffin, and simple carbs from the fruit jam. Celery sticks and tomato juice add veggies to breakfast. Necessary protein comes from the poached egg.

Carbs are just what Giraffes need—note the whole wheat English muffin and mixed fruit selection. A glass of tomato juice is a perfect Giraffe accompaniment. This breakfast uses jam instead of butter, a better Giraffe pick than fatty butter or nut butters.

the giraffe breakfast

Contains 1 whole wheat English muffin with 1 Tbsp jam, 1 cup of melon and strawberries, 1 cup tomato juice. (1 complex carbohydrate, 1 simple carbohydrate, 1 fruit, and 1 vegetable equivalent.)

FIGURE 2-5

Breakfast for Each Diet Type

Notice the transition from high protein/high fat on the Lion Diet to low fat vegetarian on the Giraffe Diet.

What animal are you?

Do you want to try to determine your Diet Type? Take the Hauser Diet Quiz! *(See Figure 2-6.)* Although this quiz has been tested and verified as very accurate compared to a person's actual Diet Typing results, the only true way to know your Diet Type is to be tested. When you take The Hauser Diet Quiz, do your best to be objective. You might be surprised how often your emotional ties to food create very subjective results. For example, we see this often with people who have followed a vegetarian diet for a number of years and actually do not know how they feel eating meat.

They tend to assume they do not do well with meat based only on the fact that they do not like the taste or prefer not to eat animal products. Other people just eat whatever they want and always feel bad, so it is more difficult to narrow down which foods are contributing just by using this quiz.

When you determine your Diet Type, be sure to read the chapter that accompanies that Hauser Diet (or read them all, just to be sure!) Good luck! And again, try to be as objective as you can. Think about how food makes *you* feel—not how you feel about the food.

if *you* eat great you'll feel **great!**

FIGURE 2-6 The Hauser Diet Quiz: What Animal Are You?

Read across the page, choosing which answer (column A, B, or C) best describes how you feel about that particular question. Circle the best answer that happens most of the time. Add up your totals for each column. See answer key below to determine your Diet Type.

A	B	C
1. High protein breakfasts, like eggs and bacon, give me the most energy in the morning.	1. Eating a variety of foods, some starchy, some fat, gives me the most energy in the morning.	1. A big glass of juice with cereal or waffles gives me the most energy in the morning.
2. If I do not eat for a few hours, I get shaky and/or irritable.	2. If I do not eat for a few hours, I feel fine. However, I do need my three meals to feel my best.	2. I can skip meals and feel fine. I could eat one or two meals per day and still feel good energy.
3. Pasta makes me tired within a short time after eating it.	3. Pasta, in small amounts makes me feel fine. I don't get sleepy.	3. Pasta gives me a lot of energy and makes me feel good.
4. I feel best when my diet consists of mostly meats.	4. I feel best with a mix of meat and veggies in my diet.	4. I feel best when my diet consists of mostly vegetables and grains.
5. When I eat pizza, I need meat on it, or my energy drops.	5. I feel good energy eating pizza with meat or veggies on it.	5. I feel good energy eating vegetarian pizza.
6. My body performs best in warm/hot weather.	6. Weather does not change the way my body performs. I feel good in any weather.	6. My body performs best in cool/cold weather.
7. I have more energy when I eat protein than any other food.	7. I have more energy when I eat a variety of foods, instead of just meat or just veggies and grains.	7. I have more energy when I eat veggies and grains, than any other foods.
8. Coffee gives me a buzz. I would never drink it before bed.	8. Coffee stimulates me a little but doesn't give me a big rush.	8. Coffee does not give me a buzz. I can drink it right before bed.
9. Eating something sweet, like dessert, would make me sleepy.	9. Eating sweets, like dessert, doesn't make me sleepy, but I can't eat them very often.	9. Eating sweets, like dessert, is fine for me. I do not get sleepy afterward.
10. I am a morning person.	10. My energy level is the same all day long.	10. I am a night person.
11. When I go to a restaurant, I feel best when I order a meat dish and stay away from breads and sweets.	11. When I go to a restaurant, I feel best when I eat a variety of meats, veggies, and starches.	11. When I go to a restaurant, I feel best when I order pasta and veggie dishes, over fatty foods or meat dishes.
12. High fat foods, like nuts, steaks, sour cream, and fried foods make me feel my best.	12. I feel fine and do not get bloated from fatty foods if I eat them in moderation.	12. I do not feel good eating high fat foods. They can give me digestive upset, like bloating.
13. I get tired in the afternoon if I eat a salad and bread at lunch.	13. I feel ok in the afternoon if I eat a salad and bread at lunch, but not my best.	13. I feel the best energy in the afternoon if I eat a salad and bread at lunch.
14. My ideal climate would be hot weather.	14. I could live comfortably in hot or cold climates. My body adjusts well.	14. My ideal climate would be cool or even cold weather.
Total for Column A:	*Total for Column B:*	*Total for Column C:*

Diet Typing Answer Key

Look at the total number of answers per column to determine your Hauser Diet Animal.

Column A: 11-14 = Lion Diet	Column C: 8-10 = Monkey Diet	A + C > B = Bear Diet
Column A: 8-10 = Otter Diet	Column C: 11-14 = Giraffe Diet	A + B > C = Otter Diet
Column B: 11-14 = Bear Diet	All Columns: 3-7 = Bear Diet	B + C > A = Monkey Diet

THE LION
DIET TYPE™

60%
protein

25%
fat

15%
carbohydrates

the lion diet type™

The Lion Diet contains the highest amounts of protein and fat of all the Diet Types. It is a highly carnivorous diet, similar to how a lion would eat. The macronutrient breakdown is 60% protein, 25% fat, and 15% carbohydrates. This diet is used therapeutically for people whose Diet Typing results show abnormalities in both the glucose tolerance test and blood pH. Two different patterns of glucose tolerance results both need the Lion Diet. A "true" Lion will be a fast oxidizer of food and have acidic blood pH. The second pattern, which is quite common in overweight America also has acidic blood pH, but the glucose tolerance test shows a slow oxidizer with high insulin levels (insulin resistance). This person also needs a Lion Diet to regain insulin sensitivity. The Lion Diet is very high in protein and fat, with a very small amount of carbohydrates. These foods help to raise blood pH and prevent blood sugar swings, along with lowering insulin levels. In other words, this diet helps to normalize the Lion's abnormal physiology. *(See Figure 3-1.)*

A Lion extracts the maximum amount of energy from food that is high in protein and fat. Why? These foods cause a Lion's acidic blood to normalize which optimizes enzyme activity in the body and ultimately energy production. Unfortunately, these people typically have a weakness for sweets and ultimately feel terrible and out of shape if they continue to eat them. A Lion really has to concentrate on staying away from starchy and sweet foods in order to be successful on this diet. Yes, it may be a challenge, but it is crucial for a Lion Diet Type to "eat like a Lion!"

What happens when a *Lion* doesn't eat like a *Lion*?

When a Lion eats too many carbohydrates, blood pH plummets to become even more acidic, and stable blood sugar levels are not established. Acidic blood pH decreases enzyme activity and thus decreases energy production in the body. This leads to fatigue, lethargy, decreased activity, and weight gain. We often see this cycle continue and lead to chronic pain, infections, and other maladies, such as Syndrome X.

FIGURE 3-1 Eating a high protein and fat diet normalizes a Lion Diet Type's physiology.

When a Lion eats like a Lion, the blood pH and oxidative rates normalize. As blood sugars and physiology stabilize, so should their overall health.

	Lion's Baseline Physiology after Eating a High Carb Diet	Lion's Physiology after Changing to a High Protein and Fat Diet
Blood pH	Acidic	Normal
Oxidative Rate	Fast or Slow with High Fasting Insulin Level	Balanced

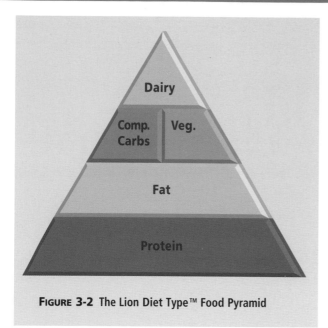

FIGURE 3-2 The Lion Diet Type™ Food Pyramid

source. When the cells no longer respond properly to insulin, this forces the body to produce more insulin to get the necessary response. When the body's cells are resistant to the action of the insulin, it is called insulin resistance (IR). Blood sugar levels stay high because the cells don't respond to insulin. If blood sugar levels go too high, diabetes forms. Therefore, people with high insulin levels have to be very careful with avoiding foods that contain simple carbohydrates such as sugar, desserts, candy, soda, white bread, white rice, pasta, and fruits, because consuming these items will cause the fasting insulin levels to remain elevated (over 15uU/ml). Foods that help lower insulin levels are protein and fat, such as meat, chicken, fish, soy, nuts, and oils. Thus, the Lion Diet is designed to put those abnormal insulin levels in check!

A person with Syndrome X will typically exhibit the following:

- Insulin Resistance (the inability to properly use dietary carbohydrates and sugars)
- Abnormal Blood Lipids (such as elevated cholesterol and triglycerides)
- Abdominal Obesity
- High Blood Pressure
- Mental Sluggishness

The condition is almost always caused by an individual's diet and lifestyle; highly processed carbohydrates and sugar, along with a sedentary lifestyle. The bad news is that if you do not make any changes in your diet and lifestyle, Syndrome X can lead to Type II (adult-onset) Diabetes, and increase your risk for other diseases. The good news is that you can reverse this phenomenon—often times with diet alone—as long as you are committed to making the appropriate changes. Never underestimate the power of food!

Keeping your insulin levels at a normal level will help to keep you healthy!

When a person eats, the body breaks down the food into usable energy. Insulin is a hormone secreted by the body to transport glucose into the cells for their energy

Food Choices on the *Lion Diet*

As you have been reading, the Lion Diet consists primarily of protein and fat, with minimal emphasis on carbohydrates. *(See Figure 3-2.)* We are soon going to take a look at a sample week's meal plan so we want to be sure you understand what this means in terms of real food. Protein includes foods such as eggs, chicken, ground beef, steak, pork, fish, and tofu. The Lion Diet requires 60% of its calories from protein, which means almost two-thirds of the food on your plate should consist of protein—every time you eat!

Fat includes foods such as olive oil, canola oil, bacon, avocado, olives, sour cream, and butter. Get the "low-fat" mentality out of your mind. This diet is not low-fat! About one-fourth, or 25%, of your diet should come from fat. You want to include these fats because your body needs them. Remember, your body needs foods that are broken down slowly so that you will have more energy and balance your blood sugar. The foods that provide this for you are proteins and fats which take longer to be processed by the body.

Foods that do not provide this type of energy for your Lion physiology are carbohydrates. Carbohydrates are divided into two categories: complex and simple, as we discussed in *Chapter 2*. In the simplest terms, complex carbohydrates are denser in fiber, while simple carbohydrates are higher in sugar without the fiber. Complex carbohydrates are foods such as oat bran, brown rice, potatoes with the skins, and whole grain bread. Simple carbohydrates are foods such as white bread or buns, potatoes without the skins, white rice, cookies, cake, soda pop, and sugar. For the purposes of the Lion Diet, fruit also acts as a simple carbohydrate, providing too much sugar for the Lion's needs. The Lion should not be eating fruit and simple carbohydrates on a daily basis.

However, the Lion has to include some complex carbohydrates on a daily basis to provide good sources of fiber. As you saw in *Figure 3-2,* the Lion Diet only allows a small amount of complex carbohydrates, such as whole grain breads, pastas, and cereals. Therefore, the Lion will also need to get fiber, vitamins, and minerals from vegetables, which we put in their own category. Vegetables include foods such as tomatoes, eggplant, dark leafy greens, carrots, bell peppers, and squash. Vegetables do not include potatoes or corn, which are actually counted as complex carbohydrates.

How does a *Lion* make vegetables taste good?

Believe it or not, this category is where a Lion really gets a tasty break! Because the Lions can have the most fat and dairy of any of the Diet Types, you can make eating vegetables very enjoyable. We'll explain… When you think of vegetables, most people prefer broccoli with cheese versus raw broccoli or green beans almandine versus plain green beans because both of these contain added fats and creaminess from cheese or butter. Since the Lion is allowed plentiful fat and some dairy, adding foods like nuts and cheese to make veggies taste better is perfectly fine. However, if you like raw vegetables, you can have them that way! If you like them lightly steamed with a little salt and pepper, you can have them that way too. But if you also like to get a little creative with your vegetable side dishes, go for it! For instance, Lions can use more butter (added fat) to flavor their sautéed carrots

and zucchini. You can sprinkle a little cheddar on your broccoli or blue cheese on your asparagus, and add a few almonds to your green beans, without worrying about going overboard with the fat. Just be sure that you do not drown your vegetables in excessive cheese and butter, for portion's sake! Doing that will put fat on anyone's hips!

How does a *Lion* make a salad?

Upcoming in this chapter we will show you a sample week's meal plan. You will see some "green salads" listed throughout the week. Each "green salad" starts with a good lettuce, such as romaine or arugula, or you can use spinach or mixed field greens. A good lettuce is dark green, not light and watery like iceberg lettuce. A good salad goes beyond the standard "dinner" salad, which is typically iceberg lettuce, a tomato wedge, and a slice of cucumber. We have included some of these favorite standard salad vegetables such as chopped cucumber, onion, tomatoes, and radishes, but we encourage you to explore the rainbow of vegetables that can be sliced and diced into your salad, such as bell peppers, carrots, and cauliflower.

In addition to creating a colorful salad, Lions can use fat to add texture and flavor to any salad. You will see in the upcoming meal plans that Lions can add nuts and seeds, such as walnuts or sunflower seeds to give their salads a little more crunch. Sprinkle a little blue cheese or add avocado slices to create a new dimension to your salad. Other Hauser Diets do not have as much leeway with adding fat and dairy products to their salads, so take full advantage. Yes, this even means you can add bacon! You'll never dread eating salad again! What's the catch? No croutons—they're simple carbs. But who needs croutons when you've got a spinach and bacon salad?!

What types of fats should a *Lion* include?

Good fats for the Lions include those from oils and plant sources, such as olive oil, walnut oil, grapeseed oil, coconut oil, olives, and avocados. A Lion will also do well with adding those otherwise sinful goodies, such as bacon, butter, sour cream, and heavy whipping cream to a meal. As you will see in the meal plans and *Chapter 9's* recipes, using fats (like bacon and oil) really add flavor and richness to your cooking. Use these to help make your meat dishes more attractive. Eating a steak, for example, is pretty plain. However, mixing a little sour cream, salt and pepper, and chives, for a dipping sauce, can help make the steak even more enjoyable. Some sauces, such as hollandaise, are all fat and protein (butter and egg yolks) so they fit the Lion Diet perfectly. You can whip up a little hollandaise sauce for your asparagus, or try it over your ham and eggs. These are examples of how a Lion should be using fat to help make this diet exciting!

On that note, let's take a look at a sample meal plan for a Lion. If you need help recalling how we define a food "equivalent," refer back to the Food Equivalent Chart in *Figure 2-2.*

LION DAILY MEAL PLAN

19	protein equivalents
13	fat equivalents
5	vegetable equivalents
2	complex carb equivalents
2	dairy equivalents
0	fruit equivalents
0	simple carb equivalents

Approximately 2,000 Calories

Drink water or herbal tea as your beverage. Coffee ought to be avoided.

Monday

Breakfast

- 3 eggs cooked in 1 tsp butter
- 2 pieces of bacon or sausage
- 1 piece of rye toast with ½ Tbsp nut butter
- 1 cup 2% milk

(3 protein, 4 fat, 1 complex carb, 1 dairy)

Lunch

- Green salad: 2 cups mescalin greens with 4 slices cucumber, 1 shredded radish, 1 chopped scallion, topped with bean sprouts
- 6 ounces grilled chicken, sliced
- ⅓ avocado, sliced
- 1 tsp oil mixed with Balsamic vinegar for dressing
- ½ cup cooked green beans

(6 protein, 2 vegetable, 3 fat)

Snack

- 2 organic beef jerky sticks

(2 protein)

* When you see an asterisk throughout the menu, look for this recipe in Chapter 9!

Dinner
- Crock Pot Beef* *(7 ounces of beef and 2 cups mixed vegetables from crock pot beef)*
- Green salad: 1 cup romaine lettuce topped with 1 chopped hard boiled egg, sliced red onion rings, and 1 tsp slivered almonds
- 1 tsp olive oil and 2 Tbsp vinegar

  (8 protein, 3 vegetable, 1 complex carb, 3 fat)

Snack
- 1 cup plain yogurt: sprinkle with cinnamon, and a dash of vanilla extract
- 1 Tbsp chopped nuts

  (1 dairy, 3 fat)

Tuesday
Breakfast
- Mexican Style Steak* *(4 ounces steak, 1 egg over easy, ½ cup salsa, 1 tsp oil, and 1 ounce shredded cheese)*
- 1 cup tomato juice

  (5 protein, 1½ vegetable, 1 fat, 1 dairy)

Lunch
- 1 cup Split Pea Soup*
- 4 ounces ham
- 1 cup raw carrots and celery

  (2 complex carb, 1 vegetable, 4 protein)

Snack
- Lettuce roll-ups: 3 large romaine lettuce leaves, 1 ounce cheese, 3 ounces turkey breast, ¼ cup shredded carrots, 2 tsp mustard

  (1 dairy, ½ vegetable, 3 protein)

Dinner
- Sautéed Sole with Mushroom Butter Sauce* *(7 ounces fish and 2 Tbsp sauce)*
- 8 sprigs of asparagus sautéed in 1 tsp lemon juice and chopped garlic

  (7 protein, 7 fat, 2 vegetable)

Snack
- 2 Tbsp nuts

  (6 fat)

Wednesday
Breakfast
- Tofu-bacon scramble: 4 ounces tofu, 2 pieces bacon scrambled and topped with 1 ounce shredded cheese

  (4 protein, 1 dairy, 2 fat)

Lunch
- Ginger Shrimp* *(4 ounces of shrimp served over ½ cup rice noodles topped with 2 Tbsp Peanut Sauce*)*
- 1 cup stir-fry vegetable blend in soy sauce and 1 tsp sesame oil

  (4 protein, 7 fat, 1 complex carb, 2 vegetable)

Snack
- 2 Deviled Eggs*

  (2 protein, 1 fat)

Dinner
- Beef taco salad: 6 ounces taco beef, 2 cups romaine lettuce, 1 medium chopped tomato, ⅛ cup chopped onion, ⅓ sliced avocado, 5 sliced black olives, 1 ounce shredded cheese, and 10 corn tortilla chips
- 1 cup raw Mexican spicy carrot-pepper mix

  (6 protein, 3 fat, 3 vegetable, 1 complex carb, 1 dairy)

Snack
- Roast beef roll-ups: 3 ounces roast beef and your favorite mustard

  (3 protein)

Thursday

Breakfast

- 4 ounces ham
- 2 poached eggs
- ½ cup grits topped with 1 ounce of shredded cheddar cheese, 1 tsp butter, and a dash of hot sauce
- 1 medium tomato, sliced and ⅓ avocado, sliced, drizzled with Balsamic vinegar, salt, and chopped fresh basil

  (6 protein, 1 complex carb, 1 dairy, 1 vegetable, 3 fat)

Lunch

- ⅛ pie slice of crustless bacon and onion quiche
- Green salad: 2 cups mixed salad greens, ¼ cup green pepper slices, 2 mushrooms, ½ cup chopped broccoli
- 1 tsp olive oil, 2 Tbsp Balsamic vinegar

  (3 protein, 4 fat, 2 vegetable)

Snack

- ½ cup cottage cheese
- 2 tsp chopped walnuts
- 2 ounces roast beef

  (1 dairy, 2 fat, 2 protein)

Dinner

- 8 ounces crock pot pork ribs
- 1 small baked potato topped with 1 Tbsp sour cream and 1 tsp butter
- 1 cup cooked green beans with 1 tsp butter
- Green salad: 1 cup spring blend lettuce, 4 cucumber slices, shredded radish, topped with sprouts
- 1 Tbsp olive oil and 2 Tbsp red wine vinegar

  (8 protein, 1 complex carb, 6 fat, 2 vegetable)

Friday

Breakfast

- 4 ounce hamburger patty
- 1 poached egg
- 2 slices bacon
- 1 slice whole grain bread
- 1 Tbsp cream cheese

  (5 protein, 3 fat, 1 complex carb)

Lunch

- Tuna salad lettuce wraps: 1 can tuna, 1 Tbsp mayonnaise, ⅛ cup chopped onion, ⅙ avocado, romaine lettuce leaves, bean sprouts, cucumber slices, and shredded carrots
- 1 medium tomato, sliced

  (6 protein, 4 fat, 2 vegetable)

Snack

- 2 organic beef jerky sticks

  (2 protein)

Dinner

- 6 ounces grilled mahi mahi with 1 Tbsp tartar sauce and lemon
- ½ medium sweet potato with 1 tsp butter
- 1 ½ cups cooked green beans with 2 tsp slivered almonds and 1 ounce shredded Asiago cheese

  (6 protein, 6 fat, 1 complex carb, 3 vegetable, 1 dairy)

Snack

- 1 cup warm soy milk

  (1 dairy)

Dinner

- 7 ounces pork tenderloin
- Green salad: 2 cups lettuce with shredded radish, sprouts, red pepper rings, and cucumber slices, 1 tsp olive oil
- 2 Tbsp wine vinegar
- ½ cup cottage cheese
- 1 cup roasted mixed veggies with 1 tsp butter and chives
  (7 protein, 2 fat, 1 dairy, 3 vegetable)

Snack

- 1 cup plain yogurt with ½ tsp vanilla extract
- 2 tsp chopped pecans
  (1 dairy, 2 fat)

Sunday

Breakfast

- Breakfast smoothie: 1 cup milk, 1 Tbsp nut butter, 1 scoop protein powder, dash of vanilla
  (1 dairy, 2 fat, 2 protein)

Snack

- 1 hard boiled egg
  (1 protein)

Lunch

- ½ turkey sandwich: 5 ounces turkey slices on 1 slice whole grain bread, with 1 tsp mayonnaise and mustard, lettuce leaves, 2 tomato slices, 4 cucumber slices, and ½ sliced avocado
- 1 cup raw carrot and celery sticks
  (5 protein, 1 complex carb, 4 fat, 2 vegetable)

Snack

- 3 ounces chicken
- 1 cup raw broccoli with 1 Tbsp homemade ranch dressing
  (3 protein, 1 vegetable, 3 fat)

Dinner

- 8 ounce ribeye steak with 1 ounce blue cheese
- 2 small red potatoes with skins topped with 2 tsp butter, 1 tsp sour cream
- 2 cups Asian spinach with 1 tsp butter
  (8 protein, 1 complex carb, 4 fat, 1 dairy, 2 vegetable)

Saturday

Breakfast

- Eggs Benedict: 2 poached eggs, 2 slices Canadian bacon, 2 Tbsp Hollandaise sauce, and ½ whole wheat English muffin
  (5 protein, 5 fat, 1 complex carb)

Lunch

- 6 ounces chicken salad served over 1 cup chopped lettuce (5 ounces chicken, 2 tsp mayonnaise, chopped onion and celery)
- 1 cup sautéed eggplant and zucchini in 1 tsp olive oil with chopped fresh basil
- 1 whole grain roll with 1 tsp butter
  (5 protein, 4 fat, 2 vegetable, 1 complex carb)

Snack

- 2 turkey jerky sticks
  (2 protein)

So do you think you're ready to eat like a Lion?

As you can see, the Lion really needs a lot of meat to optimize energy. Sorry to say, but vegetarianism was just not meant for you. We understand your boredom and frustration if you are imagining eating a plain broiled steak for dinner every night. To enjoy this diet as much as possible, you have to get creative with your cooking! *Chapter 9* is filled with recipes and tips to help you make tasty meals, while keeping on the road to better health.

Succeeding on the *Lion Diet*

Here are a few Lion tips that many of our Lion patients have found helpful:

- **Know your friends and know your enemies.**
  Lions metabolize food very quickly and thus are prone to hypoglycemia (or low blood sugar). When blood sugar gets low, it makes a person hungry. This means that Lions tend to get hunger swings throughout the day and they are prone to overeating. The secret then for the Lion is to keep blood sugars stabilized by eating a high protein and fat diet. Carbohydrates are the nemesis of the Lions.

- **Slow down!**
  Lions need to eat slowly. The majority of food recommended for a Lion is the kind of food that is broken down slowly, namely protein and fat. Your brain will not register the signs that you have eaten, until the food begins to break down. If you eat fast, but the foods you eat are broken down slowly, this may lead to overeating. In other words, Lions will start feeling full only once the protein/fats in their diets begin to be broken down by the digestive system. If they eat slowly, this will occur at the right time—when you have eaten a decent portion without overeating.

- **Perfect timing!**
  Lions typically feel best squeezing in a snack or two between their three daily meals. Many of our Lion patients feel better when they wake up iin the morning after having eaten a snack before bedtime, otherwise they wake up ravenous.

- **Dangerous drinks!**
  Lions need to eliminate caffeine and alcohol. Both of these acidify the blood, which is already too acidic in Lions. Caffeine may give the Lion a short term boost in energy but will leave the Lion extremely fatigued in a few hours. When extremely fatigued, the Lion will tend to overeat. So in the long haul, caffeine is not a good drink choice for the Lion.

- **Dairy can be scary.**
  Lions do great with full fat milk and dairy products as long as they aren't allergic to them. If you are allergic to them, dairy products will cause you to have excess swelling and weight. Thus, it is important for the Lion to get a food allergy test if allergies are suspected.

- **Lions love soy.**
  Most Lions tolerate soy products very well. Organic unsweetened soy milk is a good drink

for the Lion. You want to find a brand that contains more protein grams than sugar grams.

- **Show us those muscles!**

  Lions do well with body building/weight lifting. Since your diet consists of so much protein, it is important to give the body a place for this protein to go. The place where protein is most helpful for a Lion, long term, is into muscle tissue. The more muscle tissue the Lion has the more likely the Lion will stay fit for life. The Lion who performs no muscle-building activities will end up with a slow metabolism, even if he eats the right foods. You may struggle with how little Lions have to eat to maintain a good body weight. A better approach is to build muscle! As we will discuss in the exercise chapter, one pound of muscle consumes 50 calories per day. So if you add 10 pounds of muscle, you will increase your daily calorie food expenditure by 10 x 50, or 500 calories.

- **Do yourself a favor and add some flavor!**

  If you want to enjoy the foods you eat, a Lion needs to master spices and get different flavors from the protein and fat sources. Lions can get very tired of eating eggs and broiled steak all the time. We cannot tell you how much more you will enjoy your meat if you add a little sauce and flavor to it. See the recipe section for some delicious ideas that will get your mouth watering!

Tips for Losing Weight on the Lion Diet

- **Eat the right proportions of food.**

  Each of the Hauser Diets is a unique breakdown of protein, fat, and carbohydrates. As a Lion, your body needs the most protein and fat of any Diet Type. So 85% of your plate should have protein and fat when you sit down to a meal.

- **Eat the right portion sizes for your daily needs.**

  It should be evident from reading the food equivalent section and the meal plans that most people just eat too much food! Our bodies are not meant to take in so much food. This excessive food is stored as fat.

- **Don't drink your calories.**

  Drinks such as juice and soda are too easily absorbed and cause the blood sugar to be unstable. The Lion Diet Type focuses on trying to regain blood sugar balance. The Lion Diet Type can only have stable blood sugars by having all foods, and even liquid meals, be high in protein and fat. Lions will do better with drinks such as full fat milk or high protein soy milk.

- **Only eat carbohydrates that contain fiber.**

  This means whole grains, and carbohydrates that have at least 4 grams of fiber per serving. Fiber is necessary for proper digestion and signaling the brain that the stomach is full, among many other actions in the body.

- **Avoid coffee.**

  When you drink coffee, your insulin is raised more than if you did not have the coffee. This worsens blood sugar swings which can increase appetite. Coffee also acidifies the blood, which is already a problem for the Lion.

- **Tell others that you are on a diet.**

  Give a quick outline to people you are in contact with everyday. Tell them that you are eating a high protein diet and that you are avoiding sugary and starchy foods. Most people will get the idea that they should not offer you these foods.

- **Eat slowly.**

  This gives your stomach additional time to fill up to prevent overeating. Remember protein and fat are digested more slowly than carbohydrates, so it will take longer for you to feel full. So give yourself some time to feel the fullness before putting another helping on your plate.

- **Eat Breakfast.**
  People with the physiology of a Lion need to eat a high protein breakfast. Since you are a fast oxidizer of food, the food you ate the day before has been used up. Your energy reserves are on empty at the beginning of the day. Breakfast is a must!

- **Don't drink alcohol.**
  These simple carbs provide non-nutritious calories which can make it difficult for you to keep your blood sugar balanced and increase your appetite.

FAQ and *Lion Diet* Myths:

Won't I become constipated?

If a person on the Lion Diet is not having regular bowel movements, the first step is to increase your water intake. Next, try increasing your intake of vegetables. These foods are high in water and fiber content.

What about cholesterol?

If your physiology is that of a Lion, you will not have elevated cholesterol levels if you are eating according to your Diet Type. In fact, if someone with a Lion physiology tries to eat the Monkey Diet, that is when he or she would typically see abnormal cholesterol levels.

The Lion uses fat, protein, and cholesterol as an energy source. So by eating foods, like eggs, meats, and nuts, the Lion is getting energy foods. If a Lion eats a high carbohydrate diet, insulin levels go too high. This insulin tells the Lion's body to store fat and cholesterol. This is why when the Lion eats too many carbohydrates, weight problems, high cholesterol, insulin resistance and even diabetes are destined to follow.

How often should I eat?

Eat frequently. To avoid having blood sugar swings throughout the day, you should eat every three to four hours, and never skip meals. Breakfast should be a large meal, with lunch and dinner being moderately sized.

Can I be a vegetarian?

In our experience, vegetarian foods that are high in protein, such as legumes and soy, are typically still too high in carbohydrates to have the same effect eating meat will have. When we have seen people attempt a high protein vegetarian diet, it makes the diet extremely difficult to follow and will typically not provide the desired results.

Will I always be a Lion?

The simplest answer is: no. As you read in *Chapter 1*, there are a couple key factors that determine which diet is best for you. Typically for the Lion Diet Type, eating 60% protein, 25% fat, and 15% complex carbohydrates needs to be done until the Lion's abnormal physiology is corrected. In our experience at Caring Medical, it is best for a Lion to retest blood pH and glucose tolerance regularly until the person's health goals have been met. Most people will eventually be adjusted to the Otter Diet Type or a more balanced Bear Diet Type.

Obtaining Optimal Health on the *Lion Diet*

John the Junk Food Junkie

John was like most people who weigh 60 pounds too much. He drank soda and ate a lot of nacho chips. We did some diagnostic testing on him which showed a fasting Insulin level of 128 (normal is less than 15) and a cholesterol of 289. His glucose tolerance test was a little high (slow oxidizer) and his blood pH was very low at 7.380. He was placed on the Lion Diet Type for four months. He dropped the weight easily, his cholesterol normalized to 182, but when he was retested his blood was slightly alkaline at 7.452. If he continued on the Lion Diet Type, his blood would have continued to be more and more alkaline and he would have started feeling worse. He was switched to the Otter Diet Type and has done well since then. When he does binge on junk food, he gains some of the weight back, but at least he knows what he needs to do to lose it.

Ray and the Rice Cake Wars

Ray came to us to help lower his risk of heart disease and manage his diabetes. He was about 30 pounds overweight, especially in the mid-section, so losing weight was definitely going to help slow and reverse those conditions. Over the past few years, he had seen a dozen nutritionists, dietitians, and doctors who recommended the same traditional low-fat, high carbohydrate diet. In fact, when he showed up for his appointment, he was snacking on a bag of rice cakes! To the surprise of Ray and his family, we told him that if he kept eating those rice cakes he would never get healthy. According to his Diet Typing, his body needed some meat! Of course, Ray's wife was very concerned and called the whole diet "crazy." She refused to believe that rice cakes, fruit, and fat-free jelly beans could be harmful for anyone. After all, this is what all of those other dietitians had recommended he eat! Ray's wife truly believed that if he ate anything but fruit, salads, grains, lean meat, and fat-free snacks that his arteries would become clogged and he'd have a heart attack. The truth was that those foods were actually the ones causing his arteries to become clogged, in addition to worsening his diabetes! We argued that Ray's condition had steadily worsened since visiting with these "experts" and that he should just try the Hauser Diet approach to see if his condition would

reverse. Reluctantly, Ray's wife stopped making him eat the rice cakes and other "sissy" foods, as Ray called them. When Ray followed up a few months later, he had lost about 20 pounds, normalized his cholesterol from 260 to 180, and was starting to feel like his old self again. He was also particularly happy that he got to eat foods that he enjoyed, like steak and eggs, and let his wife eat the rice cakes!

Summary of the *Lion Diet*

If you could sum the Lion Diet up in one word, it would be *meat*. This is the meat-lover's diet! The Lion's meals should consist of mostly protein and fat, meaning meat, eggs, fish, oils, avocado, olives, cheese, milk, and other such foods. Although vegetables and some complex carbohydrates should compliment your meals, meat is always the most important part. Remember, these foods are helpful at getting your blood sugar levels in check and your acidic blood pH back to normal. Hence, your health should improve!

To succeed on the Lion Diet, you have to turn it into your lifestyle! Eating such a diet requires planning ahead and dedication! But don't get discouraged, this diet is doable and you will love the meat recipes we have in store! In the upcoming chapters we will talk more about how to grocery shop on the Lion Diet, along with turning those groceries into delicious meals. But first, we'll explore the other Hauser Diet Types and learn more about how their dietary needs are different than those on the Lion Diet.

THE OTTER
DIET TYPE™

50%
protein

25%
fat

25%
carbohydrates

the otter diet type™

The Otter Diet is carnivorous (meat-eating), but also emphasizes whole grains and vegetables. This is the most common diet type that we see at Caring Medical. The macronutrient breakdown is 50% protein, 25% fat, and 25% carbohydrates. This diet is high in protein and fat, with a moderate amount of carbohydrates. These foods help to raise blood pH and prevent blood sugar swings, along with lowering insulin levels. This diet is recommended when Diet Typing results reveal a fast oxidative rate and normal blood pH, or a balanced oxidative rate and acidic blood. Of course, there are exceptions. This diet is not as extreme as the Lion Diet (So, if a person has both a low blood pH and a glucose tolerance test that is out of the normal range, the Lion Diet is prescribed.) When only one of them is out of the normal range, the Otter Diet is recommended. The most common profile we see at Caring Medical for an Otter is a normal blood pH and a fast oxidative rate.

A person on the Otter Diet really has to concentrate on moderating starchy and sweet foods in order to have optimal health. Unfortunately, these people typically have a weakness for sweets and ultimately feel terrible if they continue to eat them. If an Otter doesn't stop eating too many carbohydrates, the blood will become more acidic, and insulin resistance may become an issue or ultimately, adult onset diabetes. If you want to feel good and maintain a healthy weight, you have to eat like an Otter!

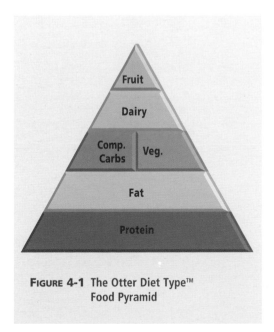

FIGURE 4-1 The Otter Diet Type™ Food Pyramid

Food Choices on the *Otter Diet*

As we have stated throughout the book, the Otter Diet is made up of primarily protein and fat, with a much smaller emphasis on carbohydrates. We are soon going to take a look at a sample week's meal plan, so you need to understand what this means in terms of real food. Protein includes foods such as eggs, chicken, ground beef, steak, fish, and tofu. Half of your daily food intake should come from protein, which means you are going to have to learn to like meat! One-fourth or 25% of your calories comes from fat, which includes foods such as olive oil, canola oil, bacon, avocado, olives, sour cream, and butter. Get the "low-fat" mentality out of your mind. This diet is not low-fat! Your body is getting most of its energy from protein and fat, so give it what it needs! *(See Figure 4-1.)*

The food that an Otter should limit is carbohydrates, because in excess, they leave the Otters feeling lethargic and overweight. Carbohydrates are really divided into two categories: complex and simple. In the simplest terms, complex carbohydrates are denser in fiber, while simple carbohydrates are higher in sugar without the fiber. Complex carbohydrates are foods such as oat bran, brown rice, potatoes with the skins, and whole grain bread. We get fiber from carbohydrate sources. Hence, an Otter has to include some of these carbohydrates. This still means less than 25% of your food per day is coming from these sources. You want to stay away from simple carbohydrates which are foods such as white bread/buns, potatoes without the skins, white rice, cookies, cake, soda pop, and sugar. Foods that are primarily simple carbohydrates like pasta, pizza, and noodle casseroles are not a good regular choice for an Otter. Meals that are planned around meat with a small side dish of complex carbohydrates are ideal, for instance, a steak with a little brown rice on the side.

The Otter will also get fiber, vitamins, and nutrients from vegetables, which we have put in their own category. Vegetables include foods such as tomatoes, eggplant, dark leafy greens, carrots, bell peppers, and squash. Vegetables do not include potatoes or corn, which are actually counted as complex carbohydrates. The Otter is also allowed a very small portion (one serving) of fruit per day, if desired. Remember that fruit and vegetables are *not* in the same category. Unlike what many generic health advertisements would have you believe, it is not necessary for all of us to have three fruits per day. This is simply too much sugar for an Otter.

We encourage Otters to get creative with your one fruit serving and use the fruit to accent your meals. For instance, stuff your pork chop with some apple slices to add a sweet flavor. You Otters should also remember that fruit is nature's ultimate dessert! You will see that we have even included a couple of Otter friendly desserts that are typically a mix of fruit, dairy, and fat, such as yogurt with nuts and berries on top. Yum!

How does an *Otter* make vegetables taste good?

You may not believe it to be possible, but vegetables can be very delicious! Because the Otters are allowed a good amount of fat and dairy, you can take the easy way out of flavoring up vegetables. When you think of vegetables, most people prefer cauliflower au gratin with cheese over raw cauliflower or green beans almondine over raw green beans. Get a little creative with your vegetable side dishes! Sauté in butter with a dash of salt to bring flavor to an otherwise dreaded vegetable! Try sprinkling a little spicy Monterey jack cheese on your broccoli or blue cheese on your asparagus, and add more almonds to your green beans. Just be sure that you do not drown your vegetables in excessive cheese and butter! You do have to watch your portions. We know there are some of you who prefer plain, raw, or lightly steamed vegetables. You can have them that way too. We want to encourage you to try new things—especially when it comes to vegetables. You will be amazed at how delicious your otherwise, ordinary vegetables can be once you learn how to add a little "extra" Otter *zest* to those veggies!

How does an *Otter* make a salad?

Coming up in this chapter we will show you a sample meal plan for one week. You will see some "green salads" listed throughout. Each "green salad" starts with good lettuce, such as romaine, arugula, spinach, or mixed field greens. A good lettuce is dark green, not light and watery like iceberg lettuce. A good salad goes beyond what you get in most restaurants which is typically iceberg lettuce, a tomato wedge, and a slice of cucumber. We have included some of old stand-by salad vegetables such as chopped cucumber, onion, tomatoes, and radishes, but we encourage you to explore the rainbow of vegetables that can be sliced and diced into your salad, such as bell peppers, carrots, and cauliflower. In addition to creating a colorful salad, Otters can use fat to add texture and flavor to any salad. You will see in the upcoming meal plans that Otters can add nuts and seeds, such as walnuts or sunflower seeds to give a salad more crunch or chop up a few feta cheese stuffed olives for a tasty twang. Other Hauser Diets do not have as much leeway with adding fat and dairy products to their salads, so take full advantage. Yes, that even means you can add bacon to your salad, and who doesn't love bacon? You'll never fear eating salad again! What's the catch? No croutons—they are simple carbs! But who needs croutons when you have walnuts and blue cheese?!

What types of fats should an *Otter* include?

Otters need a good amount of the healthy kind of fats from plant sources such as olive oil, walnut oil, grapeseed oil, coconut oil, olives, and avocados. Otters can add otherwise sinful goodies such as bacon, butter, sour cream, and heavy whipping cream to a meal. As you will see in the meal plans and the recipe chapter, using fats (like bacon and oil) really add flavor and richness to your cooking. Use these to help make your meat dishes more attractive. Eating a chicken breast, for example, is pretty plain. However, melting a little butter, feta cheese, salt and pepper, and thyme, for a sauce, can help make that plain chicken breast a little more exciting. As we just discussed, add some nuts to your salad or your sautéed vegetables to make them more interesting. These are examples of how an Otter should be using fat to help make this diet enjoyable!

On that note, let's take a look at a sample meal plan for an Otter. If you need help recalling how we define a food "equivalent," refer back to the Food Equivalent Chart *Figure 2-2* in *Chapter 2*.

OTTER DAILY MEAL PLAN

16 protein equivalents

13 fat equivalents

6 vegetable equivalents

3 complex carb equivalents

2 dairy equivalents

1 fruit equivalent

0 simple carb equivalents

Approximately 2,000 Calories

Drink water or herbal tea as your beverage. Coffee ought to be avoided.

Monday

Breakfast

- 2 eggs, any style, cooked in 1 tsp olive oil
- 2 pieces of bacon
- 1 slice whole grain toast with 1 tsp butter
- 1 cup soy milk
- 1 medium sliced tomato sprinkled with chives
  (2 protein, 4 fat, 1 complex carb, 1 dairy, 1 vegetable)

Snack

- 1 cup plain yogurt
- 2 tsp walnuts
- ½ cup chopped strawberries
  (1 dairy, 1 fruit, 2 fat)

* When you see an asterisk throughout the menu, look for this recipe in Chapter 9!

Lunch

- Green salad: 2 cups leaf lettuce, ½ sliced cucumber, 1 sliced radish, ½ medium tomato, sliced, green pepper slices, and bean sprouts
- 6 ounces roast beef
- ½ cup steamed green beans
- 2 tsp olive oil with 2 Tbsp Balsamic vinegar
  (2 vegetable, 6 protein, 2 fat)

Snack

- 1 cup of raw vegetables
- 4 tsp Ranch dressing
- 2 turkey jerky sticks
  (1 vegetable, 4 fat, 2 protein)

Dinner

- 6 ounces chicken breast cooked in 1 tsp olive oil
- 1 cup cooked brown rice
- 1 cup cooked mixed vegetables with 1 tsp butter
  (6 protein, 2 complex carb, 2 fat, 2 vegetable)

Tuesday

Breakfast

- Breakfast smoothie: ½ scoop protein powder, 1 cup soy milk, and 1 Tbsp nut butter
  (1 protein, 1 dairy, 2 fat)

Snack

- 2 hard boiled eggs
  (2 protein)

Lunch

- 1 cup vegetable soup
- 5 ounces fresh poached salmon with lemon
- Beans and rice: ½ cup black beans and ½ cup whole grain rice topped with 1 Tbsp sour cream
  (2 vegetable, 5 protein, 2 complex carb, 1 fat)

Snack

- 1 cup raw celery or carrots
- 1 Tbsp peanut butter
  (1 vegetable, 2 fat)

Dinner

- 8 ounces **Marion's Meatloaf***
- ½ cooked medium sweet potato with 1 tsp butter
- Green salad: 1 cup of dark green leafy lettuce, cucumber slices, ½ medium tomato, 1 ounce shredded cheese
- 2 tsp olive oil and 2 Tbsp vinegar
- 1 cup fresh green beans sautéed in 2 tsp butter and sliced mushrooms and garlic
  (8 protein, 1 complex carb, 6 fat, 3 vegetable)

Dessert

- ½ cup cottage cheese with ½ cup sliced peaches and 2 tsp chopped cashews
  (1 dairy, 1 fruit, 2 fat)

Wednesday

Breakfast

- Tofu scramble: 5 ounces tofu, ½ cup chopped medium tomato, ½ cup onion and green pepper mix, cooked in 1 tsp olive oil
- 1 La Tortilla Factory tortilla
- 3 slices bacon
  (5 protein, 1 vegetable, ½ complex carb, 4 fat)

Snack
- 3 ounces dried organic beef jerky sticks
  (3 protein)

Lunch
- 1 cup **Black Bean Chili***: topped with ⅓ sliced avocado and 1 ounce shredded cheddar cheese
- Green salad: 1 cup leaf lettuce, 1 chopped green onion, and 3 cucumber slices, with 2 tsp olive oil mixed with red wine vinegar as desired
- 5 organic corn tortilla chips
  (2 ½ complex carb, 4 fat, 1 vegetable, 1 dairy)

Dinner
- 8 ounces fish served on top of 1 cup cooked spinach with 2 tsp butter and juice of fresh lemon, topped with 2 tsp slivered almonds
- 1 cup cooked zucchini topped with 1 tsp olive oil and garlic
- 1 cup melon balls sprinkled with lime juice
  (8 protein, 4 vegetable, 5 fat, 1 fruit)

Snack
- 1 cup warm soy milk topped with cinnamon and a dash of vanilla
  (1 dairy)

Thursday

Breakfast
- 2 eggs, any style, cooked in 1 tsp oil
- 1 cup cooked natural plain oatmeal topped with ½ apple, chopped with a dash of cinnamon and vanilla extract, and 2 tsp chopped nuts
- ½ cup milk
  (2 protein, 3 fat, 2 complex carb, ½ fruit, ½ dairy)

Lunch
- 1 cup of **Broccoli and Bacon Salad*** served on lettuce
- 4 ounces of sliced ham
- 1 cup tomato juice
  (4 protein, 3 vegetable, 3 fat)

Snack
- Beef and cheddar roll up: 1 slice cheddar cheese, 2 slices of roast beef, 1 tsp mayonnaise, and 1 tsp mustard.
  (1 dairy, 2 protein, 1 fat)

Dinner
- 8 ounces pot roast
- ½ cup mashed potatoes with skins with 1 tsp butter and 1 tsp sour cream
- Green salad: 1 cup leaf lettuce with cucumber slices, ½ medium tomato, sprouts topped with 1 tsp olive oil with 2 tsp Balsamic vinegar
- 1 cup peas and carrots with 1 tsp butter
  (8 protein, 1 complex carb, 4 fat, 3 vegetable)

Dessert
- ½ cup plain yogurt
- ¼ cup berries
- 2 tsp chopped nuts
  (½ dairy, ½ fruit, 2 fat)

Friday

Breakfast
- Breakfast smoothie: ½ scoop protein powder, ¼ cup berries, 1 cup milk, and 1 Tbsp nut butter
  (1 protein, ½ fruit, 1 dairy, 2 fat)

Snack

- 1 hard boiled egg

  (1 protein)

Lunch

- Tuna salad: 1 can tuna, ¼ cup chopped celery, ¼ cup chopped onion, and 1 Tbsp mayonnaise served with 10 whole grain crackers with ½ sliced tomato
- ½ apple cut into slices served with 1 Tbsp natural peanut butter

  (3 protein, 1 vegetable, 5 fat, ½ fruit, 2 complex carb)

Snack

- ⅓ avocado
- 4 ounces sliced turkey

  (2 fat, 4 protein)

Dinner

- 1 ½ cups **Spaghetti Squash with Vodka Cream Sauce*** and 4 ounces Italian sausage
- Green salad: 2 cups chopped Romaine lettuce, 2 artichoke hearts, 4 onion slices, and 4 beet slices
- 2 tsp olive oil with 2 Tbsp Balsamic vinegar
- 1 whole wheat roll
- 8 ounce glass of milk

  (3 complex carb, 6 protein, 2 vegetable, 4 fat, 1 dairy)

Saturday

Breakfast

- Sausage/egg/cheese breakfast casserole: 4 x 5 inch rectangle
- 1 medium tomato, sliced

  (3 protein, 1 dairy, 1 vegetable, 1 fat)

Snack

- ½ banana

  (1 fruit)

Lunch

- 6 ounce hamburger topped with 1 slice bacon, 1 tsp mustard, pickle slices, lettuce, tomato, and onion slices
- 1 slice whole wheat toast
- 6 small black olives
- ½ cup cold marinated vegetable salad
- ½ cup cole slaw

  (6 protein, 2 vegetable, 3 fat, 1 complex carb)

Snack

- 4 tsp nuts
- cucumber slices and celery sticks
- 4 ounces beef jerky

  (4 fat, 4 protein)

Dinner

- Spaghetti and meat sauce: 1 cup whole wheat pasta with 1 cup meat sauce, topped with 1 ounce Parmesean cheese
- Green salad: 2 cups leaf lettuce, 4 cucumber slices, 6 green olives, 1 chopped green onion topped
- 2 tsp olive oil and 2 Tbsp red wine vinegar
- 1 cup cooked broccoli with 1 tsp butter and lemon wedge

  (2 complex carb, 3 protein, 1 dairy, 3 vegetable, 5 fat)

Sunday

Breakfast

- 2 eggs cooked with 1 tsp butter
- 2 slices bacon
- 1 piece of whole grain toast with 1 Tbsp nut butter
- 1 cup tomato juice

  (2 protein, 5 fat, 1 complex carb, 1 vegetable)

Snack

- ½ apple
- ½ Tbsp nut butter

  (½ fruit, 1 fat)

Lunch

- 2 cups clam chowder
- Green salad: 2 cups spinach leaves, 3 green pepper rings, 2 slices raw onion, 2 fresh mushrooms, ½ cup green peas, and 3 ounces meat or poultry
- 1 Tbsp olive oil and Balsamic vinegar with herbs

  (1 ½ dairy, 3 protein, 2 vegetable, 3 fat)

Snack

- 3 ounces organic salami slices on 5 whole grain crackers with 2 tsp mustard

  (3 protein, 1 complex carb)

Dinner

- 8 ounces of **Tarragon Chicken*** and 1 cup cooked asparagus with 1 tsp butter
- ½ cup brown rice
- Greek tomato salad: 1 sliced medium tomato, 4 Kalamata olives, 1 ounce feta cheese
- 2 tsp olive oil with 1 Tbsp Balsamic/herb drizzle
- ½ apple

  (8 protein, 3 vegetables, 1 dairy, 4 fat, ½ fruit, 1 complex carb)

So what do you think?

As you can see from these menus, the Otter needs a lot of meat with moderate carbohydrates to optimize energy. If the Otter gives in to eating too many carbohydrates, he or she will not feel well. However, the Otter Diet is not as strict as the Lion Diet which can make meal time more enjoyable because the restrictions are less. The Otter Diet can be a very fun diet, if you enjoy meat as the central part of every meal and have other foods, such as salads or grains to accompany it. Be sure to read *Chapter 9* for recipes that keep this diet delicious!

Succeeding on the *Otter Diet*

Many of the patients we see at Caring Medical type out to be Otters, therefore, we hear from them a lot! Here are some tips that we wanted to share with you to help you succeed on the Otter Diet:

- **Belly buster**

  Most Otters are fast oxidizers. If this is you, you want to aim for stable blood sugars by eating a high protein diet. Otters who eat too many carbohydrates typically gain weight around the abdomen or belly. The only way to get that weight off is to decrease the carbohydrates and increase the protein.

- **Break-the-fast**

  Otters typically need to eat a high protein breakfast and then lesser amounts of food throughout the day. Otters can do fine by eating three meals per day, plus snacks.

- **Start big and end small**

  Otters need to be careful about overeating at the evening meal. If they are not that hungry when they get home (often they wake up hungry and their appetite decreases throughout the day), then Otters shouldn't eat that much. Overeating at dinner will just put on weight.

- **Building your ideal body**

  Otters eat a lot of protein so they need weight lifting or body building—but not as much as the Lion. Whereas the Lion should consider weight lifting as their primary mode of exercise, Otters should also do it regularly but also incorporate some aerobic exercise.

- **Dangerous drinks**

  Otters should also avoid caffeine and alcohol but that won't be as devastating as for the Lion. Both acidify the blood, which may already be too acid in Otters. If you are a fast oxidizer, and have hypoglycemia (low blood sugar), these drinks will only aggravate your hunger. If caffeine gives you a short term boost in energy, but leaves you tired a couple hours later, don't drink it.

- **Bitter sweets**
  Otters can have a larger variety of foods than Lions, but often have a similar sweet tooth. Otters really shouldn't have more than one piece of fruit or sweet item per day. If they do, fatigue and weight gain become issues. Otters can look to sauces to make food taste more interesting. Like Lions, Otters must also rely on spices because the sauces have too many carbohydrates. Both Lions and Otters need to stay away from artificial sweeteners. All these will do is get them accustomed to the sweet taste and really, Otters and Lions would be better served by sour or spicy tasting foods. These are lower in carbohydrates.

Tips for Losing Weight on the *Otter Diet*

We all know that losing weight is not easy. Most of us eat too much and do not exercise enough. Following the appropriate Hauser Diet will allow your body to use the fuel that is best for your body. Here are some Otter Tips that will help you shed those unwanted pounds.

- **Eat the right proportions of food.**
  Each of the Hauser Diets is a unique breakdown of protein, fat, and carbohydrates. As an Otter, your body needs to lean toward the higher protein and fat food choices, over vegetarian food choices.

- **Don't drink your calories.**
  Drinks such as juice and soda are too easily absorbed and cause the blood sugar to be unstable. The Otter Diet Type focuses on trying to regain or maintain blood sugar balance.

- **Only eat carbohydrates that contain fiber.**
  This means whole grains, and carbohydrates that contain at least 4 grams of fiber per serving. Fiber is necessary for proper digestion and signaling the brain that the stomach is full, among many other actions in the body.

- **Avoid coffee.**
  When you drink coffee, your insulin is raised more than if you did not have the coffee. This worsens blood sugar swings.

- **Tell others that you are on a diet.**
  Give a quick outline to people you are in contact with everyday. Tell them that you are eating a high protein diet and that you are avoiding sugary and starchy foods. Most people will get the idea that they should not offer you these foods.

- **Eat slowly.**
  This gives your stomach additional time to fill up to prevent overeating. Because you are eating foods that stick with you longer (protein and fat), you may not feel full right away. Take a little rest while eating to give your body time to catch up with your brain!

- **Eat Breakfast.**
  People with the physiology of an Otter need to eat a high protein breakfast. Otherwise, your energy, mood, and hunger level are bound to send you to the vending machines mid-morning.

- **Don't drink alcohol.**
  These simple carbs provide non-nutritious calories which can make it difficult for you to keep your blood sugar balanced and increase your appetite.

- **Eat frequently.**
  To avoid having blood sugar swings throughout the day, you should eat every three to four hours, and never skip meals. Keep a couple hard boiled eggs or lunch meat in the fridge at work, or store a bag of nuts in your car. Be prepared to eat frequently, and you will succeed on the Otter Diet!

FAQ and *Otter Diet* Myths

Won't I become constipated?

If a person on the Otter Diet is not having regular bowel movements, the first step is to increase your water intake. Next, try increasing your intake of "free foods." These foods are high in water and fiber content. It may be necessary to take a fiber supplement, but it is not typical.

What about cholesterol?

If your physiology is that of an Otter, you will not have elevated cholesterol levels by eating according to your Diet Type. In fact, if someone with an Otter physiology tries to eat like a Monkey, this is when we typically see abnormal cholesterol levels because the carbohydrates end up being stored as fat.

How often should I eat?

Eat frequently. To avoid having blood sugar swings throughout the day, you should eat at least every four hours, and never skip meals. Breakfast should be a large meal, with lunch and dinner being moderately sized.

Will I always be an Otter?

The simplest answer is: no. As you read in Chapter 1, there are a couple key factors that determine which diet is best for you, one of those being blood pH. As the seasons change, our blood pH is affected. In our experience, if an Otter's blood gets too alkaline, he or she will change to a *Bear* Diet in order to acidify the blood pH into normal range. Likewise, if an Otter's blood gets too acidic, he or she will change to a Lion Diet in order to alkalinize the blood into normal range.

Can I be a vegetarian?

In our experience, vegetarian foods that are high in protein, such as legumes and soy, are typically still too high in carbohydrates to have the same effect eating meat will have. When we have seen people attempt a high protein vegetarian diet, it makes the diet extremely difficult to follow and will typically not provide the desired results.

Obtaining Optimal Health on the *Otter Diet*

Here are the stories of a couple of real patients who succeeded in achieving their health goals once they followed the appropriate Hauser Diet.

Serious Steven

We love Steven, but this guy needed a "chill pill." If there was such a pill, we would have prescribed a double dose for him. Steven is an executive and came in to see us, while continuing to work via cell phone during his appointment. He was even downright angry and rude. He had many questions. He, of course, was very skeptical that we could help him. He had been to major prestigious health care facilities that were unable to help him. Who was Caring Medical compared to these medical meccas of modern medicine? He was shocked when we told him that around 5-10% of our patient population had been to the same world-renowned medical facilities he'd been to and that we have a 95% success rate at helping these people. Seventy-five percent of our chronic pain patients are cured of their pain by using the therapies here at Caring Medical. Of course, his first reaction was "Well, I don't have chronic pain." He was right, he had been having a series of outbreaks from herpes. We did not claim that the Otter Diet or other Natural Medicine techniques were going to cure his herpes, but we did feel it would help improve his quality of life, as well as reduce many of his other symptoms.

Steven told the doctor, "I just came here to see if you could help the herpes." His new patient questionnaire revealed the following: terrible fatigue, nervousness, inability to concentrate, muscle tension, poor sex drive, and coldness in the hands and feet. He reluctantly agreed to a comprehensive Natural Medicine evaluation. His results revealed that he was an extremely fast oxidizer with a normal (neutral) blood pH. He was placed on the Otter Diet because he needed to eat like an Otter, but had been eating like a Monkey. His low hormone levels were treated with natural hormone replacement.* He also received IV therapies that helped improve his immune function. Well, we bet you're wondering what happened to Steven?

Steven quickly warmed to Natural Medicine and the Otter Diet because he lost 15 pounds and his strength returned to his body. After six months without a herpes outbreak he was amazed. "You guys are onto something. I feel 10 years younger. I hit a golf ball farther than I ever have. You have changed my life." The interesting fact about this case is how much more relaxed Steven became as a result of balancing his body chemistry. This is a good lesson to learn—how a person acts is not necessarily a personality issue. Personality and even the effects of genetics are often a result of body chemistry imbalances.

Virginia: The Vegan

Virginia came to Caring Medical looking for help for her severe pain. Her pain was not localized to a specific area where we could utilize our very successful treatment called Prolotherapy to stimulate her body to repair itself. She exhibited the classic findings of fibromyalgia with pain all over her body. She also suffered from chronic fatigue. In reviewing her medical history, she explained that she began following a vegetarian diet eight years ago. She felt that it

helped her very much. Interestingly enough, we see that sometimes a radical diet change can produce profoundly positive results initially, possibly related to detoxification or something similar. Initially, the vegan diet helped Virginia, but at this point, she was a wreck. So obviously something was wrong. Her new patient health history revealed about fifty positive findings related to ill-health. She was extremely fatigued, had irregular menses, migraine headaches, irritable bowel syndrome, and a host of other problems. Virginia needed to wake up and smell the coffee. Her health was a mess. This kind of talk may seem harsh, but Virginia needed a wake up call, and we gave it to her.

Virginia's blood testing revealed that she was a balanced oxidizer (normal glucose tolerance test), but her fasting insulin levels were slightly elevated at 28 uU/ml (Insulin Units). We like to see fasting insulin levels less than 15 uU/ml. Her blood pH was 7.390 which is below normal (acidic). Her vitamin B12 and iron stores (ferritin) were also low. Based on these findings, the best foods for her were going to be animal products. So we had to break this news to Virginia. Because she so desperately wanted to get better, she willingly made the necessary dietary changes and added meat back into her diet.

---

* **Note:** *See www.caringmedical.com for more information on the natural hormone therapy done at Caring Medical.*

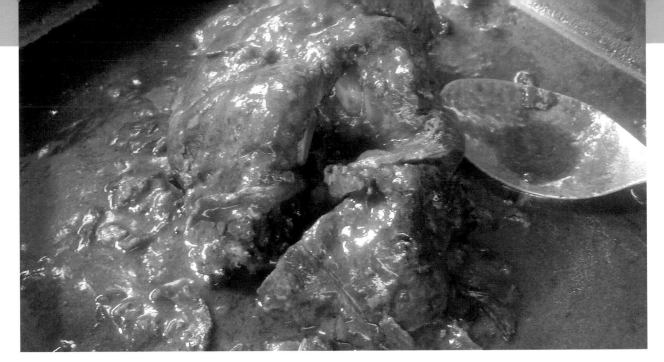

This case is interesting because over the next six months Virginia's symptoms slowly but surely improved. Her irritable bowel symptoms, migraines, body pain, and fatigue drastically improved because she was eating according to the Otter Diet. We lost touch with her for over two years, when she returned to us, again in a mess. You see, Virginia was an animal rights activist. She headed up a local society and just could not bear to eat animal products. We helped her get started on a high protein vegetarian diet. She is definitely better than she was, but not as good as she was when consuming animal products.

So are you ready to be an *Otter?*

These real life examples show you the powerful effects of diet on your overall health status. Find out how you should be eating according to your specific Diet Type—it could mean the difference between ill health and wellness!

Summary of the *Otter Diet*

The Otter Diet is a modified high protein diet. Otters should eat mostly meat, but adding in small amounts of carbohydrates and vegetables to accompany meals. This diet can be very fun, and totally do-able. Once you get cooking, you'll see how, with a little creativity,

you can make that meat especially flavorful and, served with your favorite side dishes, irresistible! The secret to success is to not let the carbohydrate portions get out of control. When your carbohydrates are under control, weight loss and energy improvement should follow. Remember, plan your meals around protein and vegetables, and the rest will fall in to place.

In the upcoming chapters we will talk more about how to create tasty, Otter friendly dishes and what foods are best to keep stocked in your pantry. But first, we'll explore the next Diet Type, The Bear Diet, and learn more about how their dietary needs are different than those on the Otter Diet.

THE BEAR
DIET TYPE™

30%
protein

20%
fat

50%
carbohydrates

the bear diet type™

The Bear Diet is a balanced diet. A Bear Diet Typing result typically shows that everything is normal (or balanced). The macronutrient breakdown is 30% protein, 20% fat, and 50% carbohydrates. The goal of the Bear Diet is to maintain balance, and this means you can eat a little of everything. The hardest challenge for most Bears is controlling portion sizes. Unlike the other Hauser Diets that typically have to either control carbs or fat, the Bear Diet is all about variety. A person on the Bear Diet really has to concentrate on moderate portions, balanced meals, and regular meal times in order to be successful on it.

Food Choices on the *Bear Diet*

We will make this easy: almost anything that is fresh and unprocessed is going to make you feel good! That's the good news! The bad news is that most people who can eat anything do not exhibit enough self control when it comes to portions and proportions. What do we mean? Bears should try and keep a good handle on a balanced, 50/50 diet: 50% coming from fat and protein, and 50% coming from carbohydrates. *(See Figure 5-1.)*

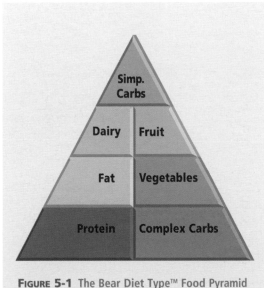

FIGURE 5-1 The Bear Diet Type™ Food Pyramid

"What does that mean in terms of real food?" Protein should be 30%, or about one-third of your food intake. Protein includes foods such as eggs, chicken, ground beef, steak, fish, and tofu. Fat should be 20%, or about one-fifth of your food intake. Fat includes foods such as olive oil, canola oil, bacon, avocado, olives, sour cream, and butter.

Carbohydrates are really divided into two categories: complex and simple. In the simplest terms, complex carbohydrates are denser in fiber, while simple carbohydrates are higher in sugar without the fiber. Complex carbohydrates are foods such as oat bran, brown rice, potatoes with the skins, and whole grain bread. Simple carbohydrates are foods such as white bread/buns, potatoes without the skins, white rice, cookies, cake, soda pop, and sugar. Bears should focus on eating plenty of complex carbohydrates, and not on the simple carbs.

Amazingly enough, somehow those foods find a way into our day. For instance, someone in the office brings brownies and you just had to have one! Or your book club goes out for dinner and you all decide to order that decadent double fudge chocolate cake! Be careful of these situations because many Bears cannot say "no"! It is not unusual for Bears to eat too many simple carbohydrates. Refer back to the Food Equivalents chart in *Chapter 2* if you have any questions about how much food actually equals the one serving you are allowed.

What about vegetables and fruits? Technically, vegetables and fruits are both considered "carbohydrates." We have, however, put each into its own category. Why? Eating fruit is not the same as eating vegetables. Fruit is much higher in sugar and calories than vegetables. On the Bear Diet, the vegetable to fruit ratio is 3:1. Vegetables include foods such as tomatoes, eggplant, dark leafy greens, carrots, bell peppers, and squash. Vegetables do not include potatoes or corn, which are actually counted as complex carbohydrates. Fruits include foods such as apples, berries, pineapple, and plums. The great thing about fruit is that it makes snacking on the Bear Diet a breeze! It's easy to keep an orange at your desk or in your gym bag.

How does a *Bear* make vegetables taste good?

We encourage Bears to really embrace different cuisines and methods of cooking, because you can eat practically anything and feel good. For instance, try a mixed stir fry using sesame oil, which is an alkalinizing fat, as well as lightly steamed vegetables with lemon, which is an acidifying food. You do not have to add fat such as butter to vegetables every night. Try serving them chopped into rice, for a vegetable pilaf, which will help keep your diet exciting and your blood pH and calorie intake balanced. When it comes to vegetable dishes, watch out for dishes that are typically really high in fat, for instance, broccoli and cheese casserole. Cheese and cream are permissible, but don't forget

that they are very high in calories that will add some very real excess weight if you do not practice self-control. We know that some of those broccoli and cheese casseroles are more cream and cheese than they are broccoli! Balance is key for Bears.

How does a *Bear* make a salad?

Coming up in this chapter we will show you a sample week's meal plan. You will see some "green salads" listed throughout. Each "green salad" starts with good lettuce, such as leaf, romaine, arugula, spinach, or mixed field greens. A good lettuce is dark green, not light and watery like iceberg lettuce. Think beyond the dinner salad served in many restaurants that is typically iceberg lettuce, a tomato wedge, and a slice of cucumber. Yes, use some of those standard salad vegetables such as chopped cucumber, onion, tomatoes, and radishes, but explore the rainbow of vegetables that can be sliced and diced into your salad, such as bell peppers, carrots, and cauliflower. A Bear who is watching his or her weight should just remember to take into consideration that while vegetables are not calorie dense, what we put on them can be—fat and sugar! Many Bears drown their traditional iceberg lettuce salads in sweet salad dressing, shredded cheese, bacon bits, and croutons. If you are having a hard time finding a vegetable in your salad that isn't covered in dressing and cheese, it is time for a salad make-over! A Bear is allowed one simple carbohydrate per day. You may want to use this to add some crunchy croutons to your salad. This is a fine thing to do, as long as you remember that those croutons are counting as a portion of your simple carbohydrate intake, so you may need to skip dessert.

What kind of fats should a *Bear* include?

Most Bears feel good eating a variety of foods. So, when it comes to your fat choices, you can certainly do the same—choose a variety of fats. Foods like bacon and sausage are not forbidden for the Bear. However, we are not encouraging you to have a BLT for lunch everyday just because you can eat anything. Eating a mix of animal and plant-based fats will probably leave you feeling your best.

On that note, let's take a look at a sample week's meal plan for a Bear. If you need help recalling how we define a food "equivalent," refer back to the Food Equivalent Chart *Figure 2-2* in *Chapter 2*.

BEAR DAILY MEAL PLAN

10 protein equivalents

10 fat equivalents

6 vegetable equivalents

5 complex carb equivalents

2 dairy equivalents

2 fruit equivalents

1 simple carb equivalent

Approximately 2,000 Calories

Drink water or herbal tea as your beverage. Coffee can be consumed occasionally.

Monday

Breakfast

- 2 pieces whole grain toast and 4 tsp 100% fruit jam and 2 tsp butter
- 2 eggs, poached
- 1 medium tomato, sliced and topped with chopped fresh basil
  (2 complex carb, ⅔ simple carb, 2 fat, 2 protein, 1 vegetable)

> * *When you see an asterisk throughout the menu, look for this recipe in Chapter 9!*

Lunch

- Beef vegetable stir fry: 4 ounces steak stir fried and 1 cup vegetables cooked in 1 Tbsp oil served atop ½ cup whole wheat noodles
  (4 protein, 2 vegetable, 3 fat, 1 complex carb)

Snack

- ½ cup blueberries and 1 tsp honey
- 2 tsp cashews
- 1 cup organic plain yogurt
  (1 fruit, ⅙ simple carb, 1 dairy, 2 fat)

Dinner

- 4 ounces **Lemon Pepper Fish***
- 1 cup brown rice
- 1 cup roasted vegetables and herbs
- Green salad: 2 cups mixed field greens, 3 tomato wedges, 1 sliced radish, 1 chopped scallion, and 4 cucumber slices topped with 2 tsp olive oil and 2 Tbsp vinegar
- 1 tsp honey
  (4 protein, 2 complex carb, 3 vegetable, 3 fat, ⅙ simple carb)

Snack

- 1 ounce cheddar cheese slices
- 1 medium sliced green apple
  (1 dairy, 1 fruit)

Tuesday

Breakfast

- 1 cup oatmeal
- ½ cup blueberries
- 1 cup milk

  (2 complex carb, 1 fruit, 1 dairy)

Lunch

- Turkey and avocado wraps: 4 ounces turkey, 1 cup sliced raw veggies, 1 ounce shredded cheese, ⅔ avocado, 2 La Tortilla Factory high fiber wraps, and 1 tsp mustard

  (4 protein, 1 vegetable, 1 dairy, 1 complex carb, 4 fat)

Snack

- 1 cup carrot sticks
- 1 apple

  (1 vegetable, 1 fruit)

Dinner

- **Asian Lettuce Wraps*** *(6 ounces chicken [or tofu], 2 cups raw vegetables per recipe, and unlimited lettuce leaves for wrapping)*
- 2 Tbsp peanut sauce
- Vegetable couscous: 1 cup couscous and 1 cup cooked vegetables and 1 tsp oil

  (4 vegetable, 6 protein, 6 fat, 2 complex carb)

Dessert

- 1 small cookie

  (1 simple carb)

Wednesday

Breakfast

- ⅛ of a pie slice of apple walnut quiche
- ½ cup orange juice
- ½ whole grain bagel with 1 tsp butter
- 2 tsp 100% fruit jam

  (3 protein, 3 fat, 1 fruit, 1 complex carb, ⅓ simple carb)

Lunch

- 1 cup of **Black Bean and Chipotle Soup***
- 1 whole grain roll
- Green salad with chicken: 2 cups mescalin greens, 3 ounces cooked chicken, 3 tomato slices, 4 bell pepper slices, 4 red onion rings, 2 Tbsp shredded carrots, with 1 Tbsp olive oil and 2 Tbsp vinegar

  (3 complex carb, 3 protein, 2 vegetable, 3 fat)

Snack

- 1 cup bell peppers, sliced

  (1 vegetable)

Dinner

- 4 ounces **Rosemary Chicken***
- 1 cup sautéed Brussels sprouts in 2 tsp olive oil and lemon
- 1 piece cheesy garlic toast: 1 whole grain roll sliced open, brushed with 2 tsp olive oil combined with 1 clove smashed garlic and 1 ounce Parmesan cheese

  (4 protein, 2 vegetable, 1 complex carb, 1 dairy, 4 fat)

Snack

- 1 cup chopped cantaloupe sprinkled with the juice of ½ lime and a dash of salt mixed with ½ cup chopped pickled beets
- 1 cup plain yogurt with 1 tsp honey

  (1 fruit, 1 vegetable, 1 dairy, ⅓ simple carb)

Thursday

Breakfast

- 1 whole wheat English muffin topped with 1 tsp butter and 2 tsp jam
- ½ grapefruit
- ½ cup cottage cheese

  (2 complex carb, 1 fat, ⅓ simple carb, 1 fruit, 1 dairy)

Lunch

- Mediterranean lamb stew: 4 ounces lamb, cubed and seasoned, 1 cup cooked Mediterranean vegetables, 1 cup couscous, and 1 Tbsp olive oil for cooking plus juice of 1 lemon.
- Green salad: 2 cups mixed greens, ¼ cup chopped cucumber, 1 chopped scallion, 1 Tbsp shredded carrots topped with 1 tsp olive oil, 2 Tbsp Balsamic vinegar and lemon juice.

  (2 complex carb, 4 protein, 3 vegetable, 4 fat)

Dinner

- 6 ounces roasted chicken with BBQ sauce
- ½ cup smashed potatoes with skins with 1 tsp butter
- ½ cup carrots and 1 cup green beans, steamed and topped with 1 tsp butter and 1 tsp slivered almonds
- Green salad: 1 cup field greens, 2 tomato wedges, 1 sliced radish, topped with 1 tsp olive oil, 2 Tbsp Balsamic vinegar, and 1 tsp honey

  (6 protein, ⅔ simple carb, 1 complex carb, 3 vegetable, 3 fat)

Snack

- 1 ounce of cheddar cheese
- 1 medium apple, sliced
- 1 Tbsp organic peanut butter

  (1 dairy, 1 fruit, 2 fat)

Friday

Breakfast

- 2 whole grain waffles with 2 tsp butter, 2 Tbsp 100% maple syrup, and ½ cup strawberries
- 1 hard boiled egg

  (2 complex carb, 2 fat, 1 simple carb, 1 fruit, 1 protein)

Lunch

- Tuna salad: 1 can tuna, 2 tsp mayonnaise, 1 Tbsp chopped onion, and 1 Tbsp chopped green pepper
- Green salad: 2 cups chopped romaine lettuce, 1 medium tomato, cut into wedges, ¼ cucumber, sliced, 6 small olives, ½ cup cold green beans, topped with 1 tsp olive oil with 2 Tbsp Balsamic vinegar
- 10 green grapes

  (6 protein, 2 vegetable, 4 fat, 1 fruit)

Snack

- 1 cup carrot and celery sticks
- ½ cup cottage cheese

  (1 vegetable, 1 dairy)

Dinner

- Spaghetti dinner: 1 cup meat sauce (3 ounces of ground beef and ⅔ cup red sauce) atop 1½ cup whole grain pasta, served with 1 ounce Parmesan Cheese
- 1 cup peas and carrots with 1 tsp butter
- Green salad: 2 cups lettuce with sliced cucumbers, grated radishes, topped with sprouts and 1 Tbsp olive oil and 2 Tbsp vinegar with Italian seasoning

  (3 protein, 3 vegetable, 4 fat, 3 complex carb, 1 dairy)

Saturday

Breakfast

- Veggie Benedict: 2 poached eggs, 2 Tbsp Hollandaise sauce, 4 slices tomato, 4 sprigs asparagus, lightly cooked, served atop 1 whole wheat English muffin
- ½ cup grits

  (3 protein, 6 fat, 2 vegetable, 3 complex carb)

Lunch

- 1 cup **Split Pea Soup***
- 1 cup fresh melon salad tossed with lime juice and salt
- 2 slices of ham, rolled up dipped in mustard
- 1 cup raw veggies (zucchini and red pepper slices)
  (2 complex carb, 1 fruit, 1 vegetable, 3 protein)

Dinner

- Sausage and cheese pizza: ¼ thin crust medium sausage (3 ounces) and onion pizza
- Green salad: 2 cups chopped romaine lettuce and 4 cucumber slices, 3 cherry tomatoes, 4 slices green pepper, 3 red onion rings topped with 2 tsp olive oil and 2 Tbsp red wine vinegar
- 1 ½ cups cooked green beans with chopped tomato garnish
  (3 protein, 1 simple carb, 2 dairy, 3 fat, 5 vegetable)

Snack

- Tofu fruit smoothie: 1 ounce tofu, ½ cup berries, ice cubes, juice of 1 lime, and ½ Tbsp almond butter blenderized into a smoothie
  (1 protein, 1 fruit, 1 fat)

Sunday

Breakfast

- 2 medium whole grain pancakes topped with berry sauce, (½ cup berries heated with 2 Tbsp 100% fruit berry jam), and 2 tsp butter
- 2 slices bacon (organic, nitrate free)
- 2 poached eggs
  (2 complex carb, 1 fruit, 1 simple carb, 4 fat, 2 protein)

Lunch

- Grilled ham and cheese sandwich: (2 slices whole wheat bread, 2 slices cheddar cheese, 2 slices tomato, 3 ounces thin slices of ham, and 2 tsp butter)
- Relishes: 2 small dill pickles, 6 black olives, and 1 cup sliced raw veggies
  (2 complex carb, 2 dairy, 2 vegetable, 3 fat, 3 protein)

Dinner

- 1 cup homemade vegetable soup
- Beet orange salad: ½ sliced orange, ½ cup sliced beets, ⅓ avocado sliced, served atop 2 cups chopped romaine lettuce, drizzled with 2 Tbsp Balsamic vinegar and sprinkled with 1 tsp slivered almonds
- 5 ounces of thin sliced roast beef with horseradish mustard garnished with onion slices
  (4 vegetable, ½ fruit, 5 protein, 3 fat)

Snack

- ½ cup cooked oatmeal
- ¼ banana, sliced
  (1 complex, ½ fruit)

So what do you think?

Of all five Diet Types, this is where most people want to be. The Bears can eat pretty much any food and feel good. It is definitely easy to manipulate recipes to be Bear friendly, because most already are. Bears have to remember to stay balanced, both in the types of food you choose and in the amounts of food you eat. Eating a meat-heavy meal, or a vegetable-heavy meal is ok. But through the rest of the day, you should focus on variety and balance within your meals. You also have to be careful not to overeat, since you do not have to stay away from any particular foods. See *Chapter 9* for some tasty Bear friendly recipes.

Succeeding on the *Bear Diet*

In seeing many Bears at our office, we noticed some trends common to most Bears:

- **Calories in, calories out.**
  A Bear would benefit from calorie counting. Since Bears can eat all foods, they tend to eat too much. You may be surprised as to how much food you actually eat. Most Bears are unaffected by the foods they eat. This means that, unless you have a food allergy, no particular foods make you more tired or give you more energy, over others. So, Bears are typically overweight because they overeat and don't exercise.

- **Listen… with your stomach.**
  Bears need to pay more attention to the sensations of eating. Once you start feeling full, you need to stop eating.

- **Carb control.**
  Typically Bears who are overweight are overemphasizing carbohydrates. Often they drink carbohydrates in the form of fruit juices and soda pop. Stopping these and drinking water or herbal teas instead jump starts the weight loss.

- **Remember why you eat.**
  Some Bears can do just fine on two meals, while others may do better with three. What is important for a Bear is that you only eat when you are hungry. Don't fall into the trap of stress eating, or eating when you aren't even hungry. This leads to overeating and thus, if this is you, consider exercise to reduce stress. Great considerations would be yoga or tai chi.

- **You might feel good now, but…**
  Bears typically aren't into food because it doesn't affect them that much. As such they typically don't cook. Well, we've got news for you! If you want to be healthy and a good weight, please start cooking your own food and start bringing your own lunch to work. You'll not only save calories, but a lot of money!

- **Think outside the box.**
  Bears can eat any food but they often eat the same things day after day. Start eating a variety and break yourself of foods and drinks you may not be aware that you are addicted to. The most common food addictions are sugar or coffee. Address these addictions and start weaning yourself off of them. Although you can have them, if you can't consume them in reasonable quantities (one or less per day), you are addicted and should cut them out completely.

- **Don't hibernate.**
  Honestly, Bears can be lazy. Bears do best to have an active lifestyle versus just doing one type of exercise. Bears who do yard work, cycle, swim, and a variety of exercises are the ones that keep the weight off the best.

Tips for Losing Weight on the *Bear Diet*

- **Eat the right proportions of food.**
  Each of the Hauser Diets is a unique breakdown of protein, fat, and carbohydrates. As a Bear, your body needs a balanced proportion of foods. Although, a Bear can technically eat a variety of foods, if there is no balance throughout the day, a person is not likely to make great strides on the diet.

- **Don't drink your calories.**
  Although a Bear can have fruit juice, it may be hard to control portion sizes. Any sort of sweet drink is best accompanied by a meal with some protein. Juice or an all fruit smoothie is not the best meal for a Bear. This is especially important for Bears that have unstable blood sugar levels.

- **Eat carbohydrates for fiber.**
  This means whole grains, and carbohydrates that have at least four grams of fiber per serving. Fiber is necessary for proper digestion and signaling the brain that the stomach is full, among many other actions in the body. Limit your simple carbohydrates, because these have little or no fiber. Although the Bear can have one serving per day, it is not necessary and may be exchanged for a complex carbohydrate.

- **If you drink coffee, use it in moderation.**
  Because coffee can raise insulin levels, it may aggravate unstable blood sugar in Bears with hypoglycemia. However, in our experience, a person with alkaline blood pH will not tend to feel stimulated, or buzzed, from coffee so it is a fine beverage to drink in moderation. So a Bear has to determine his or her true reaction to coffee and make a choice to drink it in moderation, or not at all.

- **Tell others that you are on a diet.**
  Give a quick outline to people you are in contact with everyday. Tell them that you are on a diet. Most people will get the idea that they should not offer you extra snacks or sweets.

- **Eat slowly.**
  This gives your stomach additional time to fill up to prevent overeating. Listening to these cues will help you to not overeat.

- **Don't drink alcohol.**
  These simple carbs add non-nutritious calories, especially the sugary mixed drinks. Cutting out regular alcohol consumption may cut down a few pounds relatively quickly. An occasional glass of wine should be fine for most Bears, but if you are trying to lose weight, we recommend eliminating alcohol from your diet.

- **Set goals.**
  Bears can be lazy and procrastinate. We recommend that they set weight and exercise goals right away. This could be running a 5K race in three months' time, or losing 20 pounds in three months. Bears often need accountability. Having a friend to lose weight and exercise with really helps Bears stay focused on their goals.

FAQ and *Bear Diet* Myths:

Shouldn't everyone just be on the Bear Diet?

It would be ideal if everyone could eat a variety of food and feel good. However, in our many years of clinical experience, that theory just does not hold water in the real world. We would say that most people in America eat similar to this diet style. By that, we mean they eat a variety of foods. However, look at the booming rates of obesity, diabetes, and other diseases and you will see that the Bear Diet is not appropriate for everyone. Even if the macronutrient breakdown were correct, the key to the Bear Diet (and also the other Hauser Diet

Types) is maintaining portion control. If we walk into any restaurant in America, we will see that this does not represent the concern of most patrons, where "More is better."

How often should I eat?

Bears typically do best with a routine. Typically three square meals a day with a snack is what makes a person on the Bear Diet feel best.

Can I just eat whatever I want on the Bear Diet?

The Bear Diet is not as easy as it sounds. In upcoming chapters we will discuss the need for quality food in order to obtain optimal health. This, along with portion control, is why a Bear cannot just eat "whatever." The Bear Diet focuses on a variety and balance of food, but it must be understood that the food must be quality food made from scratch, not a diet consisting of a variety of "fast" food. We will talk more about this later.

Will I always be a Bear?

The simplest answer is: no. As you read in *Chapter 1*, there are a couple key factors that determine which diet is best for you, one of those being blood pH. As the seasons change, our blood pH is affected. In our experience, if a Bear's blood gets too alkaline, he or she will change to a Monkey Diet in order to acidify the blood pH into normal range. Likewise, if a Bear's blood gets too acidic, he or she will change to an Otter Diet in order to alkalinize the blood into normal range.

How will I lose weight if I'm just eating everything?

We stress again that if you not paying attention to portion size, it is not likely that you will lose weight. As we mentioned earlier, something has to be changed about your lifestyle. Either you have to start burning more calories, which means increasing exercise, or you have to begin restricting calories. There are some exceptions. These are people who are eating the correct Hauser Diet and exercising, yet are not losing weight. From a Natural Medicine standpoint, we may then check for a hormone problem. But for most people, we can follow a food and exercise diary to target a problem that is not allowing a person to shed pounds.

Obtaining Optimal Health on the *Bear Diet*

Lois Who Just Can't Lose

Lois assured us that she couldn't lose weight. She had tried all the diets. Low carb, high carb, exercising—nothing helped. We checked her out and she was pretty balanced. Her blood pH was normal and she was a balanced oxidizer so she needed the Bear Diet. We told her that she wouldn't lose weight by following the Bear Diet. "What do you mean? Why did I spend all of this money?" The secret to her inability to lose weight was in her food allergy tests. She was allergic to a lot of different foods. When she was placed on a hypoallergenic diet, she lost 10 pounds in three weeks. Her energy level increased, so she exercised more. Of course, her hormones were low, so the little bit of DHEA, testosterone, and thyroid hormones helped too! Lois also started a supplement regime from Beulah Land Nutritionals.*

Is Lois a skinny-minny? No, she's not, but she feels much better and has energy—and that is the take-home point here. She has lost a total of 25 pounds.

* **Note:** *See www.benuts.com for more information on supplements from Beulah Land Nutritionals.*

Joan: Addicted to the Atkins Diet

Joan wanted to lose thirty pounds. She read Dr. Atkins' diet book and went right for it. She lost the thirty pounds over a three month period. People told her she was looking great. Because she felt so good on the diet, she continued to strictly adhere to it. Over time, she noticed that she was less able to handle stress. Eventually, she became a nervous wreck. She went from feeling great to feeling awful. She began experiencing aches and pains that she had never experienced in the past. She now felt she was 15 pounds underweight, but was afraid to stop the diet for the fear of gaining all of the weight back. She had terrible anxiety and was unable to sleep.

What had she done? What was happening to her? She was at a loss. This is when she decided to make an appointment at Caring Medical. On her initial visit to Caring Medical, we did some of the normal tests we do and determined that her blood pH was high at 7.477. Initially, the Atkins diet was what Joan needed to jump-start the weight loss, but it subsequently caused her blood to become too alkaline. In our experience, extremely alkaline blood can lead to symptoms of anxiety, restlessness, and insomnia. Insomnia was causing her body to stop healing. Insomnia causes a decrease in the repair hormone called Growth Hormone. Because the body could not repair itself, Joan developed all sorts of aches and pains. We recommended that Joan start on the Bear Diet, which is more of a balanced diet. We told her that she would slowly get to her ideal body weight, but that she should notice an immediate improvement in her sleep and well-being. Her anxiety was gone in a week. Joan faithfully complied with this plan and all of her symptoms eventually resolved, coinciding with a drop in her pH back to normal range. We have followed Joan for several years and she has done very well, maintaining her weight and activity level, and continues to be free of pain. She now follows the Otter Diet for maintenance.

Claude, the Canadian: Worse in the Winter

Claude's health was reasonable except during the winter. He felt sad, depressed, and with no energy in the winter. He was found to be a very fast oxidizer of carbohydrates and had a very low blood pH. He was

a teaspoon of oil, and other of the Hauser Diet Equivalents, to see how much that actually is. Compare this to your estimated caloric needs, and you may be unpleasantly surprised. If you are a Bear struggling with weight problems, it is likely that your portion sizes are to blame.

Keep a food diary in the beginning of this diet to help you become aware of how much you eat and how foods make you feel. Even within the Bear Diet population, some people feel better eating specific types of foods for certain meals. Maybe you feel best on a higher protein breakfast and prefer salads for lunch and dinner. Or maybe you like two well balanced meals through the day. These unique factors are determined by our lifestyle, culture, and physiological needs. The Bear Diet allows for flexible food choices and meal planning, as long as the ultimate goal of balance and moderation is met.

In the upcoming chapters we will talk more about how to create yummy, well balanced Bear meals. But first, we'll explore the next Hauser Diet, the Monkey Diet, and learn more about how their dietary needs are different than those on the Bear Diet.

placed on the Lion Diet, but when the summer came we received an email from him that his depression and anxiety were coming back—and this was unusual for him during the summer. We liberalized his diet to the Bear Diet to add more carbohydrates to his eating plan. We surmised that the high temperatures in the summer were raising Claude's blood pH too much, so he needed more carbohydrates in his diet during the summer to counter the effect. Claude follows this diet until November 1. So, yes, Claude follows a Bear Diet from May to November and the rest of the year he follows the Lion Diet. This keeps his blood pH in balance, as well as his mental state. Isn't this interesting? Isn't this fascinating? Don't you want to just tell all of your friends and your natural healing practitioner? Well, you should!

A Summary of the *Bear Diet*

The best way to summarize the Bear Diet is: *everything in moderation.* Your meals should be well balanced between carbohydrates, protein, and fat. Typically, there are no foods that are off limits, but the Bear Diet is not a license to gorge. Most of us have no idea how large our portions actually are! In your own kitchen, measure out an ounce of meat, a half cup of fruit,

Want to chat with other *Bears*, share recipes, and get tips for success on the

Bear Diet?

Visit us at www.hauserdiet.com

THE MONKEY
DIET TYPE™

20%
protein

15%
fat

65%
carbohydrates

the monkey diet type™

The Monkey Diet is a low fat diet that focuses on vegetables and complex carbohydrates. The Monkey Diet is typically best for people who use carbohydrates efficiently, and who have alkaline blood pH. Monkey Diet Types are typically balanced oxidizers with alkaline blood pH, or slow oxidizers (with normal insulin levels), and normal blood pH. So, for Monkeys, this diet is designed to lower blood pH into normal range and stabilize blood sugars. The Monkey Diet begins to lean toward vegetarianism, with moderate amounts of protein and fat. The macronutrient breakdown is 20% protein, 15% fat, and 65% carbohydrates. The Monkey Diet can easily turn into the "cheese pizza" diet if you forget about quality of food and strictly look at limiting the protein. There is nothing wrong with the occasional cheese pizza. However, there are a lot of pseudo-vegetarians that eat cheese pizza, or pasta, for almost every meal but claim they are healthy because they don't eat meat. This is simply not true. Many of these people do not even eat vegetables!

Food Choices on the *Monkey Diet:*

As we will be discussing throughout this chapter, the Monkey Diet is a low-fat, almost vegetarian diet. This diet allows very few animal products, especially protein and fat, while consisting mostly of plant-based foods, carbohydrates. We are soon going to take a look at a sample week's meal plan, in order to help you understand what this means in terms of real food. The Monkey Diet is 20% protein, or one-fifth of your daily intake. Protein includes foods such as eggs, chicken, ground beef, steak, fish, and tofu. The Monkey should choose mostly lean meats, such as chicken and fish, along with vegetarian protein, such as tofu. The Monkey Diet is a low-fat diet, allowing only about 15% of its calories from fat. Fat includes foods such as olive oil, canola oil, bacon, avocado, olives, sour cream, and butter. Carbohydrates are the crux of this diet and are really divided into two categories: complex and simple. In the simplest terms, complex carbohydrates are denser in fiber, while simple carbohydrates are higher in sugar without the fiber. Complex carbohydrates are foods such as oat bran, brown rice, potatoes with the skins, and whole grain bread. Simple carbohydrates are foods such as white bread/buns, potatoes without the skins, white rice, cookies, cake, soda pop, and sugar. *(See Figure 6-1.)*

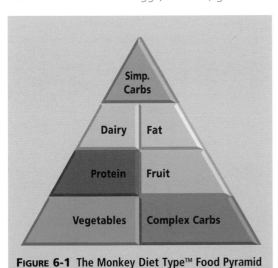

FIGURE 6-1 The Monkey Diet Type™ Food Pyramid

What about vegetables and fruits?

Technically, vegetables and fruits are both considered "carbohydrates." We have, however, put each into its own category. Why? Eating fruit is not the same as eating vegetables. Fruit is higher in sugar and calories than vegetables. On the Monkey Diet, the vegetable to fruit ratio is nearly 2:1. Vegetables include foods such as tomatoes, eggplant, dark leafy greens, carrots, bell peppers, and squash. Vegetables do not include potatoes or corn, which are actually counted as complex carbohydrates. Fruits include foods such as apples, berries, pineapple, and plums. Because there are so many vegetables and fruit servings to work into each day, you may find yourself grazing. Keep a bag of baby carrots at your desk, so you can munch while you work!

How does a *Monkey* make vegetables taste good?

As a Monkey, you have to learn to accept vegetables for what they are. There are some amazing vegetables out there that have great flavor all by themselves or with just a little kick of garlic and salt. Because you can have some fruit, let your fruits help your vegetables. Try sautéing a little orange zest in with your sautéed green beans or broccoli. The heavy green bean casserole is unfortunately not for you. Try to avoid using so much dairy food and fat, such as cream, cheese, and butter, to flavor your vegetables. A great staple for any Monkey is the basil, tomato, garlic mixture. Sauté a little sliced garlic, chopped tomatoes, and some basil and salt, in just a tad of olive oil. We use this all the time to top bagels, instead of peanut butter, or to stir into pasta noodles, instead of a heavy butter or cream sauce. Herbs and spices are definitely your friends. As you will see, throughout the book herbs and spices can really make the difference in your cooking. We look for places that sell fresh dried herbs and spices. Wow, does that make a difference compared to those old dusty dried up bottles you got for a wedding present six years ago!

How does a *Monkey* make a salad?

You will soon see a sample week's meal plan in this chapter. You will see some "green salads" listed throughout the week. Each "green salad" starts with good lettuce, such as romaine, leaf, arugula, spinach, or mixed field greens. A good lettuce is dark green, not light and watery like iceberg lettuce. Do not be fooled into thinking that iceberg lettuce, a tomato wedge, and a slice of cucumber represent a good salad. We have included some of these favorite salad ingredients—chopped cucumber, onion, tomatoes, and radishes, however, we encourage you to explore the myriad of vegetables that can be sliced and diced into your salad, such as zucchini, bell peppers, pea pods, and beets. While your salads should not be slathered in oils, nuts, or cheese, they can certainly have a little sprinkling of those fats. For added flavor and texture, add croutons and fruit, such as apple slices and kiwi. We love keeping dried fruit on hand too, such as raisins and dried cranberries for interesting flavor. You should even try some fruit juices mixed with a little Balsamic vinegar and just a little oil for your salad dressing. You'll find you don't even miss the fat!

What kind of fats should a *Monkey* include?

Monkeys typically feel best on plant-based fats, such as olive oil, walnut oil, avocados, and olives, over sour cream and butter. Not to say that a Monkey could not enjoy some bacon crumbled on a salad every once in a while, but these saturated fats are not the best choices for a Monkey. Your body does not need as many animal fats and proteins as the other diets. But you can certainly enjoy a little guacamole now and again!

On that note, let's take a look at a sample week's meal plan for a Monkey. If you need help recalling our food "equivalent" definitions, refer back to the *Chapter 2's* Food Equivalent Chart *Figure 2-2.*

MONKEY DAILY MEAL PLAN

7   protein equivalents

6   fat equivalents

8   vegetable equivalents

6   complex carb equivalents

2   dairy equivalents

4   fruit equivalents

2   simple carb equivalents

Approximately 2,000 Calories

Drink water or herbal tea as your beverage.
Coffee can be consumed occasionally.

Monday

Breakfast

- 1 cup oatmeal with ½ cup strawberries and 1 tsp honey
- 1 poached egg
  (2 complex carb, 1 fruit, ⅙ simple carb, 1 protein)

Snack

- 12 mini pretzels
- 1 cup carrots
  (1 simple carb, 1 vegetable)

Lunch

- Turkey & cheese sandwich: 1 slice whole grain toast,
  3 ounces turkey with 1 tsp mustard, lettuce leaf, 1 slice of
  tomato, ¼ cucumber, sliced, and 1 slice cheese
- Green salad: 2 cups dark leafy greens, ½ cup sliced apples,
  1 tsp pine nuts, ½ cup broccoli, ½ tomato sliced, onion slices,
  and 1 Tbsp sweet vinaigrette dressing
  *(1 complex carb, 3 protein, 3 vegetable, 1 dairy,
  2 fat, 1 fruit, ⅙ simple)*

** When you see an asterisk throughout the menu,
look for this recipe in Chapter 9!*

Snack

- 1 cup low fat yogurt with ½ banana, sliced
- 1 tsp slivered almonds
  (1 dairy, 1 fruit, 1 fat)

Dinner

- Asian-style Chicken and Cashew Salad: 3 ounces chicken and
  2 tsp cashews over a bed of dark lettuce
- 1 cup brown rice with 2 cups Asian stir-fried vegetables
  (3 protein, 2 complex carb, 3 vegetables, 2 fat)

Dessert

- Fruit roll-up: 1 whole wheat tortilla, 1 Tbsp cream cheese,
  and ½ cup strawberries with 1 tsp honey
  (1 complex carb, 1 fat, 1 fruit, ⅙ simple carb)

Tuesday

Breakfast

- 1 piece whole wheat toast with 1 tsp fruit preserves
  and ½ Tbsp almond butter
- 1 cup fresh melon
- ½ cup berries
  (1 complex carb, ⅙ simple carb, 2 fruit, 1 fat)

Snack

- 5 crackers
- 1 Tbsp cream cheese
  (1 simple carb, 1 fat)

Lunch

- 1 cup **Spicy Shrimp Soup***
- Green salad: 2 cup dark leafy greens, ½ cup broccoli florets, 3 onion slices, 3 tomato slices, 1 ounce crumbled blue cheese, 3 cucumber slices with 2 tsp sweet vinaigrette
- 1 whole grain roll with 1 tsp butter
  (3 protein, 2 fat, 1 complex carb, 2 vegetable, 1 dairy, ⅙ simple carb)

Snack

- Cheesy mixed vegetables: 2 cups steamed carrots, bell peppers, and cauliflower sprinkled with 1 ounce shredded cheddar cheese
  (4 vegetable, 1 dairy)

Dinner

- **Salmon with Fruit Salsa*** (4 ounces salmon with ½ cup fruit salsa and ½ cup black bean puree)
- Rice pilaf: 1 cup brown rice with 1 cup vegetables and 1 tsp butter
- 1 small dessert
  (4 protein, 2 fat, 3 complex carb, 2 vegetable, 1 fruit, 1 simple carb)

Snack

- ½ cup peaches, sliced, topped with ½ cup lowfat granola
  (1 fruit, 1 complex carb)

Wednesday

Breakfast

- 1½ cup high fiber breakfast cereal with 1 cup skim milk and ½ cup blueberries
- ½ bagel, 1 tsp butter, and 2 tsp jam
  (2 complex carb, 1 dairy, 1 fruit, 1⅓ simple carb, 1 fat)

Lunch

- **Arugula and Black Bean Salad*** (3 cups)
- 1 hard boiled egg
- ½ cup chopped mango
- ½ avocado
  (1 complex carb, 1 vegetable, 4 fat, 2 fruit, 1 protein)

Snack

- 2 cups mixed raw vegetables with honey mustard dipping sauce
- 6 whole grain crackers
  (2 vegetable, ⅓ simple carb, 1 complex carb)

Dinner

- **Greek Tofu Kabobs with Yogurt Sauce*** (6 ounces tofu, 2 cups grilled vegetables, and ¼ cup yogurt sauce)
- Vegetable couscous: 1 cup couscous, ½ cup mixed vegetables, and 1 ounce feta cheese
  (6 protein, 1 fat, 2 complex carb, 5 vegetable, 1 dairy)

Snack

- ½ grapefruit
  (1 fruit)

Thursday

Breakfast

- 1 medium tomato, sliced, topped with chopped basil and salt
- 1 English muffin, toasted with 1 Tbsp cream cheese
- ¾ cup orange juice
  (1 vegetable, 2 complex carb, 1 fat, 1 fruit)

Lunch

- 1 cup **Asian Sautéed Spinach***
- 3 ounces white fish, poached with lemon
- ½ cup brown rice topped with 1 tsp slivered almonds
- 1 cup fresh green beans, steamed with herbs, diced tomatoes, and a dash of Balsamic vinegar
- ½ cup **Fresh Fruit Salad***
- 1 whole wheat dinner roll and 1 tsp butter

  (4 vegetable, 2 complex carb, 3 fat, 3 protein, 1 fruit)

Snack

- 1 cup raw carrots and celery
- Herb yogurt dip: your favorite herbs mixed into ½ cup plain low fat yogurt

  (1 vegetable, ½ dairy)

Dinner

- 4 ounces roasted chicken
- 1 cup smashed Yukon gold potatoes with skins with ½ cup plain low-fat yogurt and 1 tsp butter
- 1 cup petite peas and carrots with a pinch of sugar and salt, and 1 tsp butter
- Green salad: 1 cup dark greens, ¼ cucumber sliced, bean sprouts, and diced radish with 1 Tbsp raspberry vinaigrette

  (4 protein, 2 complex carb, 2 fat, 2 vegetable, 1 simple carb, ½ dairy)

Dessert

- **Ricotta Cake with Berries***: 1 small piece served with 1 cup fresh berries

  (1 dairy, 1 simple carb, 2 fruit)

Friday

Breakfast *(Don't knock it 'til you try it!)*

- Veggie oatmeal: 1 cup cooked oatmeal, ½ cup finely chopped cooked zucchini, ½ cup finely chopped cooked broccoli, with 1 tsp butter and a dash of cinnamon and salt
- ½ grapefruit

  (2 complex carb, 2 vegetable, 1 fat, 1 fruit)

Lunch

- Beef vegetable stir-fry: 3 ounces lean beef, 1 tsp cashews, 1½ cup stir-fry veggies, with 1 tsp sesame oil, soy sauce, and Asian seasoning
- 1 cup jasmine rice
- 1 medium apple

  (2 simple carb, 3 vegetable, 2 fat, 3 protein, 1 fruit)

Snack

- 1 peach

  (1 fruit)

Dinner

- Chicken fajitas: 4 ounces diced Mexican chicken (fajita style), 2 La Tortilla Factory tortillas, 1 cup diced tomatoes, ½ cup chopped lettuce, 1 Tbsp chopped onion, 2 ounces shredded cheddar cheese, 4 Tbsp guacamole
- ½ cup refried vegetarian beans
- 1 cup **TexMex Spinach Salad*** topped with ½ cup canned pineapple

  (2 complex carb, 3 vegetable, 2 dairy, 4 protein, 3 fat, 1 fruit)

Snack

- 20 tortilla chips with tomato salsa

  (2 complex carb)

Saturday

Breakfast

- 1 cup **Ricotta Spinach Scramble***
- 1 medium tomato, sliced, drizzled with Balsamic vinegar, a pinch of salt and chopped chives
- ½ medium orange, peeled and sectioned
  (1 protein, 2 dairy, 2 vegetable, ½ fruit)

Lunch

- Turkey sandwich: 2 ounces roast turkey, 2 slices whole grain bread, toasted, with 1 tsp mustard, lettuce slice, and ½ cup cranberry sauce
- ½ sliced orange
- 1 cup **Carrot Raisin Salad*** on a bed of lettuce
- ½ cup cooked green beans, 1 tsp butter, topped with sesame seeds
  (2 protein, 2 complex carb, 1 simple carb, 3 vegetable, 1 fruit, 3 fat)

Dinner

- 4 ounce piece of **Crunchy Chicken***
- 1 cup **Squash Apple Bake***
- 1 cup brown rice
- 1½ cup grilled vegetables (peppers, onions, zucchini) with 1 tsp olive oil and sea salt
  (4 protein, 4 complex carb, ½ fruit, ⅔ simple carb, 3 vegetable, 2 fat)

Snack

- 1 cup **Savory Fruit Salad***
  (⅓ simple carb, 2 fruit, 1 fat)

Sunday

Breakfast

- Egg sandwich: 2 poached eggs, 1 plain bagel, 2 slices bacon
- 1 medium tomato, sliced, topped with chopped chives
- ¾ cup pomegranate juice
  (2 protein, 2 simple carb, 2 fat, 1 vegetable, 1 fruit)

Lunch

- Cheese onion pepper quesadilla: 1 corn tortilla, 2 ounces cheddar cheese, 1 Tbsp chopped onions, 1 Tbsp chopped green pepper, 1 tsp oil, served with 2 Tbsp salsa
- Green salad: 2 cups shredded dark greens, ¼ sliced cucumber, ¼ cup dried cranberries, ½ cup cold cooked green beans, and 1 tsp chopped pecans, served with 1 Tbsp fat-free **Vinaigrette Dressing***
  (3 vegetable, 2 dairy, 1 complex carb, 1 fruit, 2 fat)

Snack

- 1 cup berries
  (2 fruit)

Dinner

- 5 ounces lean roast beef
- 1 large baking potato with 1 tsp butter, ½ Tbsp sour cream, and chopped chives
- 1 cup sautéed zucchini with lemon and herbs
- 1 cup roasted eggplant sprinkled with Balsamic vinegar and herbs
- 1 small whole wheat dinner roll
  (5 protein, 3 complex carb, 4 vegetable, 2 fat)

Snack

- 1 cup grits with 1 tsp honey
- 1 cup sliced peaches
  (⅙ simple carb, 2 complex carb, 2 fruit)

So are you ready to start cooking?

As you can see, the Monkey Diet is a lower fat, almost vegetarian diet. In fact, people can choose to be vegetarians and do very well on this diet. A little meat

here and there is fine too, but lean meat is always preferred for Monkeys. This diet allows for some flexibility compared to the Giraffe Diet. However, you should remember that it is not as lenient as the Bear Diet and you will not feel as good if you have the amounts of fat and protein that a Bear has. Make vegetable, whole grain, and lean protein consumption a main goal of your diet. See *Chapter 9* for some scrumptious Monkey recipes that will make you go bananas!

Succeeding on the *Monkey Diet*

- **Take a break**
  Monkeys work too much and exercise too little. Monkeys are hard workers. Those who have weight issues need to work less and exercise more.

- **Getting fit**
  Monkeys do best with 50% aerobic and 50% weight lifting. Monkeys often have excessive weight in the hips. To get this off you must do some weight lifting or CORE exercises, in addition to aerobic exercise. Sorry to tell you, but you do best by exercising five to seven times per week. It will be difficult to reach your optimal health goals without the exercise.

- **Watch the cheese, please**
  You need to eat low fat and that means very little cheese. Dairy products are often your downfall because you love food. Please get a food allergy test—you may be surprised to find out that you are allergic to your favorite foods!

- **Fruit for dessert**
  Try to make your sweet choices fruit based and not sugar based. You are a slow oxidizer of food which means that food lasts in your system a long time. Fruits and sugars are therefore better tolerated by Monkeys like you, as they are metabolized more rapidly than fats and proteins.

- **One meal per day?**
  Do not eat when you are not hungry. Some of you do fine on two meals per day. If you feel like you only need to eat once per day, it means you aren't exercising enough. Get off the couch and start exercising!

- **Getting in the kitchen**
  Typically Monkeys can cook but often do not cook because they are tired. You may be tired because you are carrying around extra pounds. Your action plan should be to start an exercise program and decrease your caloric intake. Decrease the fat in your diet. This means not having seconds of those creamy sauces you put on your food and the cheese you add to every meal. A better option would be soy based products including soy milk, soy cheese, and fresh herb sauces instead of creamy choices.

- **Have a drink.**
  Monkeys typically do not drink enough water. You often become so involved in work and various projects, that you end up dehydrated. Drinking water will also help fill you up. The best drinks for a Monkey are water, herbal teas, or

iced tea. Yes it is ok to have fruit juices but if you are having weight issues, don't drink your calories. Coffee is ok in moderation, but it should be black or with a little sweetener. Cream in your coffee is only adding more fat, which you do not need.

- **Just a little something…**
Monkeys should eat a little something like an English muffin or a small bowl of cereal to get the metabolism going in the morning. You may not wake up hungry, but it is likely that you are starting your day thinking about the million things you have to accomplish. Eat a little food to give you the energy to accomplish those million things!

Tips for Losing Weight on the *Monkey Diet:*

- **Eat the right proportions of food.**
Each of the Hauser Diets is a unique breakdown of protein, fat, and carbohydrates. As a Monkey, your body needs to lean toward vegetarian food choices, over heavy protein and fat food choices.

make *optimum* health your goal

- **Eat mostly carbohydrates that contain fiber.**
This means whole grains, and carbohydrates that have at least 4 grams of fiber per serving. Fiber is necessary for proper digestion and signaling the brain that the stomach is full, among many other actions in the body.

- **Exercise everyday.**
Like we said earlier, a Monkey typically does best when exercising five to seven times per week.

- **Tell others that you are on a diet.**
Give a quick outline to people you are in contact with everyday. Tell them that you are on a diet. Most people will get the idea that a steak house is not the best place to invite you for a lunch date!

- **Eat slowly.**
This gives your stomach additional time to fill up to prevent overeating. Take a break for a few minutes during the meal to allow yourself to recognize the feeling of fullness. It is best to stop eating when you first begin to feel full.

- **Don't drink alcohol.**
Although Monkeys typically do ok with alcohol in moderation, these simple carbohydrate calories add up very quickly and will not help a person lose weight. Cutting out regular alcohol consumption may cut down a few pounds relatively quickly.

- **Know your danger foods.**

  Many Monkeys have a hard time giving up high fat foods like potato chips, fried chicken, or sour cream. Getting these foods out of your normal diet rotation will increase the chances of success on this diet.

FAQ and *Monkey Diet:* Myths:

How often should I eat?

Try to eat regularly, about three meals per day, especially if you are active. However, if you are a slow oxidizer, you will often feel fine eating fewer than three meals per day, or even being more of a "grazer," eating smaller meals throughout the day. Remember, if you can get by with one or two meals per day, it generally means your metabolism is too slow. It may be because you don't exercise enough or your hormones are too low. At Caring Medical, we see Monkeys with both tendencies and like to check hormone levels to rule out deficiencies.

Will I always be a Monkey?

The simplest answer is: no. As you read in *Chapter 1,* there are a couple key factors that determine which diet is best for you, one of those being blood pH. As the seasons change, our blood pH is affected. In our experience, if a Monkey's blood gets too alkaline, he or she will change to a Giraffe Diet. in order to acidify the blood pH into normal range. Likewise, if a Monkey's blood gets too acidic, he or she will change to a Bear Diet in order to alkalinize the blood into normal range.

Do I have to eat meat?

If a person chooses to eat all plant-based protein sources, such as tofu or tempeh, and has the physiology of a Monkey, he or she will likely still do well. Monkeys can generally get enough protein with plant-based protein, but adding some eggs and light meat are optimal for the best balance of nutrients.

Is coffee ok to drink?

Regular coffee helps to acidify your blood. So, it is ok for people who have alkaline blood pH to drink coffee in moderation. In our experience, these people do not tend to feel stimulated or buzzed, from drinking regular coffee—just minimize your use of fattening creamers! Monkeys are typically the ones who can easily drink an espresso after a nice relaxing dinner and still be able to fall asleep as soon as their heads hit the pillows!

Obtaining Optimal Health on the *Monkey Diet:*

We wanted to share some stories of successful Monkey clients to help inspire you to eat the Monkey way.

Joann: Jumping for Joy

Joann is known as JJ by her friends because of her joy. Joyous Joann was anything but joyous the last several years. She put on a good front for people, but we could see it in her eyes; they were tired. On her initial medical history forms she marked the following symptoms as severe: fatigue, lethargy, sleeplessness, aching, menstrual symptoms, anxiety and irritability. She was a biological mess. In our experience, the first place to start with someone like this is to figure out what diet they need to eat. We did the Hauser Diet Typing analysis and JJ was found to be a balanced oxidizer with alkaline blood. She was placed on the Monkey Diet. We explained to her that her alkaline blood was most likely the reason for her insomnia, irritability, and anxiety. These symptoms cleared over the next few months as JJ followed the Monkey Diet. She incorporated more vegetables and whole grains into her diet, and reduced her frequent consumption of meats. We also had her address her addiction to diet soda and eliminate it from her diet, and she started

doing some exercise. Her fatigue improved about 50% after dietary intervention alone. We checked JJ's hormones which turned out to be low. She started on natural hormone replacement therapy to achieve even more improvement in energy, vitality, and joy. Now she tells us that she is truly JJ again.

The Crashing Couple

There are times that body chemistry crashes together in a couple. Robin and Jack were just that! They both came to Caring Medical on the same day. They weren't particularly happy. Their relationship was struggling. We felt that this was due to the fact that both of them felt terrible most of the time. When you feel awful, you do not treat people the way you would like to be treated. Other people don't want to be around you. Robin and Jack recently started using herbal remedies and had become "granola" according to their friends. They were strict vegetarians. We can see your wheels turning already! Something happened to them when they made these changes that for all intents and purposes, seemed like healthy changes.

What did their testing show? Robin tested out as a fast oxidizer with with normal blood pH, making her an Otter Diet Type. She was definitely not eating nearly enough natural fats and protein, being a strict vegetarian. Therefore we started her on a supplement program which included a protein powder and essential fatty acids.* This is an example of the Monkey Diet not being right for just anyone.

---

* **Note:** *See www.benuts.com for more information on supplements from Beulah Land Nutritionals.*

Jack's testing revealed that he had normal blood pH and was a slow oxidizer. He was put on a Monkey Diet, which was very close to what he was eating. The cause of his terrible fatigue then really was due to something else. He was given a food allergy test and it turned out that he was allergic to gluten. As we discussed previously in *Chapter 1*, a food allergy test will often come back showing high sensitivity to common foods that a person is eating, such as gluten-containing items. Once the gluten containing grains (such as wheat) were omitted from his diet, his health improved drastically. He could still be primarily vegetarian, but the types of grain he ate were crucial. He avoided wheat and other gluten-containing products. The gluten-free choices are still ample, including rice, corn, potatoes, and soy. So, Jack was able to still eat the right food that he needed to keep his blood pH and blood sugar balanced, while not aggravating his food allergies. The crashing couple recovered nicely. We understand they are still together, very active, and very happy.

Paula with PMS

Paula's case is one that you must understand. She felt great except the week before her menstrual cycle. She would get bloated, irritable, start with migraine headaches, and just feel terrible. Unfortunately, the day she came to the office she looked like a million bucks and felt even better. We did all the normal tests and found her blood to be slightly alkaline, but encouraged her to get tested on her worst day. She obliged and three days before her menstrual cycle her blood pH went from the 7.451 to 7.476. This may not seem like a big jump to you but to the blood it is major! This was why during that time of the month she felt horrible.

Paula actually had to follow different diets on different days of her cycle. Days 1-14 of the menstrual cycle she ate the Monkey Diet, but days 14-28 of her cycle she needed the Giraffe Diet. She, like a lot of women with PMS, had more alkaline blood during the second half of her menstrual cycle. This could be one of the reasons why many women go crazy for chocolate during PMS which would help balance their blood pH. The problem with sweets is that they cause other problems. A better approach is to eat a diet more on the carbohydrate side throughout the menstrual cycle and really increase the whole grains, fruits, and vegetables during the second half of the menstrual cycle.

In regard to Paula's case it took two menstrual cycles to get her blood pH to the normal range throughout the cycle. Paula knew for sure that she was better when on her third menstrual cycle she got her period during a business meeting and she didn't even know it! She suffered no PMS symptoms to tell her it was coming. Perhaps this is the one downside to The Hauser Diet?

Summary of the *Monkey Diet*

Of all the Hauser Diets, the Monkey should keep the *low-fat* = *healthy* mentality. The Monkey Diet falls between a balanced diet, and a strict low-fat, vegetarian diet. Those Monkeys who choose to go completely vegetarian typically do well on this diet too. Your meals should be carbohydrate-based, including plenty of foods such as fruits, vegetables, rice, pasta,

and whole grains. While it is important to remember to get protein throughout the day, choose lean protein most often, such as chicken, fish, and tofu. With a little discipline, you can create savory dishes with all your favorite Monkey foods, even without the added fat!

In the upcoming chapters we will start cooking up tempting Monkey meals. But first, we'll explore the next Hauser Diet, The Giraffe Diet, and learn more about how and why their dietary needs are different than those on the Monkey Diet.

THE GIRAFFE
DIET TYPE™

10%
protein

10%
fat

80%
carbohydrates

the giraffe diet type™

The Giraffe Diet is a vegetarian-based diet. The macronutrient breakdown is 10% protein, 10% fat, and 80% carbohydrates. This diet is very low in fat and protein, while consisting mostly of carbohydrate (plant) foods. The Giraffe Diet is typically used therapeutically for people who have alkaline blood pH, and are slow oxidizers with normal insulin levels. Thus, Giraffes have a very abnormal physiology. Their blood pH is very high and they metabolize, or breakdown, food extremely slowly. To have optimum health, a Giraffe must consume carbohydrates which are metabolized easily and lower blood pH. As you will see from the case studies later in the chapter, this diet has also been helpful for many patients at Caring Medical with autoimmune disorders. The Giraffe Diet is a very limited diet, as it leans very far to the carbohydrate end of the Hauser Diet spectrum and can prove one of the more difficult diets to follow. Many people think that being a vegetarian is easy because "you just don't eat meat." But most vegetarians allow themselves ample plant-based protein and fat. The Giraffe Diet does not allow this same leeway with protein and fat because a person who types out to be a Giraffe needs less protein and fat in order to be healthy.

Food Choices on the *Giraffe Diet:*

The Giraffe Diet is a vegetarian diet typically used for therapeutic reasons. This is a very strict, low-fat diet that focuses on fresh vegetables, fruits, and grains. We are soon going to take a look at a sample week's meal plan, so you need to understand how this measures up in terms of real food. Protein is a very small part of your diet, only 10%. Protein includes foods such as eggs, chicken, ground beef, steak, fish, and tofu. Fat is also a small part of your diet, only 10%. Fat includes foods such as olive oil, canola oil, bacon, avocado, olives, sour cream, and butter. These are foods that you will not see a lot throughout the day. When you do eat protein and fat, it should come from plant sources, such as tofu for protein and olive oil for fat. Eighty percent or four fifths of your diet will come from carbohydrates. *(See Figure 7-1.)*

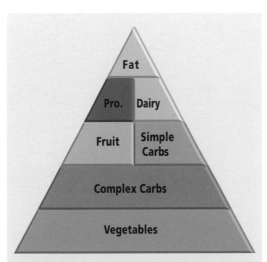

FIGURE 7-1 The Giraffe Diet Type™ Food Pyramid

Carbohydrates are really divided into two categories: complex and simple. In the simplest terms, complex carbohydrates are denser in fiber, while simple carbohydrates are higher in sugar without the fiber.

Complex carbohydrates are foods such as oat bran, brown rice, legumes, potatoes with the skins, and whole grain bread. Simple carbohydrates are foods such as white bread/buns, potatoes without the skins, white rice, cookies, cake, soda pop, and sugar. Complex carbohydrates are always the better choice, but you are allowed some simple carbs too. When you do have simple carbs, choose ones that most mimic a complex carb. By that we mean you should choose white rice instead of soda, or a slice of white bread instead of a piece of cake. See, even within this category there are some choices that are better than others! In other words, nobody should really be pounding down the sweets!

What about vegetables and fruits? Technically, vegetables and fruits are both classified as "carbohydrates." We have put each into its own category. Why? Eating fruit is not the same as eating vegetables. Fruit is much higher in sugar and calories than vegetables. On the Giraffe Diet, there are a lot of both, but still the vegetable to fruit ratio is nearly 3:1. Vegetables include foods such as zucchini, tomatoes, eggplant, dark leafy greens, carrots, bell peppers, and squash. Vegetables do not include potatoes or corn, which are actually counted as complex carbohydrates. Fruits include foods such as oranges, apples, grapes, berries, pineapple, kiwi, and plums.

How does a *Giraffe* make vegetables taste good?

No one knows vegetables like a Giraffe. We know this diet has so many vegetables that you will no doubt feel like you *are* a Giraffe! Giraffes should really learn to like vegetables raw, for easy snacking—peapods and baby carrots are easy choices! But when it comes to making dinner, try substituting excessive oil or cream sauce for something lighter, such as sautéing vegetables in broth or lemon juice. Do not rely on butter and cheese to make vegetables more palatable. Some fats are allowed, but too many of those foods will never allow you to reach your health goals. Use spices and herbs to enhance vegetable dishes, such as fresh garlic, basil, chives, cilantro, and even green onion. Try growing your own basil and other herbs. It is right there when you want to make some basil and tomato pasta or to add into a Thai vegetable stir-fry. There is nothing like fresh herbs—we love ours! Because the Giraffes can have more fruit, experiment with mixing them in with your vegetables, like sautéed apples and green beans as an interesting side dish. Even using fruit, such as sliced oranges and cranberry sauce, can help turn broccoli into something that you actually look forward to eating! So, if you can't have the fat, go for the sweet fruits to help give your vegetables a unique flavor!

How does a *Giraffe* make a salad?

Coming up in this chapter we will show you a sample meal plan for one week. You will see some "green salads" listed throughout. Each "green salad" starts with good lettuce, such as romaine, leaf, arugula, spinach, or mixed field greens. A good lettuce is dark green, not light and watery like iceberg lettuce. Do not be fooled into thinking a good salad is iceberg lettuce, a tomato wedge, and a slice of cucumber. We have included some of these favorite standard salad vegetables in our meal plans, but we encourage you, especially being a vegetarian, to explore the rainbow of vegetables that can be sliced and diced into your salad, such as shredded squash, bell peppers, carrots, beets, green beans, and cauliflower. For added flavor and texture, add croutons and fruit, such as kiwi and pear slices. We love keeping dried fruit on hand, such as dates, figs, and dried cranberries for interesting flavor.

When it comes to salad dressing, we can honestly tell you that investing in a good bottle of Balsamic vinegar is well worth it! You can buy the bottle at the supermarket for a few bucks and it will taste very acidic, or you can spend more at a specialty store, but get a good Balsamic vinegar (aged over eight years, or longer if you can find it!) and have it add a smooth, rich, sweet flavor to your foods. The Giraffe is eating so many vegetables, without the high fat flavor enhancers of cheese and butter, that you will probably start using the Balsamic vinegar daily. You can also mix this in with a little fruit juice to create a fruity vinaigrette. Remember, as a Giraffe, you'll be eating a lot of salads so experiment with ways to make them as fun to eat as possible!

What kind of fats should a *Giraffe* include?

The Giraffe typically does better with plant-based foods. Hence, a Giraffe should look for plant-based fats, rather than fats such as bacon and butter. Good fats for a Giraffe are oils, such as olive, walnut, and sesame, as well as avocados and olives. The Giraffe Diet is the lowest in fat of all the Hauser Diets, so it should take you a while to go through that bottle of olive oil! Your sacrifice is fat, but you get the carbs that other diets envy, so it is not all that bad!

On that note, let's take a look at a sample week's meal plan for a Giraffe. If you need help recalling how we define a food "equivalent," refer back to the Food Equivalent Chart *Figure 2-2,* in *Chapter 2.*

GIRAFFE DAILY MEAL PLAN

  4 protein equivalents

  5 fat equivalents

12 vegetable equivalents

10 complex carb equivalents

  1 dairy equivalent

  5 fruit equivalents

  3 simple carb equivalents

Approximately 2,000 Calories

Drink water or herbal tea as your beverage. Coffee can be consumed occasionally.

* When you see an asterisk throughout the menu, look for this recipe in Chapter 9!

Monday

Breakfast
- 1½ cup high fiber cereal with 1 banana
- 1 cup soy milk
- 1 cup tomato juice
- ½ cup berries with 1 tsp honey
  (2 complex carb, 3 fruit, 1 dairy, ⅙ simple, 1 vegetable)

Lunch
- 2½ cups lentil soup (vegetarian)
- 1 piece garlic bread: ½ inch thick slice crunchy French bread spread with 1 tsp olive oil and crushed garlic
- Green salad: 3 cups dark leafy greens, ½ cup bell pepper slices, ½ medium tomato sliced, 2 Tbsp dried cranberries, 1 scallion chopped, ⅓ avocado, and 1 Tbsp fresh chopped cilantro, sprinkled with 2 Tbsp Balsamic vinegar and juice of ½ lime
- 1 cup cooked green beans with lemon and herbs
  (5 complex carb, 6 vegetable, 1 simple, 1 fruit, 3 fat)

Snack

- 1 cup melon slices
- 2 cups jicama slices (or other crunchy vegetable)
- ½ Tbsp peanut butter for dipping
  (1 fruit, 2 vegetable, 1 fat)

Dinner

- **Asian Lettuce Wraps** *(made with tofu)** *(4 ounces tofu cooked in 1 tsp sesame oil, 3 cups vegetables, and unlimited lettuce for wrapping)*
- 1½ cups whole grain rice
- 2 medium oatmeal cookies
  (4 protein, 1 fat, 3 vegetable, 3 complex carb, 2 simple carb)

Tuesday

Breakfast

- 1½ cup cooked oat bran with 1 tsp honey and 1 cup blueberries
- 1 cup melon chunks with lime juice drizzle
- 1 cup tomato juice
  (3 complex, ⅙ simple, 3 fruit, 1 vegetable)

Lunch

- Wrapped grilled vegetable skewers with rice: 2 cups grilled vegetables, 1 Tbsp garlic butter, 1 cup jasmine rice, chopped cilantro, and 2 corn tortillas, topped with 1-2 Tbsp of salsa
- 1 medium apple
  (4 vegetable, 3 fat, 2 simple carb, 2 complex carb, 1 fruit)

Snack

- 2 cups mixed raw vegetables
- 1 medium orange
- honey mustard dressing for dipping (fat-free made from scratch)
  (2 vegetable, 1 fruit, ⅙ simple carb)

Dinner

- 2 cups couscous tofu pilaf: 1 cup couscous, 2 cups cooked vegetables, 4 ounces tofu, 1 ounce feta cheese, and 1 tsp sesame oil
- Green salad: 2 cups dark leafy greens, ½ cup sliced tomatoes, 3 cucumber slices, ½ cup black beans, ⅙ avocado, and ½ cup garbanzo beans
- 1 Tbsp fruit vinaigrette
- 1 whole grain roll
  (1 dairy, 5 complex carb, 2 fat, 5 vegetable, 4 protein, ⅙ simple)

Wednesday

Breakfast

- 1 cup fresh fruit salad
- 2 small pancakes with 2 Tbsp real maple syrup, 1 tsp butter
- 1 egg, poached
  (2 fruit, 3 simple carb, 1 fat, 1 protein)

Lunch

- Grilled Tofu and Corn Salad* *(3 ounces tofu, 4 cups lettuce, 1 cup corn mixed, ½ cup black beans, 1 medium tomato, ½ cup mandarin orange segments with 2 Tbsp fat-free dressing, ⅙ avocado)*
- 1 whole grain roll
- 1 apple, sliced (toss into the salad if desired)
  (3 protein, 4 complex carb, 5 vegetable, 2 fruit, 1 fat)

Snack

- 10 whole grain crackers, topped with tomato slices
- 1 cup snow peas, or other crisp vegetable
  (2 complex carb, 2 vegetable)

Dinner

- Italian Antipasto Salad* (without olives) *(2 cups whole wheat pasta, 1 medium sliced tomato, 8 sprigs asparagus, 10 halved grapes, and 1 cup chopped bell peppers and onions, steamed and seasoned, and 1 ounce mozzarella cheese, tossed with 1 Tbsp Italian dressing and 2 sprigs of fresh chopped basil)*
  (4 complex carb, 5 vegetable, 1 dairy, 3 fat, 1 fruit)

Thursday

Breakfast

- 1 whole wheat English muffin
- 2 Tbsp 100% fruit jam
- ½ Tbsp organic peanut butter
- ½ cup cottage cheese, low fat
- 1 medium peach, sliced
- 1 cup tomato juice
  (2 complex carb, 1 simple carb, 1 dairy, 1 fruit, 1 vegetable, 1 fat)

Lunch

- 4 ounces tofu with 2 cups sautéed Asian veggies (sautéed in 2 Tbsp soy sauce and 1 tsp sesame oil)
- 1 cup brown rice
- ½ cup chick peas (atop veggies)
- 1½ cup mixed fruit salad
  (4 vegetable, 3 complex carb, 3 fruit, 4 protein, 1 fat)

Snack

- Veggie snack wrap: 1 tomato basil tortilla wrap, 1 cup fresh sliced vegetables (peppers, onion, cucumber, sprouts, and lettuce) drizzled with Balsamic vinegar and fresh lime juice
- 1 cup tomato juice
  (1 complex carb, 2 vegetable)

Dinner

- 1 cup brown rice
- 1 medium-large baked sweet potato with 1 tsp butter and dash of cinnamon
- ⅓ cup whole cranberry sauce, tossed with 2 tsp chopped walnuts and 1 medium diced apple
- 2½ cups seasoned green beans and onions
  (4 complex carb, 1 fruit, 3 fat, 1 simple carb, 5 vegetable)

Dessert

- 1 small cookie
  (1 simple carb)

Friday

Breakfast

- Mexican breakfast wraps: 1 egg scrambled with 1 cup cooked pepper/onion mix cooked in 1 tsp oil topped with 1 medium chopped tomato, 1 Tbsp fresh cilantro, wrapped in 2 La Tortilla Factory Whole Wheat Tortillas
- 1 cup vegetarian refried beans
- ½ cup orange juice
- Add a dash or two of hot sauce or Mexican spices to liven things up!
  (1 protein, 3 vegetable, 1 fat, 3 complex carb, 1 fruit)

Snack

- 10 whole wheat crackers with ½ Tbsp peanut butter
  (2 complex carb, 1 fat)

Lunch

- Veggie-rice pita pocket: 1½ cups broccoli/cauliflower/carrot medley, steamed and seasoned, 1 cup Basmati rice, 2 whole wheat pita pockets, and 1 Tbsp cream cheese
- 1 cup vegetable soup
- 1 medium Gala apple, sliced
  (4 vegetable, 2 simple carb, 2 complex carb, 1 fat, 1 fruit)

Dinner

- 3 ounces baked tofu with lemon and dill
- 1 cup brown rice with 1 cup vegetables chopped finely
- 1 cup sauteed asparagus in 1 tsp oil with lemon zest
- 1 cup orange/beet salad: 1 medium orange and 8 sliced beets,1 tsp slivered almonds drizzled with Balsamic vinegar
- 1 small dessert
  (3 protein, 2 complex carb, 5 vegetable, 2 fat, 1 fruit, 1 simple carb)

Snack

- Soy yogurt parfait: 1 cup soy yogurt topped with 1 cup berries and ¾ cup high fiber cereal
  (2 fruit, 1 complex carb, 1 dairy)

Saturday

Breakfast

- Eggs Florentine atop bagel: 2 poached eggs, ½ cup seasoned spinach cooked in 1 tsp butter, and 2 Tbsp 100% fruit-pepper jam atop 1 whole grain bagel
- 1 cup tomato juice
- 1 medium orange, sliced
  (2 protein, 2 complex carb, 1 simple carb, 2 vegetable, 1 fruit, 1 fat)

Snack

- 1 pear
- 10 whole wheat crackers
- ½ Tbsp nutbutter
  (1 fruit, 2 complex carb, 1 fat)

Lunch

- 2 cups Lentil Soup*
- 1 whole grain roll topped with 1 tsp olive oil and herbs
- 1 cup four-bean salad in fat-free vinaigrette dressing on bed of lettuce
- 1 medium tomato, sliced
  (5 complex carb, 1 fat, 3 vegetable)

Snack

- 1 plum
- 1 cup carrot sticks
  (1 fruit, 1 vegetable)

Dinner

- Make your own shrimp and veggie pizza: 2 slices regular pizza crust topped with 2 ounces shrimp, 1 medium tomato, 2 cloves sliced garlic, and fresh basil sautéed in 1 tsp olive oil, 1 cup sautéed vegetables such as green & red peppers, onion, mushrooms, ¼ cup chopped pineapple, and 1 ounce shredded mozzarella cheese
- Green salad: 2 cup mixed field greens, ½ cup chopped strawberries, ¼ sliced cucumber, ½ cup garbanzo beans, bean sprouts, 5 olives, sprinkled with Strawberry Balsamic Vinaigrette dressing made with pureed strawberries and herbs
- 1 cup cooked Brussels sprouts with lemon and herbs
  (2 simple carb, 6 vegetable, 2 fat, 1 dairy, 1 complex carb, 2 fruit, 2 protein)

Sunday

Breakfast

- 2 butttermilk pancakes with ½ cup blueberries and 2 tsp butter
- 2 Tbsp real maple syrup
- ½ grapefruit
  (3 simple carb, 2 fat, 2 fruit)

Snack

- 1 cup bell peppers
- 1 cup carrot sticks
  (2 vegetable)

Lunch

- 2 cups vegetarian **Split Pea Soup***
- Green salad: 2 cup mixed field greens, ¼ cucumber sliced, ½ cup shredded raw carrots and zucchini, ½ cup chopped fresh mushrooms, ½ cup pickled beets, drizzled with Balsamic vinegar and lemon juice
- 1 whole grain muffin with raisins
  (5 complex carb, 1 fat, 3 vegetable, 1 fruit)

Snack

- 10 tortilla chips with tomato and avocado salsa
  (1 complex carb, 1 fat)

Dinner

- 1 cup tomato juice
- 4 ounces Tilapia with lemon and herbs
- 1 cup confetti brown rice: 1 cup whole grain rice with 1 cup peppers and onions mixed in
- 1 whole grain dinner roll
- 2 cups sautéed mixed vegetables with 1 tsp olive oil, salt, and garlic
- 1 cup fresh fruit salad with lime and salt
  (4 protein, 3 complex carb, 7 vegetable, 1 fat, 2 fruit)

Snack

- ¾ cup high fiber cereal
- 1 cup soy milk
  (1 complex carb, 1 dairy)

So... what do you think?

You're probably thinking, "Wow, that's a lot of vegetables!" It is. The Giraffes need a diet very high in vegetables, fruit, and grain. It is a truly vegetarian diet. However, the difference between the typical "vegetarian" diet and the Giraffe Diet is that there are tighter protein and fat restrictions. Remember, your body does not need as much fat as the other Diet Types. Learning new ways to cook food, without using large amounts of butter and oil, are necessary if you want to succeed on the Giraffe Diet. Turn to *Chapter 9* for recipes that will make eating vegetables a pleasure.

Succeeding on the *Giraffe Diet*

Although this diet may seem difficult, these tips for success may make things a little easier for you.

- **Couscous anyone?**

  We know you may not want to be a vegetarian but you are one. You can fight it but you need to eat vegetarian. Yes, that means breakfast, lunch, and dinner. Try learning how to cook various cuisines like Mediterranean or Thai, focusing on the vegetarian-based meals. The internet provides an unending variety of vegetarian recipes.

- **Correct carb consumption.**

  Yes, you can have pasta, but don't make every dinner a pasta dish with little else. Your meals need to consist primarily of vegetables, with grains and fruit being secondary.

- **Uproot the root cause.**

  We see many people who are allergic to wheat-containing foods, such as bread and pasta. Unfortunately, most never thought their food was the cause of their health trouble. As we previously discussed, food allergies can increase systemic inflammation, irritate the digestive system, increase body pain, and cause havoc on our overall health. The Giraffe Diet contains such a high amount of carbohydrates, so it is wise to have yourself tested for any delayed, adverse reactions to foods. If you are allergic to wheat or other grain, the Giraffe Diet is still doable, but you have to use carbohydrate sources that you are not allergic to. Otherwise, your health is not likely to improve. Food allergy testing is key to better health on the Giraffe Diet.

- **Spice it up!**

  Honestly, you need to cook. Spices are your buddies. You do not have to make the same boring vegetables day after day. As you will read later in this book, keeping an array of spices and herbs in your kitchen can add a new dimension to your vegetables.

- **Put down the butter and nobody gets hurt!**

  Do not get in the habit of using butter or cheese for enhancing the flavor of vegetables. If you have weight, or other health issues, and are supposed to be a Giraffe, your problem is you eat too much fat. Learn where the fat is in your diet and then eliminate it. If you listen to your body, you will probably realize that fatty foods give you bloating or other digestive or symptomatic complaints. Your body doesn't want fat, so don't eat it!

- **Find the right exercise for you.**

  You do very well with exercises that involve stretching. Yes, this means yoga, pilates, Tai Chi, and the like. Body building or weight lifting should be secondary. You also do not need as much aerobic exercise to be healthy. Consider though picking a type of exercise like Yoga, Pilates or Tai Chi and becoming proficient at it. You have the potential to be very fit. This will involve being a very strict vegetarian and sticking to an exercise regime. Let your body be your guide.

Tips for Losing Weight on the *Giraffe Diet*

- **Eat the right proportions of food.**

  Each of the Hauser Diets is a unique breakdown of protein, fat, and carbohydrates. As a Giraffe, your body needs a large amount of carbohydrates, mostly from vegetables and complex carbs. Although everyone needs some protein and fat, you require the least of the Hauser Diets.

- **Stay away from your danger foods.**

  Do not rely on high fat foods and condiments like sour cream and mayonnaise to make your

meals taste better. Use foods such as vinegars, fruit juices and mustards to flavor all the vegetables in your diet.

- **Tell others that you are on a diet.**
  Give a quick outline to people you are in contact with everyday. Tell them that you are eating a vegetarian diet, or a low fat diet.

- **Eat slowly.**
  This gives your stomach additional time to fill up to prevent overeating. If you listen to these cues, you will not overeat.

- **Don't drink alcohol.**
  Although Giraffes typically do ok with alcohol in moderation, these simple carbohydrate calories add up very quickly and will not help a person lose weight. Cutting out regular alcohol consumption may cut down a few pounds relatively quickly.

- **Get creative.**
  The Giraffe Diet is a lot stricter than how the average person is used to eating. It has three times the amount of vegetables the average person probably eats in a day. You have to get creative with increasing your vegetable intake. This even means incorporating vegetables into your breakfast.

FAQ and *Giraffe Diet* Myths:

How often should I eat?

Try to eat regularly, especially if you are a very active person. If you are a slow oxidizer, you will probably feel fine eating fewer than three meals per day, or even being more of a "grazer," eating smaller meals throughout the day.

Will I always be a Giraffe?

The simplest answer is: no. As you read in *Chapter 1*, there are a couple key factors that determine which diet is best for you, one of those being blood pH. If a person moves to a colder climate, or is a Giraffe in the summer months, it is likely that colder weather will produce an acidifying effect on the blood. This change in blood pH may require a person to add more protein and fat, such as switching to a Monkey Diet, in order to keep it balanced. In our experience, if the Giraffe Diet is recommended for therapeutic reasons, a person may switch to a Monkey Diet as his or her symptoms (often from autoimmune disorders) remit.

Where will I get my protein?

The Giraffe Diet is recommended for someone who does not need much protein, such as meat and eggs, as the other Hauser Diets. It should be noted here that even plant based items contain some protein—such as legumes and green leafy vegetables—although in smaller amounts than animal protein.

So, if a person has the physiology of a Giraffe and follows the diet correctly, he or she should get enough protein.

Can I drink coffee?

Drinking regular coffee (not decaffinated) in moderation is allowed in the Giraffe Diet. We do not reccomend decaffinated coffee because of the chemicals used to extract the caffeine. In our opinion, decaffinated coffee can worsen symptoms of certain autoimmune disorders.

Is this a vegan diet?

If a person chooses to be a vegan, meaning their diet consists of no animal products, this fits in very well with the Giraffe Diet. It is typically not necessary for a person with the physiology of a Giraffe to need animal products, and many do better without them. However, many people still like to eat some animal products, whether it is cheese or an occasional piece of meat. This is fine. It is ideal for a Giraffe to obtain the little amount of allowed protein from lean sources, such as tofu or white meat chicken.

Obtaining Optimal Health on the *Giraffe Diet*

Lauren with Lupus

Lauren arrived at Caring Medical for her first visit. She came to us with prescriptions for nine different medications. Her kidneys were starting to fail. Her lupus was out of control even with all of the medications. She felt terrible. She had diffuse body swelling and terrible body pain. Her fatigue was unremitting.

She underwent a comprehensive Natural Medicine evaluation. She was found to have a high blood pH at 7.469 and her glucose tolerance test showed that she was a slow oxidizer with a normal fasting insulin level. She was initially placed on the Giraffe Diet until some of her autoimmune disorder symptoms abated. Her hormone levels were very low, so she was placed on natural hormone replacement therapy, including DHEA, progesterone, testosterone, and cortisol. She was also placed on a supplement regimen from Beulah Land Nutritionals.*

Lauren continues to be a patient at Caring Medical. She has reduced her nine medications to three. She still has a ways to go, but she continues to make slow, steady progress. She and her husband are so enthusiastic about her progress. You see, we want everyone cured and sometimes it doesn't happen.

---

* **Note:** *See www.benuts.com for more information on supplements from Beulah Land Nutritionals*

She states that after 16 months on The Hauser Diet she is able to do everything she wants to do. Her body swelling is almost gone. Her weight is down twenty pounds. Her energy level has tripled. Her kidney function is just about normal. She was able to liberalize her diet because her symptoms were so much less and she now follows the Monkey Diet, with her blood pH and sugar levels stabilized. Lauren told Dr. Hauser, "Yes doctor, I have a normal life. It is because of you." No, it is because of The Hauser Diet!

Rhonda with Rheumatoid

Rhonda was diagnosed with early rheumatoid arthritis. She came to Caring Medical wanting to know if there was anything that could "cure" it. Well, there are no known cures. But like cancer, we have seen it go into "remission." She was intrigued by this. We explained The Hauser Diet and like most people with autoimmune diseases Rhonda tested out to need a Giraffe Diet.

Her hormones were low so she started on DHEA and cortisol. She was also found to have a lot of food allergies so these were eliminated from her diet. She also tested positive for mycoplasma infection and was placed on an antibiotic for that. She was followed for eight months, at which time her joint swelling and stiffness was gone and she tested negative for rheumatoid arthritis. "It is incredible!" were her first words when she found out! Will she stay rheumatoid factor negative? It is possible, but it depends on her staying faithful to her Natural Medicine program.

A Summary of the *Giraffe Diet*

The Giraffe Diet is a true vegetarian diet, and vegans can certainly thrive on this diet. In our experience, people who need a Giraffe Diet do best with the majority or all of their foods being plant-based. Protein and fatty foods are not the focus of your diet and will only work against you, in excessive quantities. Giraffes need foods that are broken down quickly, and help to neutralize blood pH. This means carbohydrates, including plenty of fruits, vegetables, breads, rice,

cereals, pasta, and whole grains. Giraffes should find the abundance of these fresh foods on this diet satisfying, even though you may have to get used to grocery shopping more often. Have fun with the diet by creating interesting salad combinations, or try new fruits and vegetables you never thought of sampling! The Giraffe Diet may get you out of your comfort zone a little at first, but take the challenge head on! Soon you won't even remember you're on a "diet!"

Next, let's learn how to grocery shop, the Hauser Diet way! We'll look closer at what foods should go in your cart, (and which should keep collecting dust on the shelf.)

Want to chat with other *Giraffes,* share recipes, and get tips for success on the *Giraffe Diet?*

Visit us at www.hauserdiet.com

shop
smart

Welcome to grocery shopping, the Hauser Diet way.

Your challenge in this chapter is to learn more about what foods you put in your cart, and ultimately in your mouth. We are focused on breaking those old shopping habits and integrating healthy ones. We understand how hard this can be at first.

It is easy to zone out when you are grocery shopping. But if you ultimately want better health, you have to stop wandering the aisles just pulling the same junky foods from the shelves. Use this chapter as a tool to help you make your list of healthy food choices.

We are going to start by making a list of good foods to buy. In our years of cooking for ourselves, family, and friends, we know all meals do not have to be extravagant to be healthy and tasteful. In fact, we specialize in simple, easy, and delicious!

One of the greatest things you can hear is a compliment about your cooking. One of the best compliments I (Marion) received came from my father-in-law when he was staying with us for a week. I cooked my usual foods, adding a little of this and that, to make the vegetables a little different and the meat a little tastier. Well, dad still talks about the food that week! He said that vegetables never tasted so good! So it is possible to make good-for-you food taste good!

By keeping a combination of certain foods in your pantry, you can improve the variety of foods you prepare and literally have a wide array of meals at your fingertips!

Following is a list of some of the items we like to keep in our kitchens.

Products that We Keep On Hand in Our Kitchens

Nuts

Nuts are good to have around as they can really dress up a main dish, salads, smoothies, as well as taste great for a healthy snack, especially for Lions and Otters, because they are high in fat.

- Almonds, slivered
- Peanuts
- Pecans, whole or chopped
- Pine nuts
- Walnuts, chopped

Dried Fruit

Dried fruit adds variety to many dishes. We like to add it to salads and our main dishes to make things more interesting. They are always good on hot cereal in the morning as well. Monkeys and Giraffes can use these more freely.

- Apricots
- Cherries
- Cranberries
- Dates
- Figs
- Raisins

Jams (100% Fruit)

Interesting sauces and marinades can be made with these jams. They can really change the taste of what you are making—a little spoonful stirred into a sauce can really dress up a dish! A little mixed in a sauce is fine for all diets, but Lions and Otters should leave the jam off the toast.

- Ancho Chili Pepper *(Marion's absolute favorite.)*
- Apricot
- Marionberry *(We had to include it with that name!)*
- Raspberry

Condiments/Sauces/Dressings

This is one of our favorite categories. We love to add a little of this and that to make interesting, fun food. Learn to experiment!

- Hot sauces
- Ketchup *(Organic)*
- Liquid smoke
- Mayonnaise
- Mustard
- Olive oil *(Cold-pressed, extra virgin)*
- Soy sauce
- Tamari sauce
- Vinegars *(apple cider, rice, Balsamic, and wine vinegars)*
- Wine

Click Tips

Visit one of our favorite spots in the world: The Mustard Museum can be found at **www.mustardmuseum.com** *for a great listing of mustards, hot sauces, and other condiments! Located in Mount Horeb, Wisconsin—check it out!*

Spices (for all Diet Types)

- Basil
- Cilantro
- Cinnamon
- Cloves
- Cumin
- Dill
- Garlic
- Ginger
- Kosher salt
- Onion flakes
- Oregano
- Parsley flakes
- Pepper
- Sea salt
- Thyme
- Vanilla extract

Click Tips

Fresh herbs taste best in a dish, but it's good to keep some dried spices for when you're in a pinch. We like to use high quality dried herbs for the great flavor, without the added chemicals. We like Penzey's Spices at **www.penzeys.com** *for very fresh and always interesting herbs.*

Canned Foods

We try to use organic canned goods which can now be purchased at most local grocery stores. Some are best eaten fresh, but these canned goods are great to have on hand to make quick meals from the pantry. As with any food, choose canned foods that fit your Diet Type.

- Artichoke hearts
- Beans (Such as black, garbanzo, pinto)
- Beef broth (Organic, without MSG)
- Chicken broth (Organic, without MSG)
- Diced tomatoes
- Mandarin orange segments
- Pineapple chunks
- Tomato sauce
- Tuna
- Vegetable broth
- Whole cranberry sauce
- Whole tomatoes

Miscellaneous

Just the basics! We all need these things. When you need to thicken up a sauce or create a breading for your eggplant parmesan, you're all ready to go!

- Baking powder
- Baking soda
- Bread crumbs
- Corn meal
- Corn starch
- Flour (Organic wheat flour, or non-wheat flours such as rice or corn)
- Sugar (Natural cane sugar and brown sugar.)

Starches

These starches make a nice addition to any meal, especially for the Bear, Monkey, and Giraffe Diets.

- Couscous
- Oat bran
- Pasta (We use different kinds of pasta such as rice, corn, and spinach pasta, in addition to regular pasta.)

- Rice (We like different kinds of rice, such as wild, brown, and jasmine.)

These items are just a sampling of things that we like to use in our cooking. The combinations of these items are endless. This list can go on and on. The reason to keep a variety of food on hand is, first of all, so you do not get bored with your meals, but secondly so that you will be encouraged to provide your family and yourself with more "home-cooked" meals. Adding a little something different can turn a boring dish into something that "wows" your family. No one wants to feel like they are dieting, and you don't have to, when you have some of these secrets up your sleeve!

Let's Go Shopping!

Upon walking into the store, many times, you are greeted by a large and tempting "Featured Items" display. These are designed for the impulse buyer. In the average grocery store, these items are donuts, cakes, or other perishable baked goods. Large grocers with in-store bakeries can make this even more tempting when they are handing out free samples. Resist it! Let's pass by the display and get to the first section—**Produce.**

Produce
Fruit

Fresh! Fresh! Fresh! To get the most nutrition out of your fruit, eat it fresh. Buy a small amount at a time because good organic fresh fruit will spoil in about four days. If you cannot get fresh fruit, frozen is next best. You should avoid regularly eating canned fruit. In small amounts, adding it to make recipes more savory is certainly okay. If you do eat canned fruits, rinse them with water to dilute, and drain those sugars and syrups used in canning. You should also try eating fruits closest to their natural state. For instance, eat an apple rather than applesauce. It is best to eliminate as many processed fruits with artificial sweeteners, colors, and flavors as possible. Read your labels. You would be amazed at what is put into canned goods these days. If you cannot pronounce it, avoid it! Fruit is allowed regularly in the Bear, Monkey, and Giraffe Diets. They are more restricted in the Otter Diet, and not allowed on the Lion Diet. Here are some great raw fruits to keep handy:

- Apples
- Apricots
- Blueberries
- Cantaloupe
- Grapefruit
- Grapes
- Kiwi
- Lemons/limes
- Nectarines
- Oranges
- Peaches
- Plums
- Strawberries
- Watermelon

Most fruits have a pretty significant number of sugars naturally. If you are limiting your sugar and carbohydrate intake, you must take the fruit you eat into the calculation. This is particularly important for Lion and Otter Diets.

Vegetables

Vegetables are permissible and encouraged on all of the Hauser Diets. Do not get tunnel vision when it comes to vegetables, only eating the same two or three, like peas and carrots. Increase your intake of dark, deeply colored vegetables. The simplest way to look at it is that you should try and eat a *rainbow* of vegetables, including red, orange, yellow, white, purple, and the obvious— green. Those different colored vegetables have a variety of benefits including vitamins and nutrients that you will not get if you limit yourself to just a couple. As with fruits, raw vegetables are better to eat than frozen or canned. We recommend this because vegetables lose vitamins, enzymes, and fiber upon being processed. We want you to get the most out of every bite.

We like to have fresh veggies on hand so that we can make interesting salads, which are a nice refreshing compliment to any meal. We also like to have fresh vegetables on hand to either stir-fry or combine with a protein such as chicken or beef. Some of our personal favorites are asparagus, broccoli, and Brussels sprouts. Cooked well, these can be absolutely delicious as well as healthy! Even potatoes go beyond the tried and true Idaho baking potato. Try red, Yukon Gold, or fingerling. We should note here that both potatoes and corn, two of the most common vegetables, are technically counted as complex carbohydrate. This is because their calorie and carbohydrate make up are more fitting in this category than with "vegetables." In addition, we count potatoes that have the skins left on as a complex carbohydrate. If you peel the skins of your potato, it is actually a simple carbohydrate, because you have peeled off the fiber. If you are eating potatoes from a box—get with it! Mashed potatoes from scratch is where it's at, so throw that box away!

It's easy to incorporate veggies into any meal, so eat up!

- Artichokes
- Asparagus
- Beets
- Bell peppers
- Broccoli
- Brussels sprouts
- Cabbage
- Carrots
- Cauliflower
- Corn
- Eggplant
- Green beans
- Green leafy vegetables
- Onions
- Peas
- Potatoes, variety
- Spinach
- Squash
- Sweet potatoes
- Tomatoes

What's in Season?

Try buying fruits and vegetables that are locally grown
and in season. Not only do they taste better, but they
are generally less expensive at their peak. If you live in
a rural area, you probably have ample produce stands
and markets run by local farmers who know the best
seasons for the crops. If you are more of a city slicker,
you may seek out the seasonal farmer's markets. We
all know how delicious those home-grown tomatoes
taste! *Yum!* We could just eat them like candy—
topped with a little sea salt, of course!

Legumes

Legumes should be a part of any diet! Many people
we see in the clinic are a bit perplexed at how to
incorporate legumes into their diets. Everyone should
have extra beans available in the cabinets, raw, or
canned for convenience, as well as for the fiber
and protein! Legumes are a great source of fiber,
folate, and iron, along with protein and complex
carbohydrates. Legumes are well suited in larger
amounts for the Bear, Monkey, and Giraffe Diets,
which allow a more balanced protein and carbohydrate
intake, and are lower in animal protein. The Lions and

Otters should eat them in moderation, as they are
considered carbohydrates. Add them to a salad, or you
can make some great soups from legumes, as well as
some great crock-pot meals! There are so many places
out there to get recipes, you just have to look. One
time I (Marion) went to the web and typed in "recipe
for lentils and sweet potatoes" and there I had it!
I did not have too much on hand, but these two
ingredients. So I ended up making something
interesting, tasty, and healthy! The best part of it
was my family asked me to make it again!

Here is a list of some of our favorite legumes that
we like to keep on hand:

- Baked beans
- Black beans
- Black-eyed peas
- Fava beans
- Garbanzo beans
- Kidney beans
- Lentils
- Navy beans
- Northern beans
- Pinto beans
- Refried beans
- Spilt peas

Grains

Although Monkey and Giraffe Diets allow some
refined grain products, you should still opt for
whole grains more often. Whole grains are a
great source of fiber, helping you feel full and
moving things along through your digestive tract.
Many of the products with refined grain products
have undesirable chemicals or other artificial
ingredients, and no fiber or other nutritional
value, which make it "junk" food.

When buying a good cereal, choose a whole
grain, high fiber cereal! A high fiber cereal will
have at least four grams of fiber per serving.
A couple brands that we like are Kashi™ and
Natural Ovens™ products, but there are many
great organic cereals and grains out there. For
those of you following the Lion and Otter Diets,
look for a cereal that contains a high amount of
protein, for example, the product should contain
at least seven grams of protein per cup.

Grains you should include:

- Barley
- Brown rice
- Buckwheat
- Couscous
- Flax
- Oats
- Polenta
- Quinoa
- Rye
- Whole grain pastas

Meat, Poultry, and Fish

Meat and fish are acceptable in most Hauser Diets, except for the Giraffe Diet, which is primarily vegetarian. Lions and Otters need meat with each meal. While Bears, can have some meat through the day, but do not need to have it with every meal. As with fruits and veggies, we recommend organic free-range meat. We have found some great organic and free-range meats from stores such as Whole Foods® and Trader Joes.® It is not typically found at traditional supermarkets. Another way to buy organic meat is to buy half or the whole animal with friends or neighbors and divide it up. *(See Figure 8-1.)*

For beef and lamb, we ideally recommend grass fed organic. The animals eat a natural diet of mainly grass, not grain. This ensures a more pure and nutritious product for your family. For instance, grass fed beef is higher in Omega 3 fatty acids which are necessary for good health. In our opinion, not only do we feel that the meat is healthier, but the taste and texture of the meat is typically superior to that of other commercial meat.

Stop beefing up the beef! Be careful of eating too many processed meats and fish. Companies add ingredients to extend shelf life of meat, add or enhance flavor, or to help bulk it up. A food manufacturer who

Click Tips

Visit any of these resources for information on great organic food:

www.localharvest.org
www.americangrassfedbeef.com
www.foxfirefarms.com

FIGURE 8-1

Meats to Eat on the Hauser Diet

- All organic meat
- Beef
- Chicken
- Fish
- Pork

Notice that this list does **not** include commercial chicken nuggets, fish sticks, or pre-made hamburgers. Take a good look at those labels. They are filled with artificial ingredients, and very often they contain very little "meat."

is more concerned with "the bottom line" does not have your best health interests at heart. This is in part why so much food is pumped full of added ingredients like broth, sweeteners, or other fillers. *(See Figure 8-2.)* A pre-packaged steak, for instance, may still be sold at the same weight with less quality beef, if the manufacturer adds some fillers. It may then be marketed as "Enhanced flavor," "Special recipe," and "Juicy." No thanks—we'll pass! We do not recommend any food that has artificial ingredients added because our bodies have to work to detoxify them. When you want a hamburger, buy ground beef. You do not have

FIGURE 8-2

Types of Meat to Avoid:

- Commercial bacon
- Commercial hot dogs
- Commercial lunch meats
- Commercial chicken
- Commercial sausage
- Other processed meats

FIGURE 8-3

"Where's the Beef?"

Here is a label we found for a very popular commercial "hamburger." We put hamburger in quotes because we just can't locate the beef! This is an extreme example of mislabeling. Someone buying this thinks he or she is about to get a beef patty on a bun. But take a look—no beef— and heaps of chemicals. Do you want your kids putting this into their bodies? Do you want to put this into *your* body?

Nutrition Facts

Serving Size 24 pieces (Pasteurized) • Servings Per Container: About 9

Amount Per Serving

Calories 310	Calories from Fat 160

	% Daily Value
Total Fat 17g	**26%**
Saturated Fat 9g	**45%**
Cholesterol 30mg	**10%**
Sodium 480mg	**20%**
Potassium 0mg	**0%**
Total Carbohydrates 23g	**8%**
Dietary Fiber 6g	**24%**
Sugars 0	
Other Carbohydrates 0	
Protein 15g	

Vitamin A 2%	Vitamin C 0%
Calcium 8%	Iron 6%

Percent daily value reflects as "packaged" food.
*Percent daily values are based on a 2,000 calorie diet. Your daily values may be higher or lower depending on your calorie needs:

		Calories:	2,000	2,500
Total Fat	Less than		65g	80g
Sat Fat	Less than		20g	25g
Cholesterol	Less than		300mg	300g
Sodium	Less than		2,400mg	2,400mg
Total Carbohydrate	Less than		300g	375g
Dietary Fiber			25g	30g

Calories per gram:
Fat 9   Carbohydrates 4   Protein 4

INGREDIENTS: Bun: Enriched Flour (Wheat Flour, Malted Barley Flour, Niacin, Reduced Iron, Thiamine Mononitrate, Riboflavin), Water, Shortening (Partially Hydrogenated Soybean, Cottonseed and/or Canola Oil), Dextrose, Yeast, Salt, Sugar, Vital Wheat Gluten, Oat Fiber, Corn Syrup Solids, Calcium Stearoyl-2 -Lactylate, Mono and Diglycerides, Isolated Soy Protein, Diacetyl Tartaric Acid Esters of Mono and Diglycerides, Polysorbate 60, Calcium Sulfate, Sodium Alginate, Ammonium Sulfate, Guar Gum, Sodium Diacetate, Monocalcium Phosphate, Calcium Peroxide, Soy Flour, Potassium Iodate, Enzyme. **Pasteurized American Cheese:** American Cheese, (Cultured Milk, Salt, Enzymes, Artificial Color), Water, Cream, Sodium Phosphate, Enzyme-Modified Cheese (Cultured Milk, Water, Cream, Sodium Citrate, Salt, Sodium Phosphate, Sorbic Acid (Preservative) Acetic Acid, Phosphoric Acid, Colored with Caritenal, Enzymes), Salt, Sorbic Acid, (Preservative), Acetic Acid, Artificial Color.

to buy the special, ready-to-grill, pre-seasoned burgers in a box. Look at the ingredient list. If you cannot pronounce any ingredient after "beef," it is likely that it is more of a chemical beef burger." *(See Figure 8-3.)*

Chicken

What's in your chicken?

Most of you have probably heard on various television shows or read in magazines or websites that most "regular" chicken comes from places where the chickens are given drugs to speed up their rate of growth. Manufacturers also inject the chickens with antibiotics because chickens are typically kept in very horrible cramped and damp conditions with no natural ventilation, allowing diseases to spread rapidly.

We recommend that you purchase organic chicken (or Amish chicken because they follow many of the same standards) in order to buy the safest form of chicken. Why? You'll not only taste the difference, your body and your family's bodies will be safer. Organic farmers do a number of things to ensure that chickens are raised as naturally as possible. Arsenic is commonly used in conventional chicken feed to ward off parasites and to promote growth. Arsenic? Yes, arsenic! Arsenic is a poison and increases our risk of cancer. Hard to believe, but it's true! Although recently many chicken producers have decided to stop using arsenic, not all of them have. The USDA does not require it at this time. But there are even more reasons to choose organic.

What is Organic Chicken?

- Chicken has always been fed only organic grains. (Organic grains—non genetically modified [GMO]; no chemicals or pesticides were used on the farm for at least three years.) Feed is checked and verified for organic standards.

- Chicken was never given any antibiotics, hormones, or drugs.

- Organic chickens are reared for at least 81 days, allowing chicks to grow at their natural rate. Most non-organic chickens sold in supermarkets have been killed after only 42 days. Not only is this inhumane, but it makes them bland, fatty, and tasteless.

- Chicken was raised humanely and in a stress-free environment.

- The bird was free-range and had access daily to fresh air and sunshine outdoors. The bird had room to move. Outdoors area was clean and safe.

Read your labels! Organic certification standards state that food must undergo as little processing as is practical. Additives that are dangerous to health such as hydrogenated fat are not permitted, as well as other dyes, fillers, and chemicals. So, organic processed foods, like organic chicken nuggets are much better for your health than the non-organic equivalent. Have you ever taken a look at processed chicken labels? You have to wonder if you are even getting any meat. We recommend that you consume food in its freshest state for your most optimal food choices.

Remember, organic standards are legally binding. All organic businesses must be licensed by law, and are fully inspected at least once a year. The bottom line: The reasons are many for why you need to purchase good quality poultry. Eating chicken out in a restaurant or fast food establishment is somewhat risky in that you do not know what type of chicken they purchase, unless it is listed on their menus. So please, beware and buy smart! Your health depends on it!

Fish

As the list of benefits grows for fish and fish oils, such as helping to decrease the risk of heart disease, there are also growing concerns over mercury contamination. Some people are concerned about mercury levels rising in fish such as tuna, which ranks in the top 10 fish with the highest mercury levels. In general, the larger

the fish is, the higher the potential mercury content. The highest amounts of mercury are actually found in swordfish, king mackerel, and shark.[1] The lowest amounts are found in smaller fish, such as sardines and shellfish. For most people, we recommend eating fish at least three times per week.

If you feel you are at risk for elevated mercury levels, discuss the concern with your Natural Medicine physician and have your heavy metal levels tested. In addition to eating fish, (or instead of eating fish), most people can benefit from supplementing with Omega 3 fatty acids such as Cod Liver oil or Super Omega* to achieve the maximum benefits of fish oils. Here are some fish that we like:

- Bass
- Cod
- Grouper
- Haddock
- Mackerel
- Salmon
- Sardine
- Shellfish
- Sole
- Tilapia
- Trout
- Tuna

Eggs

The incredible, edible egg is just that! It is a wonderful source of pure protein and vitamins and is recommended for all of the Hauser Diets, although the Giraffes probably will not do as well eating eggs everyday. Every other day or even less would be fine. Eggs have gone in and out of vogue for years. We recommend organic

* Note: *See www.benuts.com for more information on supplements from Beulah Land Nutritionals.*

eggs, for their higher Omega 3 fatty acid content. Eggs can be a permanent, regular food in most diets. What? Eat eggs freely? Won't that contribute to heart disease? Nope! Eggs are not, in fact, linked to heart disease.[2] Plus, we have to remember that part of disease prevention is eating right for your Diet Type. Eggs are just part of the puzzle.

In general, Lions and Otters are allowed more eggs than Bears, Monkeys or Giraffes. But in all diets, we recommend staying away from liquid imposter eggs. Take a look at the label of one of those products. What do you see? Chemicals and dyes. Why does the egg require additional nutrients to be added back? Because they were taken out in the processing by removing the nutrient-filled yolks! They also added corn oil and chemicals in order to preserve it and create flavor and consistency. (See Figure 8-4.) Eggs are a great source of

protein for all of the Hauser Diets, however, make sure that you are not allergic to them. Many people have undiagnosed food allergies and eggs is a common one. This is why we recommend food allergy testing for many of our patients getting Diet Typing.

Organic Dairy

- Butter
- Cheeses (mozzarella, cheddar, chihuahua, blue, gorgonzola, feta)
- Milk
- Yogurt

Dairy is recommended on all diets, although in different types and amounts. Giraffes can have nonfat dairy in moderation (one or less times per day), if desired, but should consider soy or rice based dairy products as a better vegetarian alternative. Lions and Otters can have full fat dairy while a Monkey can have low-fat dairy. The Bears can have both in moderation.

Butter versus margarine? Butter—no contest! Margarine—no way! Take a look at the labels. Butter should have two ingredients: cream and salt. Margarine is made by hydrogenating vegetable oil to make it solid. Most margarines also contain many chemicals, dyes, and many other unnatural ingredients including hydrogenated fats, which are a primary source of trans fatty acids that are now listed

FIGURE 8-4

Egg Substitutes

Egg substitutes are touted as a "healthy" alternative and are found in every grocery store next to the real eggs in the refrigerated section in little cartons. As we've been discussing, these have chemicals added, and vitamins and oils added back in because the nutrient-dense yolk has been removed.

Nutrition Facts

Serving Size 1/4 cup (61g)

Amount Per Serving

Calories 35	Calories from Fat 10
	% Daily Value *
Total Fat 15	**1%**
Saturated Fat 0.5g	**3%**
Cholesterol less than 5mg	**1%**
Sodium 210mg	**9%**
Total Carbohydrate 1mg	**0%**
Dietary Fiber 0g	
Sugars 0g	
Protein 6g	**10%**

*Percentage Daily Values are based on a 2,000 calorie diet.

INGREDIENTS: EGG WHITE, NONFAT MILK, CALCIUM CASEINATE, **MODIFIED CORN STARCH**, NATURAL AND **ARTIFICIAL FLAVORS**, CORN OIL, SALT, **MONO-AND DIGLYCERIDES**, BETA CAROTENE (FOR COLOR). VITAMINS & MINERALS: IRON (FERRIC ORTHO- PHOSPHATE), VITAMIN D3, ZINC (ZINC SULFATE), CALCIUM PANTOTHENATE, VITAMIN B2 (RIBOFLAVIN), VITAMIN B1 (THIAMINE MONONITRATE), VITAMIN B6 (PYRIDOXINE HYDROCHLORIDE), VITAMIN B12 (CYANOCOBALMIN).

on food labels. Researchers have found that trans fatty acids significantly raise LDL cholesterol levels (bad cholesterol) while lowering the HDL levels (good cholesterol). In the Framingham Heart Study (a 40 year study covering 5,209 individuals living in the state of Massachusetts) high LDL cholesterol (bad cholesterol) levels combined with low HDL levels (good cholesterol) was indicative of coronary heart disease risk. You may be thinking, "Then why does the food industry use hydrogenated or partially hydrogenated fats in food products?" For this plain and simple reason: hydrogenation extends the supermarket shelf life of products. *(See Figure 8-5.)*

Figure 8-5

Margarine

Highlighted here are the ingredients that specifically make margarine a bad choice.

INGREDIENTS: LIQUID SOYBEAN OIL, WHEY, WATER, **PARTIALLY HYDROGENATED SOYBEAN OIL,** SWEET CREAM BUTTERMILK, SALT, VEGETABLE **MONO-AND DIGLYCERIDES** AND SOY LECITHIN (EMULSIFIERS), **SODIUM BENZOATE** AND POTASSIUM SORBATE (TO PRESERVE FRESHNESS), **ARTIFICIAL FLAVOR, PHOSPHORIC ACID (ACIDULANT),** VITAMIN A PALMITATE, COLORED WITH BETA CAROTENE (SOURCE OF VITAMIN A). CONTAINS: MILK.

Back to dairy products. Dairy products are delicious! Most of us love butter and cheese because of the positive effects they have on the flavor and texture of a meal. We always recommend organic dairy when possible, and the least-processed available. We do not recommend eating dairy freely because it is a calorie-dense food. A small serving packs a lot of calories, so it is typically better to use cheese and butter to accent your foods, not as a primary part of a meal.

What about the cream in your coffee? We know those flavored creamers may taste delicious, but they are are a terrible choice. Take a look at all the chemicals and hydrogenated fats in these products. *(See Figure 8-6.)* A better choice for cream in your coffee is to use real cream, in small amounts, or use regular milk or soy milk. To make it taste a little more interesting, try adding a little dash of cinnamon or vanilla extract. See, you can make your own healthier version of these creamers, with just a little creativity!

Please note, if you suspect you have a dairy allergy or you know you have the allergy, we recommend that you avoid dairy products. Unfortunately, many people are allergic to dairy products. Try soy or rice cheeses as an alternative.

Let's Talk Soy!

Soy is highly recommended on the Hauser Diet and is also one of the most versatile and beneficial foods available. This topic is hotly debated in the field of Natural Medicine. So before you throw this book down or start e-mailing us the studies about the ill-effects of soy, please know that we are making these statements after much research on the topic.[3]

Facts About Soy:

- Organic soy is one of the best sources of protein, containing almost no saturated fat.
- Soybeans contain numerous minerals, including iron and zinc.
- Whole soybeans are a good source of fiber.

Figure 8-6

The Cream in Your Coffee...

When it comes to creamers, we do not recommend using products like non-dairy, non-fat creamers, or artificial powdered creamers. These are filled with chemicals, hydrogenated oils, and sugars. Choose milk, soy milk, or real cream instead.

Here's one popular non-dairy creamer:

INGREDIENTS: SUGAR, CORN SYRUP SOLIDS, VEGETABLE OIL (**PARTIALLY HYDROGENATED COCONUT OR PALM KERNEL AND CANOLA, HYDROGENATED PALM, SOYBEAN, COTTENSEED AND/OR SAFFLOWER**), NONFAT MILK, **MALTODEXTRIN,** LACTOSE, SODIUM CASEINATE (FROM MILK), **ARTIFICIAL AND NATURAL FLAVORS,** POTASSIUM PHOSPHATE, SODIUM CITRATE, SALT, **SODIUM PHOSPHATE, SUCRALOSE.**

- Soy is a good source of B Vitamins
- Soy isoflavones, including genistein and diadzein, are phyto-estrogens *(cancer-fighting substances)*

Products that Contain Soy:

- Soy Milk—Use this in almost any recipe as a substitute for cow's milk.
- Soy Yogurt—Makes a tasty alternative to regular yogurt.
- Ground soy—Substitute soy for ground beef in taco or sloppy joe recipes.
- Soybeans—Roasted and salted, these make a good alternative to potato chips or other snack foods with partially hydrogenated oils.
- Edamame—Soybeans, which are green and harvested before hardening.
- Tofu—Soy bean product used the same way as meat in recipes.
- As with any food, we recommend "organic" soy!

What is Tofu and Where Do I Find It?

Tofu is made of soy bean curds. The soy beans are soaked, mashed, and pressed together to form the substance. It is generally pressed into soft, silken, or firm tofu. Each is used in different styles of cooking, making tofu one of the most versatile foods available. For instance, silken tofu can be used to make smoothies or salad dressing, while firm tofu can be used for stir-frying or grilling. It can be substituted for meat in almost any dish. Another benefit of tofu is that it is a relatively inexpensive food compared to meat. If your grocer carries tofu, it will most likely be found in the refrigerated section by the pre-packaged salads and fresh herbs.

Beverages

Grocery stores generally have at least one huge aisle featuring a variety of beverages. Watch out! Be aware of the calories and ingredients in beverages too.

- **Alcohol:** We feel that alcohol is acceptable in small amounts for most people. The fast oxidizers, Lion and Otter Diets specifically, should not be consuming alcohol very often because it provides too many simple carbohydrates for these diets. These simple carbohydrates acidify the blood and aggravate hypoglycemic symptoms. For Bear, Monkey, and Giraffe Diets, alcohol may be consumed in small amounts. There are, however, reasons why people should not regularly drink alcohol—specifically those trying to lose weight—because alcohol is high in calories, while not satisfying your appetite. In addition, often harmful additives and colorings are added to alcohol containing products, including artificial colors and flavors. This is particularly true for mixed drinks that have fancy colors and are made using pre-made mixes instead of natural scratch ingredients. Did you know that a strawberry margarita-type drink contains upwards of 300 calories? And what about those "jumbo-sized" drinks? *(See Figure 8-7.)*

FIGURE 8-7

Need a Drink?

Too much alcohol can cause you to have a hangover, and your belly to "hang over." If you're watching your weight, consider decreasing or eliminating alcohol consumption.

Alcohol	Serving	Calories
Beer	12 oz	135-150
Hard liquor	1 oz	65
Light Beer	12 oz	90-100
Margarita	12 oz	350
Pina Colada	7 oz	260
Wine	4 oz	80

- **Coffee** is a substance that should definitely be limited by certain Diet Types more than others. For many people, coffee is no better than a street drug. They need it or feel they cannot make it through the day without it. The caffeine gives them a big lift but they will need to drink more in order to keep that good feeling. If this describes you, you have to stop drinking coffee, or anything caffeinated for that matter. For others, coffee does not offer that same lift. They can enjoy a cup and not need to keep refilling. These people tend to be people with a high (or alkaline) blood pH. You see, coffee helps to lower the blood pH. People who are eating a Bear, Monkey, or Giraffe Diet can have coffee. People eating a Lion or Otter Diet should not have coffee as it will make the blood more acidic and aggravate hypoglycemic symptoms.

- We are often asked about decaffeinated coffee. Typically, coffee is decaffeinated using very strong chemicals such as methylene chloride or ethyl acetate. As we keep saying, the Hauser Diet focuses on fresh, organic foods with minimal toxins and chemicals. Remember, our bodies are already bombarded with environmental pollutants that are beyond our control. Why add to the stress your body is under? What we are saying is that if your Diet Type is not supposed to drink coffee, choosing conventionally decaffeinated coffee is not necessarily

Click Tips
Visit **www.swisswater.com** *to learn more about safer methods of decaffeination and to see if your favorite brands are using it!*

a better choice. Conventionally decaffeinated coffee has also been linked to increased risks of rheumatoid arthritis. We know that we have seen this to be true in patients that we treat. So is all decaf coffee bad? There is a safer method that is gaining popularity with coffee companies. This is the Swiss Water™ method, which uses water to extract the caffeine, rather than chemicals. This is a safer alternative for people who cannot have caffeinated coffee, but still like the occasional cup. To read more about it, check out this site www.swisswater.com.

We like organic coffee best! Just like anything else, chemicals and extracting agents are added to most non-organic coffee. The best option is to purchase organic coffee. You can get this now, even at your regular grocery store.

- **Smoothies/shakes:** Ready-made yogurt smoothies, "meal" replacement drinks, and coffee drinks are not a good buy for those trying to lose weight by cutting down on the calorie intake. We do not recommend substituting a meal with a ready-made yogurt or coffee drink. Your hunger will likely sneak back up on you faster than if you eat a regular, well portioned meal. If you like smoothies, it is best to make them at home. Add protein powder or tofu to increase the protein per serving. *See Chapter 9 for recipes!*

- **Soda:** Basically, soda, whether regular or diet, is chemical water. A woman who consumes more than one soda or sugar-sweetened beverage per day has increased her risk of becoming diabetic by 83% and will gain more weight than those who do not.[4] No one should be drinking sodas, especially children!

- **Soy Milk** is a delicious way to increase protein and still be able to cook with recipes that call for "milk,"

if you are allergic to it or need to eliminate it from your diet. Be sure to find a brand with no added or artificial sweeteners. You want the protein grams to outweigh the sugar grams. Look for "organic" soy milk fortified with quality calcium, vitamin D2, and vitamin B12. We like Eden Soy® and WestSoy® unsweetened soy milk.

- **Tea:** If you love iced tea, buy it unsweetened. If you are drinking tea for the caffeine buzz, stop drinking it altogether. A better alternative is to buy herbal tea and make it yourself, which is naturally caffeine free. Try red and green teas for a delicious change with powerful antioxidants.

- **Water:** The best drink for anyone is, of course, plain, filtered water. Tap water is filled with impurities and chemicals. Consider buying a water filter, home water filtration system, or a cooler that puts extra oxygen into your water. If you have a zeal for flavor, try adding a flavored vitamin and mineral mix, such as Emer'gen-C™*. This is a great fizzy alternative to your child's soda or artificial juice drinks. If you can't get used to plain old water, add lemon or lime juice.

Frozen Foods

Fresh frozen foods may be used in moderation. The point here is to not have to run to the store when you have everything in your house already. The frozen foods we encourage are fresh frozen with no additives. If there's an ingredient list on the product with words you cannot pronounce, put it back. We find some great products available at stores such as Whole Foods®, Wild Oats®, or Trader Joe's®! *(See Figure 8-8.)*

---

* **Note:** *See www.benuts.com for more information on supplements from Beulah Land Nutritionals.*

Labels

Food labels are meant to inform the customer of the contents of the product. Unfortunately, we have been trained by most magazine and news reports to look for "Fat" and "Cholesterol" as the most important items on the label. We highly disagree. As we have been discussing the principles of the Hauser Diet, it is important for you to know that the product has high quality, natural ingredients and will fit your Diet Type. Ideally, food labels should provide us with this information so we can accurately measure the amount of what we ate and see what ingredients were used to make the food.

When you look at a label, try asking yourself: *Is this food good for my Diet Type?* Use the general food guidelines for your Diet Type to determine the foods you put in your cart. With this in mind, most people can completely disregard the Percent Daily Value (%DV) on the food labels, which is based on the USDA food pyramid. *(See Figure 8-9.)* This is because your percent daily value is most likely not going to match the generic listing on the label. Lions and Otters

---

FIGURE 8-8

What's In Your Freezer?

Stock It
- Butter
- Fruit (Keep your very perishable fruits, such as berries, good by freezing them)
- Meats (unprocessed, organic)
- Organic packaged foods without additives to use in a pinch.
- Tofu
- Vegetables

Scrap It
- Burritos or tamales
- Corn dogs
- Hamburgers (unless all meat patties)
- Packaged breakfasts
- Packaged dinners
- Pastries (dessert or meat filled)
- Pizza and pizza rolls
- Processed chicken (ex: Chicken Kiev)
- Processed fish (ex. fish sticks)

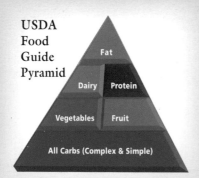

USDA Food Guide Pyramid

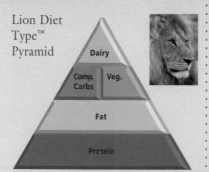

Lion Diet Type™ Pyramid

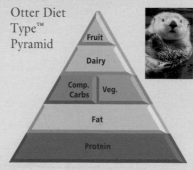

Otter Diet Type™ Pyramid

Bear Diet Type™ Pyramid

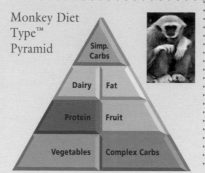

Monkey Diet Type™ Pyramid

Giraffe Diet Type™ Pyramid

FIGURE 8-9

How does the USDA match up to the Hauser Diet?

Compare the USDA food pyramid to each of the five Hauser Diets. Each Hauser Diet has a different food pyramid, based on the allowed percentages of carbs, protein, and fat.

should be looking for labels to list higher amounts of protein and fat than carbohydrates, while Monkeys and Giraffes should be looking for the low fat foods that are higher in carbohydrates. But we stress to you not to be fooled by tricky advertising. Very often foods labeled "Low Fat" or "Low Carb" contain an array of unwanted chemicals and modified ingredients. We will be discussing this more in the following pages. But if you read for the macronutrient breakdown (Protein/Fat/Carbohydrates) and the purity of ingredients listed, you will have a good handle on your food intake.

Another item on the food label you should be familiar with is the calorie count. This is especially important for people counting calorie intake. The calorie information is generally found in the top, left corner of the label. However, locally labeled foods averaged 85% more calories than stated on the label, when analyzed. Regionally labeled foods averaged 25% more calories than stated on the label. Nationally labeled foods are the most accurately labeled foods.[5, 6]

Why are manufacturers allowed to mislead consumers? The simplest answer for this question is that the laws are not very strict or clear when it comes to labeling. The FDA just does not have the time or resources to check up on every food on the market. In an ideal world, manufacturers would not use unsafe additives, understate calories or fat, or manipulate the integrity of a product to increase their bottom line. Until that time, we have written this book to increase your awareness of what is going into your mouth. We hope that you will use this information to further your knowledge of food and begin incorporating more pure foods into your diet.

Watch out for additives: the most important reason to read labels! Additives are chemicals which are added to foods during processing to enhance flavor, extend shelf life, and prevent bacteria growth. The integrity of the food is compromised when chemicals are added to it. Plus, not all additives are safe for excessive consumption. Many people are sensitive to

check the labels

FIGURE 8-10

The Different Names for MSG

Here are some common ingredient names that contain MSG:

Autolyzed yeast	Hydrolyzed protein
Calcium caseinate	Monopotassium glutamate
Glutamate	Yeast food

Here are some common names that *may* contain MSG:

Bouillon	Soy sauce extract
Broth	Yeast extract
Malt extract	Whey extract
Maltodextrin	...and flavorings—including
Smoke flavoring	"artificial flavoring."
Soy protein	

one or two, but maybe not to all. One of the food allergy panels conducted at Caring Medical checks for food chemical sensitivity. Many people can already tell which types of foods or additives make them feel terrible. As a general rule, try to eat and drink foods containing no, or minimal, additives.

Here is a list of common food additives to avoid as often as possible.

- **Bromated Vegetable Oil:** Used as an emulsifier in foods and a clouding agent in soft drinks and fruit flavored drinks.

- **Butylated Hydroxyanisole (BHA) and Butylated Hydroxytoluene (BHT):** Synthetic antioxidants used to retard rancidity in many packaged foods including cereals, chewing gum, oils, and margarine.

- **MSG:** Monosodium Glutamate is the sodium salt of glutamic acid, an amino acid which enhances the flavor of foods, but has no flavor itself. It is found in many foods including packaged food, canned food, restaurant food, drinks, candy, or sold in the spice section of the grocery store. MSG can be masked under a variety of names. *(See Figure 8-10.)*

- **Olestra:** An indigestible fat which runs through the body. It causes many to have to "run" to the bathroom. It may interfere with the body's ability to absorb fat-soluble cartenoids, such as alpha-carotene, beta-carotene, and lutein. This indigestible fat is found in popular snack foods so the product can be labeled "Fat Free." Technically, it is not "fat free," rather just indigestible fat.

- **Sodium Benzoate:** This is a very common preservative generally found in processed foods which can help to disguise poor taste. Some foods where it is found include jams, fruit juices, pickles, ketchup, tomato products, soda, and salad dressings.

- **Sodium Nitrite:** It is generally used as a preservative in bacon, ham, hot dogs, lunch meats, smoked fish, and corned beef. It also stabilizes the color in certain cured meat and gives a distinct flavor.

What do you mean by "sensitive to additives"?

Some side effects of food additives may include headaches, nausea, flatulence, diarrhea, runny nose, or allergic type reactions. The more extreme effects of high additive intake may include organ damage and cancer.

Sugar "Hides" in Many Forms.

If you think that your sugar intake is pretty low because you do not use table sugar, think again. Sugar is hiding in more foods than you may be aware. Sugar is more obvious in foods such as cookies, donuts, ice cream, soda pop, and cakes. But it is present in foods such as barbecue sauce, ketchup, relish, peanut butter, breads, jellies, cereal, sauces, canned goods, yogurt, and ready made smoothies. As a general rule, if one or more of the first three ingredients listed on a label is a sugar, or an alternative name for sugar, it is probably high in sugar, and should be avoided or only used in moderation to flavor foods. *(See Figure 8-11.)* For example, next time you reach for that name-brand peanut butter, take a look at the ingredients. We think that peanut butter should contain just peanuts, not **sugar** and peanuts! That's why we purchase natural organic nut butters!

FIGURE 8-11

Various Names of Sugars

Sugars often appear on food labels and ingredient lists under different names. Be aware when you see these kinds of terms:

Barley malt	Glucose
Brown rice syrup	High-Fructose corn syrup
Cane juice	Honey
Caramel	Lactose
Corn syrup	Malt
Dextrose	Maltose
Fructose	Milk sugar
Fruit juice	Molasses
Fruit juice concentrate	Naturally sweetened sucrose

The Sweet and Sour of Sugar Substitutes

Many patients ask us about our opinion on the use of low calorie sweeteners. In our opinion, **none** of the artificial sweeteners are worth the potential health risk. The reason is two-fold: they may create a false sense of healthy eating and the chemicals themselves may be dangerous.

Labeling foods as "Fat-free" or "Sugar-free" gives people a false sense of healthy eating which can actually lead to over consumption of food. Although a food has no sugar or fat, it still has calories. If a person eats more calories that he or she uses in a day, this equals weight gain.

Studies are suggesting that artificial sweeteners can actually alter the body's natural ability to regulate food intake.[7] In the end, people who eat food with artificial sweeteners will eat more food and calories than people who eat foods that have been naturally sweetened. We feel that many of these sugar substitutes have not been tested adequately with any long term epidemiological studies. Because of the large "diet" food industry, the rush to get a sweet product to the consumer can take precedence to proper testing. Many toxicity reactions have been reported to the FDA and other organizations.

- **Acesulfame Potassium (also Sunette® and Sweet One®):** It is an artificial sweetener 200 times sweeter than sugar. It is found in soft drinks, baked goods, chewing gum, breath mints, throat lozenges, instant coffee, instant tea, gelatin, pudding, and non dairy creamers. Though proven safe in some animal studies, it has not been thoroughly tested for humans.

- **Aspartame (Equal®):** Evidence demonstrating the toxicity of aspartame has quickly grown. In particular, recent European research shows that ingesting aspartame leads to the accumulation of formaldehyde in the brain, other organs and tissues, which has been shown to damage the nervous system, immune system, and cause irreversible genetic damage in humans.[8] Many toxicity reactions have been reported to the FDA and other organizations.

- **Saccharin (Sweet N' Low®):** This sweetener was shown to cause cancer in animals when consumed in very large quantities. It is our opinion, that this

FIGURE 8-12

The Sweetest Deal...

If you have a sweet tooth or just need to sweeten your tea, here is a kind of hierarchy of what you should reach for in order of most often to least.

1 Fruit—a small piece, a few chunks or a handful of berries

2 Honey

3 Natural Cane sugar

4 100% Maple Syrup

5 Refined (white) sugar

6 Xylitol—Derived from sugar (can be used if intolerant to cane sugar.)

7 Stevia

artificial sweetener is actually one of the better ones, if used in small amounts.

- **Stevia:** Stevia is a sugar substitute that is 100 times sweeter than sugar. In small amounts, it is generally permissible. It should not be used as a sugar substitute in large amounts or consumed more than once per day, if used at all.

- **Sucrolose (Splenda®):** Pre-approval tests indicated potential toxicity of sucralose in "independent" controlled human studies on sucralose (similar to 15 years ago for aspartame). There have been no long-term human studies of sucralose's effects, and no monitoring of health effects. Sucralose has a chemical bond that cannot be metabolized by human beings. This can't be good!

- **Sugar Alcohols:** This is the name given to sweeteners produced from carbohydrate sources, such as sucrose (sugar). However, these sweeteners such as erythritol and xylitol, do not have the effect on raising blood sugar the same way that regular sugar does, making them popular for "sugar-free" foods. In excess, some of these can cause abdominal cramping or diarrhea. However, the one we like the best is erythritol, which in our experience, has not shown to produce any GI discomfort. In small amounts, xylitol is another good choice.

When needed for cooking, it is generally acceptable to add a little bit of natural cane sugar to your dish to enhance the taste. *(See Figure 8-12.)* The idea is to avoid using too many sweetened, processed foods. Use whole foods and add in the sugar yourself! You will tend to use much less sugar than what is in a processed version of foods like sauces or smoothies.

Watch Out for Artificial Colors

Food additives are chemicals added to food to enhance flavor, extend shelf life, and prevent bacteria contamination. As a consumer, rich colors in foods make it more appealing to the eye. So, it should not be surprising that companies thrive on this. Foods with added color are on almost every shelf in the grocery store including cereals, snack foods, and sweets. Food companies even put artificial coloring into condiments we use on the already colorful food. Most of the colorings found in processed food are synthetic and may indicate that a low amount of "natural" ingredients have been used. Certain artificial colors may pose an increased risk of allergic reactions for sensitive persons. Yellow Dye #5, for instance, was associated with changes in irritability, restlessness, and sleep disturbance in some children.[9] Watch out for the artificial colors that are in your food, and also present in most beauty care products. We see many people who are sensitive to one, or many of these. We feel it is not worth the risk of having a bad reaction and/or contributing to a depressed immune system. We recommend staying away from artificial coloring in all food and beauty products.

Read your labels to check for the most common artificial colors you should stay away from. *(See Figure 8-13.)*

Artificial colors and flavors, MSG, and artificial sweeteners are toxins as well as allergens.

If the look doesn't hook you, food manufacturers want the taste to hook you. So they add excessive sugar,

FIGURE 8-13

Common Artificial Colors

Many people are sensitive to artificial colors. It is best to avoid them as much as possible. Here is a list of common ones and their typical locations.

- Blue 1 is often found in beverages, candy, baked goods, gelatin, cereals, and toothpaste.
- Blue 2 is often found in beverages, candy, and toothpaste.
- Citrus Red Dye 2 is used to color orange skins.
- Green 3 is not commonly used but can be found in some candy and beverages.
- Red 3 is often found in candy and baked goods. It is also used to give fruit cocktail cherries that alluring hue.
- Red 40 is often found in beverages, candy, gelatin, baked goods, cereals, and sausage.
- Yellow 5 is often found in gelatin, candy, and baked goods.
- Yellow 6 is often found in beverages, baked goods, candy, gelatin, cereals, and sausage.

salt, artificial sweeteners, or flavor enhancers like MSG to not only get you to buy the food but get addicted to the taste. Did you ever wonder why diet sodas and other artificially sweetened drinks never really quench your thirst? You keep drinking them because you are addicted to the taste. The artificial sweeteners are so stimulatory to your nervous system that you want that buzz. There is increasing data that artificial sweeteners are the reason for the ever-increasing number of cases of Alzheimer's Disease and progressive neurologic conditions. *(See Figure 8-14.)*

Artificial colors and chemical sweeteners are toxins—plain and simple. Would you add arsenic to your food?

FIGURE 8-14

expert
opinion

The following quote is from Dr. Ross Hauser, M.D.

"There are many in the Natural Medicine field who believe that the increase in neurological degenerative disease, like Alzheimers and Lou Gehrig's disease, not to mention the 'epidemic' of cancer, is in part due to digesting so many chemicals. For example, when artificial ingredients are loaded into "diet" products, it gives people the false belief that he or she is consuming something healthy. These products generally do very little to improve satiation. So the person will end up consuming more of these toxins. The end result is weight gain and ill health."

Why not? Then why do you add artificial colors and chemical sweeteners to your food? Both are toxins. They are toxic to your system. They destroy your body, not build it up. You eat food to give you energy. These substances take energy away from your body.

Most people don't realize that artificial colors and sweeteners can also act as allergens. *(See Figure 8-15.)* This makes sense because these are items which are not intended to be ingested. So you ingest an artificial sweetener and your body has to work to eliminate this toxin, using up precious energy. Your immune system then sees the artificial sweetener molecule as an invader and starts mounting an immune reaction. This can zap vital resources, including immune system resources and energy resources, from the body for weeks! This is why a person can feel lousy and not know why. It is because they ate "Sugar-Free" cookies or some other chemical-laden treat two days before and the body is still processing the poison. Also very common are people who drink multiple diet sodas per day. If you are one who struggles with chronic illness and drinks diet soda and consumes other chemical-laden foods, how do you ever expect to get well?

Buyer beware—artificial substances that are ingested into the body will do nothing but harm it!

What are some adverse reactions to excitotoxins like MSG or Aspartame? In sensitive persons, MSG or

Aspartame may trigger an allergic reaction due to over stimulation of the nervous system. Some of the common adverse reactions associated with a sensitivity are anxiety, arrhythmias, chest tightness, cramping, depression, diarrhea, dizziness, flu-like symptoms, flushing, hives/rash, hyperactivity, migraines, nausea/vomiting, numbness, rapid heartbeat (tachycardia), runny nose/sneezing, shortness of breath, vision disturbances, and weakness.

Reading Labels for Other Specific Diet Considerations

Your physician may recommend that you avoid foods containing gluten or casein, based on food sensitivities. The gluten-free diet is for those sensitive to wheat and focuses on omission of foods using barley, couscous, kamut, spelt, buckwheat, malt, oats, rye, wheat, semolina, farina, tabouleh, bran, and triticale. It allows food prepared with corn, potato, quinoa, rice, and soybean flour. The casein-free diet is for those sensitive to dairy and focuses on omission of products made from cow's milk, goat's milk, and foods with casein fillers or stabilizers. A gluten and casein-free diet is also a common recommendation for children to prevent or alleviate symptoms of conditions such as autism, ADHD, allergies, and eczema.

Check your labels for the following:

Gluten may be listed as:
- Flour
- Food starch
- Gluten
- Graham
- Vegetable gum
- Vegetable starch
- Wheat bran
- Wheat germ
- Wheat starch

Casein may be listed as:
- Calcium
- Casein
- Caseinate solids
- Cream
- Lactalbumin
- Lactose
- Milk
- Non-fat milk
- Sodium caseinate
- Whey

ACCEPTABLE (NEG)	LIMIT (Range +1)	AVOID (Range +2)	ELIMINATE (Range MPOS)
Acid Orange	Blue #1 Patent Blue	Blue #2 Indigo Carmine	Aspartame
Ammonium Chloride	Curv Specifear	Formaldehyde	Nickel Sulfate
Aspergillus	Green #3 Fast Green	MSG	Tolune
Bemzene	Pullularia	Red #2 Amaranth	
Benzoic Acid	Spondylcoclodium	Red #3 Erythrosin B	
Brilliant Black	Yellow #5 Taratrazine	Saccharine	
Candida Albicans		Sodium Metabisulfite	
Chlorine			
Ethylene Glycol			
Fluoride			
Mucor Racemosus			
Orris Root			
Phenol			
Phoma Herbarum			
Polysorbate 80			
Potassium Nitrite			
Red #1 Crystal Ponceau			
Rhod Glutini			
Sodium Sulfite			
Sorbic Sulfite			
Sorbic Acid			
Sporobolomyces			
Trichoderma			
Yellow #10 Quin Yellow			

The ALCAT Test®

FIGURE 8-15
The ALCAT food chemical sensitivity test is one of the food allergy tests used at Caring Medical.

What about Salt?

Many of our Caring Medical patients, as well as friends and family members feel that following a low sodium diet is in their best health interest. They purchase low sodium products right and left! In our clinical experience, as well as in the medical literature, most people do not benefit from salt restricted diets. Most published studies suggest that not much benefit comes from salt restriction with no effect on any cardiovascular events or death.

Salt is essential not only to life, but to good health. Salt maintains the electrolyte balance inside and outside of cells. Salt restriction may help a small number of hypertensive people stop their medication, but there are no other benefits. The major sources of sodium in most Americans' diets are processed, prepared foods and the salt we add to food during cooking or at meals. However, as you have read in this book, the Hauser Diet encourages you to eliminate processed foods and consume fresh, organic foods.

If you consume fresh vegetables, fruits, meats, and whole grains, follow the appropriate Hauser Diet for your Diet Type, increase your exercise efforts, and lose weight if needed, you will be on your way to preventing diseases such as high blood pressure, heart attack, stroke, diabetes, and cancer. It is not about the salt. Reducing the amount of packaged and processed foods, not only reduces sodium, but also reduces intake of bad chemicals, hydrogenated fats, and nutrient-poor foods. As we have said in this book, it is best to consume fresh, non-processed, organic (if possible) foods, including fresh fruits and vegetables, meats, fish, and poultry. These types of dietary changes are more likely to have lasting health benefits than reduction in sodium content of the diet.

In summary, restricting dietary sodium for the average healthy American is not necessarily recommended or required. We do, however, recommend that you change your overall eating habits to help prevent chronic diseases later in life.

How to Stop Stressing Over Sodium:

- Cook from scratch, utilizing fresh foods when you can.

- Reduce the amount of processed foods you consume. Read the labels first!

- Stop eating out at fast food restaurants.

- When you do eat out, chose restaurants that serve fresh food.

- Choose fresh or frozen vegetables when at all possible. Eat them daily!

- Choose fresh or frozen fish, shellfish, poultry, and meat more often than canned or processed forms.

- Snack on fresh vegetables and fruits instead of processed fatty, high sugar, chemical-laden snack foods from vending machines!

So What's the Deal with Organic?

Throughout this chapter, you have surely noticed that we keep recommending "organic" meat, vegetables, and other items. Organic foods are grown without the use of herbicides, pesticides, antibiotics, or other chemicals. The more pure a substance is that you ingest, the more nutritious and beneficial to the body. Our bodies are very good at detoxifying impurities. However, the average person is surrounded with impurities such as environmental pollution, water supply, and foods we have no control over (such as at a restaurant). Your body is constantly trying to detoxify these substances which becomes draining on your immune system. So you want to have the most potent antioxidant foods available. In general, organically grown food shows a higher amount of flavonoids than those grown commercially. In a plant, these flavonoids help ward off insects and damaging effects of the sun.[10] While in our bodies, they are powerful antioxidants and disease fighting substances. With chemical pesticides and fertilizers, the plants do not have to produce so many flavonoids in order to defend itself. Lazy defenses in the plant = lazy defenses in your body.

If you have the choice of foods grown with herbicides or pesticides, or raised on hormones or antibiotics, or an organic food, choose the organic. We know that many of you are saying "But it's so expensive." In general, organic food is more expensive than commercially grown and raised. We again need to ask where your priorities lie. Chances are your car has automatic locks and windows, airbags, and a stereo system—these all cost more than a "basic car." Chances are, you buy clothes that cost a little bit more

Click Tips

Visit **www.foodnews.org** for interactive produce and pesticide information.

if you know they are better quality than the generic alternative. So, why would you opt not to do that for your body? We believe that organic food provides you with a higher quality product. It gives your body the nutrients it needs without the chemical residues. In our opinion, that is worth the extra money.

I Just Don't Have the Time to Shop!

Because we love a variety of food, we will shop at multiple stores to get our favorites. This is not feasible for many people. In fact, many of our patients claim "I don't have time to shop well." It is very difficult to practice shopping for healthy foods when you feel you don't have time to go through the store except to grab the "essentials." Instead of reading labels and taking your time, you run through the store and pull the same junk off the shelves. The real way to be successful with any long term wellness plan, or weight loss, is to alter your habits, not just for three months, six months, or a year, but for life. These are *lifestyle* changes—not just a fad diet.

This is our recommendation for you, and you should only have to do this once:

- Assess what food you have in your kitchen. "What foods do not fit into my diet anymore?" This is definitely going to include any of your "Danger Foods." You need to throw these away!

- Set aside four hours, depending on how much food you have stored and how many people and meals you have to plan.

- Brainstorm your favorite foods and determine which are most suitable for your diet. Write them on your list. Think of other foods to compliment them. If you like shrimp, for instance, think what you can stir-fry with it.

- Write down some ideas for meals. Go through your cookbooks, recipe websites, or just make up your own. Try to think of at least five!

- Review your list for foods that really do not belong in your kitchen. Do not list pizza if you are not supposed to eat casein or gluten. Do not list chocolate chip granola bars if you are supposed to eat a high protein diet. You get the idea.

- Make a list of spices, condiments, and garnishes that you would like to dress up your food. Why is this important? If you like flavorful food, but do not cook for yourself, chances are you will keep buying pre-packaged meals because they taste good. You need to move away from high calorie, artificially flavored foods. We may not spice everything perfectly and it will take some trial and error, but we feel it is worth it!

- Congratulations, you are on your way to building a healthy food environment!

Click Tips

If getting to the store is not possible all the time, try using a grocery delivery service. In Chicagoland, we like to use **www.peapod.com**. There are also grocery chains that offer a home delivery!

Visit **www.greenpeople.org** for information on co-ops and on organic household products for you, your family, and your pets.

You Must Be Persistent.

"It's all junk food!" We hear many people say this about supermarkets when they start reading labels and making more educated food choices. When you practice separating the "good" and "not so good" foods in the grocery store, you will notice more how much the "not so good" seems to be the majority of products available. It can be discouraging when you read what is really in the common foods that you have enjoyed for years. It may be challenging to find stores close to your home which stock organic food or food that is not soaking in a chemical bath. But you should never just settle for what your local market is feeding you if you know that it is not good food. Remember, this is your health—do not cheat yourself!

Talk with the store's manager about what you would like to see more of in the store. Are they lacking in organic vegetables? Soy milk? Free range eggs? The store is there to serve the consumer demand, so demand it!

Let's review how you bring The Hauser Diet home from the grocery store.

1. Every time you plan to go shopping, bring a list and stick to it. Eventually, healthy shopping will become second nature. We cannot tell you the last time we walked down the soda pop aisle!

2. Shop when you are able to concentrate. Do not shop while hungry or in a hurry.

3. Assess your kitchen cabinets. If you find food that is "junk," throw it away!

4. Give soy a try.

5. Stop buying so many sugary products: soda, candy, pastries, and desserts. Save these indulgences for special occasions.

6. Read the labels! If you do not know what an ingredient is, research it. If you cannot pronounce it, it probably is not good for you.

7. Gradually stock up on spices and "healthy" bulk items.

8. Find, or create, a few simple recipes that you like using fresh, whole foods.

9. Stop buying chemical-laden imposters and start cooking with "real" food again: butter, cream, 100% juice or nectar, cheese, fresh vegetables and fruits, fresh meats.

10. Buy organic when you can.

Make these commitments to yourself and your family. These little conscience choices you make in the store will reflect not only in your waistline, but in your overall health.

Unless you are a natural in the kitchen, assessing your kitchen may seem like a daunting task. Either that or you may look at your margarine tub or sugar free raspberry iced tea and not think twice about how it is effecting your health. You may still be thinking that the little heart logo on the label means it is good for your heart, or the fact that it says "healthy" means it must be good. Your cooking, eating, and food shopping habits have probably been with you for years and we all know that old habits don't die easily. We hope that you are starting to look at food differently while reading this book. The truth is that a huge portion of food sold in the average supermarket is bad even though its fancy packaging says otherwise. Remember, wholesome food is not found in a three slotted microwave dinner, even if it is "low fat" or "low sodium." It is also not found in diet soda or sugar free vanilla wafers. The food that will make you feel your best is organic, fresh, whole food. Let's have a little fun now and start cooking with that good food! We're going to bring the Hauser Diet to the table in the next chapter!

These 10 steps lay the foundation for better tasting, healthier eating. In the next chapter we'll start having some fun in the kitchen when we prepare some of our favorite recipes for each Diet Type. We'll show you how to turn your fresh groceries into delicious delights that your family and friends will love to eat!

Footnotes

1. Mercury Levels in Commercial Fish and Shellfish. FDA/ Center for Food Safety & Applied Nutrition. 2004. Available at http://vm.cfsan.fda.gov/~frf/sea-mehg.html. URL as of April 20, 2005.

2. Hu F., Stampfer M., Rimm E., Manson J., Ascherio A., Colditz G., Rosner B., Spiegelman D., Speizer F., Sacks F., Hennekens C., Willett W. A. Prospective Study of Egg Consumption and Risk of Cardiovascular Disease in Men and Women. *JAMA* 1999;281:1387-1394.

3. Hauser R., Hauser M., *Treating Cancer with Insulin Potentiation Therapy.* Oak Park, IL: Beulah Land Press; 2002.

4. Schulze M.B., Manson J.E., Ludwig D.S., Colditz G.A., Sampfer M.J., Willett W.C., Hu F.B. Sugar-sweetened beverages, Weight Gain, and Incidence of Type 2 diabetes in young and middle-aged women. *JAMA* 2004; 292:927-934.

5. Allison D.B., Heshka S., Sepulveda D., Heymsfield S.B. Counting calories—Caveat emptor. *JAMA.* 1993; 270:1454-1456.

6. Young, L. Nestle, M. Food labels consistently underestimate the actual weights of single-serving baked goods. *J Am Diet Assoc.* 1995; 95: 1150-1151

7. Davidson T., Swithers S. A Pavlovian approach to the problem of obesity. *International Journal of Obesity.* 2004; 28: 933-935.

8. Gold M. Holistic Medicine Resource Center's Web site. Toxicity Effects of Aspartame Use. Available at: http://www.holisticmed.com/aspartame/. Accessed September 18, 2006.

9. Rowe K.S., Rowe K.J. Synthetic food coloring and behavior: a dose response effect in a double-blind, placebo-controlled, repeated measure study. *J Pediatr.* 1994 Nov;125(5 Pt 1): 691-8.

10. Asami D., Hong Y., Barrett M., Mitchell A. Comparison of the total phenolic and ascorbic acid content of freeze-dried and air-dried marionberry, strawberry, and corn grown using conventional, organic, and sustainable agricultural practices. *J of Agricultural and Food Chemistry.* 2003; 51: 1237-1241.

Note: *Ingredient lists in this chapter were obtained on the website www.peapod.com.*

CHAPTER

9

COOKING
RIGHT
FOR YOUR
DIET TYPE

cooking right *for your* diet type

Due to the popularity of our e-newsletters, many of our patients and readers have asked us to provide some of our favorite recipes in this book. We know how hard it can be to put a healthy, delicious meal on the table day after day. We all face distractions and "tyranny of the urgent" moments that may direct our attention away from meal preparation, therefore leading us to the fast food restaurant instead of making something at home. We want to help you avoid doing that by having enough ingredients on hand that you will be able to whip up a quick meal, even when pressed for time.

Cooking should be fun and exciting—not drudgery. We hope that by providing you with some of our favorite recipes, along with some helpful "test kitchen tips" that you will be able to view cooking as a new adventure. As a good Floridian friend of ours once said about the impending hurricane, "embrace it"… embrace the challenge of cooking. It is a great way to share time together with your family or to be alone and have a special creative moment.

These meals can be made just as delicious by the average home cook who has nothing more than a skillet, a cutting board and the desire to start making healthy home-cooked meals. Many thanks to our friend, chef Steve, for making our easy simple meals look amazingly beautiful in their presentation. He really brought out the potential in the presentation of our recipes. But let's be honest, on the average Tuesday night's dinner after a hard days' work—we too need to put a meal on the table quickly—so they don't always look as pretty as they do in these pictures! But on the other hand, many of the food photos were taken of everyday meals we prepared in our kitchens!

For people who are not familiar with much more than microwave cooking, we are hopeful that these recipes will inspire you to start making healthier meals in your own kitchen. Everyone has to start somewhere and we hope that this book is the turning point for you. Cooking takes practice, so you should not be discouraged if you try a dish and it did not turn out exactly how you had hoped. Make a goal of learning five or ten dishes that you feel comfortable making and that taste good to you. Save those boxes of macaroni and cheese (natural of course!) for a rainy day. The majority of your meals should not come from a box any more…and they definitely should not come out of the microwave oven!

Diet Rating Legend

We developed this Diet Rating Legend to help you determine which recipes are best for each of the five Hauser Diets. A rating of three green circles, similar to "go" on a stop light, means that the recipe can be eaten daily or eaten for a main meal for that particular Diet Type. Two yellow circles, similar to "yield" on a stop light, means that the recipe can be eaten as a side dish, a snack, or if eaten for a main meal, one to two times per week. One red circle, similar to "stop" on a stop light, indicates that the recipe is not a good choice for that particular Diet Type.

What do I do when I'm an *Otter* and my spouse is a *Monkey*?

If you have been reading this book thinking that you will have to start cooking two different dishes for every meal, you will be happy to know that is not the case. My husband Ross and I are a great example. I am a Monkey and he is an Otter. As you know, these are on opposite sides of the diet spectrum. But eventually, cooking for two separate Diet Types becomes intuitive. I can cook the same types of basic, home-style meals and we each pick out what our bodies need. Let's use stir-fry as an example. Sauté your meat and vegetables, accompany with rice or noodles, and you've got dinner! The Otters should be choosing the meat and vegetable portion of the dish, with minimal rice or noodles. On the other hand, the Monkey should pick a lot of vegetables and rice, with minimal meat. So in order to best prepare this meal, one just has to remember to cook ample vegetables, because all diets need vegetables. This same rule may apply for a family-style set up when at a catered event, a friend's house, or other type of buffet. Choose foods according to your dietary needs. Yes, this will take self control. Of course there are also times when you will "cheat" on your diet. But our focus is long-term change in health. Having a piece of wedding cake will not make or break your health. However, always keeping coffee cake around when your body needs protein means you are choosing to ignore your basic survival needs. It is the overall picture of your health that we are trying to improve.

Taking a look at the recipe ingredients will help you better understand why a recipe is ranked higher for an Otter compared to a Monkey. We hope that you will soon learn that you can take these recipes and manipulate them to become more "Otter-friendly" or "Giraffe-friendly" simply by changing some of the ingredients.

Tweaking for Your Type:

Our crustless sweet potato pie is a recipe where the ingredients can be tweaked to better fit each of the Hauser Diet Types. For example, sweet potatoes are allowed on all Hauser Diets, but the amount of fat and sugar require adjusting to fit each of the Hauser Diets. The yellow boxes show the fat content alterations, where the pink boxes show sugar alterations. Lions and Otters can have more fat and less sugar, where Monkeys and Giraffes can have more sugar but less fat. Tweaking for your type is not an exact science, but if you give a little thought to the basics of your Diet Type, you'll be able to analyze any recipe and determine whether it is a good choice for you. Good luck and have fun!

CRUSTLESS SWEET POTATO PIE

For Lions and Otters:

- 2 medium sweet potatoes, cooked
- ½ stick butter (4 Tbsp)
- ¼ cup sugar
- 2 eggs
- ¼ cup heavy cream
- ¼ tsp cinnamon
- ⅛ tsp nutmeg
- ⅛ tsp salt
- 1 Tbsp vanilla

For Bears:

- 2 medium sweet potatoes, cooked
- ½ stick butter (4 Tbsp)
- ¾ cup sugar
- 2 eggs
- ¼ cup 2% milk
- ¼ tsp cinnamon
- ⅛ tsp nutmeg
- ⅛ tsp salt
- 1 Tbsp vanilla

For Monkeys and Giraffes:

- 2 medium sweet potatoes, cooked
- 3 Tbsp applesauce
- 1 tsp butter
- ¾ cup sugar
- 2 Tbsp cornstarch
- ¼ cup skim milk
- ¼ tsp cinnamon
- ⅛ tsp nutmeg
- ⅛ tsp salt
- 1 Tbsp vanilla

Can you tweak for your Type? If you follow the yellow boxes, you will see how the fat was altered to fit your type. The pink boxes indicate a change in the sugar used.

What to Do:

1. Preheat the oven to 375 degrees. 2. Bake 2 medium sweet potatoes for 50 minutes in a glass baking pan with about an inch of water in the bottom. Poke a couple of fork holes through the skin of the potatoes. 3. Peel and mash cooked sweet potatoes in a medium bowl with hand mixer. Add remaining ingredients and mix well. 4. Pour into a glass baking pan or mini loaf pans and bake for 45 minutes. 5. Remove from oven and let sit to cool. Slice and serve with a dollop of whipped cream or frozen yogurt.

recipes

Our Tried and True
Favorites

The recipes in the following pages are some of our tried and true favorites. You'll see that we have provided you a rating system that tells you which recipes are best for which Hauser Diet Type. Recipes that contain primarily protein and fat are better suited for the Lions and Otters. This includes beef, chicken, pork, and other animal protein recipes, along with recipes high in fat, such as cream sauces, oils, or recipes using bacon.

As you get better at tweaking a recipe for your Diet Type, Lions and Otters will only get better at transforming a vegetarian dish into something healthier for you, just by adding meat. Bears should be looking for a way to bring balance to each meal. The good news for Bears is that all recipes in this book can fit into your Diet Type. If they are not ideal for you, perhaps because they are very high in animal fat and protein, you eat a moderate portion of the meat and fat and balance it with some vegetables or whole grains. But in general, it is very easy for a Bear to feel good on most of the recipes we've put together. The recipes that are best suited for the Monkeys and Giraffes are the low fat, vegetarian ones, high in whole grain, vegetable, and fruit content. So, keep an eye out for some great salads, tofu dishes, and snacks that are right up your alley! Many of the recipes can be tweaked for your type very easily just by omitting, or Monkeys can just minimize, the meat and adding additional vegetables and seasoning.

So let's get cookin'!

soups

Oh, so delicious! There is nothing better on a cold evening, when you are feeling run down, or as a starter to meal time! Soups are a good place to start, if you are new to cooking. "A little of this, a little of that, and presto… a meal!" You can turn any soup into a meal, but most people consider soup a starter. Most of our recipes are for about four to eight people, depending on the serving size. Flexible thinking and creativity makes most of these soups suitable for all diets.

If you are a Lion or an Otter, your Diet Type needs more meat and protein from every meal. So, add more meat or tofu to the soup, or use the soup as a starter to a meat-based entree. If you are a Monkey or a Giraffe, your Diet Type needs a lot of veggies, so add more, or make a meal of a big soup and salad platter. The following pages contain some of our favorite soup recipes. So, grab your favorite soup mug and get ready to fill up!

BLACK BEAN SOUP WITH CHIPOTLE CHILIES

ALL DIETS

This spicy Mexican-inspired soup is a wonderful alternative to traditional chili. It packs a lot of flavor and can make a meal all by itself!

Tip for Your Type

Lions and Otters can have full fat sour cream or yogurt, whereas Bears should choose 2%, and Monkeys and Giraffes 1% or fat-free.

For Bears, Otters, and Lions, top with shredded cheese.

Ingredients

- 1 Tbsp olive oil
- 2 medium red onions, chopped
- 1 medium red bell pepper, chopped
- 1 medium green bell pepper, chopped
- 4 garlic cloves, minced
- 4 tsp ground cumin
- 16 ounce package dried black beans
- 1 Tbsp chopped canned chipotle chilies
- 7 cups water
- 2 Tbsp fresh lime juice
- 2 tsp coarse Kosher salt
- ¼ tsp ground black pepper

TEST-KITCHEN TIPS

Chipotle chilies canned in a spicy tomato sauce, sometimes called adobo, *are available at Latin American markets and many supermarkets.*

• • •

We use a slow cooker for this recipe to cook the beans. You can use canned, or pre-soaked beans and make this recipe on the stove top.

What to Do

1. Heat olive oil in large skillet over medium-high heat. Add onions and bell peppers and sauté until beginning to brown, about eight minutes. Add garlic and cumin. Stir 1 minute. **2.** Transfer mixture to 6-quart slow cooker. Add beans and chipotles, then 7 cups water. Cover and cook on high until beans are very tender, about 6 hours. **3.** Transfer 2 cups bean mixture to blender; puree until smooth. Return puree to remaining soup in slow cooker. **4.** Stir in lime juice, salt, and pepper. **5.** Ladle soup into bowls. Spoon a dollop of yogurt on top of soup and sprinkle with chopped lettuce, tomatoes, and avocado as desired.

Great Additions

- plain sour cream • chopped black olives • chopped cilantro

LENTIL SOUP

Lentils are a great source of protein and fiber that will really fill you up. They are also inexpensive, making those grocery dollars go a little bit further. Include at least one dish like this per week in your meal plans.

Ingredients

- 8 ounce bag of dry lentils
- 3 strips bacon, chopped into small pieces
- 1 small onion, chopped
- 1 Tbsp canola oil
- 1 Tbsp garlic, minced

- 1 carrot, chopped
- 1 stalk celery, chopped
- 4 cups water
- 2 tsp dried thyme
- salt and pepper to taste

What to Do

1. Cook bacon pieces in a stockpot until crispy. **2.** Add oil to bacon fat in pan and sauté garlic and vegetables until tender. Add water, thyme, and lentils. **3.** Bring to a boil, then lower heat and simmer until lentils are tender, about 60 to 90 minutes. Season with salt and pepper.

Tip for Your Type

Giraffes should eliminate the bacon.

TEST-KITCHEN TIPS

Add richness to slow-cooker soups by using a mixture of half broth and half water instead of only water.

• • •

If you have an immersion blender, this soup tastes great blended too!

Mom's Chili

LION OTTER BEAR MONKEY ⦿⦿ GIRAFFE

My mom has been making this chili for years. It's a definite family favorite! We serve it with rye bread and butter for something a little different. Mom uses tomato juice versus chopped tomatoes for a more soup-like chili.

Tip for Your Type

Giraffes and Monkeys should eliminate the meat, where Lions and Otters should increase the meat to 2 pounds. Giraffes increase beans to three cans—even try a combination of beans— kidney, black, and navy beans. To add more veggies, add shredded carrots and/or zucchini. Vegetarian chili requires a lot more seasoning, so you may need to kick it up a notch with more salt and seasonings.

Test-Kitchen Tips

This can be made in the crock pot too. The longer it cooks, the better it tastes. Use water to thin if chili is too thick.

Great Additions

- black olives • scallions
- jalapeños • sour cream
- shredded cheddar cheese

Ingredients

- 1 lb ground beef
- 4 celery stalks, chopped
- 1 large onion, chopped
- 64 ounces of tomato juice
- 2 Tbsp chili powder
- 1/8 tsp dried chili peppers
- 1 tsp dried cilantro
- 1 tsp salt
- 1/4 tsp pepper
- 1/4 tsp cinnamon
- 1 tsp sugar
- 15 ounce can of red kidney beans
- 1 small can of chopped chilies

What to Do

1. Brown meat in sauté pan. Drain off excess grease. **2.** In large stockpot, sauté chopped celery and onion with about 1 cup water for about 15 minutes. **3.** Add seasonings, tomato juice, and cooked beef. **4.** Cook for at least 45-60 minutes. **5.** Add red kidney beans right before serving.

SPICY SHRIMP SOUP

LION  OTTER BEAR MONKEY GIRAFFE

This soup packs a spicy punch! It is a great soup to make when you're feeling under the weather because it really makes you sweat!

Ingredients

- 2 Tbsp olive oil
- 16-20 large, cooked shrimp, chopped into medium pieces
- 2 Tbsp garlic, chopped
- 2 tsp red pepper flakes
- 2 fresh medium tomatoes, diced
- 4 Tbsp butter
- 4 tsp fresh cilantro, chopped
- 2 cups Chardonnay wine

What to Do

1. In a large sauté pan, heat the olive oil, garlic, and red pepper flakes. When garlic begins to brown, add shrimp and sauté for another minute. **2.** Add tomatoes and continue to sauté. When shrimp is firm and tomatoes are heated, remove from heat and place cooked contents into a large bowl. **3.** Return the pan immediately to the hot stove. Deglaze the pan by adding wine and cilantro, mixing well and scraping the remains of the tomato and shrimp. **4.** Boil until the alcohol flavor is diminished. Add the butter and bring it back to a boil. **5.** Pour the wine mixture into the large bowl with the tomatoes and shrimp. Mix and serve.

Great Additions

Serve with a slice of fresh lime and chopped cilantro.

SPLIT PEA SOUP

ALL DIETS

This is one of our all-time favorite dishes. Our friends and family love it too! It is an easy, healthy thing to make—especially on the weekends!

Ingredients

- 2 cups split peas, washed
- 2 bay leaves
- 2 quarts water
- 1 ham bone (or use chopped ham or bacon)
- ¼ cup fresh parsley, chopped
- 3 stalks celery, chopped
- ½ tsp crushed oregano
- ½ tsp basil
- 1 medium onion, diced
- 3 carrots, chopped
- 1 medium potato, chopped
- ½ tsp Kosher salt
- 2 cloves garlic, minced
- pinch of cayenne or black pepper

What to Do

1. Combine all ingredients in a large stockpot on top of the stove. **2.** Bring to a boil. Reduce heat and simmer for at least 1 hour or until split peas are cooked. **3.** Remove ham bone and bay leaves before serving. Blend with a hand-held immersion blender to make a smoother soup.

TEST-KITCHEN TIPS
We recommend organic, nitrate-free bacon and ham.

Tip for Your Type
Giraffes should omit bacon or ham.

SWEET POTATO AND SWISS CHEESE SOUP

LION ●●●	OTTER ●●●	BEAR ●●●	MONKEY ○○	GIRAFFE ●

This creamy soup may sound a little strange, but it is delicious! It's a great way to use sweet potatoes for something a little different!

Ingredients

- 2 sweet potatoes, raw, peeled and cut into chunks
- 2 shallots, minced finely
- 3 cloves garlic, minced finely
- 4 cups water
- 1 cup heavy cream
- 5 slices Swiss cheese
- salt and pepper to taste

What to Do

1. Fill a saucepan with 4 cups of water. Place sweet potato chunks, shallots, and garlic in water and bring to a boil. Boil until the sweet potatoes are fully cooked or falling apart (about 20-30 minutes). Reduce heat. **2.** Stir cream into the sweet potato mixture and bring to a boil again. Remove from heat. **3.** Mix in one piece of Swiss cheese at a time, blending until smooth, using a hand held blender or immersion blender. Salt and pepper to taste. Do not boil again after adding the cheese or the bottom will burn.

TEST-KITCHEN TIPS

We like to use a handheld immersion blender to make our soup really smooth. You can pour the soup into your regular blender to liquefy as well. Be sure to vent the top of the blender if you pour hot soup into it to prevent an explosion!

VEGETABLE AND PASTA SOUP

LION ●   OTTER ○○   BEAR ●●●   MONKEY ●●●   GIRAFFE ●●●

Vegetable soup is so easy to make that you can literally toss in your favorite vegetables or those wilting salad greens, season, and heat. This recipe has some of our favorites. We love to serve this soup with fresh garlicky bread.

Ingredients

- 2 garlic cloves, minced
- 1 Tbsp oil
- 1 small onion, chopped
- 2 carrots, chopped
- 2 celery stalks, chopped
- 2 medium red potatoes, chopped
- 2 cups green beans, chopped
- 1 zucchini, chopped
- 2 tomatoes, chopped

- 14.5 ounce can of diced tomatoes
- 1 quart broth (homemade chicken stock or vegetable broth)
- 1 quart water, or more as needed
- 1 bay leaf
- ½ tsp thyme
- ½ cup fresh parsley, chopped
- salt and pepper to taste
- 2 cups elbow macaroni, cooked

What to Do

1. In a large stock pot, heat garlic, oil, onion, carrots, and celery for a couple minutes until they begin to soften. **2.** Add the remaining ingredients, minus the macaroni. **3.** Bring to a boil, and then reduce to a simmer until vegetables are cooked and soft. **4.** Stir in pasta and remove from heat. Serve.

Great Additions

- wilted salad greens • white beans
- roasted garlic cloves • Asiago cheese topping

ITALIAN BEAN SOUP

Here's another recipe that I got from my mom who has made this for years. We gave it a few minor alterations. It's delicious and a great way to get some legumes in your diet—a great source of fiber!

Ingredients

- 1 medium onion, chopped
- 2 stalks celery, thinly chopped
- 2 medium carrots, thinly sliced
- 3 cloves garlic, minced
- 1 Tbsp olive oil
- 1 Tbsp flour
- 1 tsp dried rosemary leaves
- ¼ tsp dried thyme leaves
- ¼ tsp black pepper
- 58 ounces organic chicken broth
- 15 ounce can green baby lima beans, drained
- 15 ounce garbanzo beans, drained and rinsed
- 15 ounce kidney beans, drained and rinsed
- 2 Tbsp tomato paste
- 14 ½ ounce can diced tomatoes
- 1 large Idaho potato, unpeeled, cut into small chunks
- ⅓ cup pearl barley
- 1 cup spinach leaves
- salt and pepper to taste

What to Do

1. In a large deep pan, sauté onion, celery, carrots, and garlic in oil until soft, for about 10 minutes. Stir in flour, herbs and pepper; cook until onions are tender, 2 to 3 minutes longer. **2.** Add chicken broth, beans, tomatoes, tomato paste, and potato to pan; heat to boiling. Reduce heat and simmer, for at least 50 minutes longer or pour into crock pot and simmer for 2-6 hours over low heat. **3.** Add barley and spinach during last 10 minutes of cooking time. Salt and pepper to taste. Serve.

Great Additions

If you have a ham bone left over from a ham dinner, it will taste great simmering in this soup. You can also just add chopped ham or bacon to give the soup that smoky flavor.

TEST-KITCHEN TIPS

Substitute all white beans and add ham for a delicious ham and white bean variation.

salads

We know many of you cringe at the thought of having to eat salad, but we're determined to change that! There are hundreds of ways to incorporate these tasty sides into your diet, even making them into meals.

Monkeys and Giraffes especially should make salads into meals, as well as look for salads that contain minimal cheese, meat, and oils, while emphasizing a variety of vegetables, fresh fruits, and dried fruits in every salad. When making salad dressing, use more vinegar and fruit juice than oils—instead of the other way around. Bears, as always, will have plenty to choose from in this category because our salads offer a lot of variety. Add or delete from the ingredient list as you see fit: add a hard boiled egg for more protein, some nuts for more fat, or some corn for added carbohydrates.

Lastly, Lions and Otters will learn to love salads just as much as any other Diet Type by adding delicious fats such as olives and avocado, along with protein, to the salad vegetables. Say goodbye to boring salads—we're going have some fun in this category!

ARTICHOKE HEART PASTA SALAD

LION   OTTER   BEAR   MONKEY   GIRAFFE

We love pasta salad with crunchy, flavorful veggies—a delicious way to add vegetables to any diet. Fresh basil gives this salad a delightful fresh flavor.

Ingredients

- 14 ounce can of artichoke hearts, drained and quartered
- 2 medium tomatoes, chopped
- 1 medium green pepper, chopped
- 6 raw mushrooms, sliced
- 2 cups raw spinach, cleaned
- ½ cup onion, diced
- 1 garlic clove, minced
- 6 Tbsp olive oil (divided)
- ¼ cup red wine vinegar
- 2 tsp Dijon mustard
- 2 Tbsp fresh basil, chopped (or 2 tsp dried)
- ½ tsp oregano
- salt and pepper to taste (about ¼ tsp of each)
- 2 cups pasta, cooked al dente

What to Do

1. Heat 1 Tbsp olive oil in large skillet. Sauté mushrooms for 2 minutes. Add spinach and sauté together for 1-2 minutes. Do not over cook. **2.** In large mixing bowl, whisk together red wine vinegar, remaining olive oil, Dijon mustard, basil, oregano, salt, and pepper. Add artichoke hearts, tomatoes, green pepper, and onion and mix. Add cooked pasta, sautéed mushrooms and spinach. Mix well. **3.** Serve on a bed of fresh lettuce with a lemon wedge.

Tip for Your Type

Lions and Otters should eliminate or reduce pasta dramatically and add some chicken pieces or sliced beef. Look for higher protein, whole grain pastas instead of plain white pasta.

Great Additions

- chopped green or black olives • scallions • additional fresh basil

TEST-KITCHEN TIP

For those following gluten-free diets, try rice or corn pasta. For more fiber, choose whole wheat pasta. Substitute rice if you are not a pasta fan—it's a great change!

Mix in a pinch of sugar with the vinegar and oil to help bring out the flavors in the salad.

BEET AND GOAT CHEESE SALAD

We have to admit, Chef Steve helped us with this recipe! It may sound a little weird, but don't knock it until you've tried it. Delish! This is one of Marion's all time fav's!

Ingredients

- 4 whole, cooked, canned or fresh beets
- 4 ounces goat cheese
- 1 Yukon Gold potato
- 2 Tbsp fresh dill, chopped
- 1 Tbsp fresh parsley, chopped
- 2 Tbsp white wine vinegar
- 2 Tbsp olive oil
- 1 shallot, minced
- 1 Tbsp honey
- 1 Tbsp walnuts, chopped
- mixed greens for garnish

What to Do

1. Slice 1 beet into round medallions. Dice the other beets into small squares. Boil the Yukon potato in salted water until fork tender. Remove and smash with a fork. **2.** Add goat cheese to the potato mixture and season with salt and pepper. **3.** Blend herbs, honey, shallots, and vinegar in a small mixing bowl until smooth, using a blender or whisk. Slowly add the oil until a dressing is formed. **4.** Line the sliced beets in rows. Stuff the center with goat cheese/potato mixture. Garnish with mixed greens and goat cheese over the beets. **5.** Drizzle with dressing and walnuts. Surround the plate with diced beets.

BROCCOLI AND BACON SALAD

LION OTTER BEAR MONKEY GIRAFFE ⚪⚪

Once you bring this salad to a picnic or family gathering, they won't stop asking you for the recipe! The mix of salt and sweet with the crunchy broccoli is a great combination!

Ingredients

- 4 cups fresh broccoli, cut in bite-sized pieces
- 1 small onion, diced
- ¾ cup dried cranberries
- 6 slices bacon, cooked crisp and crumbled
- ¼ - ⅓ cup mayonnaise, adjust as desired
- 2 Tbsp apple cider vinegar
- 1 Tbsp brown sugar or raw cane sugar
- ¼ cup shredded cheddar cheese
- salt and pepper to taste

What to Do

1. Combine broccoli, onion, cranberries, and bacon in a salad bowl. **2.** Combine mayonnaise, vinegar, and sugar in small bowl. **3.** Pour over broccoli mixture and stir to coat, stirring in cheddar cheese. Refrigerate. Serve chilled.

Tip for Your Type

Lions and Otters are allowed higher fat and lower carbohydrate content, therefore they can add more bacon and eliminate or reduce the dried cranberries. Monkeys and Giraffes, which are more vegetarian, could reduce or eliminate the bacon and add marinated tofu or sunflower seeds. But please note, it definitely won't taste the same without the bacon!

TEST-KITCHEN TIP

Substitute cranberry sauce for dried cranberries and sugar.

CHICKEN WALDORF SALAD

LION ●●   OTTER ●●●   BEAR ●●●   MONKEY ●●   GIRAFFE ●

Waldorf salad has been around for years. This is a nice dish to make for a bridal shower or brunch. We, of course, recommend it for everyday living too! It's especially nice in the hot weather when you don't want to have to heat up your house with the stove.

Ingredients

- 2 skinless, boneless chicken breasts, cooked and cubed
- 2 medium red and/or green apples, coarsely chopped or slivered
- ⅓ cup red grapes
- ⅓ cup pecans or peanuts, coarsely chopped
- ¼ cup celery, thinly sliced

- ⅓ cup mayonnaise
- ⅓ cup sour cream
- 1 Tbsp lemon juice
- 1 Tbsp honey
- 1 to 1½ tsp dried rosemary, crushed
- poppy seeds for garnish
- dark green lettuce leaves

What to Do

1. In a medium bowl, combine cooked chicken, apples, grapes, pecans, and celery. **2.** In a small bowl, stir together mayonnaise, sour cream, lemon juice, honey, and rosemary. **3.** Pour dressing over chicken mixture; toss gently to coat. **4.** Serve the chicken mixture on lettuce leaves. May be refrigerated overnight.

Tip for Your Type

Lions and Otters can add extra chicken, chopped olives, or avocado slices, where Monkeys can add some chopped pineapple or dried cranberries and reduce the chicken.

Monkeys and Giraffes can add 1-2 cups of cooked whole grain rice to make into a casserole or side dish that can be served cold or hot.

CRANBERRY ORANGE SPINACH SALAD WITH WARM HONEY DIJON BACON DRESSING

 LION ○○   OTTER ○○   BEAR ●●●   MONKEY ○○   GIRAFFE ●

This salad combines sweet, salt, and tart flavors for a delicious and beautiful salad that your friends and family will not be able to get enough of!

Salad Ingredients

- 6 cups spinach, washed
- ½ cup dried cranberries
- ½ red onion, chopped
- 1 orange, peeled, cut into bite-sized pieces
- ½ cup walnuts or pecans, chopped

Dressing Ingredients

- ¼ cup honey
- ½ cup orange juice
- ½ cup lime juice
- 2 Tbsp Dijon mustard
- 4 slices bacon, cooked crisp and crumbled

What to Do

1. Combine bacon with dressing ingredients and mix well. **2.** Heat in a small saucepan until warm. **3.** Pour over spinach, onion, oranges, and dried cranberries in a large salad bowl. **4.** Top with nuts. Mix and serve.

ITALIAN SALAD

 LION ○○   OTTER ○○   BEAR ●●●   MONKEY ●●●   GIRAFFE ○○

We love to serve this salad with our favorite Italian dishes, such as spaghetti and meatballs, lasagna, and penne with vodka sauce.

Salad Ingredients

- 1 small head Romaine lettuce, torn in pieces
- 1 small head of leaf lettuce, torn into pieces
- 14 ounce jar/can of artichoke hearts, drained and chopped in quarters
- 14 ounce can/jar of hearts of palm, drained and chopped into bite-sized pieces
- 1 large red onion, sliced in rings or chopped
- 4 ounce jar of chopped pimento, drained
- ½ cup fresh Parmesan cheese, shredded
- ¼ cup olive oil
- ⅓ cup tarragon vinegar (or red wine vinegar)
- salt and pepper to taste

What to Do

1. In large salad bowl, combine lettuces, artichoke hearts, hearts of palm, red onion, and pimentos.
2. Add Parmesan cheese and toss gently. **3.** In a small bowl, blend oil and vinegar, mixing well. Pour over salad and toss gently. Add salt and pepper to taste.

GRILLED TOFU SALAD WITH CORN, CILANTRO, AND JALAPENO YOGURT DRESSING

ALL DIETS

If you have been reluctant to try tofu, give this recipe a try— it's got great flavor and interesting ingredients. You may not even notice that you are eating tofu!

Ingredients

- 6 ounces tofu, cut in 1-2 inch chunks
- 1 Tbsp soy sauce
- 1 Tbsp BBQ sauce
- 1 ear corn, kernels cut off (or ½ cup)
- 1 avocado, chopped
- 1 green onion, sliced
- ¼ cup pinto beans, drained
- 1 head Romaine lettuce, torn into pieces

- 1 jalapeño, diced
- 1 clove garlic
- 1 Tbsp fresh cilantro, chopped coarsely
- 1 Tbsp honey
- ½ cup plain yogurt
- 2 tsp rice wine vinegar
- 1 pinch paprika

What to Do

1. Mix soy sauce and BBQ sauce and pour over tofu in a bowl. Let sit for about an hour. **2.** Heat a griddle on top of the stove and grill tofu until fully cooked on all four sides. Set aside. **3.** Combine the jalapeño, garlic, cilantro, honey, yogurt, vinegar, and paprika in a blender. Blend until smooth. **4.** To serve in large salad bowl, place tofu on lettuce pieces topped with avocado, corn, green onion, and pinto beans. **5.** Drizzle dressing over all.

CREAMY DATE AND CARROT SALAD

LION ●   OTTER ○○   BEAR ○○   MONKEY ●●●   GIRAFFE ○○

Ross was always purchasing this salad at the deli counter of the grocery store when we first got married. So consequently, I learned how to make it—with a few alterations! It's crunchy and sweet— a deliciously different alternative to your basic green salad.

Ingredients

- 2 cups pitted dates, chopped
- 2 red apples, chopped
- 4 cups carrots, shredded coarsely
- 1 tsp orange rind, grated
- 2 Tbsp fresh orange juice
- ½ to 1 cup sour cream or yogurt
- ¼ tsp salt

TEST-KITCHEN TIPS
Refrigerate mixed salads like this overnight to enhance the flavor.

What to Do

Mix chopped dates, apples, shredded carrots, and orange rind in mixing bowl. Add orange juice, sour cream/yogurt, and salt. Gently toss. Cover and refrigerate until chilled.

Great Additions

- chopped walnuts or pecans • chopped pineapple • dried cranberries

You can even try adding a nutty trail mix for a more unique taste!

ITALIANO ANTIPASTO SALAD

LION	OTTER 	BEAR	MONKEY	GIRAFFE

This is a great meal for a vegetarian, yet it also makes a beautiful appetizer plate. Serve on a large square plate for added effect.

Ingredients

- 8 ounces fettuccine pasta, cooked al dente
- 1 head Boston lettuce, torn into pieces
- 3 Tbsp Balsamic vinegar
- 2 tsp oregano
- 2 Tbsp garlic, minced, divided
- ¼ tsp red pepper flakes
- ½ cup olive oil
- 1 tomato, diced
- 3 leaves fresh basil, finely sliced into strips
- 6 green olives, sliced
- 1 can artichoke hearts, drained
- ½ can hearts of palm, sliced
- 3 ounces Parmesan cheese, shredded

TEST-KITCHEN TIP

You may want to double the dressing recipe for this salad if you like your salad "wet."

Tip for Your Type

For added protein required in the Lion and Otter Diets, serve with cold sliced chicken or beef.

Monkeys and Giraffes should reduce oil and olives, and increase vinegar. Add a pinch of sugar to cut the tartness of the vinegar.

What to Do

1. Whisk Balsamic vinegar with oregano, 2 tsp garlic, red pepper flakes, and olive oil until a vinaigrette dressing is formed. **2.** Place the Boston lettuce in the center of the plate. **3.** In a small bowl, toss tomato with 1 tsp minced garlic, fresh basil strips, and season with salt and pepper and place on 1 corner of the plate. **4.** Toss the olives, artichoke hearts, and hearts of palm each individually with 1 or 2 tsp of the Balsamic dressing and a sprinkle of Parmesan cheese. Place each on a separate corner of the plate. **5.** In a bowl, toss the pasta with the dressing and add more Parmesan cheese. Place in center of plate on lettuce.

Savory Fruit Salad

| LION  | OTTER ⚫⚫ | BEAR ⚫⚫ | MONKEY ⚫⚫⚫ | GIRAFFE ⚫⚫⚫ |

This is a peppery twist on the typical fruit salad style. Feel free to use your favorite fruits and don't be afraid to add a little spice to your life!

Ingredients

Varying amounts of your favorite fruits. We like:

- 3 cups watermelon, sliced into chunks
- 1 fresh pineapple, cut into chunks
- 2 mangos, sliced
- 2 peaches, sliced
- 1 cup blueberries
- 20 green grapes, halved
- 3 Tbsp honey
- ½ cup plain yogurt
- ¼ cup olive oil
- hot paprika to taste

Tip for Your Type

This salad is an acceptable meal for the Monkey and Giraffe Diets, but the Bears and Otters should only have it as a side dish. Sorry, Lions, this is too much fruit for you!

What to Do

Mix the yogurt, honey, olive oil, and paprika in a small bowl. Place all the fruit in a bowl and toss with dressing. Serve.

ARUGULA AND BLACK BEAN SALAD

Like most salad greens, arugula is very low in calories and is high in vitamins A and C.

One cup of raw arugula contains only five calories, and is a nice change from regular lettuce!

Ingredients

- 15 ounce can black beans, rinsed and drained
- ½ cup dried apricots, snipped into ½ inch pieces
- ½ bell pepper, chopped
- 2 green onions, thinly sliced
- 2 Tbsp fresh cilantro, snipped into small pieces
- 1 clove garlic, minced
- ¼ tsp Kosher salt
- 4 cups fresh arugula

Dressing

- ¼ cup apricot nectar or orange juice
- 2 Tbsp olive oil
- 2 Tbsp rice vinegar
- 1 tsp soy sauce
- 1 tsp grated fresh ginger

What to Do

1. In a large bowl, combine the black beans, apricots, pepper, green onion, cilantro, garlic, and salt.
2. In a screw-top jar combine apricot nectar, oil, vinegar, soy sauce, and ginger. Cover and shake well.
3. Pour dressing over the bean mixture; toss gently to coat. Cover and refrigerate for 2 to 24 hours.
4. To serve, add the arugula to bean mixture; toss to combine.

TEST-KITCHEN TIP

- *1 cup fresh, in season apricots instead of dried*
- *You may wish to double the recipe for the dressing if you tend to like your salads "wet."*
- *Add a teaspoon of sour cream and green onions for a richer taste!*
- *Substitute orange juice and Mandarin oranges for apricots.*

SPINACH SALAD WITH SWEET ONION DRESSING

You may think this recipe is a lot of steps, but it is so worth it! Who doesn't love onion rings?

Ingredients

- 1 cup mushrooms, cleaned and sliced
- 2 bunches fresh spinach, cleaned and dried
- 1 cup cherry tomatoes, halved
- 1 Tbsp canola oil
- ½ cup chopped walnuts
- 1 cup sweet onion dressing*
- 1 cup crispy onion rings*

Sweet Onion Dressing

- 2 large onions, peeled and chopped finely
- 1 Tbsp canola oil
- ½ cup Balsamic vinegar
- ½ cup tamari soy sauce
- ½ cup white wine
- 1 garlic clove, minced

Crispy Onion Rings

- 2 onions, peeled and sliced into rings
- ¾ cup flour
- 2 eggs, beaten
- ¾ cup bread crumbs
- 1 tsp dried oregano
- 1 tsp dried basil
- 1 garlic clove, sliced
- ½ tsp salt
- ½ tsp freshly ground pepper
- 2 Tbsp Parmesan cheese, grated

TEST-KITCHEN TIP

Use non-wheat flours if you are gluten sensitive, such as rice or corn flours.

What to Do

For Dressing 1. Sauté chopped onions in heated canola oil on medium heat, until soft and light brown, about 10 minutes. **2.** Place cooked onions, vinegar, wine, soy sauce, and garlic in a food processor or blender and puree. Can be refrigerated up to two weeks.

For Crispy Onion Rings 1. Preheat oven to 400 degrees. Lightly grease baking sheet. **2.** Set out 3 flat bowls: one for flour, one for beaten eggs, and one for bread crumbs, spices, and cheese. **3.** Dip each onion in flour, then egg, then crumb mixture. Place on baking sheet. **4.** Bake at 400 degrees for 20 minutes or until light brown and crispy.

For Salad 1. Lightly sauté the mushrooms in oil until just soft. Remove from heat. **2.** Place spinach, mushrooms and tomatoes in a large salad bowl. Toss with 1 cup of dressing. **3.** Top with onion rings and sprinkle with nuts. Serve.

TOMATO MOZZARELLA AND BASIL SALAD

LION ●●●   OTTER ●●●   BEAR ●●●   MONKEY ○○   GIRAFFE ○○

This is a great starter or appetizer, as well as a salad to serve with your favorite Italian dish! It is a great way to use those tomatoes from the garden or farmer's market. People love this dish, and it whips up in no time, so it's great to serve when you have guests coming over! It is always one of the first things to go at my house!

Ingredients

- 3 large ripe tomatoes, sliced
- 1 lb fresh mozzarella cheese, sliced
- ½ cup olive oil, cold-pressed, extra-virgin
- 2 Tbsp wine vinegar
- 2 Tbsp fresh basil, finely chopped
- Pinch of Kosher salt
- Pinch of pepper

What to Do

In a large serving dish, alternate slices of tomatoes and mozzarella cheese. Sprinkle with oil, vinegar, and basil. Season with salt and pepper.

SPINACH SALAD WITH WARM BACON DRESSING

LION ● ● ●   OTTER ● ● ●   BEAR ● ●   MONKEY ○ ○   GIRAFFE ●

Traditional spinach salad is one of our all-time favorites! Don't you just love it when you find that spinach salad is being served at a restaurant instead of boring iceberg lettuce salad? Now you can make it right in your own home!

Ingredients
- 1 large bunch of fresh spinach, washed
- 6 strips of bacon, cooked and chopped, saving bacon grease
- 2 eggs, hard boiled and chopped
- 1 small red onion, sliced in rings
- 2 tsp sugar
- ¼ tsp salt
- ½ cup Balsamic vinegar
- ½ tsp dried onion flakes
- ¼ cup natural cane sugar

What to Do

1. Combine spinach in a large salad bowl.

2. Top with cooked bacon, egg, and red onion.

3. Heat bacon grease, vinegar, onion flakes, sugar, and salt in saucepan until just bubbling. **4.** Pour warm dressing over spinach. Serve immediately.

Great Additions

- For Lion, Otter, and Bear Diets, add cheeses such as crumbled blue, goat, or feta. Use nuts such as chopped pecans, walnuts, or pine nuts.

- For Bear and Monkey Diets, add some fruit for variation, such as diced oranges, dried cranberries, or chopped dates.

Tip for Your Type

For more protein, Lions and Otters could add more meat, such as chicken slices.

Monkeys should reduce or eliminate bacon.

TEX MEX SPINACH SALAD

LION ⬤⬤	OTTER ⬤⬤⬤	BEAR ⬤⬤⬤	MONKEY ⬤⬤⬤	GIRAFFE ⬤⬤

You're going to love this salad—it is just the right mix of ingredients—spicy and sweet go so well together! It makes a great meal in and of itself!

Ingredients

- 16 ounces baby spinach
- 2 chicken breasts
- 1 small bunch cilantro, chopped
- 2 tsp garlic, minced
- 1 Tbsp cumin
- ½ tsp cayenne pepper
- ½ tsp cinnamon
- 1 red onion, chopped

- 2 Tbsp red wine vinegar
- 1 Tbsp honey
- 6 Tbsp canola oil
- 2 red chilies, diced (more or less, depending on how spicy you like it)
- ¼ cup pinto beans, cooked
- 2 apricots, diced

Tip for Your Type

Increase chicken for Lion and Otter Diets. Reduce chicken for Monkey Diet, and eliminate it for the Giraffe Diet and add more pinto beans.

What to Do

1. Preheat oven to 400 degrees. **2.** Sprinkle the chicken breast with cumin, cayenne pepper, and cinnamon and roast in oven for 45 minutes, or until fully cooked. Set aside and let the meat rest before slicing into thin strips. **3.** Blend the cilantro, garlic, honey, chili pepper, and vinegar together, slowly adding the oil until it forms a thick vinaigrette. **4.** Toss the spinach with the dressing, add the chicken slices, beans, sliced red onion, and apricots. For more spice, add the red chilies.

TUESDAY NIGHT'S SPINACH SALAD

You'll find yourself making this recipe over and over again—it's so good! Our friends ask us to make "that salad." This dressing is so simple, but so delicious. It has become a Tuesday and an every night favorite dressing!

Ingredients

- 1 bag of fresh baby spinach
- 3 large mushrooms, sliced
- 1 tomato, sliced
- ¼ cup sliced almonds
- ¼ cup blue cheese, crumbled
- 2 green onions, chopped

Dressing Ingredients

- 4 Tbsp olive oil
- 2 Tbsp Balsamic vinegar
- 1 tsp honey
- 2 Tbsp sour cream (or plain yogurt)
- salt and pepper to taste

TEST-KITCHEN TIPS

Greek yogurt has a similar taste and can be used as a substitute for sour cream, while having more protein and fewer calories.

What to Do

Mix olive oil, vinegar, and honey in a small bowl. Gradually whisk in sour cream. Toss salad ingredients together in a large salad bowl. Drizzle with dressing and serve.

Great Additions

- candied or roasted pecans
- strawberry slices
- dried cranberries
- Mandarin oranges

Use any of your favorite ingredients! You can't go wrong!

ASIAN MANDARIN ORANGE SALAD

ALL DIETS

A lot of cafes make various Asian-style salads that people just go crazy over. They're tangy, crunchy, and sweet—what's not to love?! Even better, they are a breeze to make at home! Keep a can of Mandarin oranges, and these other simple ingredients on hand, and you can whip up the same quality salad in no time!

Ingredients

- 1 bunch Romaine lettuce, chopped
- 2 green onions, chopped
- 1 can Mandarin orange segments, juice reserved
- ¼ cup slivered almonds
- ½ cup Chinese noodles
- 1 Tbsp sesame seeds

Dressing Ingredients

- 1 Tbsp sesame oil
- 1 Tbsp soy sauce
- 1 Tbsp rice vinegar
- 1 Tbsp juice from Mandarin oranges
- 1 clove garlic, minced
- 1 pinch of red pepper flakes (optional)

What to Do

1. In a large bowl, combine lettuce, green onions, orange segments, almonds, noodles, and sesame seeds. **2.** In a small bowl, whisk dressing ingredients together. **3.** Pour dressing over salad and mix well to coat.

TEST-KITCHEN TIPS

Toast the almonds and sesame seeds in a dry skillet before adding to the salad.

Tip for Your Type

Lions and Otters should use fewer or no orange segments, and try adding ½ sliced chicken breast.

Monkeys and Giraffes can decrease the almonds, sesame seeds, and oil to decrease the fat in this salad.

salad dressing 101

Imagine you have made a beautiful salad with fresh dark greens, bell peppers, tomatoes, onion, walnuts, and dried cranberries. You have grilled your favorite lemon pepper fish and baked some fresh crusty bread. As you are about to sit down and enjoy this meal, you think "Oh, I forgot the dressing. What is in the cabinet?" You then dump a quarter of a cup Ranch dressing over your otherwise perfectly good dinner. But let's rewind to 10 minutes prior and see how we can save your salad from this "chemical cover up."

It is very easy to whip up basic salad dressings that are much tastier than store bought versions. The following section contains some of the dressings we make to dress our salads, spread on sandwich bread, or dip our fruits. Once you start making your own salad dressings, you'll never go back to store-bought! Monkeys and Giraffes should make primarily lower fat dressings, using a variety of vinegars, mustards, honey, and fruit juices. Lions and Otters should make oil-based and yogurt dressings. All Diet Types should experiment with different seasonings, such as thyme, sweet curry, garlic salt, or dill.

Avocado Dill Dressing
(Ranch Dressing Alternative)

LION OTTER BEAR  MONKEY ⚪⚪ GIRAFFE ⚫

You'll find that this dressing can be used in many different capacities—as a veggie dip, as a sauce for fish, or as a sandwich spread—in addition to using it on your salad greens!

Ingredients

- 1 cup yogurt
- ½ avocado
- ½ cup sour cream
- 2 Tbsp lemon juice
- 2 Tbsp fresh dill
- 1 tsp sugar
- ½ tsp garlic salt
- ¼ tsp pepper

TEST-KITCHEN TIP

Substitute fresh cilantro or basil for dill to change the flavor to complement your meal.

What to Do

Blend all ingredients in a food processor or blender. Add more lemon juice if thinning is required. Chill until served.

Spicy Ranch Dressing

LION  OTTER BEAR MONKEY ⚫ GIRAFFE

Talk about delicious! You'll use this recipe as a dip for chips and veggies, as well as a sauce for meats and vegetables. Of course, an occasional pizza crust dipped in this sauce is a must!

Ingredients

- 3 egg yolks
- 1 Tbsp Dijon mustard
- 2 Tbsp red wine vinegar
- 1 Tbsp garlic, minced
- 1 Tbsp dill, minced
- 1 jalapeno pepper, seeded and chopped
- ½ cup canola oil
- ½ cup sour cream

What to Do

1. Blend egg yolks, Dijon mustard, and red wine vinegar in a blender until smooth. **2.** Add in garlic, dill, jalapeno pepper, and blend again. **3.** Slowly pour in oil while ingredients are blending. **4.** Add in sour cream and blend until smooth.

MOM'S THOUSAND ISLAND DRESSING

LION ●●●   OTTER ●●●   BEAR ●●●   MONKEY ●   GIRAFFE ●

*My mom has made this dressing for years and it is still a family favorite. Unfortunately you'll want to eat it with a spoon and bypass the salad! Ooh, it's **so** good!*

Ingredients

- 1 cup mayonnaise
- ½ cup chili sauce
- 1-2 hard boiled eggs, chopped
- ½ cup green olives, chopped
- 1-2 tsp sugar (to taste)
- dash of salt and pepper

What to Do

Mix all ingredients in a bowl. Thin with milk to desired consistency. Serve over your favorite crunchy lettuce with fresh tomatoes.

> **TEST-KITCHEN TIP**
> *This dressing makes a great dip and sandwich spread.*

PEANUT LIME DRESSING

LION ●●●   OTTER ●●●   BEAR ●●   MONKEY ●   GIRAFFE ●

This Thai-inspired dressing is a unique blend of ingredients that taste great together. It is not only good on a salad, but as a dipping sauce for satays or mixed into Thai noodle dishes.

Ingredients

- ¼ cup toasted sesame oil
- 3 Tbsp peanut butter
- ½ cup sour cream
- juice of 1 lime
- 1 Tbsp rice vinegar
- ½ Tbsp sugar
- 2 tsp soy sauce

What to Do

Whisk in a bowl and pour over salad. Thin with more lime juice if needed.

Sun-dried Tomato with Avocado

We love to use this dressing on spicy foods or just as a dressing for your Tuesday night salad. It's a good one to double the recipe and keep on hand in the refrigerator.

Ingredients

- 2 Tbsp sun-dried tomatoes, chopped
- 1 avocado, peeled and chopped
- 1 garlic clove, minced
- 3 Tbsp Balsamic vinegar

- 3 Tbsp olive oil
- 3 Tbsp water
- 1 Tbsp fresh basil (or 1 tsp dried basil)
- salt and pepper to taste

What to Do

Mix all ingredients in bowl. Blend with a hand-held immersion mixer for best results or place in blender or food processor. Thin with more water if needed.

Warm Orange Vinaigrette

ALL DIETS

This dressing is great on Asian salads and as a marinade for poultry and fish.

Ingredients

- ½ cup olive oil
- ¼ cup cider vinegar
- 2 Tbsp orange juice

- 1 tsp grated ginger root
- ½ tsp thyme
- salt and pepper to taste

What to Do

Mix all ingredients together in a small saucepan. Bring to a boil. Remove from heat and pour over salad.

HONEY MUSTARD DRESSING

This is a great little recipe to whip up for a two-person salad. Feel free to double or triple the recipe if you want to keep a little extra on hand for tomorrow's salad. You may want to do that because it is so simple, yet so delicious!

Ingredients

- 1 tsp mustard (apricot ginger)
- 1 Tbsp olive oil
- 2 tsp apple cider vinegar
- ½ tsp honey
- Salt and pepper

What to Do

Whisk all ingredients together in a small bowl and pour over your favorite salad.

FAT-FREE CITRUS BALSAMIC DRESSING

LION   OTTER   BEAR   MONKEY   GIRAFFE

This is an unusual but tasty dressing with a zesty zip to it! If grapefruit juice is too tangy for you, substitute your favorite fruit juice. But for those of us who love sour tastes, you'll love the combination!

Ingredients

- ¼ cup grapefruit juice
- 2 Tbsp Balsamic vinegar
- 1 tsp honey
- ¼ tsp salt

What to Do

Whisk all ingredients together in a small bowl and pour over your favorite salad.

> **TEST-KITCHEN TIP**
>
> *We like to use this dressing over a salad of arugula, orange or grapefruit slices, and sliced pickled beets! It may sound weird, but it's delicious!*

vegetable-based meals and sides

Some of these vegetable recipes may be stretched into the main dish of a meal, especially for you Monkeys and Giraffes, with a nice salad as an accompaniment. Bears may do that occasionally, if their other meals had plenty of protein, or you can add a little meat to many of these.
Lions and Otters should primarily enjoy vegetable-based meals and sides, as just that—a side dish! Your Diet Type requires your meals to be high in protein. So, you can either add meat to these recipes, or just have a small amount as a side to your meat-based main dish. Enjoy!

ASIAN SAUTÉED SPINACH

ALL DIETS

We love cooked spinach. Adding new flavors and textures continue to make it enjoyable to eat. Here is one of our favorite ways to serve spinach. This tastes delicious as a side dish with Asian shrimp over rice. Watch the spinach closely because it only takes a minute or two to cook!

Ingredients

- 4 cups fresh spinach
- 1 tsp sesame oil
- 2 cloves garlic, sliced
- 2 dashes soy sauce
- pinch of salt and pepper
- 2 Tbsp peanuts, chopped

What to Do

1. Heat oil in skillet. **2.** Add garlic and sauté for a minute. Add spinach, salt, pepper, soy sauce, and chopped peanuts. **3.** Sauté for about a minute until wilted. Serve immediately.

TEST-KITCHEN TIP

Substitute olive oil and lemon juice for the soy sauce and sesame oil for a more traditional flavor. Sautéed spinach is a great substitute for rice or pasta—serve seafood or meat atop the bed of sautéed spinach. It looks and tastes beautiful!

BABA GHANOUJ

LION OTTER OO BEAR ●●● MONKEY ●●● GIRAFFE ●●●

This is a Mediterranean dish that is deliciously garlicky and a great way to eat eggplant.

Warning: It's one of those dishes you cannot stop eating! It makes a great appetizer!

Ingredients

- 1 medium eggplant
- 2 cloves garlic, crushed
- 3 Tbsp tahini
- 3 Tbsp onion, finely chopped
- 2 Tbsp olive oil
- 1 Tbsp rice vinegar

- 2 Tbsp fresh parsley (or 1 Tbsp parsley flakes)
- juice of 1 lemon
- ¼ tsp salt
- dash of black pepper
- dash of cayenne pepper (optional)

What to Do

1. Preheat oven to 350 degrees.
2. Place eggplant on a baking sheet in oven and bake for 1-1½ hours, turning the eggplant 3 times throughout baking. The eggplant will collapse while baking and will look like a large prune. Take it out of the oven and let it cool for 20 minutes.
3. Once cooled, strip the skin and stem off the eggplant, leaving only pulp. **4.** In a food processor, blend the pulp and remaining ingredients until smooth. Serve with crackers, pita, or fresh vegetables.

GREEN BEANS ALMONDINE

Talk about comfort food! This is such a simple, yet elegant side dish guaranteed to please even the most finicky eater!

Ingredients

- 1 cup fresh green beans, washed and tips removed
- 2 shallots, minced
- 4 Tbsp almonds, slivered

- 2 Tbsp butter
- 1 Tbsp canola oil
- salt and pepper to taste

What to Do

1. Place the beans in a large saucepan and cover with water. Bring to a boil and cook until beans are tender. Drain and set aside. **2.** Add canola oil and shallots to saucepan and sauté until slightly browned. Stir in almonds and butter **3.** Add cooked green beans back into the pan, tossing to coat. Salt and pepper to taste. Serve with your favorite meat dish.

Great Additions

For an extra kick, add slivered garlic or sprinkle with grated Asiago cheese just before serving.

GRILLED SUMMER VEGETABLES

This is a great recipe to utilize some of those veggies that you get from the garden.

Don't you just love the summer freshness of home-grown vegetables?

Seasoning Ingredients

- 2 Tbsp Kosher salt
- 2 Tbsp sugar
- 2 garlic cloves, crushed
- 1 Tbsp ground black pepper
- 1 tsp paprika

Vegetable Ingredients

- 3 carrots, sliced
- 1 large zucchini, sliced
- 1 medium baby squash, sliced
- 2 bell peppers, chunked
- 2 yellow onions, chunked
- 2 medium tomatoes, wedged

- 12 12-inch wooden skewers, soaked in water for 10 minutes
- 2 Tbsp olive oil
- 2 tsp Kosher salt

What to Do

1. Mix the seasoning ingredients together in a small bowl and set aside.

2. Thread the vegetables on the skewers (except the tomatoes). Brush with olive oil and sprinkle lightly with seasoning mixture.

3. Grill vegetables on medium-high heat for approximately 5 minutes per side. Remove from grill and serve with tomato wedges.

Pan Roasted Potatoes

LION ●●   OTTER ●●   BEAR ●●●   MONKEY ●●●   GIRAFFE ●●

This recipe is a very easy side dish to make to accompany seafood, meat, poultry, or even an egg dish. It's so simple, yet so delish!

Tip for Your Type

Adding fatty foods like bacon and cheese are better suited for Lions and Otters. Additional veggies like onions and bell peppers, are better suited for the Giraffes, Monkeys, and Bears.

Ingredients

- 8 small red potatoes, quartered
- 1 medium onion, sliced thin
- 3 Tbsp butter
- salt and pepper to taste

What to Do

1. Boil the potatoes in salted water until tender. Drain and set aside.
2. Sauté the onions in butter. Add water to the pan as they are cooking to bring out the full sweetness of the onion (about a half cup). Cook for a least 10 minutes until dark brown. **3.** Add cooked potatoes and toss with salt and pepper. Heat for another few minutes and serve.

Great Additions

- bacon crumbles • blue cheese crumbles • minced garlic • chopped bell peppers

KIDNEY BEAN RELISH

LION  OTTER ● ● ● BEAR ● ● ● MONKEY ○ ○ GIRAFFE ●

This side dish goes great with Cuban-style pork! See our recipe in the Pork section.

Ingredients

- ½ lb bacon, sliced into ⅛ inch pieces
- ¼ medium onion
- 2 cloves garlic, thinly sliced
- 1 Tbsp oregano
- 1 red bell pepper, diced

- 4 fresh mushrooms, sliced
- 1 can kidney beans
- 1 can black beans
- salt and pepper to taste

What to Do

1. In a sauté pan, cook bacon until crispy. **2.** Add the onion and garlic and sauté until lightly brown. Add the oregano, bell pepper, and mushroom and cook until tender. **3.** Add the beans, salt, and pepper. Sauté until the flavors come together and the beans are hot.

Tip for Your Type

This becomes a great Giraffe recipe if the bacon is omitted and a small amount of oil substituted.

TEST-KITCHEN TIP

Add a large can of chopped tomatoes, a couple squirts of ketchup, a pinch of brown sugar, and a can of great northern beans or other favorite beans and make a great crock pot bean dish.

MASHED RED POTATOES

LION OTTER BEAR MONKEY GIRAFFE

We absolutely love these potatoes. Talk about comfort food! These team up well with homemade meatloaf. (See recipe in beef section of this chapter)

Ingredients

- 12 large red potatoes, quartered
- ½ cup butter
- ½ cup milk
- ½ tsp Kosher salt
- ¼ cup sour cream

What to Do

1. Fill a large pot with salted water. Place potatoes in the water and bring to a boil. Boil until potatoes are fork tender, about 20 minutes. **2.** Turn off heat and drain the potatoes. **3.** Add butter, salt, sour cream, and milk to potatoes in a large mixing bowl. **4.** Mash ingredients together by hand or with a hand mixer. Thin with milk as desired.

TEST-KITCHEN TIP

Homemade mashed potatoes are so easy to make. If you are a boxed potato user, you'll never go back once you've made these. There is no comparison! Try using other types of potatoes such as Yukon Gold or Fingerling to mix it up a little!

Tip for Your Type

We leave the skins on when we make mashed potatoes to keep these in the complex carbohydrate category for all Diet Types. The potato skins contain good vitamins and fiber that you don't want to scrape into the garbage can. Giraffes and Monkeys remember to reduce the fat when making this recipe!

Great Additions

- chopped green onions
- 2 cloves of minced garlic
- ½ cup of shredded cheese

CHEESY EGGPLANT

LION	OTTER	BEAR ●●●	MONKEY ●●●	GIRAFFE

My friend gave me a taste of his mother's eggplant parmesan one day. I thought I had gone to heaven, so we adapted that recipe to come up with this version of Cheesy Eggplant. To my friend's mom—thanks! You inspired us to create this wonderful tried and true favorite!

Ingredients

- 1 Tbsp olive oil
- 1 large eggplant
- 3 tsp garlic, minced
- 1 medium yellow onion, chopped
- ½ cup olive oil (divided)
- 16 ounce can chopped tomatoes

- 2 Tbsp fresh basil, chopped (or 2 tsp dried)
- 1 Tbsp fresh parsley (or 1 tsp dried)
- ¼ tsp Kosher salt, add more as needed
- ½ cup Romano cheese, shredded
- ½ cup Asiago cheese, shredded
- ½ cup Parmesan cheese, grated

What to Do

1. Wash and dry eggplant. Slice into ½ inch rings and place on paper towels. **2.** Sprinkle with Kosher salt and allow the eggplant to "sweat" for 20 minutes. Wipe collected "sweat" off eggplant slices. **3.** Cut rings into small chunks. **4.** Heat 1 Tbsp olive oil in skillet. Add onion, garlic, and spices. When garlic becomes fragrant, add eggplant. **5.** Add tomatoes and heat until bubbly. Turn off heat and stir in cheeses. Serve as a side dish, over pasta, atop crusty Italian bread, or as a main meal.

TEST-KITCHEN TIP

Thinly slice a few pieces of eggplant horizontally. Cook in a little bit of olive oil to soften on top of the stove. Wrap cooked eggplant mixture inside for an elegant presentation as seen in the photo.

Tip for Your Type

Lions and Otters can add one to two sliced cooked Italian sausages, while Monkeys and Giraffes should go easy on the cheese and avoid the added meat.

SPAGHETTI SQUASH WITH VODKA CREAM SAUCE

LION ●●○	OTTER ●●○	BEAR ●●○	MONKEY ○○	GIRAFFE ○○

This recipe is a Hauser family favorite. My good friend Pam gave me her vodka sauce recipe and I have adapted it for this dish. For those of you who are counting carbs, this is a great recipe! Squash is a very healthy food, loaded with vitamins and fiber. Once at a family gathering I set this dish on the table— they gave me "the look" because it was "different" but once they tried it, they loved it!

Ingredients

- 1 spaghetti squash, sliced in half lengthwise (Scoop out seeds.)
- 2 Italian sausages, skin removed, chopped
- 4 slices bacon, chopped into 1-inch pieces
- 1 Tbsp olive oil
- 3 garlic cloves, thinly sliced
- 1 small onion, diced

- 3 Tbsp butter
- 28 ounce can of diced tomatoes (or 6 fresh tomatoes)
- ⅛ cup fresh basil, chopped
- ¼ tsp red pepper flakes
- ½ cup heavy cream
- ¾ cup vodka
- ½ cup Parmesan cheese, grated

What to Do

1. In a large pot bring water to a boil. Submerge the squash halves and boil for 10-30 minutes, until tender. **2.** Remove the squash and submerge it in an ice bath to stop the cooking. **3.** Using a fork, scrape the inside spaghetti-like strands into a bowl. Discard the skin of the squash. **4.** Heat olive oil and cook bacon pieces in a skillet. Add garlic and onion to the pan and sauté for a couple of minutes until tender. Add sausage and break apart as you are cooking it. **5.** Add butter, tomatoes, basil, pepper flakes, and vodka and simmer until the flavors come together, about 5 minutes. **6.** Stir in cream, blend well. Stir in Parmesan cheese and remove from heat. **7.** Pour sauce over cooked squash and serve immediately. Garnish with roasted squash seeds and chopped basil if you are feeling adventurous!

Great Additions
- chopped scallions • chopped black olives • chopped pineapple

Tip for Your Type

Lions and Otters: Broil an additional Italian sausage or two and cut into disc shaped slices and serve on top of squash as shown in the picture in order to get more protein. Giraffes: eliminate sausage.

TEST-KITCHEN TIP

This dish makes a great make-ahead casserole too. Pour the cooked squash and sauce together into a greased 9 x 13 baking dish. Refrigerate until ready to cook. Heat at 350 degrees for 30-40 minutes until hot and bubbly.

SQUASH APPLE BAKE

LION	OTTER ○○	BEAR ●●●	MONKEY ●●●	GIRAFFE ○○

What a great dish to make on a crisp fall day! This dish goes great with pork and poultry.

Ingredients

- 1 butternut squash, peeled and sliced
- 3 medium apples, cored and sliced
- ½ cup brown sugar
- 2 tsp cinnamon
- 2 Tbsp butter, melted

What to Do

1. Preheat oven to 350 degrees. **2.** Place squash slices in a greased glass baking dish, and top with apple slices. **3.** Sprinkle with cinnamon and brown sugar. Pour butter over the entire dish. Cover and bake for 1 hour.

SWEET POTATO FRIES

ALL DIETS ●●●

Once you make these, you'll never stop making them! They are absolutely delicious and addicting, as well as a fun way to get more vegetables into your diet!

Ingredients

- 6 large sweet potatoes, peeled and sliced like steak fries
- 2 tsp Kosher salt
- Olive oil for lightly coating the fries
- Mexican spice mix (optional)

What to Do

1. Preheat oven to 425 degrees. **2.** In a large mixing bowl, drizzle oil over the potatoes and toss to coat. Add salt and any additional seasoning, and toss. **3.** Place sweet potato fries in one even layer onto a baking sheet, keeping space between the potato slices to ensure a crisp fry. **4.** Bake for 10 minutes, then flip the fries. Bake for an additional 10 minutes, until browned on the outside and soft on the inside. Cool the fries for 5 minutes.

TEST-KITCHEN TIP

Bake these potatoes in batches to avoid overcrowding the baking sheet and mushy fries. You may substitute with Idaho potatoes. However, shorten the second cooking time to 5 minutes.

Great Additions

Try one of our dressing recipes for a dipping sauce.

VEGETABLE KUGEL

LION ●   OTTER ○○   BEAR ●●●   MONKEY ●●●   GIRAFFE ●●●

Since some of my family is Jewish, I have tried my hand at making some traditional dishes and love them. This Kugel recipe is not just for the holidays—it's a great way to get your fruits and vegetables. We like serving it for a brunch or as a side dish.

Ingredients

- ½ cup butter, melted
- 2 medium Granny Smith apples, chopped
- 2 medium sweet potatoes, peeled and grated
- 1 carrot, grated
- 1 cup matzo meal
- 1 tsp Kosher salt

- 1 tsp baking soda
- 1 tsp ground cinnamon
- ¼ tsp nutmeg
- ½ cup sugar or honey, optional
- ¼ cup raisins

What to Do

1. Preheat oven to 350 degrees. **2.** In a medium bowl, combine all ingredients and gently mix. **3.** Pour into a greased 9 x 13 baking dish and sprinkle a pinch of sugar over the top and bake for 40 minutes. Serve warm.

TEST-KITCHEN TIP

Use olive oil instead of butter to make this recipe vegan for Jewish holidays.

Great Additions

- chopped dates or figs
- dried cranberries
- chopped walnuts or pecans

OVEN ROASTED BRUSSELS SPROUTS

ALL DIETS

Before you turn up your nose to this recipe, give it a try. Roasting these cabbage-like vegetables brings out their flavor and makes them sweeter tasting.

Ingredients

- ½ to 1 lb fresh Brussels sprouts, halved lengthwise, stems trimmed
- 1-2 Tbsp olive oil
- Kosher salt
- pepper to taste
- red pepper flakes, as desired

What to Do

1. Preheat the oven to 400 F. 2. Toss sprouts in olive oil and add salt, pepper, and red pepper flakes to taste.
3. Spread sprouts cut side up in a single layer on a baking sheet. 4. Bake 400°F for 20-30 minutes, until browned. Serve immediately.

TEST-KITCHEN TIP
Try out one of our dressings or dipping sauces from this chapter with these tasty gems! You may even like them for an appetizer! We also like adding shredded Asiago cheese right at the end of the roasting period!

chicken

This might be one of the first diet books you have read that did not focus all protein intake on chicken! It is a great protein, but we like to include a variety of animal protein and rotate our diets frequently. Eating chicken everyday can become very boring, especially when you run out of ideas for serving it. These are some of our favorite ways to serve chicken and we hope they give you some new ideas for dressing up that chicken breast!

Chicken, like all animal meat, is excellent for Lions, Otters, and Bears. Because chicken is a lean meat, it is also good for Monkeys to accompany a vegetable-based meal or salad. Giraffes—we are sorry—but this section is not for you. If you find a recipe that sounds tempting, we recommend substituting the chicken with tofu or added vegetables. If you use enough seasonings, this can be delicious. But if you don't, these recipes will be bland for a Giraffe. Use your imagination and have fun!

ASIAN LETTUCE WRAPS

We love this recipe! It's a great appetizer, as well as a unique main course and a great alternative to fried egg rolls!

Ingredients

- 6 to 8 lettuce leaves, rinsed and dried (Boston or leaf lettuce)
- 1 Tbsp sesame oil
- 1 medium yellow onion, chopped
- ½ cup water
- 2 Tbsp soy sauce
- 1 lb ground chicken or turkey (optional: tofu)
- 1 Tbsp garlic, minced
- ⅛ tsp red pepper flakes

- ⅛ tsp Five-Spice Powder
- ⅛ tsp salt
- ⅛ tsp pepper
- 1 cup carrots, grated
- 1 cup mung bean sprouts
- 4 radishes, sliced
- 1 cucumber, diced
- 2 green onions, chopped finely
- 1 red bell pepper, chopped
- ½ cup peanuts, chopped

Tip for Your Type
Giraffes substitute tofu for chicken.

What to Do

1. Heat sesame oil in skillet, and sauté onion until browned. Add water and soy sauce, along with chicken and spices, stirring frequently. Remove from heat when chicken is done. **2.** Arrange chicken filling, chopped vegetables, lettuce leaves, and nuts on a platter. **3.** Place a spoonful of the chicken mixture and a little of each of the veggies in a lettuce leaf, wrap, and enjoy! Dip lettuce wraps in your favorite dipping sauces. *(See below.)*

TEST-KITCHEN TIPS

You can modify this recipe by stir-frying the vegetables in with the chicken. Then scoop the entire mixture in the lettuce, wrap, and enjoy!

Homemade Oriental Sauce

- 1 tsp ginger, freshly grated
- 1 tsp garlic, minced
- 1 Tbsp fresh cilantro, chopped

- ⅛ tsp Five-Spice Powder
- pinch of red pepper flakes

- 2 Tbsp soy sauce
- 1 tsp brown sugar

What to Do
Mix well and serve with lettuce wraps.

CHICKEN AND ASPARAGUS WITH CREAMY DIJON SAUCE

LION ●●●   OTTER ●●●   BEAR ●●●   MONKEY ●●   GIRAFFE ●

This dish is an alternative to the more traditional Chicken Divan. The asparagus tastes divine with this sauce! Delish! It is a great dish to serve guests that is easy to make and that can be made ahead of time.

Ingredients

- 4 chicken breast halves, split lengthwise
- 2 Tbsp olive oil
- 1 lb asparagus, cut into 2 inch lengths

- 1 small onion, finely diced
- 2 cloves garlic, finely minced
- ½ cup dry white wine
- 1 cup chicken broth

- 2 Tbsp Dijon mustard
- ½ cup sour cream
- 2 Tbsp chopped chives

What to Do

1. Heat the olive oil in a large sauté pan over medium-high heat. Season chicken with salt and pepper and sauté on both sides until golden brown, about 2-3 minutes per side. Transfer the chicken to a platter and keep warm in a 200 degree oven. **2.** Cook asparagus in ½ inch of water in a saucepan for about 3 minutes. Drain and set aside. **3.** Heat pan that chicken was cooked in and cook onions for about 5 minutes, then add garlic and cook for 1 minute more. Add wine, and cook until wine is almost completely evaporated. **4.** Add the chicken broth and cook until it is reduced by half. Whisk in the mustard, sour cream and half of the chives, stirring until the sauce is smooth and creamy. **5.** Add the chicken and asparagus to the sauce to heat a minute or two. Garnish with remaining chives and serve with Jasmine rice as allowed on your diet.

TEST-KITCHEN TIPS

Cut chicken breasts horizontally into thin pieces, pound with a meat mallet for thinner chicken pieces that cook faster, are more tender, and keep the portions smaller.

CROCK POT CHICKEN CURRY

LION OTTER BEAR MONKEY ⚪⚪ GIRAFFE ⚫

This mouth-watering Asian dish goes great with rice and is quick and easy enough to make any night of the week.

Ingredients

- 1 onion, thinly sliced
- 3 cloves garlic, minced
- 1 Tbsp fresh gingerroot, grated
- 2-inch long cinnamon stick
- 2 tsp curry powder
- ½ tsp red pepper flakes
- 3 ½ lbs chicken pieces, rinsed and dried
- 2 cups chicken broth or water
- 2 Tbsp cornstarch
- ¼ cup cold water
- ¼ cup cilantro leaves, chopped
- ½ cup green onions, sliced
- ½ cup apricot jam

What to Do

1. Combine the onion, garlic, gingerroot, cinnamon, curry powder, and red pepper flakes in 3-4 quart crock pot. Top with chicken pieces. Pour chicken broth over all, cover, and cook on low for 7-8 hours. **2.** Remove chicken from crock pot and keep warm in 200 degree oven, covered. **3.** Pour crock pot juices into a large saucepan. Combine cornstarch and cold water in a small bowl. Stir into juices. Increase heat to high and cook, uncovered, for 15-20 minutes or until sauce is thickened. Stir in apricot jam. **4.** Serve chicken with sauce. Garnish with cilantro and green onions. Goes nicely with Basmati rice or couscous.

CROCK POT SWEET AND SOUR CHICKEN STEW

LION ●●● OTTER ●●● BEAR ●●● MONKEY ○○ GIRAFFE ●

We love this recipe because it is simple and can be cooking in the crock pot waiting for you when you return home from work. It's delicious served over Basmati or Jasmine rice if your diet allows for it!

Ingredients

- 2 skinless, boneless chicken breast halves, cut into cubes
- 4 cups carrots, sliced
- 2 cups chicken broth
- 1 Tbsp fresh gingerroot, minced (or 1 tsp cinnamon)
- 1 Tbsp packed brown sugar
- 2 Tbsp soy sauce or Tamari

- 1 clove garlic, chopped
- 1 tsp Five-Spice Powder
- 3 dashes red pepper flakes
- 1 Tbsp cornstarch
- 8 ounce can pineapple chunks, juice reserved
- 1 red bell pepper, diced

What to Do

1. Mix chicken, carrots, broth, gingerroot, brown sugar, soy sauce, garlic, Five-Spice, and red pepper flakes in a crock pot. Cover and cook on low heat setting 7 to 8 hours. **2.** Mix cornstarch and reserved pineapple juice in a small bowl; gradually stir into chicken mixture. Add pineapple and bell pepper. Cover and cook on high heat setting about 15 minutes longer or until slightly thickened and bubbly. **3.** Serve over Basmati or Jasmine rice.

Tip for Your Type

Lion and Otter Diets can modify the amount of rice allowed based on your diet. For Monkey and Giraffe Diets, reduce or eliminate meat or substitute tofu, and add more vegetables.

CRUNCHY CORN FLAKE CHICKEN

LION ●●○ OTTER ●●○ BEAR ●●○ MONKEY ○○ GIRAFFE ●

This is a great alternative to the processed frozen chicken tenders loaded with chemicals and preservatives, or deep-fried, fast food nuggets. Kids love to help make this recipe. What a great way to spend quality time together!

Ingredients

- 3 cups corn flakes
- 3 Tbsp all-purpose flour
- 1 tsp paprika
- ½ tsp onion powder
- ¼ tsp ground sage
- ¼ tsp garlic
- salt and pepper to taste
- ⅔ cup milk
- 2 ½ lbs bone-in chicken parts (breasts, wings, drumsticks, thighs) or cut up boneless chicken breasts into strips

What to Do

1. Preheat oven to 375 degrees. **2.** Pour corn flakes into zip lock gallon plastic bag and roll with a rolling pin or your hands to crush the cereal. Add flour, seasonings, salt and pepper to taste, reseal, and shake until well combined. **3.** Rinse the chicken pieces. Pour the milk into a shallow bowl. Dip chicken pieces in milk, then drop in the bag of corn flake mix, and shake until chicken is thoroughly coated. Place the chicken on an ungreased baking pan. Repeat until all the pieces are coated. **4.** Bake for 50 minutes at 375 degrees. **5.** Serve with your favorite sauces. *(Check the Sauces section for more great ideas.)*

TEST-KITCHEN TIPS

Try adding BBQ seasoning powder from Penzeys Spices. See the site www.penzeys.com. This recipe can also be used with fish such as grouper fillets, whitefish, or cod.

MJ's Chicken Casserole

LION ●●●   OTTER ●●●   BEAR ●●●   MONKEY ●●   GIRAFFE ●

MJ is a dietitian that I used to work with at Hines VA Hospital—the "queen of coupon clipping," we used to call her. She gave me this recipe and we adapted it for the Hauser Diet. It is really rich, but oh-so-good!

Ingredients

- ½ stick of butter
- 2 Tbsp olive oil, divided
- 1 medium onion, chopped
- 2 cloves garlic, sliced
- 10 fresh mushrooms, washed, chopped (1 whole package)
- ¼ tsp salt
- ¼ tsp pepper

- 6 chicken breasts, boned, cut in half widthwise (making 12 thin chicken breasts)
- 16 ounce carton of sour cream or plain yogurt
- 1 can water chestnuts, sliced and drained
- 1 cup cereal, crushed (such as corn flakes, Puffins)
- 1 Tbsp cane sugar (optional)

What to Do

1. Preheat oven to 350 degrees. **2.** Heat 1 tsp of olive oil in medium saucepan. Sauté onion and garlic for 2 minutes, adding mushrooms and sautéing for another 1-2 minutes. Remove from pan, set aside in a separate bowl. **3.** Heat 1 tsp olive oil and 2 Tbsp butter in medium sauté pan. Brown chicken breasts until nearly fully cooked (about 7 minutes), turning regularly. Place chicken in a greased 9 x 13 baking dish. **4.** Pour onion/mushroom mixture into food processor. Add sour cream and water chestnuts. Pulse to mix until just slightly chunky. Add some milk or soy milk to thin as needed. Pour mixture over chicken. Turn chicken to coat both sides. Sprinkle with crushed cereal mixed with cane sugar. Drizzle 2 Tbsp olive oil over the entire mixture (or 2 Tbsp melted butter). **5.** Bake 30 minutes at 350 degrees until hot and bubbly. Garnish with chopped scallions or black olives. Serve with rice and colorful vegetables.

Test-Kitchen Tip

To reduce the fat, cut oil/butter in half and use low fat yogurt instead of sour cream.

ROSEMARY CHICKEN

LION ●●● OTTER ●●● BEAR ●●● MONKEY ○○ GIRAFFE ●

These whole chickens are just wonderful, and oh so tasty! Cooking a whole chicken locks in the flavors and juices! This is such an easy and delicious dish to make for a family of four or for two people to have leftovers.

Ingredients

- ¼ cup extra virgin olive oil
- needles of 2 fresh rosemary sprigs
- 4 large garlic cloves, cut in half and then pressed with the side of a knife to mash
- 3 or 4 full sprigs of fresh rosemary
- 1 6-lb roasting chicken, washed and dried, giblets removed
- salt and pepper to taste

What to Do

1. Preheat oven to 450 degrees. **2.** In a medium skillet, heat olive oil. Add rosemary and mashed garlic and cook for about 2 minutes, sprinkle with a pinch of salt and pepper. **3.** Salt and pepper cavity and skin of chicken. Stick 3 or 4 sprigs of rosemary in the cavity. Tie legs of chicken together with kitchen twine. Place chicken in oven-proof baking dish. **4.** Rub half of the rosemary-garlic oil across the skin of the chicken, covering all parts of the chicken. Bake on lower rack of the oven with legs toward back of oven for 20 minutes in a 450 degree oven to brown. Turn oven down to 350 degrees. Rub with remaining oil. Cook until tender another 1 hour and 15 minutes. Remove and place chicken on platter. **5.** Pour pan juices into a glass measuring cup while chicken rests. Carve chicken, spooning juices over the chicken. Garnish with remaining rosemary sprigs. This dish goes great with roasted or mashed potatoes and vegetables!

CHICKEN WITH FETA CHEESE OVER RICE

LION ●●○ OTTER ●●● BEAR ●●● MONKEY ○○ GIRAFFE ●

This recipe is a tasty counterpart to those using processed condensed soups. We've made this chicken with all different vegetables and even substituted feta cheese with gorgonzola. Though the ingredient list seems long, various substitutes can be used if you keep a decent selection of spices in your cabinet and some dairy products to make it creamy. Be creative and have fun!

Ingredients

- 2-3 chicken breasts, cut horizontally
- 3 stalks celery, chopped
- 1 medium onion, chopped
- 1 head of broccoli, chopped
- 3 garlic cloves, sliced
- 3 Tbsp butter
- 1 Tbsp oil
- 1 cup chicken broth
- ½ cup plain yogurt
- ½ cup feta cheese, crumbled
- 2 Tbsp flour
- 1 tsp rosemary, divided
- 1 tsp thyme, divided
- 1 tsp salt, divided
- ½ tsp pepper
- juice of 1 lemon
- brown rice, cooked

What to Do

1. Sauté celery, onion, broccoli, garlic, and half of the spices in the butter and oil, until fragrant and slightly softened. Remove vegetables and set aside. **2.** Return the skillet to the heat and add chicken broth, the remaining spices, lemon juice, and the chicken breasts. Poach until chicken is cooked through. Do not overcook chicken. **3.** Whisk in a little flour in the skillet, to thicken the broth. Turn the heat to low, and add yogurt and feta cheese. Remove from heat. **4.** Mix the vegetables back in the skillet to cover in sauce. Serve over appropriate amount of brown rice for your Diet Type.

TEST-KITCHEN TIPS

Making a basic white sauce with soy or regular milk and adding some plain yogurt or sour cream makes for a delicious, much healthier cream sauce that you can use in many recipes that called for canned cream soup.

ROASTED CHICKEN WITH SUN DRIED TOMATO RELISH

LION ●●● OTTER ●●● BEAR ●●● MONKEY ○○ GIRAFFE ●

The relish stuffed in this bird is a tasty alternative to the traditional white bread stuffing, especially for the Lions and Otters. Serve it with polenta or mashed potatoes and a green salad. Yum!

Ingredients

- 1 whole chicken
- ¾ stick butter, softened
- ¼ cup sun dried tomatoes, softened
- 1 sweet onion, chopped
- 1 small bunch fresh basil, chopped
- 5 cloves garlic, sliced
- 1 tsp thyme
- ½ tsp paprika
- ½ tsp garlic powder
- ¼ tsp cayenne pepper
- salt and pepper to taste

What to Do

1. Preheat oven to 350 degrees. **2.** Rub butter over chicken. Let the rest of the butter sit in the bottom of the baking dish. **3.** Mix seasonings in a small bowl, and then sprinkle over the chicken. **4.** Stuff with sun dried tomatoes, onion, basil, and half of the garlic. Sprinkle the other half of the garlic over the bird. **5.** Cover and bake at 350 degrees for 1 hour, then uncovered for another 30 minutes. Remove the chicken from the oven and let it rest for 10 minutes. Remove relish and serve as a side dish. Carve chicken into pieces and serve.

GREEK LEMON CHICKEN

LION  OTTER BEAR MONKEY ○○ GIRAFFE ●

My good friend Pam gave me a version of this recipe that her parents John and Georgia have made for years. She served this to us one day at her house and it was so delicious and easy to make, that we had to share it with you.

Ingredients
- 1 whole 6 lb organic chicken, washed, giblets removed
- 2 Tbsp olive oil
- 1 Tbsp Greek Seasoning (oregano, thyme, pepper)
- 1 whole lemon
- 2 sprigs fresh rosemary
- 2 Tbsp flour
- 1 cup organic chicken broth
- salt and pepper to taste

What to Do

1. Preheat oven to 350 degrees. **2.** Rub olive oil over entire chicken and sprinkle with Greek seasoning, salt and pepper to taste. **3.** Stuff chicken with fresh rosemary. Insert fresh whole lemon into chicken cavity. **4.** Roast for 90 minutes. Let rest for 10 minutes prior to carving. Remove whole lemon. **5.** Carve chicken into pieces, place on serving platter and squeeze juice of whole lemon from cavity over all of the chicken. Garnish with fresh rosemary. **6.** To make gravy, heat chicken drippings from roasting pan in a sauce pan with 1 cup chicken broth. Whisk in 2 Tbsp flour to thicken. Salt and pepper to taste. **7.** Serve with couscous or rice pilaf and roasted vegetables as your diet allows.

TEST-KITCHEN TIPS

Letting the chicken rest after roasting is key to sealing in the juices.

beef

An American staple! Many of us, especially in the Midwest, were raised as "meat and potato" people. So these recipes will quickly become family favorites! Beef recipes are geared toward the higher protein diets, such as Lion and Otter Diets who do well on heavier protein meals, and can have red meat regularly. Bears should eat beef in rotation with other meats, and the meat should always be part of a balanced meal. Monkeys and Giraffes should not rely on beef as a primary source of protein, though Monkeys can have lean beef occasionally. Monkeys and Giraffes may be able to substitute some of these recipes with tofu, or added vegetables. Just as we mentioned with our chicken recipes, be sure to use enough seasonings, even more than listed in the recipes, so the recipes do not turn out too bland. Beef has a lot of flavor, and only needs a little seasoning to make it taste even better. If you are new to cooking meat, beef is a great place to start!

BEEF TACOS

Who does not love tacos? Here is a much healthier version of the fast food that even your kids will love. My nephews love making these with me!

Ingredients

- 2 lbs ground beef
- 1 tsp salt
- 2 Tbsp chili powder
- 2 Tbsp paprika
- 1 tsp cumin
- 1 tsp garlic powder or 2 cloves, minced
- 15 ounce can chopped tomatoes
- 1 bell pepper, chopped
- 1 onion, chopped
- 1 Tbsp cilantro, chopped
- corn tortillas
- 1 head Romaine lettuce, chopped
- 1 tomato, chopped
- ½ cup cheddar or Chihuahua cheese, shredded
- 1 lime, cut into wedges

What to Do

1. Cook ground beef in a skillet. Drain grease. Add bell pepper, onion, salt, chili powder, garlic, cumin, paprika, and tomatoes. Bring to a boil and then lower heat to simmer for 30 minutes. **2.** Spoon beef into the tortillas. **3.** Garnish with tomato, lettuce, cheese, cilantro, and lime. **4.** Serve with rice and refried beans as allowed on your Hauser Diet.

Great Additions

- guacamole • sour cream • black olives

CROCK POT BEEF

LION OTTER BEAR MONKEY GIRAFFE

This is the perfect dish to put in the crock pot before work and walk into a wonderfully fragrant kitchen when you get home! You can chop the vegetables the night before so it will take under 5 minutes to prepare in the morning.

Ingredients

- 2 lbs beef roast (we like shoulder cut)
- ¼ lb bacon, or salt pork, chopped
- 4 carrots, chopped
- 1 onion, chopped
- 4 tomatoes, chopped
- 2 bay leaves
- ½ tsp cinnamon
- ⅛ tsp cloves

- 2 tsp salt
- ¼ tsp freshly ground pepper
- 1 bottle red wine
- 16 ounces organic beef stock
- water

TEST-KITCHEN TIPS

This beef is great served over mashed potatoes with a fresh crunchy green salad topped with Mom's Thousand Island Dressing.

What to Do

1. Place beef roast in crock pot, along with carrots, onion, tomatoes, and bacon. **2.** Fill crock pot with ⅓ beef stock, ⅓ wine, ⅓ water. (You probably will have enough wine leftover to serve a couple of glasses with the meal, if your crock pot is small!) Add spices. **3.** Cook on low for 8 hours, or until the beef is tender and falling apart.

LASAGNA

LION ●   OTTER ○○   BEAR ●●○   MONKEY ○○   GIRAFFE ●

This basic lasagna recipe is great to use when you need to feed a group. Everyone loves it!

Ingredients

- 1 package (32 ounces) lasagna noodles, uncooked
- 1½ cups ricotta or cottage cheese
- 1 egg
- ¼ cup Parmesan or Romano cheese, grated
- ¼ cup fresh parsley, chopped
- 28 ounce can tomato sauce
- 28 ounce can crushed tomatoes
- 1 lb ground beef, cooked and drained
- 2 Italian sausages, skinned, chopped, cooked, and drained

- 2 cloves garlic, crushed
- ⅛ tsp red pepper flakes (if you like it a little spicy)
- 1 tsp sugar
- ½ red bell pepper, chopped finely
- ½ medium onion, chopped finely
- ½ cup black olives, chopped finely
- ¼ cup fresh chopped basil (or 2 tsp dried basil)
- 1 lb mozzarella cheese, shredded
- ½ lb provolone cheese, shredded

What to Do

1. Preheat oven to 350 degrees. **2.** In large skillet, cook ground beef and Italian sausage until done. Drain grease. **3.** In a large pot, simmer sauce with vegetables, meat, and seasonings for 30 minutes. **4.** In a mixing bowl, combine ricotta, egg, Parmesan cheese, and parsley. **5.** Layer lasagna by spooning a few tablespoons of meat sauce in the bottom of the dish. Place one layer of uncooked lasagna noodles on top of the sauce. Spread a layer of ricotta mixture on the noodles. Top with a layer of meat sauce mixture. Top with a layer of cheese mix. Continue layers until all the ingredients are used, ending with a layer of sauce. **6.** Bake for 45 minutes or until sauce begins to brown on top. Let sit for 15 minutes before serving.

Tip for Your Type

Monkeys should reduce the meat in this recipe. Recommended in moderation for Otters just as is, or add more meat and skip a layer of noodles to better suit your low-carb needs. Giraffes can make this recipe with tofu—see soy section.

TEST-KITCHEN TIP

Make lasagna in two 8 x 8 pans and freeze one for later.

MARION'S HOMEMADE MEATLOAF

| LION ●●● | OTTER ●●● | BEAR ●●● | MONKEY ○○ | GIRAFFE ● |

We just love this "comfort food." We serve it with mashed red potatoes and spinach salad with hot bacon dressing.

Ingredients

- 2 lbs organic ground beef
- 1 green pepper, chopped small
- 1 medium onion, chopped small
- 1 egg
- ¼ cup ketchup
- ½ cup bread crumbs, finely chopped
- ¼ cup Parmesan cheese, finely grated
- 2 cloves garlic, minced
- couple dashes of hot sauce *(optional)*
- ¼ cup fresh parsley (or 3 tsp dried)
- 1 tsp Kosher salt
- pinch of pepper

Topping

- 1 tsp olive oil
- 2 cloves garlic, sliced
- 8 ounce can of chopped tomatoes

What to Do

1. Preheat oven to 350 degrees. **2.** Mix all ingredients, except the last 3 ingredients, in a large bowl, using your hands. Press the mixture into a loaf pan. **3.** Bake for 1 hour. Let cool for 10 minutes before serving. **4.** Add 1 tsp olive oil to a saucepan and sauté garlic for a minute or two. Add canned tomatoes and heat through. Salt and pepper to taste. **5.** Slice meatloaf and top with tomato mixture.

SWISS ENCHILADA BAKE

LION ●●●   OTTER ●●●   BEAR ●●●   MONKEY ○○   GIRAFFE ●

My very good friend Marla gave me this recipe many years ago because it was a great crowd-pleaser, inexpensive to make, and a dish that even the kids love. We have made a few adaptations to the original recipe, but give it a try. It tastes like a Mexican lasagna!

Ingredients

- 1 ½ lbs ground beef
- 1 large onion, diced
- 2 Tbsp cilantro, chopped
- 1 Tbsp of Mexican seasoning (or 1 tsp cumin, 1 tsp chili powder, 1 tsp oregano)
- 2 cloves garlic, chopped
- ½ tsp pepper
- ⅛ tsp red pepper flakes for increased "heat"
- 2-10 ½ ounce cans of diced tomatoes
- 2 cups milk (substitute soy or rice milk if needed)
- 10-14 flour or corn tortillas
- 10 ounces Monterey Jack, cheddar cheese, Mexican Chihuahua cheese, or combination

What to Do

1. Preheat oven to 350 degrees. **2.** Brown beef in sauté pan. Drain grease. Add onion and sauté for 1-2 minutes. Stir in seasonings, add tomatoes and simmer for 15 minutes. **3.** Place 2-3 spoonfuls of beef mixture in tortilla and roll it up. Place in greased 9 x 13 pan. Repeat until the pan is filled with tortillas rolled side by side. Pour remaining sauce over the tortilla rolls. Pour milk over the entire dish. Top with cheese. **4.** Bake for 45-60 minutes. Serve with rice or chopped lettuce salad.

Great Additions
- chopped black olives • chopped scallions • sour cream • guacamole

MEXICAN BEEF POSOLE

| LION ●●● | OTTER ●●● | BEAR ○○ | MONKEY ○○ | GIRAFFE ● |

Serve this dish when you want a little something different—a Mexican twist on a more traditional pot roast, served with hominy which can be found at your local grocery store in the Latin American section.

Ingredients

- 2 lbs beef ribeye or sirloin, cubed
- 1 Tbsp flour
- 2 tsp chili powder
- 1 tsp cumin
- ¼ tsp pepper
- 1 Tbsp olive oil
- 1 large onion, chopped
- 1 large bell pepper, chopped
- 4 ounce can of green chilies, chopped
- 2 cloves garlic, finely chopped
- ½ tsp salt
- ⅛ tsp pepper
- ¼ cup fresh cilantro, chopped
- 15 ounce can chopped tomatoes
- 2 ounces tomato paste
- 1 cup water (more or less)
- 1 can hominy

What to Do

1. In a mixing bowl, mix flour with chili powder, cumin, and pepper. Add beef and toss to coat well. **2.** Sauté beef in olive oil until just done. Add onion, green pepper, chilies, garlic, salt, pepper, and cilantro and continue sautéing for about 5 minutes. Add tomatoes and tomato paste and simmer for 30 minutes. **3.** Meanwhile, in a medium saucepan, heat the hominy, adding a small amount of water to the bottom of the pan. Serve the stew with hominy or add hominy into the stew.

TEST-KITCHEN TIP

Beef stew meat or skirt steaks are tougher cuts of meat that are not recommended for this recipe.

Tip for Your Type

This recipe is best for Lions and Otters, however, only with small portions of hominy. Bears can have a moderate amount of both, where Monkeys should have a small portion of meat. Giraffes could substitute tofu for the beef for a better-suited recipe for your Diet Type, but you will want to add much more seasoning.

STEAK AND EGGS

We especially like this dish after a long run or bike ride when we have a big appetite for breakfast. Now that's satisfying!

Beef and Marinade Ingredients

- 1 Tbsp olive oil
- 2 Tbsp lime juice
- 2 cloves garlic, minced
- 2 scallions, thinly sliced
- 1 lb skirt steak
- salt and pepper to taste

Eggs and Stew Ingredients

- 4 tsp olive oil, divided
- 1 medium onion, chopped
- 6 ripe plum tomatoes, seeded and diced
- 2 scallions, chopped
- 1 clove garlic, minced
- 4 eggs
- 2 Tbsp water
- 1 Tbsp fresh cilantro

What to Do

1. Mix marinade ingredients in a bowl. Add steak and marinate for at least 1 hour or overnight. **2.** Sauté onion in skillet with 1 tsp oil until soft, about 5-6 minutes. Add tomatoes, scallions, and garlic and continue cooking for about 10 minutes. **3.** In the meantime, in a separate skillet, heat 1 tsp oil over high heat. Remove meat from marinade and add to the skillet. Cook to desired doneness, about 2-3 minutes per side. Slice meat into strips.
4. In the first skillet, you have two options with the eggs: for a sunny side up version, take the tomato mixture out of the skillet. Crack eggs into the pan and add water. Cover and cook for 3-4 minutes. For a scrambled version, add the eggs into the tomato mixture and lightly scramble until the eggs are cooked. Serve sliced meat with eggs and tomato mixture. Garnish with cilantro.

TEST-KITCHEN TIP

Serve with dipping sauces like Salsa Verde and Guacamole from this recipe chapter.

GARLIC DIJON SIRLOIN ROAST

LION ●●◯	OTTER ●●◯	BEAR ●●◯	MONKEY ◯◯	GIRAFFE ●

This is a very easy and delicious recipe that is great to make for a group of people who love a good piece of meat. The gravy adds a little different taste to an old stand by. Serve with homemade mashed potatoes and roasted vegetables! Now that's good eating!

Ingredients

- 6 lb sirloin tip roast, room temperature
- 6 cloves garlic, sliced in thirds
- 4 Tbsp Dijon mustard, divided
- 6 strips organic bacon
- 1 cup of wine (your favorite red or white, or water if you don't have wine)
- Salt and pepper to taste
- Flour for thickening

What to Do

1. Preheat oven to 325 degrees.
2. With a sharp knife, make slits in the roast and insert garlic slices throughout the roast. **3.** Rub Dijon mustard all over the roast to coat. **4.** Lay bacon slices across roast, tucking them underneath the roast. **5.** Roast in a baking pan until the internal temperature reaches 160 degrees for medium, approximately 1 hour and 20 minutes depending on your oven. **6.** Let roast rest before slicing. Remove from pan to a cutting board, slice and serve. **7.** To make gravy, deglaze roasting pan on top of the stove with 1 cup of wine, scraping the drippings from the bottom of the pan. Heat on top of stove until liquid is reduced by half. Whisk in 2 Tbsp Dijon mustard. Season with salt and pepper to taste. Thicken with a couple teaspoons of flour if needed.

fish

Fish can be a little intimidating to people when they first start cooking. Many of our friends and family don't really know what to do with it, which is unfortunate. Fish is very tasty and healthy, once you get a few favorite recipes down. The key to good fish is purchasing it fresh. Try shopping at a local fresh fish market and ask the seller to suggest a way to serve it. Often times they have some great, simple ideas! You will be pleasantly surprised at how easy fish is to cook. In this section, we've included some recipes that have changed the minds of even the most stubborn fish skeptics! Fish is a fantastic protein and contains beneficial fatty acids, which makes it an excellent choice for the Lions, Otters, and Bears. Monkeys can also eat fish regularly because it is a very lean meat. Giraffes should not eat fish daily, but can certainly have fish occasionally over any other animal meat.

ASIAN GINGER FISH

This Thai-inspired fish cooks up very quickly and is absolutely delish!

LION ●●●   OTTER ●●●   BEAR ●●●   MONKEY ●●●   GIRAFFE ●●

Ingredients

- 2 lbs whitefish fillets, rinsed and dried
- 5 Tbsp dry sherry
- 2 tsp peanut oil
- 1 Tbsp soy sauce

- 1 piece fresh gingerroot, 2 inches peeled and sliced
- 5 green onions, chopped
- ½ cup red bell peppers, chopped

- ½ cup pineapple, diced
- cooked Jasmine rice

TEST-KITCHEN TIP

Substitute 1 to 2 tsp vanilla extract or apple juice for 2 Tbsp sherry.

What to Do

1. Heat the peanut oil, sherry, and soy sauce in a large skillet. Add ginger and lightly sauté. **2.** Add fish fillets and cook for 2-3 minutes per side over medium heat. **3.** Sprinkle onions, peppers, and pineapple over fish. Cover and cook for another 5-7 minutes.

Great Additions

- chopped peanuts • fresh cilantro
- pea pods

Tip for Your Type

Fish is a lean source of protein, rich in essential fatty acids and vitamins that can be used by all Diet Types, but only minimally by the Giraffes.

BAKED GROUPER WITH CAPERS

LION ●●● OTTER ●●● BEAR ●●● MONKEY ○○ GIRAFFE ○○

Grouper is a delicious mild-tasting fish popular in Florida and one of our all-time favorites.

We know you will love it too!

Ingredients

- 2 fresh 6-8 ounce grouper filets
- 2 medium tomatoes, chopped
- 1 small onion, chopped
- 4 cloves garlic, sliced

- 2 Tbsp capers
- 4 Tbsp butter, melted
- 2 Tbsp olive oil
- 1 tsp thyme

- ¼ tsp salt
- ⅛ tsp black pepper
- ½ large lemon, wedged

What to Do

1. Preheat oven to 400 degrees.
2. Combine tomatoes, onion, garlic, capers, melted butter, olive oil, thyme, salt, and pepper in medium bowl. Spoon half of mixture into glass baking dish. Place grouper in baking dish, flipping to coat. Top with remaining tomato mixture. Squeeze lemon over dish.
3. Bake for 20 minutes. Serve with rice pilaf or garlic mashed potatoes and fresh asparagus.

TEST-KITCHEN TIPS

This recipe is also quite delicious, made with very thin pieces of chicken breasts.

BRAISED MUSSELS WITH CHARDONNAY WINE SAUCE

LION ●●● OTTER ●●● BEAR ●●● MONKEY ●●● GIRAFFE ○○

This dish is easy to prepare, fun to serve, and delicious to eat. Your guests will love it and will be impressed by your culinary skills!

Ingredients

- 1 lb Prince Edward Island mussels
- 2 Tbsp olive oil
- 4 garlic cloves, slivered
- ½ tsp red pepper flakes
- 14 ½ ounce can chopped tomatoes

- 1½ cup Chardonnay white wine
- 3 Tbsp butter
- 1 Tbsp bread crumbs
- 1 cup fresh Italian parsley, chopped

What to Do

1. In a large sauté pan, heat the olive oil, garlic, and red pepper flakes until garlic is a light brown color. **2.** Add the mussels, tomatoes, and white wine and cover. Cook on high until the mussels are fully opened. Remove the mussels from the pan into a bowl using a slotted spoon. **3.** Continue boiling the broth, add butter. Heat until reduced by half. **4.** Once reduced, add the bread crumbs and parsley. Finish with salt and pepper to taste and pour over mussels.

TEST-KITCHEN TIPS

When cooking mussels, wash mussels thoroughly under cold water to rinse away any sand and to make sure any are not alive. If the shells are open, discard.

CAJUN STYLE TUNA LOIN

This dish goes great with a sautéed potato salad! See our vegetable-based meals and side dish section for the recipe. This tuna uses very high-quality, sushi-style tuna. It is a delicious treat for a special occasion.

Ingredients

- 6 ounce center cut tuna loin
- 4 asparagus spears, blanched
- 2 tsp red wine vinegar
- 1 Tbsp Dijon mustard
- 1 Tbsp honey
- 3 Tbsp olive oil
- ½ tsp cayenne pepper
- 1 tsp cumin
- 1 tsp ground coriander
- 1 tsp ground oregano
- salt and pepper to taste
- 2 scallions, chopped

What to Do

1. In a bowl, whisk the red wine vinegar, mustard, and honey together. Slowly add the olive oil to form a vinaigrette. **2.** Stuff the cooked asparagus spears into the tuna loin by first taking a sharp knife and stabbing the tuna loin lengthwise forming a hole. **3.** Blend dry spices together. Transfer spices to a plate. Roll tuna loin in the spices. **4.** Heat a sauté pan for about 1 minute, then sear the outside of the tuna. **5.** Slice, garnish with dressing and scallions, and serve!

HERB CRUSTED SCALLOPS WITH CAPER SAUCE

LION ●●● OTTER ●●● BEAR ●●● MONKEY ●●● GIRAFFE ●●

Scallops provide a good lean protein source and are a great food for entertaining. They freeze well and are a good item to keep on hand in your freezer because they are so easy to make!

Ingredients

- 12 sea scallops, large
- 2 Tbsp olive oil
- 3 tsp garlic, minced and divided
- 1 bunch parsley, chopped
- 1 sprig fresh oregano, chopped
- 6 Tbsp bread crumbs

- 2 eggs, beaten
- 4 Tbsp butter
- 2 Tbsp shallots, minced
- 1 medium tomato, diced
- 4 Tbsp capers

What to Do

1. Whisk 2 Tbsp olive oil with 1 tsp garlic, parsley, and oregano until smooth. Add bread crumbs and stir.
2. Dredge the scallops into the beaten eggs, then into the bread crumb mixture, forming a crust. **3.** Heat 1-2 Tbsp olive oil in a sauté pan. Once the pan is hot, sear the scallops on both sides, heat until cooked, about 2 minutes. Remove the scallops from the pan. **4.** Add butter, shallots, and remaining garlic to the pan. Cook until the butter is brown in color. Add the tomato and capers and warm. Pour over the scallops and serve.

HONEY PECAN CATFISH

We had a similar dish in a restaurant in Florida and recreated our version of it.

Now just pretend that you are looking out over the sunset on the Gulf of Mexico!

Ingredients

- 6 Tbsp Dijon mustard
- ½ cup milk
- 2 Tbsp honey
- 1 cup pecans, ground in food processor
- 2 tsp grated orange peel
- ¼ tsp salt
- Dash of pepper
- 4 catfish filets, 6-8 ounces each

TEST-KITCHEN TIPS

Serve this dish with homemade bean relish for something unique and delicious

What to Do

1. Preheat oven to 450 degrees. Grease a baking pan. **2.** Whisk Dijon mustard, milk, and honey together and pour into a shallow dish. **3.** Mix ground pecans, orange peel, salt and pepper in another shallow dish. **4.** Dip filets into mustard mixture, then roll in ground pecan mixture, shaking off excess. Place on prepared baking sheet. **5.** Bake for 10 to 12 minutes or until catfish flakes easily.

KISSING GINGER SHRIMP

LION OTTER BEAR MONKEY GIRAFFE

We love this dish served over fresh sautéed spinach. It really makes the presentation appealing!

Ingredients

- 1 pound cleaned, peeled, uncooked, shrimp (16-20 count)
- 1 Tbsp sesame oil
- 1 Tbsp fresh cilantro, chopped
- 3 Tbsp garlic, minced
- 1 Tbsp ginger, chopped
- 1 Tbsp soy sauce
- ½ tsp red pepper flakes
- pinch of salt and pepper

What to Do

1. Heat the sesame oil in a large skillet or wok over medium-high heat. Add shrimp and sauté for about 1 minute. **2.** Add the soy sauce, garlic, ginger, cilantro, red pepper flakes, pinch of salt and pepper. Cook shrimp another 2 minutes, but do not overcook. **3.** Remove shrimp from pan. Add about 4 Tbsp water, followed by 1 Tbsp cornstarch to juices in the pan to make a sauce to drizzle over the shrimp. Serve immediately on a bed of cooked spinach or rice.

LEMON PEPPER FISH

LION OTTER BEAR MONKEY ●●● GIRAFFE

This is a beautiful one-pan dish that is great to serve guests. It is light, tastes great, and looks wonderful on the plate.

Tip for Your Type
Monkey and Giraffe Diets may wish to reduce the oil and butter to 1 Tbsp each.

Ingredients

- 4 6-ounce pieces whitefish
- 1 fresh lemon, cut in half
- ½ tsp salt
- ⅛ tsp fresh ground pepper or to taste
- 2 cloves garlic, crushed

- 2 Tbsp olive oil
- 2 Tbsp butter, melted
- 1 cup white wine
- 2 beefsteak tomatoes, chopped

What to Do

1. Preheat oven to broil or 500 degrees. **2.** Place fish in shallow greased baking dish. **3.** Squeeze juice of one half of lemon into small mixing bowl. Cut the remaining half plus the squeezed half into rings or wedges. Set aside rings. Add salt, pepper, garlic, olive oil, melted butter, and wine to lemon juice and whisk. Pour over fish, flipping to coat. **4.** Top with lemon rings or wedges followed by ½ of the chopped tomatoes. Broil for 5-10 minutes or until opaque. **5.** Garnish with remaining chopped tomato and your favorite vegetables, such as cooked asparagus.

TEST-KITCHEN TIPS
Fish cooks quickly. Be careful not to overcook it or it will be dry and tough.

SALMON WITH FRUIT SALSA AND BLACK BEAN PUREE

LION ●●●   OTTER ●●●   BEAR ●●●   MONKEY ○○   GIRAFFE ○○

A popular Chicago restaurant serves a dish much like this one—so, of course, we took the idea and made our own version. Who says salmon has to be boring? This recipe combines spicy and sweet providing a unique, flavorful dish.

Ingredients

- 4 4-ounce salmon filets
- 1 lemon, cut into wedges

Salsa

- ½ cucumber, chopped in small pieces
- 1 green bell pepper, diced
- 1 peach, diced
- 2 kiwis, diced
- 1 Tbsp fresh cilantro, chopped
- 2 scallions, chopped, use entire scallion
- 1 lime, wedged
- 1 tsp olive oil
- 1 Tbsp honey

Black Bean Puree

- 2 Tbsp garlic, sliced
- 2 tsp olive oil
- 15 ounce can black beans
- Pinch of oregano
- Pinch of red pepper flakes (optional)
- Pinch of cumin
- Dash of salt and pepper

What to Do

1. Mix all salsa ingredients well in a small mixing bowl. Squeeze juice from 2 lime wedges over salsa and mix. Set aside. **2.** Heat oil in a skillet. Add sliced garlic until lightly browned, then add black beans, spices, and a touch of water. Heat for a few more minutes.
3. Use hand-held blender to puree the black bean mixture or pour into a blender or food processor and puree.
4. Salt and pepper the salmon filets. Add olive oil to the bottom of a baking dish. Squeeze lemon juice over the fish and drop lemon wedges over the fish to cook together. Bake in 400 degree oven for about 7 to 8 minutes. **5.** Serve salmon on top of black bean puree, topped with salsa.

"Sanibel" BBQ Shrimp with Bacon Served with Pineapple Pepper Kabobs

Lion ● ● ●   Otter ● ● ●   Bear ● ●   Monkey ● ●   Giraffe ●

We were inspired to create this recipe from one of our favorite restaurants in Sanibel Island, Florida. You can create a little sunset on the beach with these tasty treats that can be used as an appetizer or main dish. They will disappear quickly if you serve them at parties!

Ingredients

- 24 16-20 count shrimp, peeled, deveined, washed and dried
- 12 slices bacon (organic nitrate free)
- ⅓ fresh pineapple (we like it fresh, but canned will do)
- 1 small can water chestnuts, sliced
- 1 green pepper, chopped in chunks
- 1 onion, chopped in chunks

BBQ Sauce

- 1 cup ketchup
- 1 tsp mustard
- 1 Tbsp dried onion flakes
- 2 Tbsp brown sugar
- 1 Tbsp soy sauce
- 1 Tbsp Worcestershire sauce
- ½ tsp garlic powder

Test-Kitchen Tips

BBQ sauce can burn very easily when grilling. Brush lightly and watch closely. It is best to baste a number of times versus slathering with sauce.

What to Do

1. Preheat oven to 400 degrees. 2. Cook bacon on a cookie sheet at 400 degrees until partially cooked, but not brown. 3. Skewer alternating pineapple, onion, green pepper, and water chestnuts. Place off to the side. 4. Combine all of the BBQ sauce ingredients together in a small bowl. Dip shrimp in BBQ sauce and coat. 5. Wrap a half-piece of bacon around each shrimp. Repeat for all shrimp, then skewer. Brush with BBQ sauce. Broil or grill skewers for approximately 3 minutes per side. Brush again with sauce. Serve with baked sweet potato or salad! *Yum!*

Sautéed Sole Filet with Mushroom Butter Sauce

LION	OTTER	BEAR	MONKEY	GIRAFFE ●

I made this dish for some "finicky eater" friends and even they loved it! Even the worst fish-haters will love this dish. The fish is very mild and takes on the taste of the other ingredients. It's not only delicious, but looks great and cooks up fast!

Ingredients

- 2 8-ounce Dover sole filets
- 2 Tbsp olive oil
- 1 cup Chardonnay wine
- 2 shallots, peeled and chopped
- 4 fresh mushrooms, sliced
- 2 plum tomatoes, diced
- 1 sprig of fresh thyme, minced
- 2 Tbsp butter

TEST-KITCHEN TIPS

Serve with Green Beans Almondine from our vegetable section.

What to Do

1. Preheat oven to 400 degrees. **2.** Pour 1-2 Tbsp oil in the bottom of a baking pan. Roll fish in oil, then salt and pepper to taste. Bake for 10 minutes, or until the fish is white. Remove from oven and set aside. **3.** Heat 1 Tbsp olive oil in a saucepan and add shallots. Heat for 1-2 minutes. Add mushrooms, heating for 2 minutes, then add tomatoes and wine, heating until sauce is reduced by half. Add butter and thyme. **4.** Pour sauce over the fish and serve with your favorite rice and vegetables.

SHRIMP AND PORTABELLO BROCHETTE

| LION | OTTER | BEAR | MONKEY  | GIRAFFE |

Quick, delicious, nutritious, and good for all Hauser Diets! You'll step up the backyard BBQ with this lovely dish!

Ingredients

- 12 uncooked shrimp, deveined *(See note below.)*
- 2 red bell peppers, sliced into medium-sized chunks
- 1 onion, sliced to medium-sized chunks
- 1 portabello mushroom, sliced into medium-sized chunks
- 1 cup spinach leaves, whole
- 4 cloves garlic, sliced
- 4 Tbsp olive oil, divided in half
- a couple dashes red pepper flakes
- a couple drizzles of Balsamic vinegar

What to Do

1. Preheat oven to 450 degrees or low broil. **2.** In a medium bowl, toss the red bell pepper, onion, and mushroom with 2 cloves garlic, dash of chili flakes, 2 Tbsp olive oil, salt, and pepper. **3.** Skewer the shrimp and vegetables and place on baking sheet. Broil or grill the skewers for 3 minutes per side or until desired doneness. **4.** In a sauté pan, heat 1 Tbsp olive oil over medium high heat. Sauté 2 cloves garlic and a dash of chili flakes for 2 minutes. Add the spinach and lightly sauté until just wilted. **5.** Serve skewers atop bed of spinach and drizzle with Balsamic vinegar.

TEST-KITCHEN TIPS

To de-vein shrimp, wash the shrimp and remove the dark vein by making a shallow cut lengthwise along the back of the shrimp's body and pulling out the vein upward once it is exposed. Discard the vein. Many shrimp come already deveined.

SPICY SHRIMP OVER JASMINE RICE

Lion	Otter ○○	Bear	Monkey ○○	Giraffe

You'll love making this spicy Thai-inspired dish for your friends when they come over for movie night. Try eating with chop sticks on cute square plates. Remember, a great presentation makes the food taste even better!

Ingredients

- 16 uncooked, washed, deveined, large shrimp
- 3 Tbsp cornstarch
- 2 Tbsp sesame seed oil
- 2 red bell peppers, chopped into 1-inch chunks
- 1 Thai chili pepper, chopped into 1-inch chunks
- 3 Tbsp peanuts
- 2 Tbsp scallion, chopped finely
- 1 Tbsp garlic, minced finely
- 1 Tbsp fresh ginger, minced (or 1 tsp dried)
- 4 Tbsp brown sugar
- 4 Tbsp soy sauce
- 1 cup water
- ½ cup fresh cilantro, chopped coarsely (or 2 Tbsp dried)
- 1½ cups jasmine rice, cooked

Tip for Your Type

Lions and Otters reduce or eliminate the rice. Monkeys and Giraffes may increase veggies and reduce shrimp.

What to Do

1. Place the cornstarch in a small bowl and roll shrimp in cornstarch to coat. Set aside. **2.** Heat the sesame seed oil in a wok or sauté pan. Add shrimp and quickly move it around the pan until skin just starts to turn pink. Remove with a slotted spoon and set aside. **3.** Add peppers and cook quickly until slightly brown. Add garlic, ginger, brown sugar, and soy sauce and bring to a boil. **4.** Mix in 1 cup of water and simmer around 1-2 minutes. Add back the cooked shrimp, cilantro, scallions, and peanuts. Cook until the sauce is thick, about 1-2 more minutes, being careful not to overcook the shrimp. Serve immediately over jasmine rice.

Tuna Salad with a Twist

LION OTTER ●●● BEAR ●●● MONKEY ○○ GIRAFFE ●

Tuna salad is one of those things you can make from ingredients that you keep on hand. Sometimes you just feel like having tuna salad. We like to experiment and try different things in our tuna salad. Here's one of our favorites.

Ingredients

- 6 ounce can water packed tuna
- 2 Tbsp mayonnaise
- 3 Tbsp almonds, slivered
- 3 Tbsp carrots, grated
- 3 Tbsp celery, chopped finely
- 1 small onion, chopped finely
- 10 grapes, halved

What to Do

Mix all ingredients together in a bowl.
Serve on lettuce leaves or whole wheat toast.

Tip for Your Type

Tuna is a high protein fish that contains 2-3 times as much protein per ounce compared to other fish. Therefore tuna salad is an especially great food for the Lions and Otters!

Test-Kitchen Tips

Instead of 2 Tbsp of mayonnaise, substitute 2 Tbsp olive oil, 1 tsp vinegar, and a pinch of salt and sugar.

Great Additions

- chopped pineapple • dried cranberries
- green pepper

pork

This is quite a tasty category. Who doesn't love a good pork chop? They are quick and simple to make after a long day of work—and they taste great! Many cuts of pork can be lean, making it a better choice than fattier meats for Monkeys. It is still not a great meat for a Giraffe to have regularly. Pork is best suited for the Lions, Otters, and Bears. The recipes we have included are not going to leave much room for substitutions using tofu or added vegetables. These recipes are very high in protein which means the Lions, Otters, and Bears should be satisfied. But the Monkeys and Giraffes, may find some inspiration from the seasoning in order to create an interesting tofu or lean meat dish.

BACON-WRAPPED PORK LOIN WITH APPLE STUFFING

LION ●●●   OTTER ●●●   BEAR ●●●   MONKEY ●   GIRAFFE ●

Liven up the flavor of your average pork roast. This is a great recipe to make for a crowd.

We made it for a group of hungry athletes after a long race and they gobbled it up!

Rub Ingredients

- ½ tsp salt
- ⅛ tsp pepper
- ½ tsp cinnamon
- ⅛ tsp chili powder
- ⅛ tsp paprika
- ⅛ tsp garlic powder
- ⅛ tsp cumin
- ⅛ tsp cayenne pepper

Meat

- 2 pound pork loin
- 4 pieces of bacon

Stuffing

- 1 sweet apple, thinly sliced
- 1 medium onion, thinly sliced
- 1 Tbsp Dijon mustard
- 1 Tbsp brown sugar
- 1 tsp cinnamon

What to Do

1. Preheat oven to 375 degrees. **2.** Slice pork loin longways so that it opens like a book. Mix rub ingredients together and cover the outside of the pork with the rub. Sprinkle extra rub in the bottom of the 9 x 13 roasting pan. **3.** Lay the pork open and spread one side with Dijon mustard and rub in. Sprinkle both sides with brown sugar. Place apple and onion slices inside, sprinkle with 1 tsp cinnamon, then fold the pork closed. Tie roast tightly with twine. **4.** Heat 1 Tbsp oil in skillet. Using large kitchen tongs, sear all sides of the wrapped pork for 1-2 minutes per side. **5.** Place pork in the roasting pan and lay bacon slices lengthwise over the top of the pork. Thread bacon through twine or T-tie the bacon with new twine. Roast for 50 minutes or until pork reaches 140 degrees with a meat thermometer. Do not undercook. Let roast rest 15 minutes before serving. This will increase the tenderness of the meat.

Great Additions

For an easy sauce: heat 1 can of whole cranberries. Add 2 chopped apples. Blend with immersion blender. Serve with the roast.

TEST-KITCHEN TIPS

This meat goes great with mashed red potatoes or sweet potatoes.

CATHY'S HAM AND PEA CASSEROLE

LION ○○	OTTER ○○	BEAR ○○	MONKEY ○○	GIRAFFE ●

Cathy, our friend and clinical manager at Caring Medical, has adjusted many of her family's favorite recipes to be casein and gluten-free, due to food allergies. This is a wonderful example of how a recipe can be adapted for those following a casein-free diet who still crave the occasional creamy dish. This is a great mid-week meal that your family will love.

Ingredients

- 2 cups milk
- 3 ½ Tbsp butter, divided
- 5 Tbsp flour
- 1 Tbsp fresh thyme
- 1 tsp fresh rosemary

- ¼ pound ham, cooked and cubed (Organic is best.)
- ½ tsp salt and pepper
- 1¼ cups shelled peas
- ½ cup freshly grated Parmesan cheese (optional)
- 8 ounces of cooked elbow pasta

What to Do

1. Preheat oven to broil or 500 degrees. **2.** In a large saucepan, melt 2 ½ Tbsp butter. Vigorously stir in flour. Gradually add milk, stirring constantly, until thickened. **3.** Add in thyme, rosemary, ham, salt, pepper, and peas. Cook for a few minutes. Add pasta and mix. **4.** Pour into greased baking dish. Sprinkle with cheese and broil uncovered for 3-5 minutes. Remove and serve!

Tip for Your Type

This recipe is recommended for Lions and Otters if meat to pasta ratios are altered. Use less pasta and more meat. Choose whole grain, high protein organic pastas for a complex carbohydrate. Monkeys reduce ham and increase peas.

TEST-KITCHEN TIPS

Use soy milk for casein-free diets and quinoa pasta for gluten-free diets!

CUBAN PORK TENDERLOIN

LION ●●○ OTTER ●●● BEAR ●●● MONKEY ○○ GIRAFFE ●

This dish is a tasty Sunday night dinner idea that is nicely accompanied by the kidney bean relish from the vegetable section of this chapter.

Ingredients

- 12 ounce pork tenderloin
- 2 tsp cumin
- ½ tsp black pepper
- 2 cloves garlic, chopped
- 2 tsp salt
- 1 tsp dried oregano
- ⅓ cup orange juice
- 3 Tbsp fresh lemon juice
- 2 Tbsp olive oil

What to Do

1. Combine cumin, pepper, garlic, salt, and oregano in a small bowl. Stir in orange juice, lemon juice, and olive oil. Pour citrus marinade over meat and seal. Refrigerate for 12 to 24 hours. **2.** Preheat the oven to 325 degrees. **3.** Transfer pork and marinade to a roasting pan and roast in oven for about 2 ½ hours, basting with pan juices occasionally until thermometer in the center reads 140 degrees. **4.** Add small amount of water to the pan if it dries out. Transfer the pork to a carving board and let rest for 15 minutes. Carve and serve.

GINGER PORK WITH MANGO CHUTNEY

LION OTTER ●●● BEAR ●●● MONKEY ○○ GIRAFFE ●

Our friend Eva knows how much we love a good recipe. Here is an Asian-inspired recipe that she gave us that is quite tasty!

Ingredients

- 1 lb boneless pork tenderloin
- 1 Tbsp olive oil
- ½ cup mango chutney
- ¼ cup orange juice

- 1 tsp fresh gingerroot, grated
- ¼ tsp Allspice
- pinch of salt and pepper
- dash of hot sauce (optional)

What to Do

1. Cut pork crosswise into 1-inch thick slices. Season with salt and pepper. **2.** Heat oil in large skillet over medium-high heat. Add pork, cook quickly on both sides until browned. **3.** Combine chutney, orange juice, ginger, Allspice, and hot sauce (optional) in small bowl, pour over pork. Reduce heat to low. Stir occasionally, for 4-6 minutes, until pork is fully cooked. **4.** Remove pork from skillet. Increase heat to medium-high. Cook sauce, stirring frequently for 2-3 minutes or until slightly thickened. Pour sauce over pork before serving. Serve with mashed sweet potatoes and your favorite vegetable dish!

TEST-KITCHEN TIPS

Substitute other favorite fruits such as apple, pineapple, or peaches.

Great Additions

sautéed fresh apples

egg dishes

*If you are an Otter trying to add protein to your diet, or a Monkey just maintaining some lighter forms of protein, eggs are a delicious way to eat according to your Diet Type. As you read in the meal plans for the individual Diet Types, slicing a hardboiled egg into a salad can add a nice taste and texture to your typical side salad. Their high protein, low carbohydrate content makes them the ideal mid-day snack for a Lion, Otter, and even a Bear who typically feel great eating eggs in moderation. We love making unique deviled eggs to keep on hand for a yummy snack around 3 o'clock in the afternoon. Eggs are, of course, best known as a breakfast food, but there are limitless ways to enjoy eggs beyond just scrambling them. That's why we included some interesting quiche and breakfast casserole recipes that will surely satisfy a crowd, or even just your own inner food critic. We hope you enjoy these **egg-cellent** recipes!*

APPLE SPINACH WALNUT QUICHE

LION OTTER BEAR MONKEY ◯◯ GIRAFFE

We love all kinds of quiche recipes. They are simple and almost anything you have available can be added. Quiche makes a great dish for a brunch or breakfast for a large crowd. Make ahead of time and heat before company arrives. Serve with some fresh fruit or sliced tomatoes! Fabulous!

Ingredients

- 6 eggs
- 1 Tbsp raw cane sugar
- 2 tsp cinnamon
- 1 tsp nutmeg
- 1 tsp salt
- 1 Tbsp butter

- 2 small apples, chopped
- 1 cup raw spinach, chopped
- 1 small sweet onion, chopped
- ½ cup walnuts, chopped finely
- 1 cup heavy cream or half and half

What to Do

1. Preheat oven to 350 degrees. **2.** Whisk together the eggs, cream, cinnamon, nutmeg, and salt in a large bowl. **3.** Sauté apples, onion, and sugar in butter for about 5-10 minutes to soften. Add the spinach at the last minute. Remove from heat. Add walnuts. Pour into greased pie pan. **4.** Pour egg mixture over ingredients. **5.** Bake for 50 minutes. Let stand for 10 minutes before serving.

Tip for Your Type

Lion, Otter, and Bear Diets could add meat to this recipe—we love Amy's Apple and Gouda Cheese Chicken Sausages in this recipe. Slice and cook up 2 sausages and add into the quiche before baking.

Monkeys and Giraffes should choose lower fat dairy products and avoid meats.

TEST-KITCHEN TIPS

Other great combinations:

- *Chopped fresh tomatoes, basil and garlic, topped with Asiago cheese*
- *Chopped apples, pecans, and blue cheese topped with chopped scallions*

CRUSTLESS BROCCOLI CHEDDAR QUICHE

LION OTTER BEAR MONKEY ●●● GIRAFFE ○○

We cannot tell you how popular these easy crustless quiches are! Brunch with friends is a great way to entertain—fast and inexpensively!

Ingredients

- 6 large eggs
- ½ cup half and half
- ½ tsp salt
- dash of pepper or to taste

- dash of red peppers flakes (if desired)
- 1½ cups fresh broccoli, chopped coarsely
- 1 small onion, chopped finely
- ¾ cup cheddar cheese, shredded

What to Do

1. Preheat oven to 350 degrees. **2.** In a large bowl, whisk together eggs, half and half, salt, pepper, and red pepper flakes. Stir in broccoli, onion, and cheese. **3.** Pour into greased pie pan. Bake until golden brown about 50-60 minutes. **4.** Serve with crusty bread and a mixed green salad for brunch or sliced tomatoes and toast for breakfast.

DEVILED EGGS

LION ●●●   OTTER ●●●   BEAR ●●●   MONKEY ◐◐   GIRAFFE ●

Here are three delicious recipes that can liven up traditional deviled eggs. We have also used these recipes to help inspire more tempting egg salads. Long gone are the days of only eggs and mayonnaise! Eggs can be enhanced by almost any flavor that you have a taste for such as sun-dried tomatoes, chives, or crabmeat, so be creative! Enjoy!

Spinach and Bacon Egg Ingredients

- 6 hard boiled eggs, peeled
- ¼ cup spinach, cooked and chopped
- ⅛ cup mayonnaise
- ⅛ cup sour cream
- 1 Tbsp lemon juice or vinegar
- 2 pieces bacon, cooked and crumbled
- 1 tsp brown sugar
- salt and pepper to taste

Salsa Egg Ingredients

- 6 hard boiled eggs, peeled
- ⅓ cup pico de gallo, or drained salsa
- 1 tsp Tabasco sauce
- ½ tsp garlic powder
- 1 Tbsp sour cream
- salt and pepper to taste
- Garnish with chopped green onion and/ or crushed tortilla chips.

Horseradish Egg Ingredients

- 6 hard boiled eggs, peeled
- ⅛ cup sour cream or mayonnaise
- 1 Tbsp mustard
- 2 Tbsp horseradish
- salt and pepper to taste

What to Do

Cut eggs in half. Spoon out yolks and place in mixing bowl.
Place remaining ingredients in bowl and mix well.
Spoon mixture into hollowed out egg halves.

Easy Breakfast Casserole

LION ●●●	OTTER ●●●	BEAR ●●●	MONKEY ○○	GIRAFFE ●

Adults love this dish too, but it is especially great for kids. We make dishes like this every few weeks to break up the breakfast monotony. It makes providing a hot meal very easy. You may substitute with your choice of meats, cheeses, and veggies.

Ingredients

- 2 cups raw red potatoes, sliced very thinly or grated
- ½ cup onion, chopped
- 2 Tbsp butter
- ½ pound ground sausage, cooked, drained, and blotted for grease
- ⅓ cup cheddar cheese, shredded
- ⅓ cup mozzarella cheese, shredded
- 6 eggs
- ½ cup milk or soy milk
- 1 Tbsp fresh basil, chopped or 2 tsp dried
- 1 tsp dried oregano
- 1 Tbsp fresh parsley, chopped (or 2 tsp dried)

Great Additions

- diced apple • red pepper flakes
- cubed ham • chopped bacon

Tip for Your Type

Lions and Otters add more meat and reduce potatoes. Monkeys and Giraffes reduce meat and add more veggies.

What to Do

1. Preheat oven to 350 degrees. **2.** Cook potatoes and chopped onion in butter over medium heat for about 10 minutes. Press potato mixture evenly into the bottom and sides of a 9-inch greased pie pan. **3.** Spread cooked sausage evenly over the potatoes. Sprinkle cheeses evenly over the sausage. **4.** Beat eggs and milk in a bowl. Add herbs. Pour egg mixture evenly over cheeses. **5.** Bake for 40 to 45 minutes or until the center is set. Tastes great topped with your favorite salsa.

EASY ASPARAGUS FRITTATA

LION ●●●   OTTER ●●●   BEAR ●●●   MONKEY ●○   GIRAFFE ●

Our good friend Pam's dad, John, showed us the art of the perfect frittata when we were visiting with them in Florida. The beauty of this dish is that you can use whatever you have on hand—plus everything cooks all in one pan!

Ingredients

- 2 Tbsp olive oil, separated
- 1 pound fresh asparagus, washed and chopped
- 3 cloves garlic, chopped
- 3 scallions, chopped
- 1 Tbsp fresh basil, chopped
- 6 large eggs
- ¼ cup water
- ⅔ cup Asiago cheese, shredded
- salt and pepper to taste
- 1 medium tomato, sliced thinly

What to Do

1. In medium skillet, heat 1 Tbsp olive oil over medium-high heat. Add chopped asparagus, garlic, and scallions. Cook for 2-3 minutes to desired doneness. **2.** Remove from heat and scrape into a bowl and set aside. Stir in basil. **3.** Whisk eggs and water together in a small bowl. **4.** Reheat skillet with 1 Tbsp olive oil over medium heat. **5.** Pour in egg mixture. Cover and cook for 2-3 minutes spreading eggs evenly over the pan. Sprinkle asparagus mixture over eggs. Cover and continue to cook lifting sides of eggs to ensure even cooking for about 5-7 minutes. **6.** Top with cheese, tomato slices, then more cheese. Cover and cook 1-2 more minutes. To brown the top, stick entire pan in a 450 degree oven for 1 minute. Cut into pie wedges and serve.

Great Additions

Top with Ancho Chili Pepper jam or your favorite chutney or salsa.

TEST-KITCHEN TIPS

Use stainless steel, not Teflon-coated pans for cooking. The key to the eggs not sticking is to cook over low-to-medium heat. Be patient and let this cook slowly.

EASY SPINACH COTTAGE CHEESE QUICHE

LION ●●●	OTTER ●●●	BEAR ●●●	MONKEY ●●	GIRAFFE ●

One of my dietitian co-workers gave me a version of this recipe many years ago at my first hospital job. It makes a great brunch entrée or an easy breakfast to eat during the week for a change of pace! This is a great dish to serve for when all your Lion or Otter friends come over because cottage cheese is a high protein dairy food!

Ingredients

- ½ medium onion, chopped finely
- 10 ounce package frozen chopped spinach, thawed and drained well, or 1 bag fresh spinach, lightly sautéed
- 8 ounces cottage cheese
- ½ cup Parmesan cheese plus 1 Tbsp
- 4 eggs, beaten
- 6 Tbsp cream or milk
- salt and pepper

What to Do

1. Mix all ingredients together in a bowl. **2.** Add the mixture to a greased pie pan and top with remaining Parmesan cheese. **3.** Bake at 325 degrees for about 40-45 minuttes. Let set for 5 minutes before slicing. **4.** Serve with sliced tomato topped with chopped fresh basil or chives.

TEST-KITCHEN TIPS

Add chopped red bell peppers or mushrooms or any of your other favorite veggies.

RICOTTA SPINACH SCRAMBLE

LION ●●	OTTER ●●	BEAR ●●	MONKEY ●●●	GIRAFFE ●●●

We love to whip up a veggie cheese scramble. These taste so good for breakfast, especially after a hard workout, served with a piping hot cup of your favorite coffee (Monkeys and Giraffes)! Ooh, what a reward for working out!

Ingredients

- ½ medium onion, chopped
- 1 bag fresh spinach, cleaned
- 1 medium tomato, chopped finely
- ½ sweet red pepper, chopped finely
- 2 Tbsp fresh basil, chopped
- 6 ounces ricotta cheese, low fat
- 4 eggs
- 6 Tbsp milk, low fat

What to Do

1. Mix all ingredients together in a bowl, except spinach. **2.** Heat 1 tsp oil in a sauté pan over medium heat and lightly sauté the spinach. **3.** Pour remaining ingredient mixture into sauce pan with spinach and scramble to desired doneness. **4.** Serve with whole wheat English muffin and sliced tomato topped with chopped fresh basil or chives.

EGGS BENEDICT

| LION | OTTER | BEAR | MONKEY ● | GIRAFFE ● |

LION ●●●   OTTER ●●●   BEAR ●●●   MONKEY ●   GIRAFFE ●

We would be remiss if we did not include Eggs Benedict in our recipe section. This has got to be one of our all-time favorites, not just for special occasions any more! Once you purchase an egg poacher, this recipe becomes as easy as 1-2-3! Wow, is this good!

Ingredients

- 4 whole eggs
- 3 egg yolks
- ¼ cup butter (½ stick), cut into 4 chunks
- 2 Tbsp lemon juice
- couple dashes of hot sauce
- 1 medium tomato, sliced
- 4 thin slices Canadian bacon or ham
- 2 whole wheat English muffins, toasted

What to Do

1. Bring a 2 quart pan full of water to boil. You will use this for the hollandaise sauce. **2.** For the sauce: Separate three eggs, discarding the whites, placing the yolks in a small metal bowl. Whisk in lemon juice and hot sauce. Set aside. **3.** Grease inside of egg poacher cups with butter or oil. **4.** Fill sauce pan part of egg poacher half full with water. Heat over medium heat. **5.** Crack eggs one at a time into a small bowl. Pour 1 egg into each of the greased egg poacher cups and set in water in sauce pan. Repeat for all eggs. Cover and cook for 3-4 minutes over medium heat. **6.** Hold metal bowl with yolk mixture over 2 quart boiling water pan. Add butter, one chunk at a time, whisking until melted, about 1 or 2 minutes total. Remove from heat. Do not let eggs curdle. **7.** Place four English muffin halves on a plate. Top each half with a slice of ham or Canadian bacon, then a tomato slice, then the poached egg. Pour sauce over each half. Garnish with a few dashes of hot sauce and a dash of parsley flakes.

Great Additions

- cooked spinach
- cooked asparagus
- lox and onion

snacks

It is okay to snack, and in fact, for some people, it is necessary. You can snack the healthy way by keeping portions small and choosing the right snacks for your Diet Type. While Lions and Otters may do well with chicken slices, natural beef jerky, or nuts, Monkeys and Giraffes will do better with carrot sticks or a piece of fruit. Bears can have a variety of snacks and feel good, such as a trail mix of dried fruit, nuts, and pretzels. We have included some of our favorite snack recipes that you can make ahead of time and keep in your office, car, purse, or gym bag. In addition, some snacks we included are better left in the refrigerator. There is something for everyone here. What you need to realize, if you have not already, is that it is better to make your own snacks at home versus making a trip to the vending machine every afternoon for that cheese popcorn, cookie, or chocolate bar!

Veggie Pita Snacks

This is a great way to get your kids and your spouse to eat more vegetables! Using whole wheat pita bread makes a quick and healthy snack, that is fun and easy to make, but definitely more Bear-Monkey-Giraffe friendly, since they are complex carbohydrates. Otters can use them occasionally, where Lions need to avoid using them, but could substitute a high protein, high fiber cracker. Here are a few versions for you to try—but feel free to make your own combos!

MEDITERRANEAN PITA SNACKS

| LION | OTTER | BEAR | MONKEY  | GIRAFFE  |

Ooh, I just love these—every time I think of this recipe I want to make them! Of course, the recipe includes four of my favorite ingredients—fresh tomato and basil, garlic and olive oil! Yummy!

Ingredients

- 2 whole wheat pita breads, sliced open and quartered
- 2 tsp olive oil
- 2 Tbsp chopped fresh basil
- 16 cherry tomatoes, halved
- ¼ tsp Kosher salt
- dash of garlic powder and pepper
- 2 Tbsp Parmesan cheese, shredded

Great Additions

For a little extra creaminess, spread pitas with a layer of goat cheese or cream cheese before adding the topping.

What to Do

1. Preheat oven to 350 degrees. **2.** Place pitas on a baking sheet. Lightly brush pitas with olive oil and sprinkle with Kosher salt. **3.** Place chopped basil, then tomato halves on each pita wedge. Sprinkle with garlic powder and pepper to taste. Sprinkle with Parmesan cheese. **4.** Bake until cheese is browned slightly and tomatoes are soft, about 5 minutes. Serve warm or at room temperature.

CREAM CHEESE AND CUCUMBER MINI PITAS

LION OTTER BEAR  MONKEY  GIRAFFE

These little cucumber sandwiches have special meaning to me. My mom used to make these for me when I came home from school as a youngster!

Ingredients

- 2 whole wheat pita breads, quartered but left intact as a pocket
- 4 Tbsp cream cheese
- ½ tsp dill (optional)
- ¼ tsp Kosher salt
- 1 medium cucumber, peeled, thinly sliced
- 1 small onion, cut into very thin rings

What to Do

Spread inside of pita quarters with cream cheese. Sprinkle with dill and salt. Insert cucumber and onion slices. There you have it—mini pita snack sandwiches!

PEANUT BUTTER AND APPLE MINI PITAS

LION OTTER BEAR MONKEY  GIRAFFE

Kids especially love these little pitas. It's a fun thing to make and a great way to get in some extra fruits and vegetables. Make up a batch the night before and the kids can stuff the pitas and chow down when they get home from school.

Ingredients

- 2 whole wheat pitas, quartered but left intact as a pocket
- 3 Tbsp organic peanut butter
- 1 medium apple, cored, thinly sliced
- 1 stalk celery, thinly chopped
- ¼ tsp salt
- 1 tsp honey (if desired)
- dash of lemon juice
- 1 Tbsp raisins

Tip for Your Type

Lions could substitute lettuce leaves for pita bread to make a mini-lettuce wrap.

TEST-KITCHEN TIPS

Use mini pitas instead of whole pitas if you can find them.

What to Do

Place apples, celery pieces, salt, honey, dash of lemon juice, and raisins in a small bowl and combine. Spread pitas with peanut butter. Stuff pita quarters with apple mixture. Serve. Yummy!

Meat Roll-ups

These little roll-ups are so easy to make and easy to carry with you. They are generally best for the higher protein Lion and Otter Diets. Use your imagination and your favorite combinations! Here are some of our favorites.

CREAMY HAM ROLL-UP

 LION ● ● ○ OTTER ● ● ○ BEAR ○ ○ MONKEY ● GIRAFFE ●

Ingredients

- 2 slices organic ham, thinly sliced
- 1 Tbsp cream cheese
- 1 Tbsp chopped chives
- 4 green olives, chopped

What to Do

Spread cream cheese on slices of ham. Sprinkle with chopped chives and olives. Roll and eat!

SPICY TURKEY CRAN ROLL-UP

 LION ● ● ○ OTTER ● ● ○ BEAR ○ ○ MONKEY ● GIRAFFE ●

Ingredients

- 2 slices organic turkey, thinly sliced
- 2 tsp spicy cranberry stone mustard
- 1 Tbsp almonds, slivered
- 1 leaf Romaine lettuce, chopped

What to Do

Spread turkey slices with mustard. Sprinkle with almonds and chopped lettuce and roll!

BEEF AND BLUE ROLL-UP

LION  OTTER ● ● ● BEAR ● ● MONKEY ● GIRAFFE ●

Ingredients

- 2 slices organic roast beef, thinly sliced
- 1 Tbsp blue cheese, crumbled
- 1 Tbsp red onion, chopped
- 1 gerkin pickle, halved

What to Do

Spread blue cheese on beef slices. Top with red onion and pickle slice. Roll and eat!

GRANOLA PEANUT BUTTER BALLS

LION OTTER BEAR MONKEY ● ● GIRAFFE

These are a great after school snack or little dessert.

They're even good for a quick breakfast on the run!

Ingredients

- 2 Tbsp honey
- ¼ cup organic peanut butter
- 1 cup granola or your favorite healthy cereal
- 2-4 Tbsp soy milk, or as needed
- Shredded coconut or chopped nuts as desired

What to Do

1. In a large bowl, mix peanut butter with 2 Tbsp milk. Using a spatula, stir in granola or cereal. **2.** Form into balls. Chill. If balls are not sticking together, add more peanut butter. **3.** Roll the balls in shredded coconut or chopped nuts for added protein.

TEST-KITCHEN TIPS

This is a great way to get some fiber in your diet if you choose cereal with at least 4 grams of fiber per serving. Use gluten-free cereal if you have allergies.

Tip for Your Type

This is a high fat snack, so Lions and Otters do best with this. Adding dried fruits plus cereals make it more Monkey friendly. Adding more nuts make it even more Lion and Otter friendly.

HOMEMADE GRANOLA

LION   OTTER   BEAR ●●●   MONKEY ○○   GIRAFFE

One of my good friends gave me this recipe. It's a favorite that Kurt's grandma and mom used to make. He was nice enough to pass it along to us.

Ingredients

- 3 cups old-fashioned oats
- ½ cup chopped walnuts
- ½ cup chopped pecans
- ½ cup sliced almonds
- ½ cup hazelnuts
- ½ cup bran
- 1 cup shredded coconut
- 2 tsp ground cinnamon

- ½ tsp ground nutmeg
- ¼ tsp ground cloves
- ½ cup butter
- 2 Tbsp lightly packed brown sugar
- ¼ cup honey
- 2 tsp pure vanilla extract
- ¾ cup dried cranberries

What to Do

1. Preheat the oven to 325 degrees. Line a baking sheet with parchment paper and set aside. **2.** In a large bowl, combine the oats, nuts, bran, coconut, and spices. Set aside. **3.** In a small saucepan, melt the butter. Add honey, brown sugar, and vanilla extract, and mix well. Pour over dry ingredients and toss well. **4.** Spread the granola on the prepared pan and bake for about 30 minutes, stirring every 10 minutes. Remove from the oven and allow to cool. Mix in cranberries or raisins. Store in an air-tight container.

Tip for Your Type

Otters eliminate dried fruits and sugar and increase the nuts. Monkeys and Giraffes reduce the nuts and coconut, and add more fruit.

HEALTHY HIGH FIBER SNACK MIX

LION ●   OTTER ○○   BEAR ●●●   MONKEY ●●●   GIRAFFE ○○

Most of us have tried "Chex Mix" or made it for a party. Put a bowl out and watch it disappear! This is a healthier alternative to the traditional snack mix. Feel free to use your imagination and try other ingredients!

Ingredients

- 4 cups high fiber health cereal
- ½ cup cashews
- ½ cup sunflower seeds
- ½ cup raisins or dried cranberries
- ½ cup dried chopped apricots
- ½ cup mini pretzels
- ½ cup sesame sticks

What to Do

Mix all ingredients together and store in a zip-lock bag or plastic container.

QUICK AND EASY SNACK IDEAS

Sometimes you just can't eat another rice cake or celery stick. Here are five of our favorite quick and easy snack ideas that we use ourselves, as well as recommend for our clients.

Five Easy Lion and Otter Friendly Snack Ideas

- Organic turkey or beef jerky or cheese sticks
- Hard boiled eggs (or try deviled eggs)
- Cashews, peanuts, or almonds
- Whole ricotta cheese topped with cinnamon and slivered almonds (add a pinch of stevia for sweetness if needed)
- Green olives stuffed with blue cheese, wrapped in a basil leaf

Five Easy Bear Snack ideas

- Almond butter spread on organic toasted wheat crackers
- Peanut butter spread on celery sticks, topped with a couple of raisins (ants on a log!)
- ¼ cup cottage cheese topped with a dollop of crushed pineapple
- Mini pizza crackers: whole grain crackers, spread with a tsp of tomato sauce or a thin slice of fresh tomato, a slice of fresh mozzarella cheese, and a fresh basil leaf. Toast in the toaster oven for a minute.
- Sliced avocado sprinkled with Balsamic vinegar and salt alone or atop ½ whole grain English muffin.

Five Easy Monkey and Giraffe Friendly Snack Ideas

- Plain yogurt (1 cup) blended with your favorite herbs and spices. Serve with raw veggies such as red and green pepper slices, broccoli, or cherry tomatoes.
- Plain Greek yogurt (1 cup) mixed with a tsp of honey and cinnamon. Serve with fresh berries, peach or apple slices.
- Shredded Romaine lettuce sprinkled with Balsamic vinegar topped with fresh tomato slices and Kosher salt.
- ¼ cup low fat cottage cheese topped with pickled beets
- 1 whole grain La Tortilla Factory tortilla topped with vegetarian refried beans, fresh salsa, and chopped cilantro

legumes

Legumes are a great source of plant-based protein, though technically we have classified them as a complex carbohydrate, because they are high in carbs. This means legumes are great for Bears, Monkeys, and Giraffes. Lions and Otters can have them as a side dish to a meaty main course.

Legumes provide our diets with a lot of vitamins and fiber, and they can easily make meals more interesting by being added to a green salad, rice pilaf, or a hot soup. Legumes are also very affordable, especially when purchased dried in a bag. With all of these great qualities, we're surprised that more people do not regularly eat legumes. Other cultures eat them daily, but many Americans do not have a single legume in their kitchen! We think that it is simply because people just do not know how to make legumes taste good. Possibly all you think of when you hear the word "legume" is boiled, flavorless lima beans that your mother used to make you eat before leaving the dinner table. Well, we promise you that our recipes will make you look at legumes in a whole new light and actually want to eat them!

BLACK BEAN BURGERS

LION OTTER BEAR  MONKEY GIRAFFE

Black bean burgers are a great vegetarian substitute for hamburgers, yet do not contain the preservatives and chemicals that some of the packaged vegetarian "burgers" contain.

Ingredients

- 15 ounce can of black beans, drained
- 1 small onion, chopped
- ½ cup walnuts, chopped
- 2 cloves garlic, sliced
- 1 tsp cumin
- 1 tsp oregano
- ½ tsp chili powder
- ¾ cup bread crumbs (more if burgers are too wet)
- 1 egg
- salt and pepper to taste
- dash of hot sauce
- 1 Tbsp olive oil

What to Do

1. Place onion, garlic, and walnuts in food processor. Process until diced. Add black beans, bread crumbs, spices, and hot sauce. Blend for a moment. If you are not using a food processor, dice the onion and garlic, and use a masher. **2.** Beat egg in medium mixing bowl. Add bean mixture from the food processor and mix with hands. Form mixture into 4 patties, depending on your size preference. **3.** Stack the patties in a food storage container with a piece of waxed paper between them. Refrigerate at least 1 hour. **4.** Heat oil in skillet on medium heat. Cook each patty for about 5 minutes per side. Serve on a whole grain bun or topped with salsa on a bed of lettuce.

TEST-KITCHEN TIPS

Feel free to experiment with this recipe. For a total vegan burger, try using silken tofu instead of the egg. Try sunflower seeds instead of walnuts or use half corn and half onion. You can also experiment with your favorite ingredients, such as sun-dried tomatoes.

Great Additions

- dollop of yogurt • slice of cheese
- diced tomatoes • avocado slices
(or make guacamole) • chopped cilantro

BLACK BEAN ENCHILADAS WITH SALSA VERDE

LION OTTER ⚫⚫ BEAR ⚫⚫⚫ MONKEY ⚫⚫⚫ GIRAFFE ⚫⚫⚫

The ingredient list is long but these are very common ingredients. Most of the ingredients are just duplicated in the salsa. So you can do all the dicing at the same time.

Ingredients

- 8 soft corn tortillas
- 10 ounces grated cheese, cheddar, Chihuahua, or your favorite

Black Bean Filling

- 1 Tbsp olive oil
- 2 cloves garlic, minced
- 1 small onion, finely chopped
- 1 jalapeno, seeded and minced
- ½ red bell pepper, finely chopped
- 2 15-ounce cans of drained black beans, mashed
- 1 tsp ground cumin
- 2 Tbsp tomato paste
- 1 tsp salt or to taste
- 1 Tbsp lime juice
- few dashes of your favorite hot sauce (optional)

Salsa Verde

- 6 tomatoes, halved
- 2 tsp olive oil
- 2 cloves garlic, minced
- 1 small onion, minced
- 1 jalapeno, seeded and minced
- 14 to 16 ounces of vegetable or chicken broth
- ½ cup fresh cilantro, chopped
- 1 tsp ground cumin
- 1 avocado, mashed
- ½ tsp salt

What to Do

1. Heat oven to 250 degrees. Place tortillas in oven until ready to be filled. **2.** Heat oil in large skillet and add garlic, onion, and jalapeño. Cook for 2 minutes. Add red bell pepper, mashed black beans, cumin, tomato paste, salt, and lime juice. Stir while heating. Set aside. **3.** To make salsa verde, blend tomatoes well in food processor or blender. **4.** Heat oil in large saucepan. Add garlic, onion, jalapeño and cook for 2 minutes. Add blended tomatoes and cook for 3-5 minutes. Add broth, cumin, cilantro, and mashed avocado. Stir. Remove from heat. **5.** Remove tortillas from oven. Heat oven to broil or 500 degrees. **6.** Spread a layer of salsa into the bottom of a 9 x 13 baking dish. Place tortillas in a line and scoop black bean filling and a sprinkle of cheese into each. Roll each tortilla, placing seam down in the baking dish, cover with remaining salsa and cheese. Broil until cheese is melted. Garnish with cilantro and sour cream to serve.

HUMMUS

Hummus is a great dip for veggies or a spread for a sandwich instead of mayonnaise! Store-bought is available, but it is so easy to make at home that you will be making your own varieties in no time.

Ingredients

- 1 can of chickpeas (garbanzo beans), drained
- ⅓ cup of lemon juice
- 3 Tbsp of tahini (sesame paste)
- approximately 4 Tbsp olive oil
- 2 garlic cloves
- salt and pepper to taste

What to Do

1. Blend all ingredients together in a food processor or blender except the olive oil. **2.** Gradually drizzle olive oil into mixture until it reaches a smooth consistency. **3.** Place hummus in a serving bowl and sprinkle with paprika and a drizzle of olive oil, garnishing with black olives or tomatoes. Serve with your favorite pita chips or veggies.

Great Additions

- roasted red bell peppers • sun-dried tomatoes
- black olives

Blend these into your hummus for added flavor.

RED BEANS AND RICE

LION OTTER BEAR  MONKEY GIRAFFE

This dish is not only something a little different, but a spicy one to make when you are cooking from ingredients in your pantry when you are down to the bare bones in your refrigerator.

Ingredients

- 3 cups cooked brown rice
- ½ tsp salt
- 1 Tbsp olive oil
- 1 small onion, diced
- 2 large garlic cloves, minced
- 2 15-ounce cans of red kidney beans
- 4-6 slices of Canadian bacon, chopped
- 1 celery stalk, chopped
- ½ green pepper, diced
- ½ tsp Tabasco sauce (we like the chipotle)
- ¼ tsp cayenne pepper
- 1 cup water

What to Do

1. Heat oil in a large skillet. Add onion and garlic. Stir frequently until onion is tender, about 4 minutes. **2.** Add beans, Canadian bacon, celery, green pepper, Tabasco sauce, and cayenne pepper. Stir in 1 cup water. Simmer, stirring occasionally, until well heated and liquid has thickened. You can mash up some of the beans while heating, to help this along. **3.** Serve over cooked rice. Talk about comfort food!

Tip for Your Type

Adjust the amount of rice down and add more meat for Lions and Otters. Monkeys and Giraffes reduce Canadian bacon to 1 piece for flavor and add more veggies.

LENTIL RICE CASSEROLE

My friend Sheila gave me this recipe years ago. It is a great way to incorporate legumes and fiber into your diet, as well as feed a family on a budget. We've tweaked it a little, but it has been an old favorite of ours for years. Feel free to add other veggies as you desire. This dish goes well with green salad, sliced tomatoes and crunchy Italian or corn bread.

Ingredients

- 3 cups organic chicken or vegetable broth
- 1 cup lentils, dried
- 1 medium onion, chopped
- 1 Tbsp fresh basil, chopped (2 tsp dried)
- salt and pepper to taste
- 2 tsp fresh oregano, chopped (or 2 tsp dried)
- 2 tsp fresh thyme, chopped (1 tsp dried)
- 2 cloves garlic, chopped
- 1 ½ cups brown rice, uncooked
- 1 cup shredded mozzarella or cheddar cheese (or combination)

What to Do

1. Preheat oven to 350 degrees. **2.** Mix all of the above ingredients in a bowl except cheese, then pour into greased 2-quart casserole dish and bake for 2 hours. **3.** After one hour, mix in 1 cup of shredded cheese. **4.** Add additional veggies as desired and bake additional 1 hour.

Great Additions

- chopped red bell peppers • black olives
- mushrooms

Add these for added texture and color!

Tip for Your Type

Lions and Otters, add some chopped ham and reduce or eliminate the rice to increase the protein in this recipe and make it better suited for your Diet Type.

FOUR-BEAN SALAD

LION ●●●	OTTER ●●●	BEAR ●●●	MONKEY ●●	GIRAFFE ●●

This is not your usual multi-bean salad. It's definitely got a taste of its own. You'll love it!

For a special meal, hollow out the core of a tomato and serve the salad inside of the tomato on

a bed of dark green lettuce.

Ingredients

- 6 slices uncooked nitrate-free bacon, diced
- 1 large red onion, diced
- 1 red bell pepper, diced
- 1 cup cooked split peas
- 1 cup cooked chick peas

- 1 cup cooked black eyed peas
- 1 cup cooked red kidney beans
- 3 Tbsp fresh basil, chopped
- 3 tsp fresh mint, chopped
- 6 Tbsp olive oil

- 2 Tbsp Balsamic vinegar
- 1 tsp lemon juice
- 2 tsp ground cumin
- 1 tsp garlic powder
- salt and pepper to taste

What to Do

1. Cook bacon until crisp in a small sauté pan, adding the onion and peppers and lightly cooking for 1 minute. **2.** Combine cooked bacon, onions, and peppers with the peas and beans, basil, mint, oil, vinegar, lemon juice, and seasonings. Mix well. **3.** Refrigerate overnight for best flavor enhancement.

Great Additions
- hard-boiled egg slices
- pickled beets.

BRUSCHETTA WITH WHITE BEAN SPREAD

LION ● OTTER ● BEAR ○○ MONKEY ●●● GIRAFFE ○○

Italians cook with white beans very frequently. We think you'll find this recipe refreshingly delicious and good for you! It makes for a great snack or appetizer for Monkeys and Giraffes!

Ingredients

- ¾ cup white beans, cooked and cooled with 1 cup cooking liquid reserved (or substitute canned beans)
- 6-10 black olives
- 1 tsp Balsamic vinegar
- 4 cloves garlic, minced (divided)
- 2 Tbsp fresh basil leaves, minced, plus a few extra leaves for garnish

- ½ cup extra-virgin olive oil, plus additional for spreading on bread
- ¼ tsp Kosher salt
- fresh ground black pepper
- 1 loaf thick Italian bread

What to Do

1. Preheat the oven to 425 degrees. **2.** Puree the beans in a food processor until smooth, adding the reserved liquid, as necessary, for a finished consistency that is spreadable but not too thin. **3.** Add olives, Balsamic vinegar, 2 cloves minced garlic, and basil. Puree again. **4.** Gradually add extra-virgin olive oil and salt and pepper to taste. Set aside. **5.** Cut the Italian bread into thick slices, brush each slice with olive oil and top with a little minced garlic. Toast or grill until light brown and crispy. **6.** Spread bread with the White Bean spread. Finish with a pinch of Kosher salt, freshly ground black pepper, and fresh basil for garnish.

Great Additions

- shredded Asiago or Parmesan cheese
- roasted red bell pepper slices
- chopped fresh tomatoes

SPLIT PEA BURGERS

LION   OTTER   BEAR ●●●   MONKEY ●●●   GIRAFFE ●●●

Okay—green burgers? Weird, we know. But these are delicious and inspired by a recipe we saw while watching one of our favorite TV stations—Food Network! This is a great alternative to regular burgers for Monkeys and Giraffes.

Ingredients

- 3 Tbsp olive oil
- 1 medium yellow onion, chopped
- ½ red bell pepper, chopped finely
- ¼ tsp Kosher salt
- freshly ground black pepper
- 2 tsp garlic, minced
- 4 white mushrooms, minced
- 3 cups vegetable broth

- 1 cup dry split peas, picked and rinsed
- ½ cup dry brown rice
- 2 Tbsp fresh cilantro, chopped (2 tsp dried)
- 1 tsp ground cumin
- couple dashes red pepper flakes
- juice of 1 lime
- ¾ cup plain dry bread crumbs, plus ¼ cup for coating

What to Do

1. Heat 1 Tbsp olive oil in a large saucepan over medium heat. Add the onion, pepper, and Kosher salt and cook for 5 minutes until the onions are soft. **2.** Add the garlic and mushrooms and continue to cook for another 4 minutes. **3.** Add the broth, peas, rice, cilantro, cumin, and red pepper flakes. **4.** Increase the heat to high and bring to a boil. Decrease heat to low, cover and cook at a simmer for 1 hour or until the rice and peas are tender. **5.** Remove from heat and gently pour the mixture into the bowl of a food processor and process until just combined. Do not puree. **6.** Pour this mixture into a bowl and stir in ¾ cup of the bread crumbs. Season, to taste, with salt and freshly ground pepper. Refrigerate for 30 minutes. **7.** Shape the mixture into patties and dredge on each side in the remaining ¼ cup of bread crumbs. **8.** Heat 1 Tbsp of olive oil in a medium sauté pan over medium heat and sauté until brown on each side, approximately 3 to 4 minutes per side. To grill, cook on high for 3 to 4 minutes per side as well. Serve immediately.

Great Additions

Top with BBQ sauce or hummus. Garnish with chopped olives and scallions.

TEST-KITCHEN TIPS

These burgers go great with our homemade sweet potato fries, sliced tomatoes, with or without a bun!

SLOW COOKIN' WHITE BEANS

LION ⬤⬤   OTTER ⬤⬤⬤   BEAR ⬤⬤⬤   MONKEY ⬤⬤⬤   GIRAFFE ⬤◯

Yup, we have some unique ingredients in this recipe. But don't turn up your nose until you have tried it. Of course, this recipe was developed out of a couple of other recipes and goes very nicely with pork. Feel free to tweak it a little more to your taste.

Ingredients

- ¾ lb dried Great Northern beans
- ½ lb uncooked nitrate-free bacon, diced
- 1 large yellow onion, chopped
- 1 tsp cayenne pepper
- 1 tsp oregano
- 1 tsp thyme
- 2 tsp salt
- ½ tsp ground black pepper
- 2 cloves garlic, minced

- 14.5 oz can diced tomatoes, save juice
- 12 oz bottle beer or ale
- ½ cup cane sugar
- ½ cup packed light brown sugar
- 1 cup organic chicken broth
- 2 Tbsp whole grain mustard
- 1 Tbsp Worcestershire sauce
- 2 bay leaves

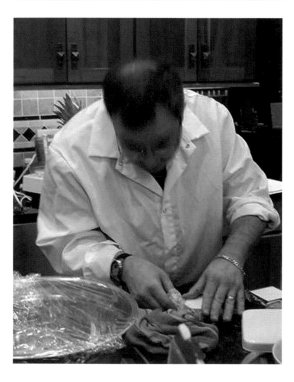

What to Do

1. Place the beans in a large pot and cover with water by 3 inches. Bring to a boil. Reduce heat to medium-low and simmer, covered, until the beans are just tender, about 1 hour and 20 minutes, stirring occasionally. Drain and set aside.
2. In a large pot, cook the bacon pieces over medium-high heat until brown about 6 minutes. Add the onions, cayenne, herbs, salt and pepper, and cook, stirring until the onion is soft, about 4 or 5 minutes. Add the garlic and cook quickly, about 30 seconds. **3.** Add the tomatoes and juices and cook for another 2 minutes. **4.** Add the beer, sugar, chicken broth, mustard, Worcestershire, and bay leaves. Stir well and cook for 1 minute. **5.** Add the beans and bring to a boil. Reduce the heat to medium-low and simmer covered for 1 hour, stirring occasionally. Remove the lid and continue to simmer until tender, about 30 minutes to 1 hour, stirring occasionally and adding more water as needed to cover the beans. Beans should be thick. **6.** Adjust seasoning as desired. Serve with pan roasted pork chops or sliced ham.

THREE BEAN CHILI

LION   OTTER  BEAR   MONKEY  GIRAFFE

One of my dietitian friends gave me a version of this recipe many years ago. It is a favorite to bring to picnics because everyone loves it! It's a great source of fiber using all the different varieties of beans. Feel free to mix them up as you like!

Ingredients

- 1 ½ lbs ground beef
- 4 bacon slices, chopped
- 1 medium onion, chopped
- 3 cloves garlic, minced
- 16 ounce can lima beans, drained
- 16 ounce can red kidney beans, drained
- 16 ounce can garbanzo beans, drained
- 15 ounce can tomatoes, chopped

- 15 ounce can tomato sauce
- ¼ cup chili sauce (or ketchup)
- 2 Tbsp brown sugar
- 1 Tbsp mustard
- 1 Tbsp chili powder
- 1 Tbsp oregano
- 2 Tbsp fresh cilantro, chopped (1 Tbsp dried)
- 1 tsp Kosher salt

What to Do

1. Brown ground beef and bacon in a sauté pan until done. Add garlic and onions and sauté for 2 more minutes.
2. Add all ingredients to crock pot and cook on low for 8 hours, stirring occasionally.

Tip for Your Type

Giraffes can make this dish if they eliminate the meat. Monkeys should reduce the ground beef to ½ pound and the bacon to 1 slice for flavor.

Great Additions

- dollop of sour cream • fresh chopped cilantro
- shredded cheddar

SOY

Adding more soy to your diet can be as easy as substituting soy milk for cow's milk or keeping soy nuts around for a snack. Most regular grocery stores have some soy products available. Ideally, you want to purchase only organic soy foods. Soy is a great alternative for people with allergies to dairy or wheat. Soy is a versatile Diet Type food, meaning if you are drinking soy milk, it is counted as a dairy. If you are eating tofu, it is counted as a protein. We hope that you will give soy, such as tofu, a try in your cooking because it is quite tasty and good for you! As with any new style of cooking, give an honest effort when cooking tofu and use plenty of seasoning, because it does not have much flavor on its own. The fun part of cooking with tofu is that you get to determine the flavor it takes on. The more you cook with it, the tastier the dishes you will create!

GREEK-STYLE TOFU KABOBS WITH YOGURT SAUCE

ALL DIETS

This is a beautiful vegetarian dish with a Greek twist, served with a tangy yogurt sauce that is absolutely delicious!

Ingredients

- 1 lb block of tofu, pressed and cubed
- 2 tomatoes, sliced into wedges
- 2 bell peppers, chopped into large chunks
- 1 medium onion, chopped into large chunks
- fresh basil leaves
- olive oil
- salt and pepper to taste

Yogurt Sauce

- 1 cup yogurt
- 1 Tbsp honey
- ½ lemon, juiced
- 1 clove garlic, minced
- a couple leaves of fresh mint or basil, finely chopped
- salt and pepper to taste

What to Do

1. Preheat oven to 350 degrees. **2.** Soak wooden skewers in water for 30 minutes. **3.** In skillet, heat olive oil and sauté onion for a couple minutes. Add in tofu and sauté until lightly browned. Be careful to maintain the shape of the tofu. **4.** Remove onion and tofu from skillet and alternate slices of tofu, veggies, and basil leaves on skewers. Drizzle with olive oil. Sprinkle with salt and pepper. **5.** Bake skewers in oven for about 25 minutes. **6.** In medium bowl mix together ingredients for yogurt sauce. **7.** Serve skewers with yogurt sauce.

TEST-KITCHEN TIPS

Try Greek yogurt available now in many health food, as well as regular grocery stores. It has a delicious, creamy taste that you'll love.

STIR FRY TOFU, PORK, AND VEGGIES

ALL DIETS

This is one of our all-time favorite meals to make. We make some version of this dish every week. So feel free to use your imagination as well as fresh veggies that you have on hand. This recipe can be easily adjusted according to your Diet Type.

Ingredients

- 1 cup chicken broth
- 1 Tbsp soy sauce
- 2 tsp sesame oil
- 4 tsp cornstarch
- 1 tsp chili-garlic sauce
- 1 Tbsp peanut oil (or canola oil)
- ½ lb pork loin, finely chopped
- 2 tsp garlic, minced
- 1 tsp red pepper flakes
- 1 lb firm or soft tofu, cubed
- 8 oz can bamboo shoots, drained
- 4 scallions, cut into 2 inch pieces
- 2 cups cooked rice

Stir Fry Veggies

- 3 Tbsp soy sauce
- 1 Tbsp sherry
- 1 Tbsp cornstarch dissolved in 3 Tbsp cold water
- 1 Tbsp honey or sugar
- 1 tsp garlic powder and/or ginger powder to taste
- 2 cups of vegetables cup up into bite sized pieces such as red bell peppers, mushrooms, carrots, peapods, and broccoli

What to Do

1. Combine the chicken broth, soy sauce, sesame oil, cornstarch, and chili-garlic sauce in a small bowl. Set aside. **2.** Heat wok or large frying pan to medium hot. Add the peanut oil, pork, garlic, and pepper flakes. Stir frequently to prevent garlic from burning and cook until pork is cooked through and lightly browned. **3.** Add the tofu and bamboo shoots and stir gently until heated through, only about 1 minute. **4.** Stir the sauce one last time in the bowl and pour over meat/tofu mixture in the wok or pan. Stir gently until sauce is thickened and the tofu and pork is totally covered by sauce. Serve on rice, topped with scallions. **5.** To make veggies: mix first 5 veggie ingredients well in a small bowl and set aside. **6.** Heat same wok or large frying pan. Stir in sauce and add vegetables quickly to cover. Toss lightly. Sauce thickens quickly, add more water if too thick. Cook for 2 minutes. Serve along side tofu and rice.

Tip for Your Type

Lions and Otters reduce or eliminate the rice. Giraffes eliminate the meat in the recipe.

Great Additions

- crushed peanuts • chopped fresh cilantro

THAI TOFU BROCCOLI

ALL DIETS

The sauce in this recipe goes great with any variety of vegetables, meat, and noodles. You will probably find many of these Asian ingredients in your local supermarket. They will not be a waste of money! Many Asian recipes call for some of these items, like fish sauce.

Ingredients

- 1 lb tofu, cubed
- ½ tsp red curry paste (or dare to add more!)
- 1 cup coconut milk
- 1 Tbsp fish sauce
- 2 Tbsp soy sauce, divided
- pinch of Asian Five-Spice

- 2 Tbsp sesame oil
- 1 head bok choy, chopped
- 2 carrots, thinly sliced
- 2-3 green onions, chopped
- 1 cup broccoli, chopped

What to Do

1. In a small saucepan, stir together the red curry paste, coconut milk, fish sauce, 1 Tbsp soy sauce, and Five-Spice, stirring in the curry paste well. Bring to a boil over high heat, cook for a minute and remove from heat. **2.** In a separate skillet or wok, heat the sesame oil and remaining soy sauce. Add in the tofu and vegetables, carefully sautéing until the tofu is slightly browned and the bok choy has started to wilt. **3.** Add the curry sauce mixture to the tofu and vegetables, tossing gently until well coated. Serve over Japanese noodles or as is.

Great Additions

- chopped cilantro • sesame seeds • chopped peanuts
These are great to use to top the food.

Tip for Your Type

Monkeys and Giraffes may wish to substitute soy milk for coconut milk for a lower fat sauce. Lions and Otters should not have noodles.

TOFU ASPARAGUS SCRAMBLE

ALL DIETS

This is a great substitute for eggs and a tasty way to get soy into your diet! You may like this so much, you switch permanently to soy! Give it a try!

Ingredients

- 1 lb firm tofu, drained and cut into 16 cubes
- 1 Tbsp grapeseed or canola oil
- 3 scallions, finely chopped
- 1 clove garlic, minced
- ¼ tsp ground turmeric
- ½ tsp salt
- 1 cup asparagus, cut into 1-2 inch pieces
- 4 fresh mushrooms, finely chopped
- 1 Tbsp parsley, finely chopped
- ½ cup Fontina or Muenster cheese, shredded

What to Do

1. Squeeze each tofu cube gently but firmly in your hand until it crumbles slightly and water drips out, removing about half its liquid. Set aside in a medium bowl. **2.** In a medium skillet, heat oil over medium heat. Add the scallions and garlic and cook for 30 seconds. **3.** Add tofu to the pan, sprinkle with turmeric and salt and cook, gently tossing with a wooden spoon, for approximately 3 minutes. **4.** Add the asparagus, mushrooms, parsley, and cheese and cook until cheese melts about 1 minute. Serve immediately.

> **TEST-KITCHEN TIPS**
>
> *Serve with sliced tomatoes topped with chopped basil and a toasted whole wheat English muffin if allowed on your Diet Type.*

TOFU STEAKS WITH SAUTÉED SPINACH

This probably doesn't sound like your typical soy protein dish. That's because it isn't! We hope to show you how you can utilize soy in many different ways—including this "steak alternative" dish!

Ingredients

- 2 lbs firm tofu
- 1 Tbsp butter
- 1 Tbsp canola oil
- ¼ cup flour
- 4 slices bacon, cut into pieces

- 2 scallions, chopped
- 1 tsp garlic, minced
- 1 bunch fresh spinach, washed and chopped
- 2 Tbsp soy sauce
- 1 tsp balsamic vinegar (aged, preferable)

What to Do

1. Wrap tofu in paper towel and set aside for 15 min. **2.** Cut tofu in half, horizontally. Dust with flour. **3.** Heat 1 Tbsp butter and 1 Tbsp oil in a frying pan and sauté tofu for 2 minutes per side. Remove tofu and set aside. **4.** Sauté bacon in frying pan on high heat for about 2 minutes. Add scallions and garlic and sauté for 1 minute. Add soy sauce and balsamic vinegar, followed by fresh spinach and sauté quickly. Remove from heat. **5.** Serve sautéed spinach mixture atop tofu steaks.

Tip for Your Type

This is a great recipe that can be used by all Diet Types. Giraffes will unfortunately need to eliminate the bacon from the spinach mixture. Try substituting a squeeze of fresh lemon juice.

Soy Tacos

Tacos are a flavorful way to incorporate soy into your diet. This recipe is so delicious you won't even notice you are using tofu instead of meat!

Salsa Ingredients

- 3 large tomatoes, diced
- ½ medium onion, diced
- 1 jalapeño pepper, finely diced
- ½ cup fresh cilantro, chopped
- ½ cup canned black beans, drained
- 1 garlic clove, minced
- ¼ tsp chili powder
- 1 lime, juiced
- salt and pepper to taste
- ½ cup corn, fresh or frozen

Taco Ingredients

- tortillas, corn or flour, soft or hard shells
- 1 lb tofu, crumbled
- 2 Tbsp olive oil
- 12 ounce can of diced tomatoes
- ¼ tsp cumin
- ¼ tsp garlic, crushed or powder
- ¼ tsp red pepper flakes
- ¼ cup fresh cilantro, chopped
- few dashes of hot sauce
- salt and pepper to taste

What to Do

1. Mix all of the salsa ingredients together and refrigerate salsa for at least one hour. **2.** Heat oil in a skillet, add tofu, tomatoes, and seasonings. Mix well while heating. **3.** Assemble tacos using your favorite lettuce, chopped tomatoes, and onions as desired.

Great Additions

- sour cream • chopped black olives
- shredded cheddar cheese
- chopped green onions

Tip for Your Type

Lions can have soy tacos without the shells. Serve atop lettuce for taco salad. Otters should use high fiber, high protein tortillas such as La Tortilla Factory.

VEGETABLE AND TOFU LASAGNA

LION ●	OTTER ○○	BEAR ○○	MONKEY ○○○	GIRAFFE ○○○

Everyone loves lasagna for its robust flavors. Substituting tofu for beef provides you with a great vegetarian dish to shake things up a little!

Ingredients

- 12 lasagna noodles (cooked)
- 8 ounces Provolone cheese, shredded
- 8 ounces Mozzarella cheese, shredded
- 8 ounces Romano cheese, shredded
- 1 cup Parmesan cheese, grated
- 3 Tbsp olive oil
- 1 large onion, chopped
- 4 to 5 garlic cloves, sliced

- 4 large fresh tomatoes, chopped
- 12 ounce can Italian style tomato paste
- 2 tsp oregano
- 1 tsp salt
- 2 tsp fresh thyme or 1 tsp dried
- ½ tsp black pepper
- ¼ tsp red pepper flakes
- 2 Tbsp fresh basil, chopped

Tofu Filling

- 2 Tbsp fresh basil, chopped
- 15 ounce carton ricotta cheese
- 12 ounce package firm tofu, crumbled
- 1 cup fresh parsley, chopped
- 3 cups fresh raw spinach, chopped

What to Do

1. Preheat oven to 350 degrees. Combine 4 cheeses together in small mixing bowl and set aside. **2.** Heat olive oil in medium pan, add onion and garlic and sauté for a few minutes. Add fresh tomatoes, cooking a few minutes until soft. Stir in tomato paste until well-blended. Add herbs and seasonings. Simmer for 20 minutes, stirring occasionally. **3.** While sauce is cooking, combine basil, ricotta cheese, and crumbled tofu for filling. Stir in fresh parsley and spinach. Remove sauce from heat. **4.** Cover bottom of 9 x 13 baking dish with a thin layer of sauce. Cover the bottom of the pan with four lasagna noodles, top with ⅓ of the tofu filling, followed by the cheese mixture, topped with sauce. **5.** Repeat three times. **6.** Bake for 45 minutes. Let stand for 10 minutes prior to serving.

TOFU TOMATO VINAIGRETTE SALAD

Feel free to use your culinary skills with this recipe and substitute some of your favorite veggies in this dish. Marinated cold tofu is a great way to incorporate soy into your diet. Try different veggies or even different types of vinegar.

Ingredients

- 1 lb firm tofu, cut into bite-sized pieces
- 2 ripe tomatoes, cut into rounds
- 2 cloves garlic, chopped
- 3 Tbsp soy sauce

- 1 Tbsp sesame oil
- 2 Tbsp rice wine vinegar
- 1 Tbsp fresh cilantro, chopped
- chopped lettuce leaves

What to Do

1. In small saucepan, heat small amount of oil and sauté garlic. Scrape into small bowl. **2.** Add soy sauce, vinegar, and sesame oil to make dressing. **3.** Place tofu and tomatoes on a bed of lettuce on a plate. Pour the dressing over the salad and top with fresh cilantro.

TEST-KITCHEN TIPS

Tofu can be marinated in the dressing overnight and then served atop tomatoes. Adding other veggies can create variety or double the dressing recipe for more robust flavor.

smoothies

Smoothies come in many variations that are as unique as your taste buds and dietary needs. Just like any other food, smoothies can take on an unhealthy twist very easily, so you have to be careful what you put in them. They can easily be as high in calories as an entire meal, so these are typically recommended as meal replacements, such as breakfast on the go. If your diet does not allow much fruit, many smoothies will be too high in sugar. Pick smoothie ingredients that best fit your personality as well as your Hauser Diet. Here are some that we and our co-workers enjoy!

"Movin' and Shakin' "Breakfast Drink

Lion	Otter	Bear ● ●	Monkey	Giraffe

Smoothies for breakfast are great for people who are always on the move. Here is one of our favorite concoctions that will keep you movin' and shakin'!

Ingredients

- 1 scoop whey protein (12 to 25 grams protein/scoop)
- ½ cup organic plain soy milk
- 1 Tbsp natural peanut butter
- 1 Tbsp high lignan flax seed oil
- ¼ cup coffee
- Stevia for sweetening if needed
- ice

What to Do

Pour ingredients into shaker or blender. Shake/blend well. Drink up!

"Doug's a Nut" Morning Shake

Lion ● ●	Otter ● ● ●	Bear ● ● ●	Monkey ● ●	Giraffe

Doug is an Otter who was very successful losing weight on the Hauser Diet. He still drinks this shake for breakfast even though he has reached his goal weight. We hope you like it. Doug's definitely a little nutty—so watch out—it might rub off on you!

Ingredients

- 8 ounces plain organic soy milk
- 1 heaping Tbsp nut butter (macadamia, cashew, peanut, or almond)
- ½ banana (or substitute with ½ cup berries or apple)
- ½ scoop protein powder (soy or egg protein)

What to Do

Place all ingredients in blender and blend on high until smooth.

Tip for Your Type

Lions eliminate fruit from this recipe.

MARION'S BERRY BREAKFAST SMOOTHIE

| LION ● | OTTER ● | BEAR ●●● | MONKEY ●●● | GIRAFFE ●●● |

Marion is a Monkey, therefore this recipe contains more fruit and low fat dairy. This smoothie will give a Monkey or Giraffe energy, but will cause a Lion or Otter to fall asleep by 10:00 AM!

Ingredients

- ½ cup strawberries or raspberries
- ½ banana
- ½ cup organic plain low fat regular or soy yogurt
- ⅓ cup low fat milk or soy milk
- 1 tsp honey

What to Do

Place all ingredients in blender and blend on high until smooth.

Dr. Ross' "Wake Up" Smoothie

Lion	Otter	Bear	Monkey	Giraffe

Dr. Ross loves protein shakes and smoothies, therefore, he's always coming up with different concoctions. Most of his smoothies contain peanut butter, but this is one of his more Monkey friendly recipes!

Ingredients

- ½ cup organic peach mango applesauce
- 6 strawberries
- 1 cup plain organic soy milk
- 1 scoop protein powder (12-25 grams protein/scoop)
- 5 ice cubes

What to Do

Place all of the ingredients in a blender and blend until smooth. Add more soy milk if smoothie is too thick.

NICOLE'S "FEEL GOOD" SMOOTHIE

LION ●	OTTER ○○	BEAR ●●●	MONKEY ●●●	GIRAFFE ●●●

Nicole is always inventing new culinary concoctions. And this is one of them.

Ingredients

- ½ mango (¼ cup), peeled and chopped
- ½ banana
- ¼ cup blueberries
- ½ tub of silken tofu (about 8 ounces)

- 1 Tbsp heavy whipping cream (omit for casein-free)
- 1 cup organic plain soy milk
- 5 ice cubes (depending on size)

What to Do

Place all ingredients in blender and blend on high until smooth. Makes 2-3 servings.

Great Additions

Add 1 tsp honey, a pinch of cinnamon, cloves, and a dash of salt for that extra herbal taste!

desserts

Desserts compliment some of our favorite times whether it is sharing a piece of pie with a friend after dinner, or enjoying fruit slices, fresh from the farmer's market, with yogurt dip. While Giraffes and Monkeys will typically feel best eating desserts or any sweet food, we still do not recommend large quantities of dessert daily for any Diet Type. Think of desserts more for a special occasion. The sweeter or fruitier the dessert, the more it is likely better suited for a Monkey or Giraffe. The higher fat and protein desserts are the ones better suited for a Lion or Otter, although neither of these diets should eat dessert every day. The recipes we've included will satisfy any sweet tooth! Throw away those commercial coffee cakes, fat-free cookies, and microwave brownies and get ready for some gourmet treats using real ingredients.

AUTUMN BAKED APPLES

LION ●   OTTER ○○   BEAR ●●●   MONKEY ●●●   GIRAFFE ●●●

We love making baked apples for a quick and very easy dessert. It's a great way to use the apples you picked at the apple orchard in the fall. Kids love this recipe too!

Ingredients

- 6 large Rome or Fuji apples, cored
- 4 tsp honey
- ¼ cup orange juice
- 1 tsp sugar
- ¼ tsp cinnamon
- 6 tsp butter
- 1 orange

What to Do

1. Preheat oven to 400 degrees.
2. Set apples in a greased baking dish. Combine honey and orange juice and pour into centers of cored apples. Put 1 tsp butter inside each core hole. Pour a little hot water in the bottom of the pan. 3. Bake for 50 minutes or until apples are tender. Remove from oven and sprinkle the tops with a little sugar and cinnamon. 4. Broil to glaze for 1-2 minutes. 5. Quarter orange slices and tuck them into the center of the apples after glazing.

Great Additions

- ice cream • whipped topping • raisins • oats • dried cranberries • chopped pecans • peanuts
These can all be great toppers.

OLD FASHIONED PEANUT BUTTER PECAN CHEESECAKE

| LION | OTTER | BEAR | MONKEY ● | GIRAFFE |

Okay, who doesn't love cheesecake? Well, our friends the Lions and Otters wanted us to come up with something that they could eat for dessert, hence this recipe was born. This recipe is also gluten-free. Thanks also to Chef Joe for sharing his family secret cheesecake recipe. Our food photographer, Chef Steve, loved this recipe so much, he is now using it himself!

TEST-KITCHEN TIPS
Make individual cheese cakes by baking in mini-pie plates.

Ingredients

- 1½ cups organic peanut butter
- 1½ cups pecans, chopped
- 3 8-ounce packages cream cheese, softened
- ¾ cup sugar
- 1 tsp vanilla
- 3 large eggs
- 8 ounces sour cream
- 4 Tbsp sugar

What to Do

1. Preheat oven to 350 degrees. **2.** In a small bowl, blend the peanut butter and chopped pecans together until smooth. Mixture will be very thick. Press mixture into 9-inch springform pan to form a crust. **3.** Beat softened cream cheese in a medium mixing bowl until smooth. Mix in sugar and vanilla. Beat in one egg at a time, mixing thoroughly. **4.** Pour batter into pan covering the crust and bake for 35 minutes. **5.** While cheesecake is baking, combine sour cream with 4 Tbsp sugar. Set aside. **6.** Carefully remove cheesecake from oven. Spread sour cream mixture over cheesecake and bake for another 30 minutes. **7.** Refrigerate for 4 hours before serving.

BAKED RICOTTA CAKES WITH BERRY SAUCE

LION	OTTER	BEAR ●●●	MONKEY ●●●	GIRAFFE

This is another very unique, but relatively healthy dessert that is very delicious.

Nicole loves this recipe so much, she makes it nearly once per week!

Ingredients

- 1 cup ricotta cheese
- 2 egg whites, beaten
- 4 Tbsp honey
- 4 cups mixed berries

What to Do

1. Preheat oven to 350 degrees. **2.** Place ricotta cheese into medium mixing bowl. Stir in beaten egg whites and honey. Mix until smooth. **3.** Spoon the ricotta mixture into a greased 8 x 8 square baking dish. Bake for 20 minutes until golden and risen. **4.** Reserve about one fourth of the fruit for decoration. Place the rest of the fruit in a saucepan with a little water. Gently heat until softened. Sweeten with honey if too tart. Serve sauce warm or cold over the ricotta cakes. Garnish with reserved berries.

Tip for Your Type

Monkeys and Giraffes should use skim milk ricotta, where Lions and Otters should use whole milk ricotta.

TEST-KITCHEN TIPS

Try adding a pinch of cloves and cinnamon for added flavor.

BANANA DELIGHT WITH LEMON FROSTING

LION ●●   OTTER ●●   BEAR ●●●   MONKEY ●●●   GIRAFFE ●●●

We love lemon and orange cakes because they are so refreshing. We found the combination of banana and lemon in this delightful dish to be equally as good as cake! Because this recipe calls for tofu and nuts, it is something that that Lions and Otters can have once in a while. Try it—you might like it!

Ingredients

- 10 ½ ounce package firm silken tofu, drained
- 2 bananas, roughly chopped
- 1 lemon, juiced
- 1 Tbsp almond butter
- 1½ Tbsp honey
- 1 tsp vanilla

Lemon Frosting

- 1 Tbsp butter, melted
- 2 ½ tsp vanilla soy milk
- 2 ½ tsp lemon juice
- 1 tsp lemon zest
- 3 Tbsp sugar or stevia
- ¼ tsp cream of tartar

- ½ tsp salt
- ⅓ cup water
- 2 tsp honey
- 2 egg whites
- 1 tsp vanilla

What to Do

1. Preheat oven to 350 degrees.
2. Mix cake base ingredients together in a large mixing bowl using a hand blender. Pour into a greased springform pan or flan pan and bake for 45 minutes.
3. For frosting, blend with a hand mixer, butter, soy milk, lemon juice and zest. Gradually add sugar, cream of tartar, salt, water, honey, egg whites, and vanilla.
4. Frost cake and chill at least 2 hours before serving.

TEST-KITCHEN TIPS

Leave pan to cool before removing cake from pan.

CREAMY COCOA RICOTTA WITH TOASTED ALMONDS AND COCONUT

LION OTTER BEAR MONKEY ○○ GIRAFFE

This dessert is something that Lions and Otters can make because the ingredients contain protein and fat, with smaller carbohydrate amounts. All of the ingredients are quite good for you—so there you have it—good for you and good-tasting as well! Give it a whirl!

Ingredients

- 1 lb whole milk ricotta cheese
- ¼ cup sugar
- 3 Tbsp dark cocoa powder

- 3 Tbsp brandy (optional)
- ¼ cup almonds, coarsely chopped and toasted
- ¼ cup unsweetened coconut flakes, toasted

What to Do

1. Roast coconut and nuts in a small saucepan over medium heat for 5-7 minutes, stirring frequently. Set aside when done. **2.** Combine ricotta with sugar, cocoa, and brandy in a medium bowl, stirring well. **3.** Refrigerate ricotta mixture. **4.** To serve, spoon mixture into small bowls or plates, sprinkle with roasted nuts and coconut. Drizzle a small amount of liquor across the top and on the plate for garnish.

Tip for Your Type

Lions and Otters use whole milk ricotta cheese, whereas Monkeys and Giraffes should use skim milk ricotta for this recipe. Lions and Otters may want to try substituting Xylitol for sugar.

Great Additions

Serve with a few berries on the side or top with slivered almonds.

EHLING'S APPLE EXPLOSION

LION ●   OTTER ◐◯   BEAR ◐◯   MONKEY ◐◯   GIRAFFE ●

Our friend Kurt Ehling, a very well-respected chiropractor in the Peoria, Illinois area, made this pie for us. We have never seen such a reaction from Dr. Hauser! He just loves this pie—it is delicious and easy! No need for ice cream with this pie—it's all in there!

Crust Ingredients

- ½ cup sesame oil
- 1½ cups flour
- 2 Tbsp half and half
- ½ tsp salt
- 1 tsp sugar

Apple Filling

- 5-7 Granny Smith green apples, peeled and quartered
- ¾ cup sour cream
- ¾ cup half and half
- 1 Tbsp butter
- 1 tsp salt
- ½ cup sugar
- 2 Tbsp flour

Topping

- ½ cup sugar
- 1 tsp cinnamon

What to Do

1. Preheat oven to 400 degrees.
2. Mix all crust ingredients together in a pie plate and press into plate.
3. Arrange quartered apples in a circular fashion within the unbaked pie crust.
4. Heat sour cream, half and half, butter, salt, sugar, and flour on top of stove until it thickens, stirring frequently. Pour over apples in the pie. **5.** Sprinkle with topping. **6.** Bake for 50-60 minutes until apples puff out and topping bubbles. Let sit 15 minutes before serving.

TEST-KITCHEN TIPS

Fruit for pies should fit snugly in the pan so that they brown evenly and do not float into the batter. Start at the center of the pan and arrange slices in concentric circles.

FLOURLESS CHOCOLATE CAKE

LION OTTER BEAR MONKEY ● GIRAFFE ●

We have to thank Chef Steve for this recipe idea—as many of his customers just love flourless chocolate cake—and it is gluten-free! This is another dessert recipe that the Lion-Otter spectrum can have occasionally.

Ingredients

- 8 large eggs
- 1 lb bittersweet chocolate, coarsely chopped (not semi-sweet)
- ½ lb butter (2 sticks)
- ¼ cup strong coffee or liqueur (if desired)

What to Do

1. Move oven rack to lower middle position and preheat oven to 325 degrees. **2.** Grease and flour 8-inch springform pan on bottom and sides. Cover pan under and along sides with sheet of heavy-duty foil and set in large roasting pan. **3.** Bring water to boil to be used later. **4.** Beat eggs with hand-held mixer at high speed until volume doubles, about 5 minutes. **5.** Set large heat-proof bowl over pan of almost simmering water. In the bowl melt chocolate and butter, stir in coffee or liqueur. Remove bowl from heat. Using large rubber spatula, fold beaten eggs into chocolate mixture, one-third at a time until only a few streaks of egg are visible and mixture is homogenous. Do not cook eggs! **6.** Pour into prepared springform pan. Set roasting pan on oven rack and pour boiling water into roasting pan until it is halfway up the sides of springform pan. Bake 22 to 25 minutes, until cake has risen slightly and looks similar to a brownie. **7.** Set pan on wire rack to cool to room temperature. Cover and refrigerate overnight. **8.** To serve, remove springform pan sides, invert cake on waxed paper and turn cake right side up on serving platter. Sprinkle with confectioners sugar or unsweetened cocoa powder over cake to decorate. Garnish with a couple of raspberries on the side and a sprig of mint. Wow!

> ### TEST-KITCHEN TIPS
> *If you use a 9-inch springform pan instead of the preferred 8-inch, reduce the baking time to 18 to 20 minutes.*

FRESH FRUIT SALAD WITH LIME

| LION ● | OTTER ○○ | BEAR ○○ | MONKEY ○○○ | GIRAFFE ○○○ |

One of our absolute favorite things to make is fresh fruit salad. You can make this fruit salad with virtually any fruits. Pick what's in season or available at your local farmer's market. It makes a great side dish, lunch, brunch item, or even dessert.

Ingredients

- juice from 1-2 limes
- ¼ tsp salt
- 1 fresh pineapple, chunked
- 1 bunch seedless grapes, halved
- 1 cup bing cherries, pitted and halved
- 1 pint strawberries, sliced
- 1 pint blueberries
- 2 kiwi, peeled, sliced, and halved
- 2 star fruit, peeled and sliced
- ½ cantaloupe and/or honeydew, peeled and chunked

What to Do

Slice or chop all fruit into bite-size pieces. Sprinkle lime juice and salt over the fruit and toss in the bowl.

Great Additions

- yogurt • raisins • dates • nuts

Yum!

ALMOND SUGAR FREE FUDGE

LION ●●●   OTTER ●●●   BEAR ●●●   MONKEY ●●   GIRAFFE ●●

Lions and Otters find it difficult to find something to satisfy their sweet tooth. Try this recipe out for size. Even Dr. Hauser has made this and enjoyed it with no carb-crashing side-effects!

Ingredients

- 1 cup virgin coconut oil, melted over very low heat
- ½ to 1 cup almonds, chopped
- 1 tsp vanilla

- ½ cup unsweetened coconut
- ½ cup to 1 cup of chopped nuts
- ½ cup erythritol granular sugar substitute

What to Do

1. Pour melted coconut oil into a mixing bowl and thoroughly mix in nut butter using a heavy spoon.
2. Stir in coconut, nuts, and sweetener. **3.** Spread mixture into an 8 x 8 glass baking dish. **4.** Refrigerate for at least 2 hours until hardened in a covered container. These melt very quickly if left out!

TEST-KITCHEN TIPS

You can make this fudge with pecans, almonds, walnuts, cashews, or whatever nuts you have on hand.

Great Additions

Lions and Otters top with toasted coconut, chopped almonds, or melted nut butter. Monkeys and Giraffes top with sliced bananas or berries for added flavor.

LEMON SORBET

| LION | OTTER ● | BEAR ○○ | MONKEY ○○○ | GIRAFFE ○○○ |

Sorbet is such a wonderful dessert—it's so light and cleanses the palate, especially after a nice dinner on a summer night.

Ingredients

- 1 cup sugar
- 1 ¼ cups water
- 4 lemons, well scrubbed
- 1 egg white

What to Do

1. Dissolve sugar in 1¼ cups water in a saucepan. Bring to a boil, stirring occasionally until the sugar has just dissolved. **2.** Using a vegetable peeler, pare the rind thinly from two of the lemons into the pan. Simmer for 2 minutes without stirring, then take the pan off heat. Leave to cool. Place pan in refrigerator to chill. **3.** Squeeze the juice from all the lemons and add to chilled syrup mixture. **4.** Strain the syrup into a shallow freezer-proof container, reserving the rind. Freeze the mixture for 4 hours, until it is mushy. **5.** Process the sorbet in a food processor until smooth. **6.** Lightly whisk the egg white with a fork until it is just frothy. Return the sorbet to the container, beat in the egg white and return the mixture to the freezer for 4 hours or until firm. **7.** Scoop the sorbet into bowls or glasses and decorate with sugared lemon rind.

TEST-KITCHEN TIPS
Serve lemon sorbet with fresh raspberries.

COCONUT PUDDING

| LION | OTTER  | BEAR ● ● | MONKEY ● | GIRAFFE |

Another Lion and Otter friendly dessert that is one of Dr. Hauser's favorites! The toasted coconut really adds a great flavor and makes for a pleasing presentation.

Ingredients

- ½ cup cold water
- 2 tsp unflavored gelatin powder or 1 packet
- 1 can coconut milk (13.5 to 15 ounce)
- 3 Tbsp sugar
- ½ tsp vanilla
- Pinch of salt
- ¼ cup unsweetened coconut flakes

What to Do

1. In a small bowl, stir gelatin powder into ½ cup cold water. Set aside. **2.** Combine coconut milk with sugar and vanilla in small saucepan. Bring to a boil, reduce heat, then gradually stir in the gelatin and water mixture. **3.** Remove from heat, stir in the coconut flakes and salt. Refrigerate at least four hours. **4.** To toast coconut, heat ¼ cup coconut in a small saucepan over high heat. Stir continuously. When coconut begins to brown, remove from heat. Continue to stir. This whole process takes about 2 minutes—so watch closely! **5.** Top with chopped nuts or toasted coconut if desired.

Tip for Your Type

Lion and Otter Diets substitute Xylitol or Erythritol for sugar.

LOW FAT CHOCOLATE PUDDING

LION	OTTER ●	BEAR ◐◐	MONKEY ◐◐	GIRAFFE ◐◐

Okay, lest you think it is all about the Lions and Otters, this delicious chocolate pudding is simple, easy, and will be something you Monkeys and Giraffes will find yourself making very frequently for that little something sweet after dinner.

Ingredients

- 3 Tbsp cornstarch
- 3 Tbsp sugar
- 2 Tbsp baking cocoa
- 2 cups skim milk
- 1 tsp pure vanilla extract

What to Do

1. In a saucepan, thoroughly combine the cornstarch, sugar, and cocoa. Pour in the milk and stir until very smooth. **2.** Cook on medium heat, stirring constantly until the pudding comes to a boil. Lower the heat and simmer gently, stirring continuously for 3-4 minutes. Stir in vanilla. **3.** Pour hot pudding into a serving bowl or individual custard cups. Serve warm or chill for about 2 hours until cold and set.

TEST-KITCHEN TIPS

Try 1 tsp mint extract instead of vanilla for a chocolate mint flavor!

Great Additions

- whipped cream • berries • bananas

NICOLE'S PUMPKIN PIE

LION OTTER BEAR MONKEY GIRAFFE

Pumpkin pie is one of America's favorites and this recipe is no exception. This pie is not only good at the holidays but any time of year. To save calories, try making it without a crust! It works out just fine!

Crust Ingredients

- ½ cup sesame oil
- 1 ½ cups flour
- 2 Tbsp half and half
- ¼ tsp salt
- 1 tsp sugar

Filling

- 2 cups plain pumpkin puree (or 15 ounce can)
- ¾ cup packed dark brown sugar
- 2 tsp ground ginger
- 2 tsp cinnamon
- 1 tsp fresh grated nutmeg
- ¼ tsp ground cloves
- ½ tsp salt
- 1 cup half and half
- 4 large eggs, beaten lightly

Topping

- 1⅓ cup heavy cream, cold
- 1 Tbsp confectioners sugar (or regular sugar)
- 1 Tbsp brandy (or other liquor)

What to Do

1. Preheat oven to 375 degrees. **2.** Mix all of the crust ingredients in a 9-inch pie plate. Press dough into the pan. **3.** Mix pumpkin, sugar, spices, and salt in a bowl. Stir in half and half. **4.** Beat eggs with a fork in small bowl. Stir into pumpkin mixture. **5.** Pour filling into pie shell. Bake about 70 minutes until firm. Cool on a wire rack for at least 1 hour. **6.** In a cold bowl and using cold beaters (refrigerate these ahead of time), beat cream at medium speed to soft peaks; gradually add sugar, then brandy. Beat on high to form stiff peaks. Accompany each wedge of pie with a dollop of whipped cream.

BERRY UPSIDE-DOWN CAKE

| LION ● | OTTER ● | BEAR ○○ | MONKEY ○○○ | GIRAFFE ○○○ |

Pineapple upside down cake is an old time favorite for many people. Here's a variation of it that your friends and family will love. Try making it in individual mini-pie pans as a special touch!

Ingredients

- 3 Tbsp butter, divided
- ⅓ cup natural applesauce (no added sugar)
- ½ cup light brown sugar
- 1 pint fresh blueberries
- ½ pint fresh raspberries
- ½ cup milk

- 1 large egg
- ½ cup granulated sugar
- 1 cup flour
- ¼ cup cornmeal
- 1 tsp baking powder
- ½ tsp salt

What to Do

1. Preheat oven to 350 degrees. **2.** Melt 2 Tbsp butter and pour into a 10-inch baking pan. Sprinkle the bottom of the pan with brown sugar. Top with berries, start in the middle and form concentric circles, fitting the pieces snugly together. **3.** Melt remaining 1 Tbsp butter in medium saucepan over medium heat, add applesauce. Remove from heat. Whisk in milk, egg, and sugar until sugar is mostly dissolved. **4.** Stir together flour, cornmeal, baking powder, and salt in a separate bowl. **5.** Slowly whisk flour mixture into milk mixture. Pour batter over fruit and spread to the edge of the pan. **6.** Bake 35 to 45 minutes until cake is lightly golden and firm to the touch. Cool pan on wire rack for at least 10 minutes. When cool, invert cake quickly onto a large plate. Serve warm topped with whipped cream or low fat frozen yogurt.

TEST-KITCHEN TIPS

Try making this with some of your other favorite fruits: Peaches, plums, pineapple—all work well!

VANILLA-BEAN CUSTARD

LION ●●   OTTER ●●   BEAR ●●   MONKEY ●   GIRAFFE ●

This is a very simple dessert that can be made with almost no effort at all. You can dress it up with extra toppings, use it as a pie filling, or eat it plain—just as is! It's a good dessert for Lions and Otters due to the high protein content.

Ingredients

- 6 large egg yolks
- ½ cup sugar
- 1 ¼ cups heavy cream

- 1 ¼ cups milk
- 1 whole vanilla bean, split (or 2 tsp pure vanilla extract)

What to Do

1. Heat oven to 300 degrees. **2.** Fill a small roasting pan halfway with water to hold 4 6-ounce custard cups. Place pan without cups in the oven. (**Note:** if you don't have custard cups, use an 8 x 8 glass baking dish.) **3.** In a medium bowl, whisk together the yolks and sugar until light and fluffy. Set aside. **4.** Combine cream, milk, and vanilla bean in a medium saucepan, bringing it to a boil. Remove from heat. Remove vanilla bean from milk mixture. **5.** Slowly whisk the hot milk mixture into the egg-sugar mixture until completely combined. **6.** Pour into custard cups and place them in the pan of hot water.   Bake on the lower rack until the custard has set and is no longer jiggly—30 to 40 minutes. **7.** Remove   pan from the oven, remove cups from the water, and place on wire rack to cool. Serve at   room temperature or chilled.

Tip for Your Type

Lions and Otters top with crushed nuts or coconut flakes. Bears may wish to serve with sliced fresh strawberries.

TOFU BROWNIES

| LION | OTTER ○○ | BEAR ●●● | MONKEY ●●● | GIRAFFE ●●● |

These low-fat brownies are a cinch to make, yet are very tasty and Giraffe-friendly.

You'll see a few ingredients that might seem a little strange—but this makes them okay

for Giraffes to eat.

Ingredients

- 1 ⅓ cups cake flour (or regular flour)
- ½ tsp baking soda
- ½ tsp cinnamon
- ¼ cup unsweetened applesauce
- 1 tsp canola oil

- ¾ cup sugar
- 1 pkg Silken Lite Firm Tofu
- 1 tsp vanilla extract
- ⅓ cup cocoa powder
- 2 Tbsp chopped walnuts (*optional*)

What to Do

1. Preheat oven to 350 degrees.
2. Grease and flour an 8 x 8 inch baking pan on bottom and sides. **3.** Mix flour, baking soda, and cinnamon together in small bowl. Set aside. **4.** Mix the applesauce, canola oil, sugar, tofu, vanilla, and cocoa together and stir until very smooth, scraping the sides of the bowl. Add dry mixture all at once, blending until just moistened.
5. Pour into prepared pan, sprinkle with nuts. Bake for 22 minutes. Cool for 15 minutes before cutting.

TEST-KITCHEN TIPS

Dust the plate with extra cocoa powder, fresh strawberry slices, and even a little scoop of sorbet for a beautiful dessert presentation.

sauces

One thing we love is a good sauce! Nothing quite compliments a piece of meat or fresh vegetables like a delicious sauce. The problem is, however, that the food industry has gotten its hands on these. If you walk down the grocery store aisle, you'll see a wide array of prepackaged sauces that contain MSG and a lot of other chemicals. We want to show you how easy it is to make a delicious sauce that will bring a whole new dimension to your meal. So toss out those bottled marinades and dried sauce mixes because the home cooked versions are 100% better tasting and 100% simple to make! Like our other recipes, stocking up on a few ingredients will ensure that you can make your favorite sauce over and over again. Making your own sauces from scratch will prove less expensive in the long run versus purchasing pre-made sauces and dry mixes. Monkeys and Giraffes should try and keep the oils and fat to a minimum when making a sauce, while Bears can typically make the recipes as is, but be cautious of using moderate portion sizes. Lions and Otters, this is a great section for you to get ideas on how to dress up all that meat in your diet so it does not become boring!

BASIC WHITE SAUCE

LION ●●●   OTTER ●●●   BEAR ●●●   MONKEY ○○   GIRAFFE ●

I've been making this white sauce for as long as I can remember. Listed here are the basic ingredients, but feel free to add herbs, spices, cheeses, mushrooms, tomatoes, or whatever you like to change the taste of it. You will never need to use cream of chicken soup from a can again! This is a great starter for all of those casseroles you used to make with creamed soup!

Ingredients

- 2 Tbsp butter
- 2 Tbsp flour
- 1 cup milk
- salt and pepper to taste

What to Do

1. Melt butter in a medium sauce pan over medium heat. **2.** Whisk in flour to form a paste. **3.** Immediately pour milk into paste and stir vigorously, incorporating the paste into the milk. **4.** Heat until thick and bubbly. Salt and pepper as desired. Thin with milk as needed.

Great Additions

• cheddar cheese • Asiago cheese • garlic • chopped mushrooms

TEST-KITCHEN TIPS

If you are making a cheese sauce, add 1-2 cups of shredded cheese and stir into hot bubbly sauce. Remove immediately from heat. This recipe can be easily doubled or tripled depending on the amount of sauce you need.

Tip for Your Type

Lions and Otters can use higher fat milk, where Bears should choose 2% and Monkeys low fat milk. Sorry, Giraffes, this sauce tends to be high in fat and dairy, which you don't need a lot of.

Asian Butter Sauce

Lion 	Otter	Bear	Monkey	Giraffe

You will find yourself using this sauce over and over again. It's so simple, yet so delicious.

This tastes especially great with chicken or seafood.

Ingredients

- 1 cup chicken broth
- 5 Tbsp oyster sauce
- ¼ cup fresh lemon juice
- 1 Tbsp sugar
- 1 tsp Chinese Five-Spice powder
- 2 green onions, thinly sliced
- ½ cup butter

What to Do

Boil chicken broth, oyster sauce, lemon juice, sugar, and Five-Spice in small saucepan until reduced to ¾ cup, about 12 minutes. Reduce heat to low. Add green onions and butter, stirring until butter melts. Spoon sauce over dish.

Tip for Your Type

Monkeys and Giraffes can use this recipe if butter is reduced to 1 Tbsp.

Apple Cranberry Sauce

Lion	Otter	Bear 	Monkey	Giraffe

This is a delicious sweet and sour sauce that can really change the taste of your food. We like it particularly with pork, ham, chicken, turkey, and even beef.

Ingredients

- 1 large green apple, peeled and diced
- ½ red onion, diced
- ½ cup unsweetened apple juice
- ¼ cup dried cranberries
- 1 tsp fresh ginger, grated
- 1 Tbsp balsamic vinegar

What to Do

Combine all ingredients except vinegar in a medium saucepan. Cover and cook over medium heat for 10-12 minutes, stirring occasionally. Remove from heat and let stand for 5 minutes. Stir in vinegar and serve over your favorite meat.

AVOCADO YOGURT SAUCE

LION ●●○ OTTER ●●○ BEAR ●●○ MONKEY ○○ GIRAFFE ●

This is one of those recipes that you will find yourself making very frequently. It is very easy and very versatile. Use it where you might normally use ranch dressing. It tastes great with fish and chicken, or even as a dipping sauce.

Ingredients

- 1 avocado, mashed
- 8 ounces plain yogurt
- ½ tsp salt
- pinch of raw cane sugar or honey

What to Do

Blend all ingredients together by hand or in the food processor. Refrigerate and serve.

Great Additions

- chopped green onion • garlic • fresh cilantro
- basil • dill

This is great for a salad dressing, dip, or sauce.

TEST-KITCHEN TIPS

If you like your sauce a little thinner, gradually stir in some milk.

BALSAMIC BROWN BUTTER SAUCE

| LION  | OTTER ●●● | BEAR ●● | MONKEY ● | GIRAFFE ● |

Here's another easy recipe that can add a little extra zip to beef, fish, chicken, or even vegetables. Most people have these ingredients on their shelves, so it is fast and easy to put together.

Ingredients

- ½ cup (1 stick) unsalted butter
- 3 Tbsp balsamic vinegar
- 1 Tbsp honey
- 1 Tbsp Dijon mustard

What to Do

Simmer butter in medium saucepan over medium heat until deep golden brown, swirling pan occasionally, about 6 minutes. Remove from heat. Whisk in vinegar, honey and mustard. Season sauce with salt and pepper. Serve with your favorite beef, fish, chicken, or vegetables.

CITRUS BUTTER SAUCE

| LION | OTTER | BEAR | MONKEY | GIRAFFE |

This quick little sauce is great on fish or other seafood, as well as pork. You might want to double or triple the recipe for those sauce-loving friends!

Ingredients

- 1 Tbsp olive oil
- 1 Tbsp orange peel, grated
- 2 tsp lemon peel, grated
- 2 garlic cloves, minced
- ¼ cup chicken broth
- 2 Tbsp (¼ stick) butter

What to Do

Heat oil in saucepan over medium-high heat. Add orange peel, lemon peel, and garlic and stir about 1 minute. Add broth and simmer for another minute. Whisk in butter. Immediately spoon over dish. Garnish with lemon and orange slices.

CHILI LIME CREAM SAUCE

LION	OTTER ⚫⚫⚫	BEAR ⚫⚫⚫	MONKEY ⚪⚪	GIRAFFE ⚫

This is a very flavorful sauce that will give your fish, seafood, or chicken a real boost.

Ingredients

- ¼ cup dry white wine
- ¼ cup fresh lime juice
- 1 Tbsp peeled fresh ginger, chopped
- 1 Tbsp shallot, minced or green onion

- ⅓ cup whipping cream
- 2 Tbsp chili-garlic sauce
- 6 Tbsp (¾ stick) unsalted butter, room temperature, cut into ½-inch pieces

What to Do

1. Combine white wine, lime juice, ginger, and shallots in small saucepan. Boil over high heat until reduced by half, about 3 minutes. **2.** Add cream and boil until reduced by half, about 2 minutes. Reduce heat to low. **3.** Mix in chili-garlic sauce. Add butter, 1 piece at a time, whisking just until melted before adding next piece. **4.** Serve immediately over your dish.

> **TEST-KITCHEN TIPS**
> *Chili-garlic sauce is available in the Asian foods section of many supermarkets and at Asian markets.*

CITRUS VINAIGRETTE

LION	OTTER ⚪⚪	BEAR ⚪⚪	MONKEY ⚪⚪	GIRAFFE ⚪⚪

This recipe is excellent atop fish or vegetables. It makes a great marinade for pork dishes as well. You'll even like it as a salad dressing. You may want to double this recipe because it is so delicious!

Ingredients

- 3 Tbsp canned pineapple in juice, crushed
- 3 Tbsp fresh orange juice
- 2 Tbsp fresh lemon juice
- 2 Tbsp fresh lime juice
- 1 Tbsp wine vinegar or malt vinegar
- ⅓ cup extra-virgin olive oil

- ¼ green bell pepper, finely diced
- ¼ red bell pepper, finely diced
- ¼ yellow bell pepper, finely diced
- 1 scallion, minced
- 1 Tbsp fresh cilantro, finely chopped

What to Do

1. Whisk together pineapple, citrus juices, and vinegar. **2.** Add oil in a slow stream, whisking until emulsified. **3.** Stir in remaining ingredients and season with salt and pepper. Serve over your favorite dish.

GARLIC BALSAMIC VINAIGRETTE

LION 	OTTER	BEAR	MONKEY	GIRAFFE

This is another great recipe that you will find 1001 uses for! It is especially good with fish or chicken, but you'll also like it as a salad dressing or marinade.

Ingredients

- 2 garlic cloves, minced very finely
- ¼ tsp salt
- 1 Tbsp shallot, minced
- 3 Tbsp balsamic vinegar
- ¼ cup extra-virgin olive oil

What to Do

1. In a bowl, whisk together, minced garlic, salt, shallots, and vinegar. **2.** Add oil in a stream, until emulsified.
3. Cover and refrigerate. **4.** Bring vinaigrette to room temperature and whisk well before using.

GINGER CREAM SAUCE

LION	OTTER	BEAR 	MONKEY	GIRAFFE

This recipe is excellent with fish or chicken.

Ingredients

- 1 cup dry white wine
- ⅓ cup shallots, chopped
- ⅓ cup fresh ginger, thinly sliced
- ½ cup whipping cream

Tip for Your Type

Monkeys may wish to substitute lower fat milk for whipping cream.

What to Do

1. Combine wine, shallots and ginger in small, heavy saucepan over high heat. **2.** Boil until liquid is reduced to ¼ cup, about 5 minutes. **3.** Add cream and boil until liquid is reduced by half, about 3 minutes. Remove from heat.

HERBED VINAIGRETTE

 LION ●●● OTTER ●●● BEAR ○○ MONKEY ○○ GIRAFFE ●

Here's another unique and flavorful sauce that you will find yourself making again and again. The olives and herbs add an extra flavor that give it that Mediterranean flair.

Ingredients

- 4 tsp Dijon mustard
- 3 Tbsp white wine vinegar
- ½ cup extra virgin olive oil
- 2 Tbsp fresh basil, minced
- 1 Tbsp fresh chives, minced
- 1 Tbsp fresh parsley, minced
- ¼ cup red bell pepper, finely diced
- ¼ cup black olives, pitted and finely diced
- salt and pepper to taste

What to Do

1. Whisk together mustard and vinegar in a small bowl. Salt and pepper to taste. **2.** Add the oil in a stream, whisking until emulsified. **3.** Whisk in the herbs, bell pepper, and olives. Talk about delicious!

TEST-KITCHEN TIPS

You're going to love this recipe. We have taken chopped fresh garden tomatoes and mixed them with this sauce to make a cold salsa or heated it atop some pasta cooked al dente! Use your imagination! Herbs can be varied per your tastes. We have made this with mint and tarragon for a more Greek style sauce.

LEMON VINAIGRETTE

 LION ●●● OTTER ●●● BEAR ●●● MONKEY ○○ GIRAFFE ●

This is a great recipe that can be used with fish, chicken, or vegetables that can be easily made with ingredients you have on hand. It gives the dish a little added zing!

Ingredients

- 1¼ cups extra-virgin olive oil
- ½ cup plus 2 Tbsp fresh lemon juice
- 2 Tbsp fresh basil, chopped
- 1 clove garlic, minced
- ½ tsp sugar

What to Do

Whisk all ingredients in medium bowl to blend. Season dressing to taste with salt and pepper. Cover and refrigerate. Rewhisk before using.

GUACAMOLE

| LION ●●● | OTTER ●●● | BEAR ●●● | MONKEY ●● | GIRAFFE ○○ |

Okay, once you have made your own guacamole, you will want to eat it everyday! It's so good! We've eaten a lot of this during our book editing! You can use this guacamole atop vegetables, fish, or salads, or on its own. It's great with Mexican food, steak, or chicken too. Thin it down and you have a great salad dressing.

Ingredients

- 2 avocados, mashed
- ½ cup onion, finely diced
- 2 Tbsp cilantro, finely chopped
- ½ tsp cumin
- 1 medium tomato, diced
- ½ tsp salt
- pinch of garlic powder
- 1 Tbsp fresh lime or lemon juice
- ½ to 1 hot pepper diced

Great Additions

- additional chopped tomato or ½ cup Pico de Gallo for a chunkier salsa-guacamole
- ½ cup sour cream or plain yogurt for a creamier guacamole or dressing

  Or add both for a creamy, salsa-guacamole dip!

What to Do

Mix ingredients in a bowl until smooth and creamy. Serve in a festive bowl, garnished with chopped cilantro or lime wedges or atop your favorite food.

Tip for Your Type

Giraffes can probably tell that this is a high-fat food. But you can add much more tomato and onion, to make this more of a pico de gallo with avocado chunks.

TANGY ASIAN SAUCE

LION ●●●   OTTER ●●●   BEAR ●●●   MONKEY ●●   GIRAFFE ●●

These are some of our most favorite ingredients all combined to make a great little sauce. These ingredients all pack a flavorful punch, so you'll notice that this is a rather small recipe. Feel free to double the recipe! We like to use it with pork, chicken, shrimp, tofu, or any Asian dish we make! It's a great sauce to serve with pot stickers or egg rolls too!

Ingredients

- 1 tsp fresh ginger, finely minced
- 1 tsp fresh garlic, minced
- 1 Tbsp fresh cilantro, chopped
- Pinch of Chinese Five-Spice powder
- Pinch of red pepper flakes
- 2 Tbsp soy sauce
- 2 Tbsp olive oil

What to Do

Mix all ingredients together in a small bowl. A little goes a long way! Serve with your favorite Asian dishes.

YOGURT SAUCE

LION ●●   OTTER ●●●   BEAR ●●●   MONKEY ●●●   GIRAFFE ●●●

This is a great recipe to use with Greek food, lamb, pork, and beef. It can also be used as a dressing for salads and veggies.

Ingredients

- 1 cup yogurt
- 1 Tbsp honey
- Juice from ½ lemon
- 1 clove garlic, minced
- couple of leaves of fresh basil or mint, finely chopped
- dash salt and pepper

What to Do

Mix ingredients well in bowl and serve!

Great Additions

Add chopped cucumber to make Greek sauce!

MISO SESAME VINAIGRETTE

| LION ●●● | OTTER ●●● | BEAR ●●● | MONKEY ●●● | GIRAFFE ● |

This recipe has an Asian flair to it and is great served with Thai, Chinese, or Japanese food or with fish, chicken, or other seafood to give that Asian taste.

Ingredients

- 3 Tbsp seasoned rice vinegar
- 3 Tbsp water
- 2 Tbsp red or white miso (fermented soybean paste)
- 1 Tbsp sugar
- 2 Tbsp fresh ginger, finely grated
- 4 tsp Tahini
- 3 Tbsp sesame or vegetable oil

What to Do

Purée all vinaigrette ingredients in a blender until smooth. Serve.

PEANUT SAUCE

| LION ●●● | OTTER ●●● | BEAR ●●● | MONKEY ○○ | GIRAFFE ● |

We use this recipe with our Asian dishes and as a dip for chicken satays or chicken fingers.

It is one of our tried and true favorites, guaranteed to be a crowd pleaser!

Ingredients

- 1 cup organic peanut butter
- ¼ cup milk
- 1 Tbsp sesame oil
- 2 Tbsp soy sauce
- juice from 1 lime
- 1 tsp red pepper flakes
- 1 Tbsp fresh cilantro, chopped
- 2 tsp fresh garlic, chopped finely

What to Do

1. Heat peanut butter in a small saucepan for 2-3 minutes, just to warm it up. Turn off heat. **2.** Slowly incorporate the milk, sesame seed oil, soy sauce, garlic, red pepper flakes, cilantro, and lime juice, blending till smooth. **3.** If still very thick because of the type of peanut butter you use, add more milk until smooth.

TEST-KITCHEN TIPS

If your sauce "breaks" then just heat on the stove again and blend and it should come back together.

RED BELL PEPPER CREAM SAUCE

| LION ●●○ | OTTER ●●● | BEAR ○○ | MONKEY ● | GIRAFFE ● |

This provides a great combination of flavors that makes for a delicious Mediterranean taste.

Tastes great on just about anything, but particularly fish, seafood, and beef.

Ingredients

- 3 large red bell peppers
- ½ cup pine nuts, toasted
- ½ cup Parmesan cheese, grated
- ¼ cup olive oil
- 1 Tbsp garlic, chopped
- 1 cup whipping cream

What to Do

1. Move oven rack to highest shelf. Preheat oven to broil (or 500 degrees). **2.** Place peppers directly on the oven rack. Char peppers until blackened on all sides, turning every couple of minutes to char each side well. **3.** Remove from oven and immediately immerse peppers in ice bath using tongs for 1-2 minutes. Peel, seed and coarsely chop peppers. **4.** Transfer to a food processor. Add pine nuts, Parmesan cheese, olive oil and garlic and process until peppers are finely chopped. **5.** Transfer mixture to large bowl. Stir in whipping cream. Season with salt and pepper. Cover and refrigerate. Serve with your favorite meat, fish or poultry.

> ### TEST-KITCHEN TIPS
>
> *You can purchase red bell peppers that have already been roasted to save time making this recipe.*

WARM TOMATO OLIVE VINAIGRETTE

LION	OTTER	BEAR 	MONKEY	GIRAFFE

Here's another one of our Mediterranean inspired favorites! Try it atop chicken, fish, seafood, lamb, or even vegetables or pasta.

Ingredients

- 4 Tbsp extra virgin olive oil
- 2 large garlic cloves, minced
- 5 or 6 plum tomatoes, diced
- ½ cup pitted Kalamata olives, coarsely chopped
- ½ cup fresh basil, thinly sliced
- 1 Tbsp red wine vinegar

What to Do

1. Combine oil and garlic in small saucepan. Heat over medium heat until garlic is fragrant, about 1 minute.
2. Mix in tomatoes, olives, basil, and vinegar. Stir vinaigrette until heated through, about 2 minutes.
3. Season with salt and pepper. Serve atop your favorite entrée.

RED WINE REDUCTION

LION	OTTER	BEAR	MONKEY	GIRAFFE

This recipe is fabulous with beef, as well as chicken. Use as a reduction sauce or marinade or both. You'll find you can take those steaks up a notch with this sauce.

Ingredients

- 1 large onion, chopped
- 2 small celery stalks, finely chopped
- 2 carrots, chopped
- 3 garlic cloves, chopped
- 1½ Tbsp olive oil
- 1½ (750-ml) bottles dry red wine (4½ cups)
- 750-ml ruby port wine (3 cups)

What to Do

1. Sauté onion, celery, carrots, and garlic in oil in a 6-quart pot over moderately high heat, stirring, until golden, about 10 minutes. 2. Add wines and simmer, stirring occasionally, until mixture is reduced to 1 quart, about 1 hour. 3. Pour through a sieve into a saucepan and simmer until reduced to 2 cups. 4. Reheat reduction and season with salt and pepper before using. Delicious with red meat!

TOMATO BASIL VINAIGRETTE

LION OTTER BEAR MONKEY GIRAFFE ●

This is one of our all-time favorites that you will find a use for on anything you eat. It is even good as a sauce over pasta or atop French bread as a bruschetta. Of course, it is great with chicken and fish as well!

Ingredients

- 10-12 red cherry tomatoes, halved
- 10-12 yellow cherry tomatoes, halved
- ½ cup red beefsteak tomato, diced
- ½ cup yellow beefsteak tomato, diced
- 1 shallot, minced

- ¼ cup fresh basil leaves, cut julienne
- ⅓ - ½ cup extra virgin olive oil
- ¼ cup balsamic vinegar
- 1 tsp fresh lemon juice
- salt and pepper to taste

What to Do

1. In a large bowl, combine shallots, basil, olive oil, balsamic vinegar, and lemon juice. **2.** Add tomatoes and season with salt and pepper, mixing well.
3. Cover and refrigerate until ready to serve. Warm in a saucepan before serving.

Tip for Your Type

Giraffe Diets can make this by reducing or eliminating the oil.

WHERE CAN I GO FOR RECIPES?

One of the many great things about the internet is that it gives people from all different areas of the globe the opportunity to share ideas. Recipes are no exception. This is the first place to try when you are not sure what to do with that chicken you do not want to deep fry because you learned it was not healthy! Search for recipes that are best suited for your type or ones that can be tweaked to your type. For instance, if you are making chicken and rice, but should not have much rice, either do not make so much rice, or just do not serve yourself so much rice. In general, Lions and Otters should be looking at meat based meals, while Monkeys and Giraffes should be looking at vegetarian based meals, and Bears can do a mix of either. Look for recipes that are using mostly fresh foods. Avoid making recipes that call for items like "artificial cheese products" or commercial "condensed soups," unless you feel inspired enough to make your substitutes from scratch. Try some of these websites to help get your creative juices flowing.

Click Tips

Here are some wonderful sites to help you explore the world of great, healthful recipes.

www.allrecipes.com   **www.cooks.com**   **www.epicurious.com**

www.foodnetwork.com   **www.hauserdiet.com**   **www.recipesource.com**

A SPECIAL
appreciation

We wanted to give a special *thank you* to Chef Steve who gave us a lot of excellent tips about how to put that *special something* into our cooking, as well as his willingness to share some tricks of the trade, educating us on everything from chopping garlic to aged balsamic vinegar. He took many of the beautiful food photographs in this book. Steve, you made the food photography sessions fun, educational, and down right gluttonous! Thanks for sharing your uniqueness, great food styling, and capturing the essence of our recipes—taking any dish and making it gourmet! Every session with you was always fun and inventive!

If we could give one bit of advice to any home chef— take a couple cooking classes from a professional chef! Continually improving our culinary skills has made us even better home-chefs than we were before…
If you apply these things daily, you will be inspired to want to make these recipes and get cooking!

About Chef Steven Chiapetti:

A South-side native, Chef Chiappetti's completed his formal education at The Culinary School at Kendall College, but his real learning came from helping his mom in the kitchen at home. Being of German, Italian, and French descendants, Chef Chiappetti discovered the greatness of simple food that satisfied the soul. Chiappetti represented the United States in the Bocuse d'Or, one of Europe's most prestigious competitions and was nominated for the James Beard's Foundation Rising Star Chef Award in 1997. Having worked with some impressive culinary talents such as Fernand Gutierrez at the Ritz Carlton Dining Room and Chef Paul Bartolotta at Spiaggia, Steve opened his own three-star restaurant, *Mango,* in 1995. Mango was an American Bistro characterized by a warm, hip dining room with an eclectic menu. *Grapes* was next, a three-star Mediterranean café, and a funky, neighborhood place with a colorful dining room. Chiappetti joined forces with the Chicago Symphony when he opened *Rhapsody*; a three-star Contemporary American, upscale place for symphony goers and Loop diners. Steve is an avid food photographer and has been featured at galleries in Chicago and Oak Park for his Edible Art series.

Chef Chiappetti and his wife Leslie currently own and operate Banana Bakery in Westchester, IL, a modern bakery with a focus on family and homemade, fresh ingredients. Chef Chiappetti is currently at Viand Bar and Kitchen in the heart of Chicago's Gold Coast.

get
moving!

We could say, "exercise or die!" We can confidently say—exercise or you'll never be in the shape you wish to be. There are so many positive outcomes from regular exercise such as increased self-esteem, better fitting clothes, higher activity level, increased metabolism, decreased disease incidence, and a better quality of life. Who would not want these things? As you have heard us say numerous times already in this book, people need to *Get Moving!*

People don't exercise because they are tired! Lack of energy is one of the primary reasons people give for not exercising. Interestingly enough, it is also the primary reason patients request Diet Typing at Caring Medical! Eating according to the Hauser Diet will help give you energy. It is key for you to focus on your diet first. The next step, however, is to use that improved energy to start building muscle and speeding your metabolism.

The more muscle mass you have, the better able you are to burn energy—i.e., your metabolism is faster. *(See Figure 10.1.)* Now, isn't that a good reason to start exercising? An interesting study published in the May 2003 edition of the *Journal of Anthropological and Applied Human Science* looked at two groups of exercisers—one group who performed only aerobic exercise—the other group that performed aerobic exercise with strength training, and compared them to a third group—the non-exercisers. The study revealed that cross-training programs integrating vigorous aerobics and strength-training exercise are your best bet for burning off fat. Results showed that those who did both aerobics and strength training burned significantly more subcutaneous abdominal fat and visceral fat (the deeper fat within the abdominal region) than the aerobics-only exercisers.

Did You Know...

The typical woman in America carries about a whopping 36% body fat and the average man is not too far behind at 31%! This means the average person in America is one-third fat!

FIGURE 10-1 # Muscle Can Speed Your Metabolism

	Fast Metabolism	Slow Metabolism
Muscle Mass	High	Low
Percent Body Fat	Low	High
Calories Burned at Rest	High	Low
Calories Consumed to Maintain Body Weight	High	Low
Appearance	Thin/Muscular	Fat/Puffy

A healthy woman who has awesome energy generally has about 20% body fat, and a man 15%. A woman in what we would consider *optimum* shape would have 15% body fat and a man 10%. We do not expect you to get down to 15% body fat, but we know it is possible. Dr. Hauser currently is steady at 7%. When he started, he was your typical man at 31% body fat!

What is the secret to success? Consistency! Your goal should be to do some form of exercise everyday. It must be planned into your day. Although it is often tough to wake up early, the best time for most people to exercise is in the morning. This leaves the rest of your day free. The longer you wait through the day, the more likely other distractions come up and seem to take that time away that you meant to exercise.

Home Equipment

We find that it is nice to have a small amount of reasonably priced exercise equipment at home to use whenever you have the time. Instead of just sitting idly watching TV; you can pick up some weights and do some lifting! It's all about consciously trying to incorporate exercise into your daily routine. We found that easier to accomplish when we had these things at home. There are some really good products out there! We recommend that you consider getting the following pieces of equipment:

- Two sets of dumbbells (one light and one heavy set. A four pound and eight pound set are typical.)
- Exercise mat
- Jump rope
- Bosu Ball
- Exercise Bands
- A good pair of running shoes (It is best to buy these from a running store, not a department store.)

The above equipment will set you back about $300. The investment is worth it.

Get into the Program!

A good exercise program would include doing something *aerobic* (heart rate increased) four to five times a week, as well as weight lifting two times per week. *(See Figure 10-2.)* It is important to include weight lifting in your fitness plan, otherwise when you lose weight you may lose some muscle with the fat! We need you building muscle while you are losing fat. The other reason to weight lift is that it will help you lose weight. The circulation of muscle tissue is many times that of fat tissue, so building muscle tissue will increase your metabolism. It will cause more calories to be burned while you are doing nothing—thus you will lose weight quicker. The other benefit of weight lifting is that it makes you look fabulous. Most people like looking fabulous! We know we do!

Initially, you may do each workout for five minutes. The next week, do six minutes and so on. The idea is to gradually get to the point where you workout at least one hour per day. When you are tired and want a day off, take a day off, no biggie! Let's look at each of these workouts:

Figure 10-2 A Good Workout Week

Monday:	Run/walk
Tuesday:	Bosu Ball
Wednesday:	Core Strengthening Program
Thursday:	Jump Rope
Friday:	Run/walk
Saturday:	Run/walk
Sunday:	Dumbbell workout on Bosu Ball

Run/Walk

In June 2001, Ross and Marion Hauser could not run a block. They then started on the Jeff Galloway program of run/walk. This started out as jogging two minutes then walking two minutes. Eventually, it became—run seven minutes and walk one minute. Marion has now run numerous marathons, half marathons, Olympic Distance Duathlons, and a wide array of 5K and 10K races. Ross has also run numerous marathons, ultra marathons, and completed multiple Ironman Triathlons! Nicole was always a good swimmer,

but she hadn't competed since high school. She set her mind to training for a triathlon. The run was really tough for her, having really never been a runner. She kept working at it and has since completed numerous 5K and 10K races, in addition to Olympic Distance Triathlons. Don't tell us you can't do it! We're living proof that anyone is capable of amazing feats! We are just normal people who have to go to work everyday, just like you do. But we just started out slowly and worked our way up to it!

So start out with jogging two minutes then walking two minutes. You could start with two sets of this or eight minutes of exercise. Increase the jogging by one minute each week until after five weeks you are jogging for seven minutes and walking two minutes. If you are still doing it and feeling better, you may want to go on the internet and sign up for a 5K race, giving yourself two months to train. Then—just go for it! You are on your way to great health!

Bosu Ball

The Bosu Ball is amazing! It can give you a cardiac aerobic workout, help with core stabilization (abdominal/back muscles), as well as help you increase your balance tremendously. We recommend getting a Bosu Ball and a couple of tapes to follow which will help motivate you to use the Bosu Ball.

The workout schedule in *Figure 10-2* lists two workouts on the Bosu Ball. The first workout is an aerobic workout. It is like doing step aerobics except you are

doing it on the Bosu Ball. Because it is a ball, it will be hard for you to balance when you first start. This will cause your hip and abdominal muscles to fire. So even though you are doing an aerobic workout you will also be strengthening your core muscles. You want to make sure you are wearing very supportive shoes because you will be amazed at how much of a workout the feet get with the Bosu Ball.

The second workout will involve doing various weight lifting maneuvers on the Bosu Ball. The Bosu Ball comes with a list of exercises that you can do at home. Doing weight-lifting exercises, such as bicep-curls on the Bosu Ball will cause the core muscles to be engaged. The largest muscles in the body are the core muscles. So, any strength training program has to make sure the core muscles are targeted. The most important fact in building muscle is that the exercise must be done to the point of fatigue. So if you are doing bicep curls, it is necessary that you do enough slow repetitions to the point that the muscle quivers. If you never get the muscle to quiver it means you did not fatigue the muscle enough. The muscle must be totally fatigued, otherwise the benefits of the exercise will not be optimal.

Core Strengthening

The core muscles are those that stabilize the spine. The primary ones are the abdominal, hip, and back muscles. (*See Figures 10-3A and B.*)

Any weight lifting program must include strengthening of these muscles because these are the bulkiest muscles on the human body! The core muscles make up most of the muscle weight of the body. To learn more about Core Strengthening we recommend a consultation with a personal trainer, or someone from your local gym. You can also come in for a consultation with Dr. Hauser at Caring Medical.

Muscle Burns More Calories than Fat—

Consider this:

Fact: You burn 50 calories per pound of muscle per day.

Fact: You must reduce your caloric intake by 3500 calories to lose one pound of weight or 500 calories per day times seven days per week.

What does this mean to me? A woman weighs 180 pounds, but should weigh 140 pounds. She starts weight training and does not change her eating habits at all. If she converts five pounds of her weight into muscle, she will lose an extra half pound of weight per week keeping everything else the same.

Say what? In other words, 5 pounds x 50 calories/pound = 250 calories per day x 7 days per week which equals 1750 calories equivalent to 1/2 pound per week of weight loss. So it would take 80 weeks to lose the 40 pounds.

Gain More Muscle? Take this one step further—the same woman increases her muscle weight 10 pounds. If you burn 50 calories per pound of muscle, she will burn 500 calories per day or one pound per week. So it would take her 40 weeks to lose those extra 40 pounds (3/4 of a year).

Core Muscles: Back

FIGURE 10-3A

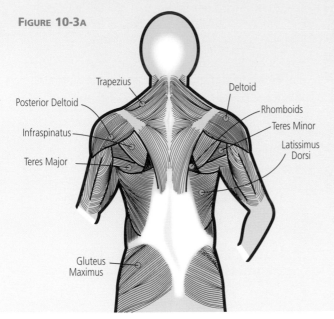

- Posterior Deltoid
- Trapezius
- Deltoid
- Rhomboids
- Teres Minor
- Infraspinatus
- Latissimus Dorsi
- Teres Major
- Gluteus Maximus

Core Muscles: Abdominal

FIGURE 10-3B

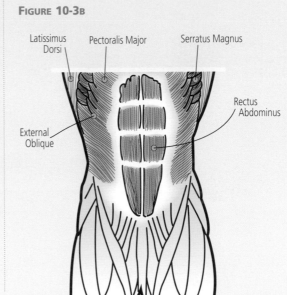

- Latissimus Dorsi
- Pectoralis Major
- Serratus Magnus
- External Oblique
- Rectus Abdominus

Jump Rope

Everyone knows how to jump rope. They also believe it is a great workout, but no one does it! Well, we want you to do it! Please try to do it, though, while wearing cushioned running shoes and on a softer surface. If you don't have a soft surface, you can do it on a carpeted floor, in the back yard, or buy a rubber mat for it.

For an extra workout, buy a jump rope with a weighted handle. Try to increase your jump rope tolerance each week. Start with 10 minutes and work your way up! If you do make it up to an hour, congratulations! You are then in a select group. Only one person in a thousand can jump rope for one hour!

Osteoporosis and Aging

Everyone, especially women, needs to make the time to start exercising. Women need to be especially concerned about weight-bearing exercise to strengthen our bones and prevent osteoporosis. We need to strength train at least one to two times per week. Yes, this means weight-lifting! This does not just mean bicep curls of three pound weights. You may have to start there, but you should be working toward sets of 60-80% of your one rep maximum. This should be done through various exercises including a leg press, knee extensions, and back extensions. For example, if you can lift 20 pounds one time, your goal would be to lift 12-16 pounds, eight times in a row, or one set. Do this set three times. You need to challenge your body. This is how you build bone density and lean muscle mass. Your balance will also improve. Having good balance along with strong bones and muscles will keep you more independent and active.

Include Aerobic Activity

In addition to strength training, we need to do a sustained exercise for at least 20 minutes three times per week where we reach at least 75% of our maximum heart rate. One hour of aerobic exercise is even better! This is considered aerobic activity. This helps strengthen your heart, improve circulation, and improve lung function and endurance.

Click Tips
Visit the Polar Heart Monitor's web site at
www.PolarUSA.com.

FIGURE 10-4

Heart Rate Goals, as a Percentage of Maximum Heart Rate, According to Age

Age	60% Max/ Minute	75% Max/ Minute	85% Max/ Minute	100% Max/ Minute
20	120	140	170	200
25	117	137	166	195
30	114	133	162	190
35	111	130	158	185
40	108	126	153	180
45	105	123	149	175
50	102	119	145	170
55	99	116	140	165
60	96	112	136	160
65	93	109	132	155
70	90	105	128	150

How do I find my maximum heart rate?

Take your age and subtract it from 220. Multiply this number by the percent heart rate you want to reach. *(See Figure 10-4.)* It is best to monitor this by purchasing a heart rate monitor. You can get one for less than $50 made by Polar. Basically, this device involves wearing a strap around your chest and a heart rate watch on your wrist.

When you exercise, your body secretes a lot of adrenaline that stimulates the beta receptors on the fat cells to release fat. Some people claim that they exercise, but still look heavy. The main reason for this probably is that they are not getting their heart rates up high enough. It is important for most people to get their heart rate up to at least 75% of maximum heart rate (aerobic zone) for as long as possible (generally an hour per day is sufficient) to maximize fat release from *adipocytes* (fat cells). Most sports physiologists recommend that the majority of your training be in the aerobic zone. This is 75-85% of your maximum heart rate. For example, a person who is 40 years old should keep their heart rate between 126-153 while aerobically training. This will help them mobilize fat as an energy source and, as a side benefit, get rid of the fat!

Wow! This is a lot of exercise! We know that weight loss is certainly not the only reason to exercise. However, for many of us, we are desperately trying to maintain our weight or even lose a few pounds. The rest of the lucky ones are trying to just get in good shape. But remember, just because your weight is within normal limits, does not mean that your body is necessarily healthy.

We know these figures can get depressing, but you need to realize this. In order to lose one pound, you must burn 3500 calories. So if you are trying to lose one pound per week, you either need to reduce your caloric intake by 3500 calories per week or 500 calories per day or you need to burn an extra 3500 calories per week. *(See Figure 10-5.)*

Our point is that we all need to get up off the couch or out of bed in the morning and start doing some activities. The activities cannot just be strolling around the block for 10 minutes. It's simply not enough to accomplish the health goals that you desire.

FIGURE 10-5

Amount of Calories Burned in Different Activities

Activities	Number of Minutes	Calories Burned
Biking (10-12 mph)	60	340
Biking (14-16 mph)	60	612
Office work	60	107
Running (5 mph)	60	572
Sitting (watching TV)	60	71
Standing	10	14
Stairmaster	30	525
Swimming (50 yards/min)	60	476
Walking, (less than 2mph)	60	143
Walking (4.5 mph)	60	322

Am I active enough?

The *Dietary Guidelines for Americans 2005* gives science-based advice on food and physical activity choices for health. The *Dietary Guidelines* describe a *healthy diet* as well as encourage Americans to increase their physical activity. They recommend engaging in at least 30 minutes of moderate physical activity on most days of the week. To lose weight and gain fitness, engage in 60 minutes per day of moderate to vigorous activity five or more days per week. We have talked to you about Caring Medical's approach to a healthy diet in this book. Basically it involves figuring out your Diet Type so that you will know what kinds of food will give you the maximum amount of energy. After you do this, it is up to you to control the portion sizes and incorporate activity into your lifestyle. Unfortunately, however, many times what one person calls "physical activity" is really just activities of daily living—*not* actual exercise. Physical activity simply means movement of the body that uses energy. Walking briskly, pushing a baby stroller, house-cleaning, climbing the stairs, playing soccer, or dancing the night away are all good examples of being active. And it is certainly good to become more active, adding in walking when you might normally drive, for an example.

In order to achieve health benefits, such as cardiovascular protection, osteoporosis prevention, and weight management, physical activity should be *moderate* or *vigorous* and be sustained for at least 30 minutes per day, or 60-90 minutes per day if you would like to lose some weight or are trying to achieve maximum fitness.

The United States Department of Agriculture (USDA) defines physical activities as follows:

Moderate Physical Activities:

- Walking briskly (about 3½ miles per hour)
- Hiking
- Active Gardening/yard work
- Dancing
- Golf (walking and carrying clubs)
- Bicycling (less than 10 miles per hour)
- Weight training (general light workout)

Did You Know...

- 15 minutes of jumping rope is equivalent to one mile of running.
- One mile of swimming is equivalent to four miles of running.

Vigorous Physical Activities:

- Running/jogging (At least 5 miles per hour or 12 minutes/mile)
- Bicycling (more than 10 miles per hour)
- Swimming (freestyle laps)
- Aerobics
- Walking very fast (4½ miles per hour)
- Heavy yard work, such as chopping wood
- Weight lifting (vigorous effort)
- Basketball (competitive)

Some physical activities are not intense enough to help you meet the recommendations. Many of our patients will tell us that they have started an exercise program, but the amount of actual activity that they perform is very minimal. Don't get us wrong, it's great that you are working at becoming more active. However, we want you to realize that you really need to get M-O-V-I-N-G to achieve the health benefits that you want.

Remember, that although you are moving, these activities do not increase your heart rate, so you should not count these towards the 30 to 60 minutes per day—or even the 90 minutes—that you want to reach. Activities such as walking at a casual pace, such as while grocery shopping, and doing light household chores do not count as physical activity.

As you know, many of the patients at Caring Medical come to see us because they are in pain or have sustained an injury. Many of our patients, therefore, state that exercise is very difficult for them to incorporate into their lifestyle plans. As you may or may not know, we utilize an injection treatment called Prolotherapy to stimulate the body to repair the injured areas. Prolo is short for "proliferate" or to grow. Prolotherapy causes your body to re-grow damaged ligaments, tendons, and cartilage. So if you are unable to incorporate exercise into your life because you are hampered by an injury or pain, give Caring Medical a call—the world experts in Prolotherapy are there to treat you!* Nearly all of our patients are able to improve their level of activity after receiving treatment. If you have still not come in to Caring Medical for Diet Typing, come on in! Get yourself moving!

Top 10 Activities to Do Instead of Watching TV

Note: You can, however, do most of these while watching TV!

1. *Walk—fast!* A 20 minute brisk walk burns about 100 calories (walking at 4.5 mph). Go to the mall and park at the opposite end of the store you need to go to. Walk briskly through the mall for 20 minutes to get to the store.

2. *Ride!* Moderately biking for 60 minutes burns about 340 calories.

3. *Buy some home equipment!* Some simple equipment is all you need to keep you active when it's not possible to get to the gym or exercise outside.

4. *Jump!* Jumping rope for 15 minutes is equal to running one mile and burns about 120 calories.

5. *Step!* Doing step aerobics for 30 minutes burns about 300 calories. Try this on a Bosu ball and really strengthen your core muscles!

6. *Kick!* Kickboxing for 30 minutes burns 300 calories.

7. *Climb!* Climbing stairs for 30 minutes burns about 150 calories. Using a Stairmaster burns even more!

8. *Lift!* Strengthen your core muscles by doing weight training that concentrates on your back, hips, and abdomen.

9. *Stretch!* Don't forget to stretch after all of your aerobic and strength training. It helps to tone your body. It is the perfect way to wind down after a great workout.

10. *Pop in an exercise video if you must watch the TV!*

Like your diet, it is very important to continue to add an exercise routine to your life, particularly as you age. Exercise keeps your joints from stiffening, as well as increases muscle and bone strength. If you are just starting an exercise routine, you want to make sure you choose activities that aren't too hard on your body. You will be surprised, however, what you are able to accomplish. Never in Marion's wildest imagination did she think that she could run a marathon, but she did it several times! That's 26.2 miles! Nicole, on the other hand, was able to master the accomplishment of open-water swimming of 2.5 miles and her first-ever Olympic Distance Triathlon! Now that's amazing! How did we do it? We started small and worked our way up to it!

Physical activity is a wonderful thing. Don't you feel better after working out? We know we do! We feel so much better. Physical activity helps slow the aging process, as well as jump start the metabolism. There are a number of activities that will provide the exercise you need and are low impact and less strenuous. Swimming, elliptical trainers, and race-walking are just a few of them. A combination of proper care, nutrition, and exercise will help you to make your body last as long as possible.

We want our clients at Caring Medical to remain active and to enjoy life to its fullest! That is why we do what we do.

---

* Note: See www.prolonews.com for more information.

We *want our clients at* Caring Medical *to remain* active *for* life

12:29:33

I WANT TO
GET HEALTHY:
WHERE DO
I START?

I want to get healthy *where do I start?*

How would you answer the question, "Are you healthy?" Most people think that they are relatively healthy. Most people figure that they are not going to have a heart attack anytime soon. Cancer is a problem for other people—it's not going to get me. Unfortunately, we all have these delusional thoughts, until one day we wake up and bammo!—we are the ones lying in the hospital with a heart attack or we are the ones wondering, "How did I get cancer?"

Many medical conditions, such as heart disease, diabetes, hyperinsulinemia, cancer, autoimmune disorders, and others, are significantly affected by what you eat. In other words, what you put in your mouth will have a long term effect on your health for the rest of your life. Eating is the number one variable that we all have the most control over to become healthy. That is definitely something to consider the next time you reach for that box of donuts!

Health is not the absence of disease. I (Marion) have run numerous marathons and Ross is an Ironman numerous times over. This and we are both over 40! Perhaps your goal is not to do triathlons or marathons but surely having energy at the end of the day to enjoy family is a good goal? What about finally picking up tennis as a leisure activity? Perhaps you need to concentrate better or drop a few pounds? Optimum health and wellness doesn't occur by accident. *This book has given you the tools you need to select the best diet for your metabolism.*

This book is written for you—for all of us, actually. Many of us need a lifestyle change. We are all so busy that we figure we don't have the time to make the change. We don't have time to shop for good food. We don't have time to cook. We don't have time to exercise. We basically just don't have time. We find that we are guilty of thinking like this as well. Yes, we are very busy. We do not have a lot of extra time. However, we need to ask ourselves, "Is it worth it to just go on the way I have been? What price will I be paying later on in life?" We have a greater than 66% chance of getting cancer and/or heart disease. Fifty percent of us will actually die a premature death from a disease process that may be halted by simple dietary changes. When you think about these facts, you realize that it is worth it to do something about it now, before it's too late. We see the results of people not taking it seriously everyday at Caring Medical and Rehabilitation Services, our Natural Medicine clinic in Oak Park, Illinois. Many people realize too late that they should have been taking care of themselves a lot sooner.

is it
too late
for me?

You may ask yourself, "Is it too late for me? I might as well continue to sit on the couch eating corn chips, and watching the latest reality TV program—because it's too late for me anyway." **It is not too late!** There is no time like the present to start. That's the problem—starting! Once you start, it may be difficult to stay on the path to a healthy lifestyle, but it is not as hard as starting. We want to help you succeed at disease prevention, as well as health preservation, and have a little fun along the way!

A Fresh Approach to Your Health...

As you have read thus far, the Hauser Diet is a whole different way of thinking. You may be saying to yourself, "It sounds interesting. How do I get started? So what is the first step?" First of all, you need to find a Natural Medicine physician to head up your health management program. We are talking about an M.D. or a D.O. who has experience in using nutrition, herbs, vitamins, exercise, and Natural Medicine testing and treatment procedures to manage your health in the most effective, yet least invasive manner. The physicians at Caring Medical and Rehabilitation Services do exactly that. They try to figure out what is wrong with you if you come in with a medical condition.

That sounds really strange, but think about it. Typically when you go to a physician's office, you leave with a prescription for some type of medication or expensive test. Most likely you did not come in with a "medication deficiency." You have some underlying problem that needs to be fixed. Often this underlying problem is left undetected, and the patient is sent out with a prescription for the latest anti-inflammatory medication or the latest ulcer medication. In reality, the answer to most medical problems involves first taking a very detailed medical and dietary history. It may then involve some specialized laboratory testing to help determine the treatment plan. You may need to change your diet. Most people do! Hence, this book! You may be required to take some nutritional supplements. You may need to decrease your stress. The physician may recommend that you receive a treatment that addresses the underlying cause of your condition. This is what happens in a Natural Medicine office.

Natural Medicine is sort of a misnomer for what we are trying to convey here. We use the terms "Natural Medicine" because we try to utilize a more natural approach when we are dealing with nearly every human disease. We try to answer the question, "What caused you to get this problem in the first place?" The answer often lies in the areas related to one or more of the following:

1. Inappropriate diet for the person's particular Diet Type
2. Presence of an allergy related to food or environment
3. Some sort of infection, including but not limited to fungus, bacteria, or viruses
4. Hormone imbalance
5. Structural weakness in a body part
6. Nutrient deficiency

Natural Medicine physicians offer solutions to these problems. By correcting these areas, many times the underlying problem is also corrected. This is not to say that people never require surgery or medications. But we are saying that often times the actual cause of the problem may be overlooked. If you follow the principles of this book, you will see that many chronic health conditions can be alleviated by simple dietary changes.

How Do I Find A Natural Medicine Physician?

We can tell you that it is not that easy to find a qualified Natural Medicine physician these days. Fortunately, however, more and more physicians and health care professionals are realizing that what they were taught in school may not be what is best for their patients. They are taking matters into their own hands and learning alternative approaches to helping their patients. They know that the traditional approach does not always work.

You want to go to a clinic where each person is treated as an individual and where Natural Medicine is the heartbeat of the clinic. You do not want to go to a clinic that just prescribes the normal medications for you. You want someone who "thinks outside the box."

Six Tips For Finding A Good Natural Medicine Clinic or Doctor

1. M.D. or D.O. licensed to practice medicine.

Your physician's actual residency training really doesn't matter that much, because most doctors learn about Natural Medicine after they have completed their traditional training. You might find a Natural Medicine physician who is an internist, family practitioner, physiatrist, psychiatrist, neurologist, surgeon, orthopedist, sports medicine physician, allergist, rheumatologist, dermatologist, and the list goes on. Basically, you want to find someone who has experienced the healing power of Natural Medicine and went on to learn all he/she could about it and incorporate it into his/her medical practice. Obviously, it goes without saying, that the physician should have a medical license that is current and active in the state in which he/she practices. You can't be too sure of people these days. There are many out there who pretend to be "doctors" who are not.

2. Choose a doctor trained in Natural Medicine.

You want to ask your potential physician's office where the doctor(s) received their training in Natural Medicine. Most of them will have attended courses by the American College for the Advancement in Medicine (ACAM) or other courses taught by other more experienced Natural Medicine physicians. In our case, we attended these courses, as well as traveled around

the world to train with some of the most experienced physicians in their respective fields. It takes a lot for your physician to embark on this approach to medicine. They have to do it on their own. All the same, you should find out how they were trained.

3. Clinic determines the root cause of your problem.

Ask the clinic if they will utilize the least invasive, yet most effective means for treating your medical condition(s). Find out what is causing your problem. You do not want a clinic whose first line treatment is to prescribe the latest drug on the market and to send you on your way, only masking the problem. Sometimes drugs are needed, but often simpler, less toxic solutions exist for many problems, including hormone imbalances, food allergies, eating the wrong foods for your Diet Type, nutrient deficiencies, and the like. We try to use prescription drugs minimally.

4. Natural Medicine is the primary practice.

There is a good chance that a clinic that emphasizes the natural approach to disease is one that knows what they are doing. A clinic that dabbles in Natural Medicine as evidenced only by a little "blurb" on their website is not one that really understands the power of Natural Medicine to get to the root cause of disease. So please find a "true" Natural Medicine clinic.

5. Clinic provides a caring atmosphere.

This used to go without saying that you could expect your physician's office to exhibit a caring attitude and make you feel special. We all know that this does not always happen in the doctor's office. Most people want to feel comfortable with the doctor and the staff. We work very hard at Caring Medical to establish the atmosphere of caring, compassion, and respect. We realize that everyone will not like us or get along with us. But we try to treat every person with respect and ask the same in return. We will work hard to figure out our patients' problems. We often see patients who have already been to five or 10 different doctors and/or clinics, including some of the very famous ones! Many times patients are just frustrated that nobody will listen to them. You want to find a place where the doctors and the entire team will listen and care for you to the best of their abilities.

6. Do your homework.

We love it when our patients come in well-educated on the treatments that we do. We encourage our patients to ask questions, understand the treatments they are receiving and the rationale behind them. These days, patients have to take matters into their own hands. Having accompanied family members for visits to the traditional medical system, I have experienced this first hand. Ask questions about everything that you are going to have done. Research it on the web. This is the information age. Be well-informed. This is why Caring Medical provides so much information in books and websites. Patients want to know.

Unfortunately, the current medical system is not optimal. Many doctors are forced to see volumes of patients, cut costs, and sacrifice quality for quantity. We could get into a long discussion about this topic, but we won't do that right now. Let's just say that it is not necessarily the doctors' faults. They are a product of the "system" which is need of some drastic changes.

Until then, take responsibility for writing down questions and bringing the list with you to your appointments and making sure you get answers that you understand. Research the clinics that you will be visiting on the web. Develop a satisfaction that you are going to put yourself under the care of the best clinic you can find.

We feel that we offer the best a Natural clinic can offer. We would love to be given the opportunity to help you achieve optimal health!

So are you ready to embark on a new adventure with us? You will be happy you did! You will feel great about yourself. The first step is working on areas that are under your control. This starts with the foods you put in your mouth and the activities you spend your time doing. It is possible to feel better and have more energy, allowing you to do things that you never thought you could do. We do not know of any other clinics that do things the *Hauser Diet* way. It's unique, interesting, practical, and totally do-able!

Please contact us to learn more about our clinic.

Caring Medical and Rehabilitations Services
715 Lake St., Suite 600,
Oak Park, IL 60301
Ph: 708-848-7789
Web: www.caringmedical.com
Email: info@caringmedical.com

How Can I Optimize My Health?

Many people come to Caring Medical and Rehabilitation Services before they are sick. They actually want to prevent a future illness from occurring. They may be motivated to do this for different reasons. One person may be taking care of a parent who is now debilitated due to adult onset diabetes or stroke.

SUMMARY:
How *do* I find a good doctor?

1 Choose an M.D. or a D.O. who is licensed to practice medicine.

2 Choose a doctor trained in Natural Medicine.

3 Clinic determines the root cause of your problem.

4 Natural Medicine is the primary practice.

5 Clinic provides a caring atmosphere.

6 Do your homework.

Another person may be helping a spouse or child with cancer fight for their lives. Others may be helping a high school or college friend recover from a serious illness.

Sometimes all it takes is examining yourself in the mirror and realizing that you are not getting any younger. You determine that you would like to be around for your children, so you can see your grandchildren be born and grow up. Most of us do not want to be a burden to family and friends as we age. We would all like to have a happy, healthy, active retirement. Of course, there are people who are just health conscious, and have been planning their wellness check-ups all along. However, not too many—unfortunately—fit into the latter category.

Are You As Healthy As You Think You Are?

How do you know you are healthy? You could feel great, yet be harboring a cancer in your system that will kill you in six months if not treated. Not to be so morbid, but it *is* true isn't it? Let's try to be a little more optimistic and realistic.

Before a disease actually develops, your physiology is changing so as to allow the disease process to be harbored. We're not saying that we have all of the answers to complete disease prevention or that you will never get heart disease or cancer. But there are some steps that everyone should take in order to create a healthy physiology.

If your mother or father died at an early age with cancer most likely you have inherited their cancer physiology. That is the bad news. The good news is that this cancer physiology can be reversed with diet, supplements, and lifestyle changes. The *Hauser Diet* recommendations are a good first place to start. An even better place to start is to get an evaluation by a medical doctor that specializes in Natural Medicine to get your blood tested to see if you really are as healthy as you think.

The number one killer of people is atherosclerosis (heart disease). Number two killer is cancer. We believe it is helpful for everyone to get a baseline study (blood tests) to see if they have the physiology that can lead to these conditions. These conditions don't just pop up, they start years and even decades before the disease actually develops. The subtle changes start in the blood and can be seen by various blood tests. Once the abnormalities are seen, recommendations are made including the proper Hauser Diet, supplements, and lifestyle changes. Then the blood is retested to make sure the blood looks healthy. Because of the epidemic of horrible conditions, everyone needs some basic lab work done.

America is getting to the point where a *typical* 60 year-old person is suffering from at least one chronic medical condition that affects his/her life on a regular basis. Because of this, many people are turning to more natural remedies to treat these conditions because the traditional allopathic methods are suboptimal, producing very few long-term cures and, at best, typically only provide temporary help. Natural Medicine strives to correct the underlying cause of the problem, which is likely an altered biochemical state. By changing this, we can often reduce symptoms and improve quality of life much more safely, and with a substantially lower risk compared to standard treatments.

Whatever your reason for reading this book, the rest of this chapter will provide you with a guideline to help you determine what type of laboratory testing and check-ups you should be getting and at what point in your life it is best to do them. This topic is actually hotly debated within medical circles. What is actually optimal for the patient is not always what is recommended by the primary care physician. The reasons for this are many and we don't have the space to discuss it—but much of it relates to the health insurance industry.

The information presented here is based on the experiences of the physicians and team at Caring

Medical and Rehabilitation Services, along with practical research to determine what we feel is best for our patients. As one of the largest and most experienced Natural Medicine clinics, we feel that these guidelines are appropriate for most people. However, as we always recommend, please review your complete medical history with your physician and use this information to help you take charge of your life.

What tests do I need?

We are going to outline the tests that you may need throughout your life span, so you can start planning now! Many of these laboratory tests are only available in a Natural Medicine office/laboratory. Your primary care or HMO/PPO doctor may not even know about some of these. So you must be prepared for that.

You may be thinking that this all sounds great, but wondering if insurance covers these types of tests? That is a good question. The answer is, "we don't know." Seriously, because Natural Medicine physicians are typically not part of PPO/HMO/Medicare plans, the patient must typically go "out of network" in order to see the Natural Medicine physicians. This may mean that the patients' responsibility for coverage is likely going to be larger than if the HMO/PPO doctor prescribed it. The patient may end up paying for some or all of these tests out of their own pockets.

At this point, since you are the one ultimately in charge of your own health, you have to figure out what that's worth to you. Most of our patients come to a point when they realize that they will very willingly pay out-of-pocket money for things that many might consider "frivolous" such as fancy cars, nice vacations, clothes from a designer shop, nice meals out in restaurants, and the list goes on, yet they may need to also spend the money on their health. What good is all of the above "stuff" if you are sick and feel terrible all of the time? Until the system changes, you may have to choose this option. You are the only one who cares about you as much as *you*. You cannot let your insurance company dictate what you are going to do about your own personal health. It's up to you to make that choice to spend some extra dollars on your health. Think about the long-term benefits that could save your life.

The Hauser Diet Wellness Check List

What we have put together here is what we call our *Hauser Diet Wellness Check List*. As we age, we all will experience changes within our bodies. Some can be seen visibly from the outside, and some we cannot see. We all know that we definitely feel different than we did when we were teenagers. Did you know that our hormone levels start decreasing at the age of 25?! Just when we have finally reached the much-desired "adulthood," things start turning south! Guess that shows us that God certainly does have a sense of humor! Yes, hormones start to decline in the mid to late twenties when the aging process sets in. People maintain fairly healthy hormone levels until age 35-40; that is about how long we could be expected to live until about 100 years ago. The effects of declining hormones have only been a problem since we started living longer. Declining hormones, coupled with poor lifestyle, improper diet, lack of exercise, and stress are largely responsible for the health problems and frailties of later years. **The good news is these signs of aging can be reversed and/or slowed down.** *(See Figure 11-1.)*

What does this matter? Well, take women, for example. As estrogen levels decrease with age, old bone is broken down faster than new bone can be made which may result in osteoporosis (a disease characterized by low bone mass and deterioration of bone tissue). Bone loss begins around age 35 and accelerates 1-3% during and after menopause. This acceleration of bone loss occurs in the first 5-10

you are the only one who cares about you as much as you

Hormone Rates in Women

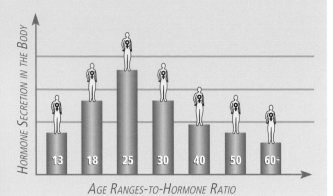

FIGURE 11-1

Because hormones start to decline at the early age of 25, it is in everyone's best interest, young and old, male and female, to get their hormones checked.

years after menopause. As women approach older ages, they may have lost 35 to 50% of their bone mass. Isn't that depressing? We will show you in this chapter what you can do to help prevent conditions such as osteoporosis and others from accelerating the aging process.

Screening tests can give us some good information about our health risks. As the saying goes, "when you've got your health, you've got everything." Many people want to know more—they want to know if something might be wrong. The risk of cancer generally increases with age. Not all cancers can be easily detected, and symptoms may not appear until it is too late. So, it is important to get regular cancer screening blood tests. *(See Figure 11-2.)* We want to show you how you can take control of your health so that you can reduce the chances of being surprised by things like cancer or heart disease later in life.

Testing Procedures and Laboratory Tests from the Hauser Diet Wellness Check List

Now let's take a closer look at each of the tests on our Hauser Diet Wellness Check List.

1. **General Physical Exam:** Your doctor should do a head-to-toe physical exam that includes:

   a. **Vital Signs:** check your blood pressure, heart rate, respiration rate, temperature, height and weight.

   b. **Neurological Exam:** Check your reflexes, eye movement, hearing and sense of balance.

   c. **Cardiovascular Exam:** Check your heart and lungs with a stethoscope, as well as check the arteries in your neck for any abnormalities.

   d. **Skin Exam:** Check to see if there are any changes in the color or texture of your skin as well as check any moles for changes.

   e. **Diet and Exercise History:** Review your diet, exercise and any risk factors you might have for cancer, diabetes, or heart disease.

   f. **Psychological History:** Review if you have been feeling depressed, anxious, or irritable.

2. **Cardiac Risk Profile:** At Caring Medical, we have combined a number of tests that we feel can best assess our patients' risk for heart disease and stroke.

   a. **Lipid profile:** The lipid profile measures total cholesterol, triglycerides (TG), high density lipoprotein (HDL or "good cholesterol"), low density lipoprotein (LDL or "bad" cholesterol) and very low density lipoprotein (VLDL).

Total cholesterol cannot be considered the sole measure of cardiac risk. Unfortunately, the general population is obsessed with their total cholesterol levels. Have you ever been to a cocktail party where everyone at the party is discussing their lab results? Scary! Makes you want to scream! But anyway, we digress…

The components of measured total cholesterol (LDL, HDL, triglycerides) include HDL which correlates inversely with cardiac risk. In other words, high HDL

Desirable Ranges for Lipid Profile
- **Total Cholesterol <200 mg/dL**
- **HDL > 40 mg/dL**
- **LDL <100 mg/dL**
- **Triglycerides <150 mg/dL**

FIGURE 11-2 THE HAUSER DIET WELLNESS CHECK LIST*

Tests	20-29 Years	30-39 Years	40-49 Years	50+ Years
1 General Physical Exam	• Baseline, then every 2-3 years	• Every 2-3 years	• Every 2-3 years	• Every 2-3 years
2 Cardiac Risk Profile	• Baseline, then every 5 years	• Every 2-3 years	• Every 1-3 years	• Every 1-3 years
3 Comprehensive Metabolic Profile	• Baseline, then every year	• Yearly	• Yearly	• Yearly
4 Fitness Assessment	• Baseline, then every 2-3 years	• Every 2-3 years	• Every 2-3 years	• Every 2-3 years
5 Saliva Hormone Screening	• Baseline, then every 5 years	• Every 5 years	• Every 3 years	• Every 3 years
6 Insulin Levels	• Baseline, then every 2 years	• Every 2 years	• Every year	• Every year
7 Hauser Diet Typing	• Baseline, then every 5 years	• Every 5 years	• Every year	• Every year
8 Allergy Testing	• Baseline, then every 5 years	• Every 5 years	• Every 5 years	• Every 3 years
9 Self Breast Exam	• Monthly	• Monthly	• Monthly	• Monthly
10 Self Testicular Exam	• Monthly	• Monthly	• Monthly	• Monthly
11 Pelvic Exam & Pap Smear	• Yearly	• Yearly	• Yearly	• Yearly
12 Prostate & Rectal Exam & PSA	• Only if problematic	• Only if problematic	• Baseline, then every 3 years if normal	• Every 3 years if normal; yearly if elevated
13 Blood or Urine Hormone Levels	• Only if problematic	• Only if problematic	• Initial, then every 1-3 years	• Initial, then every 1-3 years
14 Cancer Markers	• Only if high risk	• Only if high risk	• Baseline, then every 5 years	• Baseline, then every 3 years
15 Bone Density	• Only if problematic	• Only if problematic	• Baseline at menopause, then every 5 years	• Baseline at menopause, then every 5 years
16 Ultrafast CT Scan of the Heart	• Only if high risk	• Only if high risk	• Baseline, then every 5 years	• Every 5 years, if normal; yearly if abnormal
17 Occult Blood Testing	• Only if high risk	• Only if high risk	• Only if high risk	• Baseline, then every 5 years
18 Mammogram	• Only if high risk	• Only if high risk	• Only if high risk every 5 years	• Baseline, then every 5 years until age 75
19 Flexible Sigmoidoscopy or Colonoscopy	• Only if high risk	• Only if high risk	• Only if high risk	• Baseline, then every 5 years; 10 years for a colonoscopy if normal

* Note: *These recommendations are based on the physical examination and various tests being within the normal range. If an exam or test is abnormal, typically the physician would recommend earlier follow-up than the timeline seen here.*

(See text for details.)

cholesterol levels are protective against heart disease. Low-density lipoprotein (LDL) cholesterol levels vary directly with heart disease risk and are considered a direct cardiac risk factor. A very convenient way of expressing your risk of heart disease which takes into account both the total cholesterol and HDL (good) cholesterol is the ratio between the two. We like to see these ratios under 4.5, although a better score would be under 3.5. For example, if your total cholesterol is 200 mg/dl and your HDL 50 mg/dl, your ratio is 4. But if your total cholesterol is 200 and your HDL is 35, your ratio is 5.7, which may be considered an increased risk for cardiac disease.

Some labs will also calculate the LDL/HDL ratios to determine cardiac risk. The LDL/HDL ratio is a better indicator of cardiac risk than total cholesterol. The LDL/HDL ratio is actually a more pure ratio than total cholesterol/HDL.

Research suggests that the LDL/HDL ratio is also predictive of cardiac risk. Data from the Lipid Research Clinics and the Framingham Heart Study suggest that the LDL-to-HDL-cholesterol ratio may have greater predictive value for heart disease and stroke than serum total cholesterol or LDL-cholesterol alone. The normal levels of cholesterol ratios of LDL to HDL should be less than 2.5. [3]

A number of research studies, including the Framingham Study, suggest that serum triglycerides may be important predictors for heart disease in men or women, but not consistently in both sexes. Despite these observations, the current consensus holds that elevated levels of serum triglycerides represent a risk marker for obesity, glucose intolerance, and low HDL levels, all of which contribute to risk for heart disease and, to the extent possible, deserve preventive attention.

So, the bottom line is this: Elevated LDL and TG levels are bad and indicate a positive heart disease risk. Elevated HDL levels, on the other hand, are good. These are protective against heart disease. So remember, it's not all about the total cholesterol level. Your total cholesterol could be slightly elevated (say around 220 mg/dL), but your HDL is 68, your ratio is 3.23, which is outstanding. So be careful not to just look at total cholesterol. *Look at Figures 11-3A and 11-3B for the Chol/HDL ratios and LDL/HDL ratios.* [4]

b. **Homocysteine Levels:** Another test gaining importance is serum homocysteine. Homocysteine is an amino acid that comes from the normal breakdown of proteins in the body and appears to be a better test than cholesterol for predicting risk for heart disease, stroke, and reduced blood flow to the hands and feet.

Normal Homocysteine Values
- **Male: 6.3-15.0 µmol/L**
- **Female: 4.11-12.4 µmol/L**

c. **Lipoprotein(a):** Lp(a), is a lipoprotein consisting of an LDL molecule with another protein, Apolipoprotein(a), attached to it. Lipoprotein(a) is similar to LDL but does not respond to typical strategies to lower LDL such as diet, exercise, or most lipid-lowering drugs. Since the level of Lp(a) appears to be genetically determined and not easily altered, the presence of a high level of Lp(a) may be used to identify individuals who might benefit from more aggressive treatment of other risk factors. Normal values range from 0-3 mg/dl.

d. **C-reactive protein:** C-reactive protein (CRP) may be measured on apparently healthy patients to determine if they are at risk for a coronary event, even if their lipid levels are normal or borderline

Fig. 11-3a Men's Risk of Heart Disease According to Lipid Ratios

Risk Group	Chol/HDL	LDL/HDL
Below Average (Protective)	3.4 & below	2.4 & below
Average	3.5-4.7	2.5-4.9
Moderate	4.8-5.9	5.0-7.1
High	6.0 & above	7.2 & above

Fig. 11-3b Women's Risk of Heart Disease According to Lipid Ratios

Risk Group	Chol/HDL	LDL/HDL
Below Average (Protective)	2.9 & below	2.4 & below
Average	3.0-3.6	2.5-4.1
Moderate	3.7-4.6	4.2-5.6
High	4.7 & above	5.7 & above

elevated. Inflammation plays a role in the initiation and progression of atherosclerosis, the chief underlying cause of heart attacks. CRP levels as low as <1.0 mg/L can be detected. CRP, a sensitive marker of systemic inflammation, has emerged as a powerful predictor of cardiovascular diseases, particularly of coronary heart disease (CHD). C-reactive protein is a powerful predictor of first and recurrent cardiovascular events. Inflammation from other sources may cause these test results to be non-predictive of heart disease.

An article appearing in the November 14, 2002[5] issue of the *New England Journal of Medicine* confirms that an elevated blood level of C-reactive protein (CRP) in women (they were the population studied) is strongly predictive of future cardio-vascular events (such as heart attack and stroke.) These results came from an analysis of over 20,000 blood samples taken from women enrolled in the Women's Health Study, a long-term study which enrolled and followed apparently healthy women for a number of years. While elevated CRP levels have been known to be associated with cardiovascular risk for several years, this report offers interesting evidence that elevated CRP may be just as important as elevated LDL cholesterol levels; and that furthermore, high CRP levels may identify high-risk patients who might be missed if only cholesterol levels were tested. CRP is a

protein released into the bloodstream any time there is active inflammation in the body. (Inflammation occurs in response to infection, injury, or various conditions such as arthritis.) Evidence is accumulating that atherosclerosis (coronary artery disease) is an inflammatory process. The fact that elevated CRP levels are associated with an increased risk of heart attack tends to support the proposed relationship between inflammation and atherosclerosis. *Interestingly enough, at Caring Medical, we often find elevated CRP levels in patients with food allergies. Once they remove the allergens from their diet, the CRP levels can normalize to below <1.0mg/L.*

e. **Platelet Aggregation Study:** The platelet aggregation test measures the rate and degree to which dispersed platelets in a sample of plasma (the liquid portion of blood) form clumps after the addition of a material that normally stimulates aggregation (clumping). A machine measures the changes in turbidity (cloudiness) and prints a graphic recording of the results. Excessive thickness in the blood, i.e., abnormal platelet aggregation studies, may be a risk factor for coronary disease.

3. **Comprehensive Metabolic Profile:**

The Comprehensive Metabolic Profile (CMP) is a group of tests that has become standardized throughout the United States and is generally recognized by most insurance carriers and Medicare. The CMP is a frequently ordered panel that gives your doctor important information about the current status of your kidneys, liver, electrolytes, blood sugar and blood protein levels. Our Caring Medical panel also includes a thyroid panel, a CBC, lipid profile, ferritin (storage form of iron), and urinalysis. Abnormal results—especially combinations of abnormal results—can indicate a problem that needs to be addressed.

The CMP is used as a broad screening tool to evaluate organ function and check for conditions such as diabetes, liver disease, and kidney disease. The CMP may also be ordered to monitor conditions, such as high blood pressure, and to monitor patients taking specific medications for any kidney or liver related side effects. The CMP is routinely ordered as part of a blood work-up for a medical exam or yearly physical and is usually collected after a 10 to 12 hour fast (no food or liquids other than water). While the individual tests are sensitive, they do not usually tell your doctor specifically what is wrong. Abnormal test results or groups of test results are usually followed-up with other specific tests to confirm or rule out a suspected diagnosis.

4. **Fitness Assessment:** This analysis involves reviewing your health history, current level of fitness, nutrition and exercise habits. From there weight resistance and aerobic programs can be customized especially for your body and goals. Some fitness assessments involve a body composition analysis where the body is measured with calipers and the measurements are then calculated against age and gender. *See Chapter 10* for more information on exercise.

5. **Saliva Hormone Levels:** Saliva testing is a simple and convenient way to test the bioavailable portion of sex and adrenal hormones, such as estradiol, estrone, estriol, progesterone, testosterone, DHEA, DHT, and cortisol. Caring Medical utilizes saliva hormone testing as a screening tool for assessing baseline levels of active hormones.

6. **Insulin Levels:** Insulin is a hormone released from the beta cells of the pancreas. Insulin's most important function is to facilitate glucose (blood sugar) uptake by a variety of tissues, especially adipose (fat) and skeletal muscle. Insulin also stimulates the synthesis and storage of triglycerides and proteins. Insulin is the most important regulator of blood glucose. High blood glucose (such as exists shortly after a meal) stimulates the release of insulin, whereas low blood glucose levels inhibit insulin release.

    The most important reason for measuring the blood insulin level is the diagnosis or evaluation of abnormalities in blood sugar levels.

Insulin levels measured while fasting can give information about the body's sensitivity to insulin. High insulin, even with normal blood sugar, may indicate that the pancreas is working harder than normal to get the blood sugar level down. This situation is usually caused by the body being resistant to insulin's effect—a condition called "insulin resistance syndrome" or "metabolic syndrome" or "Syndrome X." It is a very common feature of obesity and of hormonal problems such as polycystic ovary syndrome. We like to see fasting insulin levels <15 uU/ml.

7. **Hauser Diet Typing:** Caring Medical's Hauser Diet Typing is a series of tests that allow the physicians to determine the best diet for your individual metabolism, which is what we have been discussing throughout this book. Balancing your body chemistry will help you feel better, achieve optimum health, and prevent disease.

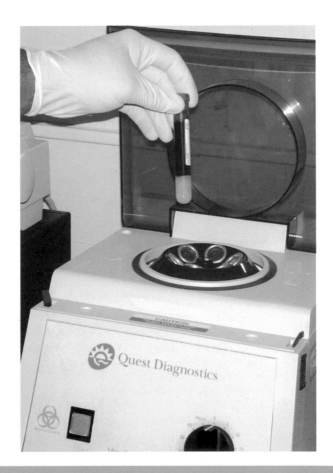

The benefits of eating according to your Diet Type are not just weight loss. Diet Typing has been used by our healthcare practitioners to help many conditions including weight problems, chronic fatigue, allergies, chronic pain, diabetes, heart disease, and autoimmune disorders, to name a few.

We analyze your blood pH, oxidative rate (using a glucose tolerance test), and may add a food allergy panel or blood insulin level based on your history. We put all of this information together to determine the best diet for your particular Diet Type. *(More information throughout the book on this topic.)*

8. **Allergy Testing:** We utilize a 95 (or 190) food test that determines the level of sensitivity, or allergy, to 95 of the most commonly eaten foods. Most people associate food allergies with foods that cause an immediate response, like hives, such as from eating shellfish or peanuts. While this is useful information, we feel that it is important for everyone to test for delayed reactions to foods that we eat everyday, such as wheat and dairy. As we discussed in *Chapter 1,* our test looks for a specific type of reaction that can be delayed in the body, often causing allergic symptoms up to 48 hours or more after a person ingests the food. The most common symptoms noted by a person with this type of food allergy include fatigue, itchy/runny nose, body pain, and diarrhea, to name a few.

9. **Breast Self-Exam:** Examining your breasts is an important way to find a breast cancer early, when it's most likely to be cured. Not every cancer can be found this way, but it is a critical step you can and should take for yourself. Below are some links to sites that show you exactly how to perform the exam.

Women's Health Information:
www.fwhc.org/health/self-breast-exam.htm

Susan B. Komen Breast Cancer Foundation:
www.komen.org/bse/

BreastCancer.org:
www.breastcancer.org/dia_detec_exam_idx.html

10. **Self Testicular Exam:** Just as it is important for women to examine their breasts, men should examine their testes. Detecting testicular cancer at the early stages is a key factor in prevention. Here are some links that provide instruction on how to perform the exam:

The Testicular Cancer Resource Center
http://tcrc.acor.org/tcexam.html

The Cancer Network:
www.cancernetwork.com/PatientGuides/Testes_Examination.htm

11. **Pelvic Exam and Pap:** It is generally recommended that women get yearly pelvic and pap exams. These exams can pick up early cervical cancers and obviously other sexually transmitted diseases and problems. If you are monogamous and have only had one partner in your life who is also monogamous, chances are you are not going to have an abnormal pelvic exam, so you may not need to be tested as frequently. Discuss this with your doctor.

12. **Prostate/Rectal Exam and PSA:** Due to the increasing cases of prostate cancer, it is recommended that men periodically receive a physical prostate/rectal exam as well as a blood test which measures the level of prostate-specific antigen (PSA), a substance produced by the prostate and some other tissues in the body. Increased levels of PSA may be a sign of prostate cancer. The exam involves an examination of the lower rectum to check for hemorrhoids, anal fissures and stool abnormalities such as frank or occult blood. *(See #17 for the definition of occult blood.)* The term "digital" refers to the clinician's use of a lubricated finger to conduct the exam.

This examination is also used to evaluate the prostate gland in males.

13. **Blood or Urine Hormone Markers:**
The hormone panel is used to determine the sex hormone status of a person or monitor progress in those receiving hormone replacement therapy. Sex hormones play a vital role in overall health of a person. Low sex hormones can cause a lack of energy, decreased libido, poor memory, low muscle mass, and bone loss.

14. **Cancer Markers:** At Caring Medical, we find that patients sometimes do not know what to do to not only prevent cancer, but to determine if their bodies are already moving in the direction of developing cancer. We utilize these laboratory blood tests to screen for cancer, as well as test response to cancer treatments. There are a host of other blood cancer marker tests that can show elevations in blood levels, such as in the case of lung, skin, liver, gastric, blood, pancreas, and uterine cancers. See your Natural Medicine physician to get these tests or other cancer marker tests ordered.

For males:
a. AFP and Beta hCG for testicular cancer.
b. PSA and PAP for prostate cancer.
c. CEA for colon cancer.

For females:
a. CA 27-29 and CA15-3 for breast cancer.
b. CA 125 for ovarian cancer.
c. CEA for colon cancer.

At Caring Medical, we test for what we call cancer physiology, in other words, certain metabolic findings that may lead to development of cancer in the future. Our experience reveals that these factors may be related to blood thickness, glucose intolerance, alkaline blood pH, and other factors, depending on the case.

15. **Bone Density Test:** One of the best ways to determine bone density and fracture risk for osteoporosis is to have a bone mass measurement (also called bone mineral density or BMD test). *(See Figure 11-4.)* General recommendations are the following:

• All women aged 65 and older regardless of risk factors

Bone Density Test DEXA (Dual Energy)
Bone Mineral Density Performed on Hologic QDR 4500 A/SL

Region	BMD	T-Score	% Peak	Z-Score	W.H.O. Interpretation*
Spine: L1-L4	1.008	-0.36	96	+0.23	Normal
Femoral Neck:	0.715	-1.20	84	+0.62	Osteopenia
Total:	0.779	-1.34	83	+0.96	Osteopenia

* World Health Organization Definitions: T-Score Greater than -1.0 = Normal Bone Mass
T-Score of -1.0 to -2.5 = Osteopenia
T-Score of less than -2.5 = Osteoporosis

Highlighted areas indicate abnormal results.

FIGURE 11-4
Here is an example of a wake up call to this woman. She needs to start exercising to build muscle and to begin a bone building supplement regimen.

- Younger postmenopausal women with one or more risk factors (other than being white, postmenopausal, and female)

- Postmenopausal women who present with fractures (to confirm the diagnosis and determine disease severity)

- Estrogen deficient women at clinical risk for osteoporosis

- Individuals with vertebral abnormalities

- Individuals receiving, or planning to receive, long-term glucocorticoid (steroid) therapy

- Individuals with primary hyperparathyroidism

- Individuals being monitored to assess the response or efficacy of an approved osteoporosis drug therapy.[6,7]

There are several ways to measure bone mineral density. The tests measure bone density in your spine, hip and/or wrist, the most common sites of fractures due to osteoporosis. Recently, bone density tests have been approved by the FDA that measure bone density in the middle finger and the heel or shinbone. Your bone density is compared to two standards, or norms, known as "age matched" and "young normal." The age matched reading compares your bone density to what is expected in someone of your age, sex, and size. The young normal reading compares your density to the optimal peak bone density of a healthy young adult of the same sex.

The information from a bone density test enables your doctor to identify where you stand within ranges of normal and to determine whether you are at risk for fracture. In general, the lower your bone density, the higher your risk for fracture. Test results will help you and your doctor decide the best course of action for your bone health.

16. **Ultrafast CT Scan of the Heart (*Heart Check America*):** The centers that perform this testing specialize in the detection and measurement of disease before the onset of symptoms. A fast, painless scan using revolutionary electron beam technology can now provide the patient and physician with critical information regarding the presence or absence of coronary disease, and thereby enhance the patient's chances of living a long, healthy, productive life. If the test reveals that you have some calcium forming in your coronary arteries, you will have time to address them with an aggressive Natural Medicine regimen. Some feel that the word is still out on this procedure, fearing that it may produce some "false positive" results. Discuss this with your doctor. See Heart Check America's website for more information. *(Note the Click Tip).*

Click Tips
*Visit **www.heartcheckamerica.com**, where you can learn more about heart health.*

17. **Occult Blood Testing:** A fecal occult blood test (FOBT) is a noninvasive test that detects the presence of hidden (occult) blood in the stool. The patient is given a card to take home and instructed to place a smear of stool onto the card. The card is returned to the lab where reagents are dropped onto the card to detect the presence of blood. It is generally recommended that the patient complete three separate samples. Such blood may arise from anywhere along the digestive tract. Hidden blood in stool is often the first, and in many cases the only, warning sign that a person has colorectal disease, including colon cancer. Usually if FOBT is positive, your doctor will order further testing such as a flexible sigmoidoscopy or colonoscopy as discussed in the following pages.

18. **Mammogram:** A mammogram is an x-ray of the breast and is the principle method of detecting breast cancer in women. Mammograms are made using a special type of x-ray machine that is used

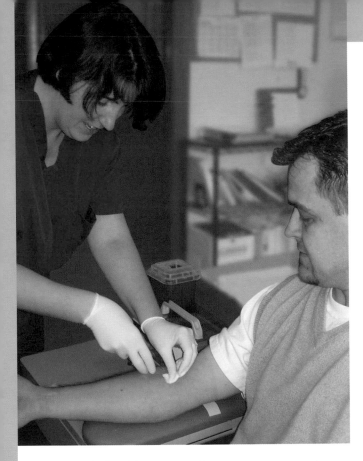

a flexible, lighted tube called a sigmoidoscope. The doctor may collect samples of tissue or cells for closer examination and remove some polyps within view. A colonoscopy is an endoscopic procedure in which a thin, flexible, lighted viewing tube (a colonoscope) is threaded up through the rectum for the purpose of inspecting the entire colon and rectum and, if there is an abnormality, taking a tissue sample of it (biopsy) for examination under a microscope, or removing it. It is used for detecting colon cancer, polyps, diverticulitis, and other colon abnormalities. The Center for Disease Control recommends baseline testing for those over 50 years of age. Those with no abnormalities should repeat either a flexible sigmoidoscopy every five years or colonoscopy every 10 years. A barium enema (a colon x-ray) may be considered if a colonoscopy cannot be performed.

** People with a family history of colorectal cancer or polyps: People with a first-degree relative (parent, sibling, or child) with colon cancer or polyps diagnosed at less than 60 years of age or with two first-degree relatives diagnosed with colorectal cancer at any age should be advised to have a screening colonoscopy starting at age 40 years or 10 years younger than the earliest diagnosis in their family, whichever comes first, and repeated every five years according to CDC guidelines.

People with one first-degree relative with colon cancer or adenomatous polyp diagnosed at less than 60 years of age or two second-degree relatives with colorectal cancer should be advised to be screened as average risk persons, but beginning at age 40 years.

only for this purpose. A mammogram can show a developing breast tumor before it is large enough to be felt by a woman or even by a highly skilled health care professional.

Here is what the Center for Disease Control has to say about mammograms: "Mammography every one to two years is recommended for all women beginning at age 50 and concluding at approximately age 75 unless pathology is detected. Obtaining 'baseline' mammograms before age 50 is not recommended. For the special category of women at high risk because of a family history of premenopausally diagnosed breast cancer in first-degree relatives, it may be prudent to begin regular clinical breast examination and mammography at an earlier age (e.g., age 35).[8]

19. **Flexible Sigmoidoscopy/Colonoscopy:**
A flexible sigmoidoscopy is a procedure in which the doctor looks inside the rectum and the lower portion of the colon (sigmoid colon) through

Click Tips

The CDC website lists a lot of references that describe the rationale for these testing recommendations. Visit it for more details: www.cdc.gov.

People with one second-degree relative (grandparent, aunt, or uncle) or third-degree relative (great-grandparent or cousin) with colorectal cancer should be advised to be screened as average risk persons.[9]

As We Age…

The Twenties:

These are exciting times…the twenties. Your body is maturing, as well as your personality. You are becoming an individual. You are moving from childhood into adulthood. For most people, these are very fun days filled with change and newness of life. The twenties are also a time where you are carving out a place for yourself. Not only are you doing this with your education, your job, getting married, or starting a family, you are doing this with your body as well. *Many times people feel like they are invincible during these years.* You have a lot of energy, you feel like you can eat whatever you want, and sporting activities are a part of life. It would be great if everyone would say to themselves, "Hey, I had a nice childhood. Now it is time for me to take responsibility for myself, as well as my health. I want to live as long as I can. Tell me what to do."

It would be very idealistic to think that most twenty-year-olds would think proactively. However, there may be a few of you out there. For those of you who are looking to start now, here is the plan. As you can see from the Hauser Wellness Check List, you should be getting tests numbers #1 to 11. *(See Figure 11-2.)*

We recommend that you meet with a Natural Medicine physician to review your test results and devise an optimal health plan. If everything is within normal limits, good for you! What do you need to do to keep them there? If some abnormalities are discovered, you want to deal with them as soon as possible. At Caring Medical we generally recommend things such as the following:

1. Take a good daily multi-vitamin.
2. Change your diet to eat according your specific Diet Type. If you don't cook, learn now!
3. Get on a good exercise program.
4. Start supplements for aiding recovery after workouts.
5. Change your lifestyle if any laboratory abnormalities are found. For example, we commonly see elevated liver enzymes in this population, which may be due to excessive alcohol or sugar consumption or may be due to a fatty liver from obesity. We also see elevations in glucose, lipids, and blood pressure levels even in the 20s! If these types of things are already happening to you, it's time to run to a Natural Medicine clinic such as Caring Medical.

Age 30-39:

The thirties become a time where people start getting really busy. They are immersed in their careers and family and find that they often do not have time to stay healthy. Things like exercising may go by the wayside. Many people feel that these are the most exciting

times of their lives. However, others feel that it only gets better with age! Either way, it is a time where most people are very busy and it takes careful planning to continue to work at your health plan with due diligence. By the end of your thirties, you will realize that it is time to get on the "wellness bus," before you end up on the "sickness bus."

What tests do I need? As you can see on the Hauser Diet Wellness Check List, you will focus on tests #1-11. *(See Figure 11-2.)* Disease physiology typically begins in the 30s. So get your blood levels checked!

At Caring Medical we generally recommend the following:

1. Take a good daily multi vitamin, with some additional supplements to help keep your blood thin and immune system strong.

2. Change your diet to eat according your specific Diet Type. If you don't cook, learn now!

3. Get on a good exercise program.

4. Begin a good supplement program for aiding recovery after workouts.

5. Change your lifestyle if any laboratory abnormalities are found. The disease process is in full swing in the 30s if you allow yourself to eat poorly and become sedentary. Don't let it take a hold of you. You have a lot more living to do!

Age 40-49:

The forties are typically when both men and women start to feel their bodies changing the most. Healthy people will also feel the change, so don't think you are invincible. Things will start to sag and you will feel like your body is not your own. What happened? You woke up one day and looked in the mirror and you saw your parents! Welcome to the 40s! During the 40s, hormones start to drop, stress levels rise, dreams may be unrealized, marriages may head south…You forty-somethings really need to sit up and take notice. You really need a tune up.

What tests do I need? As you can see on the Hauser Diet Wellness Check List, you will focus on tests #1-11. *(See Figure 11-2 .)* However, this is the time where you will need to start looking into some of the other tests that can detect risk for developing "the diseases of aging." How depressing is that? But don't fret! We're here to help you stay as active and as healthy as possible! People in their 40s now will add tests #12-19.

At Caring Medical, we generally recommend that the 40-something crowd:

1. Get on a good disease prevention supplement program, including heart, cancer, and osteoporosis prevention.

2. Find out your Diet Type and start eating accordingly. If you don't cook, learn!

3. Get on a good exercise program and get off the couch, taking supplements that aid recovery post-workouts.

4. Listen to your body. If you are experiencing changes, don't fear, come get things checked out—especially your hormone levels.

6. Change your lifestyle if any laboratory abnormalities are found. If these types of things are already happening to you, it's time to run to a Natural Medicine clinic such as Caring Medical.

Age 50 Plus:

Many patients that we see at Caring Medical and Rehabilitation Services who are aged 50 and over are so happy that they are in this stage of life. Their children are starting families, they are having fun with the grandchildren, they can take trips that they never took during the busy years, and life is generally very good. We know that each and every one of you must desire to be able to enjoy these years. All family members today have more years together as adults now than they did during the early 1900s. With this extension of longevity comes a new situation for us that we may/may not feel prepared to handle. It is when we hit our 50s that many of us are faced with caring for elderly parents, which is about the time we are beginning to experience our own health difficulties.[10]

Think about these figures for a minute. For Americans born in 1900, the average life expectancy was just below 50 years. The early decades of the 20th century brought such huge advances in the control of diseases of childhood that life expectancy at birth increased to 70 years by 1960. Rapid declines in mortality from heart disease—the leading cause of death—significantly lengthened life expectancy for those ages 65 or older after 1960. By 1998, life expectancy at birth was nearly 77 years. An American woman who reached age 65 in 1998 could expect to live an additional 19 years, on average, and a 65-year old man would live another 16 years. In 2000, average life expectancy at birth hit record highs, with men at 74.1 years and women at 79.5 years. A century earlier, life expectancy was 48 years for men and 51 years for women. Those who reach age 65 now live to an average age of 81 for men and 84 for women. In 2001, for men, life expectancy rose from 74.3 in 2000 to 74.4 years in 2001. Women's life expectancy rose from 79.7 to 79.8 years. White women have the highest life expectancy, 80.2 years,

followed by black women (75.5 years), white men (75 years), and black men (68.6 years).[10] See Figure 11-5.

How long these trends will continue is partly up to *you*. You can take control of your lives now to try and be as healthy as you can be. Many of our patients (over 50) have been thankful that they made the decision to put their health under the care of our natural medicine clinic. Many have come in with a variety of conditions that were reversed with a comprehensive natural medicine program—abnormal cancer physiology, elevated lipid levels, clogged arteries, inactivity, fatty liver, diabetes, and the list goes on.

What tests do I need? Again, as seen on the Hauser Diet Wellness Check List, you will focus on tests #1-11. *(See Figure 11-2.)* However, you will be regularly checking some of the other tests (#12-19) that can detect risk for developing "the diseases of aging." We're here to help you stay as active and as healthy as possible!

At Caring Medical, we generally recommend that those in the over 50 crowd pay particular attention, for example:

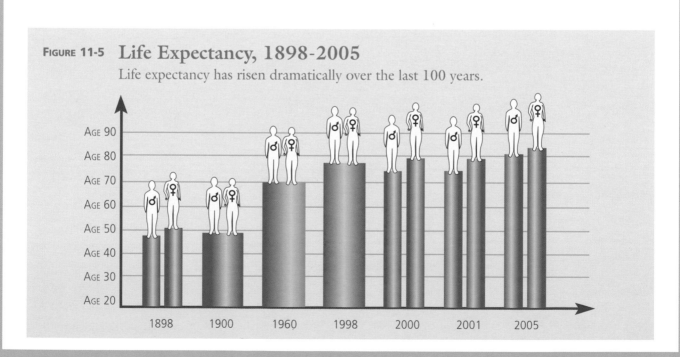

FIGURE 11-5 **Life Expectancy, 1898-2005**
Life expectancy has risen dramatically over the last 100 years.

She did not want to experience what her sister was going through, so she came in to get herself checked out. She heard we had written the book, *Treating Cancer with Insulin Potentiation Therapy* and wanted to know what she could do to prevent the disease.

The consultation went something like this. "Sue, we first need to make sure that you are cancer free now. As you know, before a cancer occurs, like with your sister, it was likely growing for 10 years. In order to test this, we will do blood cancer markers and get some x-ray studies of your breast. You can get either a mammogram or MRI. Then we will test you for cancer physiology. When all of the tests come back, we will put together a cancer prevention plan for you."

At minimum, we recommended that she start following the basic principles of the Hauser Diet. Most people with cancer physiology require a higher protein diet that is low in simple carbohydrates. Sue's test results revealed that she was a slow oxidizer, but had a high fasting insulin level. Therefore, we recommended that she start following the Otter Diet to start, which is a diet higher in protein, lower in carbohydrates.

Sue did not have any evidence of an active cancer, but she did have quite a bit of "pro-cancer physiology." Her platelet aggregation study revealed that her blood was very thick and her lactic acid levels were slightly elevated, suggestive of *anaerobic metabolism*. Normal cells live off of oxygen via process called *aerobic metabolism*. Cancer cells live off of carbohydrates (sugar) via a process called anaerobic metabolism. Sue's body was definitely headed in the wrong direction.

Other interesting findings were high insulin and estradiol levels, both feeders of breast cancer. She was told to stay on the Otter Diet and to increase consumption of soy (which has some anti-breast cancer effects). She was placed on six nutritional supplements. After several months on the program, besides feeling

1. Get on a good disease prevention supplement program, including heart, cancer, and osteoporosis prevention.

2. Find out your Diet Type and start eating accordingly. If you don't cook, get back to it!

3. Start exercising and throw away the remote!

4. Listen to your body. If you are experiencing changes or feel that things just are not quite right, don't fear, come get things checked out.

5. Change your lifestyle, especially if any laboratory abnormalities are found. If these types of things are already happening to you, it's time to run to a Natural Medicine clinic such as Caring Medical. Lives can be changed—at any stage!

Knowing more may add to your longevity.

Sue: A Strong Family History of Cancer

Sue came in as a patient to Caring Medical with a very strong family history of breast cancer. Her mother died at the age of 67 from the disease and her sister had a mastectomy and was getting chemotherapy.

great and losing 20 pounds, her cancer physiology had completely reversed. All of her blood work normalized. She understood that we could not guarantee that she wouldn't get cancer, but she now realized there was a lot that she could do about it. Sue continues to follow-up yearly—and she is grateful that she does!

Bill: Scared to Death

Bill, like Sue, did *not* have longevity in his family history. His father died at the age of 62 and his brother just succumbed to a heart attack at age 56. Bill was 54 and was scared to see doctors because of what they might find wrong. He knew that we did Natural Medicine, so he felt somewhat more comfortable seeing us.

As with Sue, we said, "Bill, we first need to see if you have heart disease. So we are going to order a non-invasive test called a *heart scan* which will tell us whether or not you have calcium in your coronary arteries. If you do have calcium deposits, it will give us the amount and how you compare to people of your sex and age. We will also run some tests which will tell us whether you have heart disease physiology or not." As you can imagine, Bill was eager to get going.

On his one month follow-up appointment, his heart scan unfortunately showed some calcium in his coronary arteries. His tests showed a significant amount of heart disease physiology. But the good news was that his high homocysteine level, abnormal cholesterol profile, hyperinsulinemia, and thick blood could all be reversed by following the appropriate Hauser Diet, in combination with a nutritional supplement program. We told Bill we cannot guarantee that his coronary artery disease would not progress, but we would do all we could to help reverse it. So far, he is doing great and his cardiac risk factors in his blood are reversing. Bill is another one who was so thankful that he finally overcame his fear of doctors and got on a good "health" program, instead of waiting until he was in "sick mode."

Greg: "I just don't feel good!"

Greg came in to see us at the recommendation of a friend. Greg was always proud of how healthy he was. Indeed, Greg *looked* good, but he had no idea what was going on inside of him. He wanted the Cadillac program! He wanted to find out everything there was to find.

Greg was astounded to find out that the tests revealed that he was not as healthy as he thought. As a matter of fact, the tests showed that though he was biologically the age of 48, chemically (blood tests) he was actually 56. He immediately began to follow his appropriate diet (Monkey Diet) and started taking natural hormone replacement and supplements. His repeat tests after three months were impressive. He was passionate about following the program and followed up with the office every six months.

Greg was doing so well, that we told him that he didn't have to return for a year. Wow! When we saw Greg the next year, you would not believe what we saw! You would have thought he had plastic surgery to his entire body! He looked great and felt great! His friends commented that he looked 10 years younger. We must admit, he did look 10 years younger.

In Summary

Run, run, run to your Natural Medicine physician's office today! It's not too late! Part of a comprehensive Natural Medicine program involves getting the appropriate lab tests that will help detect processes that you might not even be aware are going on within your body. Get started now on a program that will help you stay healthy, fit, and happy for your entire life. We hope to help you keep active for the rest of your life.

Footnotes

1. Catalog of Services. Beverly Hills, CA. Immunosciences Lab, Inc.; 2001.

2. Hauser, R. *Treating Cancer with Insulin Potentiation Therapy*; Beulah Land Press. 2002, pp.137.

3. Kinosian, B. Cholesterol and coronary heart disease: predicting risks by levels and ratios. *Annals of Internal Medicine*. 1994; 121: 641-647.

4. Merck Medicus: http://merck.micromedex.com/index.asp?page=bhg

5. Ridker, P. et al. Comparison of C-reactive protein and low density lipoprotein cholesterol levels in the prediction of first cardiovascular events. *NEJM*. 2002; 347:1557-1566.

6. U.S. Preventative Services Tasks Force. Screening for osteoporosis in postmenopausal women: recommendations and rationale. *Am Fam Physician* 2002 Oct 15;66(8):1430-2.

7. U.S. Preventative Services Tasks Force. Screening for osteoporosis in postmenopausal women: recommendations and rationale. *Am Fam Physician* 2002 Oct 15;66(8):1430-2.

8. Cancer Prevention and Control. Center for Disease Control; www.cdc.gov.prevguid. 2005

9. Colorectal Cancer Prevention and Control Initiatives. Center for Disease Control: www.cdc.gov.prevguid. 2005.

10. How population aging will challenge all countries. Population Reverence Bureau. www.prb.org.

What to do?

1. Get a comprehensive natural medicine evaluation by a qualified M.D. or D.O.
2. Get Diet Typing to determine how you should eat and cook your own food!
3. Test your physiology for the presence of disease.
4. Keep exercising—or start!
5. Do not ignore signs of ill health. Act now.

OVERCOMING
YOUR DIET
CHALLENGES

overcoming
your
diet challenges

You have heard people say "You're in or you're out." This is a good way to look at your diet and lifestyle choices. There are people who want to know what they "should" do but who will not actually start doing it. They buy a membership to the gym, but never actually go. They spend money on finding out how to eat nutritiously, but never break the old habits. There is no buttering up the fact that if you want serious results, you have to get serious! We believe your very life in the future will depend on your decisions today.

Make these 10 promises to yourself today:
• I will eat whole, natural foods.

• I will eat according to my Diet Type.

• I will learn to cook my own meals.

• I will eat out less often.

• I will exercise to the best of my ability.

• I will not let food control me emotionally.

• I will not make nonsense excuses for having a sedentary lifestyle.

• I will eat my proper portion sizes.

• I will get back on track, when I see my old habits sneaking back in.

• I will succeed!

You will succeed! You have read through this whole book, which already shows you have dedicated yourself to learning what you need to do. The road to better health takes discipline and positive thinking. It is not always easy to get motivated to exercise, or to turn down desserts, or stop eating foods you are allergic to. But what might be satisfying in the short term could be having long term damaging effects. We hope that the information presented in this book will help to turn back the aging clock, or at least extend how long that clock ticks. But you have to remove this phrase from your vocabulary: "I'll start tomorrow." Eventually, we all run out of "tomorrows." Start today!

"But I cannot start today…"
There you go again, thinking negatively. Maybe you cannot run out to the store right now and buy organic vegetables or come in to Caring Medical to have lab work. How about starting a food diary today? You can start a food diary to get the facts of what you eat. This is not as easy as you think, but it can be a valuable tool in analyzing your diet. Write down exactly what you eat everyday. Be conscious of the portion sizes. Just by doing this, you will better be able to analyze where you can improve, based upon the Hauser Diet principles discussed

FIGURE 12-1
Jane's Original Food Diary
Monday June 3

7:00am:	½ of a large white bagel with 2 Tbsp cream cheese
Through-out AM:	3 cups of coffee with aspartame sweetener and powdered creamer
9:00am	2 handfuls of almonds
12:30pm	1 tuna salad sandwich on white bread with iceberg lettuce, 1 American cheese single slice, 1 20 oz soda, 1 snack bag of barbeque chips
2:00pm	16 oz latte, 1 raspberry pastry
5:15pm	3 tacos (ground beef, onion, iceberg lettuce, cheese, sour cream, and flour tortillas) 1 cup rice, 1 large glass of 2% milk
9:00pm	1 bowl of sugar-coated corn flakes flakes with 1 scoop white sugar, 2% milk
9:30pm	20 oz soda

FIGURE 12-2
Jane's Diet Makeover
Monday June 10

7:00am:	½ of a large large whole wheat bagel with 2 Tbsp natural peanut butter, 1 cup of coffee with 1 tsp cane sugar and 1 Tbsp cream
9:00am	1 handful of almonds, 1 large glass of water
12:30pm	1 tuna salad sandwich on whole grain bread with romaine lettuce, tomato, 1 slice of cheddar cheese, 1 glass of water with lemon, 1 snack bag of carrots, ¼ cup of roasted and salted sunflower seeds
2:00pm	1 cup of herbal tea, 1 handful of raspberries
5:15pm	3 tacos (ground beef, onion, romaine lettuce, red bell pepper, cheese, and corn tortillas), ½ cup rice, ½ cup black beans, 1 glass of water
9:00pm	1 glass of herbal tea

in Chapter 2 and throughout this book. The next step is to follow through. Once you get an idea of how to improve in your diet, you have to make that a reality through buying better quality foods, increasing home-cooked meals, and eating right for your Diet Type. Here is an example of a food diary and how it can be cleaned up a bit, without being excessive.

Let's analyze this food diary. (*See Figure 12-1.*) How could we make general improvements, even without looking at Diet Type?

1. Vegetable intake is low. Even if Jane was on the Lion Diet, which recommends the most modest amount of vegetables, this menu falls short.

2. Waterintake is low. One glass right before bed is not sufficient. She would be dehydrated.

3. Too many sugary, caffeinated drinks throughout the day. Heavy use of artificial sweeteners and processed creamer.

4. Anabundance of low quality carbohydrates, including that late night snack attack for cereal.

5. Too many dairy products for any of the Hauser Diets.

6. This diet does not promote many whole foods that are rich in fiber. Instead, it is very high in processed, chemical-laden foods.

That Following Week...

1. Jane added water and herbal tea to her day, instead of mostly coffee. This will greatly help her hydration status, which is vital to optimal functioning, weight loss, and health. (*See Figure 12-2.*)

2. She replaced the artificial, chemical-laden creamer and sweetener with regular cream and sugar.

3. She exchanged the potato chips that contained partially hydrogenated (bad) fats, for some sunflower seeds and carrots. This provides more good fats, dietary fiber, and vegetable nutrients.

4. She exchanged white bread for whole grain bread. This will add fiber and vitamins that the white bread lacks.

5. She exchanged a raspberry pastry and latte for fresh raspberries and herbal tea. This not only saved her a lot of calories, but the fruit and herbal tea provides an antioxidant boost!

6. She added legumes with dinner for added fiber and protein, and changed from flour to corn tortillas.

7. She chose better quality lettuce in the lunch and dinner.

8. She added in some red bell pepper for vegetable variety and added vitamins.

9. Jane realized she generally ate at night because she was bored, so she replaced the snack at the end of the night with herbal tea.

Jane is a great example of how to refocus a diet. She increased her water and whole food intake and decreased her processed food and beverage intake. The next step for her is Diet Typing. This will determine if Jane should focus more on protein/fat or carbohydrates. But this is a great start!

Confronting the "Enemy"

Do you have a weakness in your diet? Most of us do. It is not usually as simple as "I enjoy a hot dog now and then" or "I know I shouldn't eat this ice cream cone but…." Just as food is fuel to our bodies, it can also be a drug. Don't beat yourself up about having one slip up in your diet. Hey, we all have our bad days.

Sometimes you are at a dinner party that is serving fried, high calorie meat with cheesecake for dessert you can't refuse, or you are on the road and only have fast food tacos or burgers to choose from. The same is true for exercise. Sometimes you are just feeling run down and cannot think about exercising. You may take a business trip and not have the ability to exercise for a couple days. Our point is not to let those bad days get you off track for days at a time.

Out with the Old and In with the New…

What you have read in this book may be very different than how you have been feeding yourself and your family, for years. Your dietary habits are probably decades old! It is hard to change these overnight. Many of your favorite family recipes may call for MSG containing soups or highly processed and preserved meats, or maybe you always serve chips, dip, and coffee cake for every gathering. Eating is a very emotional ritual for many people. For others, it is based on the path of least resistance. Becoming conscious of your food choices and reading labels is a great way to take small steps to bettering your health. If you learn to recognize unhealthy foods and eating habits, you have the power to change them.

"But I have the rest of my family to feed!"

Do you remember a time when food was "provided" to children and they were not allowed to go into the fridge in search of extra snacks? Things have changed quite a bit in most households. Kids are the reason why people stock their kitchens with artificial juice boxes, macaroni and cheese, pizza rolls, cookies, and candy. Think about this for a minute: why do you allow your children to run your food inventory? Part of taking control of your health, is taking back control of your kitchen!

If you are serious about making a positive change in your diet, your family will have to commit too! This is how you will succeed. There is an obvious correlation between having junk food in the house and eating it, and not having junk food in the house and not eating it. Many people trying to lose weight, or practice good eating habits, admit that "if the food is there, I'll eat it." Can you relate? Maintaining good eating habits is hard enough when you have outside temptations such as dining out or holiday feasts. You need to make your home a Temptation-Free Zone.

We each have our individual favorite foods that tempt us. What is tempting to your family, might not be to you. If you cannot have fudgesicles in the house without eating half of the box, then stop buying fudgesicles! If you can easily pass over the fudgesicles, but can't resist binge eating on potato chips, you have to stop buying potato chips. If your family members want to eat the food, they must do it outside of the house. Why don't you make a list of "Forbidden Foods"

and discuss it with members of your household? This will include all the foods you compulsively overeat that you know are holding you back.

You can start building a foundation for healthier foods for your family, not just by getting rid of the more obvious junk foods, but by upgrading basic foods that your family can still consider "normal." In this example, we've chosen a typical sandwich lunch. *(See Figure 12-3.)* Walk into any grade school classroom, and many workplace lunchrooms, and you will see a plethora of bad food, such as white bread, soda, sugary treats, and fried foods, and of course, the dreaded soda pop! But we guarantee even the picky eaters will get satisfaction from these sandwich improvements…

Five Steps to Improving a Sandwich Lunch:

1. Start with the bread. Use high fiber, whole grain bread instead of low quality white bread.

2. Choose a good meat. Use minimally processed meats like organic turkey, instead of heavily processed meat products, like bologna.

3. Choose fresh toppings. Opt for plenty of veggies like dark green lettuce, tomatoes, and onion.

4. Choose better condiments. Try new and interesting mustards, instead of loading up on high-calorie mayonnaise regularly.

5. Accompany with a tasty side. We love fresh veggies, like carrots and cucumbers with homemade dressings/dips, or some sliced fruit. Leave the cookies and potato chips behind the next time you are food shopping for lunch essentials! *(See Figure 12-4.)*

"Can't I ever buy junk food again?"

We hear this from clients who just realized what they will actually have to do in order to improve their health. It's a sign that he or she may not be fully ready or willing to implement lifestyle changes.

Attention Jones Family:

These foods are no longer permitted in the household:

- Potato chips
- Milk chocolate bars
- Ice cream sandwiches
- Fruit punch
- Soda
- Cookies

If we said to you "Yes, you can start buying potato chips in six months," what is your attitude going to be? You will think, *Oh, I'll just try this diet for a few months and then I'll be able to eat potato chips again as a reward for losing weight.* It's those rewards that can get you. If you are a frequent "dieter" you have probably rewarded yourself with a trip to the ice cream parlor or a double cheeseburger and fries in the past. *I lost five pounds; let's celebrate with a hot fudge sundae!* In reality, a potato chip snack or a small sundae will not make or break your health. The same is true for following any Animal Diet Type. A *Lion* is not committing a crime by eating a slice of cake, nor is a *Giraffe* by eating pork roast. However, we are encouraging you to make long term eating and lifestyle changes according to your Diet Type. So this means that the *Lion* is not eating cake everyday, nor is the *Giraffe* eating pork roast every night. Once you have mastered your new eating habits and are starting to reap the benefits, think outside the food box when considering a reward. Let your reward be a trip to a sports store for new equipment or a new, smaller pair of pants. We have had many clients find rewards in the back of their closets in the form of an old favorite pair of jeans that fit again!

FIGURE 12-3 Lunch #1: A Typical American Lunch

FIGURE 12-4 Lunch #2: An Updated, Healthier Lunch

Adjusting your attitude and squelching your stress is necessary for good health!

If you are a high-stress person, your "wiring"—being prone to stress—is likely one of the causes of your poor health. Stress may increase your tendency to gain weight. People who react strongly to stressful situations increase the level of the hormone cortisol, which has many effects in the body, ranging from mobilizing energy stores for activity to raising blood pressure and ultimately increasing abdominal fat. We do need cortisol to wake us up in the morning. But cortisol levels should go down in the evening, helping us get a good night's sleep and restoring the body while resting. Proper balance of this hormone is essential. Anyone who feels like stress is ruining your life or that you are on the breaking point should get hormone levels (including cortisol) checked and visit with a Natural Medicine physician.

If you are often too busy during stressful times or feel pulled in many different directions with conflicting responsibilities, you may feel that your only option is to abandon your exercise and eating plans. Believe us, we know how that goes. It's a constant battle to stay on track. Sometimes you just want to say, "Just forget it. It's not worth it…pass the chips please, with extra sour cream!" Unfortunately, dropping your exercise and eating plans during times like these is exactly the opposite of what you should be doing. Exercise and a balanced eating plan will help keep your hormones and your overall body chemistry in the proper condition to be able to handle the stress being put on the body.

Do you need to learn to say _no_?!

It's one of the hardest words to say for many people. You may be completely stressed, fatigued, overweight, or suffering from chronic pain. But when someone asks you to do something, you just can't say "no" and when it comes to taking care of yourself... well, you don't. For instance, you take everyone else to the doctor but yourself. You make sure everyone eats a good dinner but you. You drive 10 hours a week to make sure the kids get to every sporting event the school offers, but you haven't gone for a jog in 10 years.

Answer these five questions to see how your health may be affected by concentrating on others before yourself.

1. Can you think of ten nice things you did for other people today but not one nice or nurturing thing for yourself?

2. Do you put in 100% effort at work but don't have the energy to cook yourself dinner when you get home?

3. Did you find excuses to not exercise? Or do you just put it off until the day is over and think you can do it tomorrow?

4. Do you continue to eat foods that make you feel sick, tired, or bloated?

5. Have you been told which foods are best for your weight loss or general health, but do not bother to actually start planning them in your meals?

If you are answering "yes," then step one is starting to respect yourself and your health needs. When you have learned to say "No" to junk food, excuses, and

those who abuse your time and energy you have gained the will power you need to succeed. Focusing on self improvement will not only boost your self respect, it will likely attract the respect and attention of others. Others will want to know your secret, and we want you to be the envy of your friends! In all seriousness though, many clients who have emotional eating problems have the tendency to fall "off the wagon," and let his or her life be controlled by the doings of others. In the end, they have very low self-respect and self-discipline. You have to allow yourself to change and be willing to confront the reactions of those who might not want you to change. Usually those people do not want you to change because they are on the taking end of what you are giving.

I feel it's all beyond my control.

If you are feeling powerless to change certain aspects of your life, you may need to consider therapy as a means to work through stressful relationships, obsessions, or unresolved issues.

Here are our Ten Tips for Tackling Stress:

1. Take time for yourself. This may require you to actually block time out of your schedule for enjoyable activities, but make it a priority.

2. Limit alcohol and caffeine to only occasional use. Do not use alcohol to cope with stress or caffeine for a rise in energy.

3. Laugh! Watch funny movies, read funny books, and don't let current events such as featured in the evening news or newspaper get you depressed. Jokes, stories, pictures can stimulate laughing, which in turn will relax the muscles, lower the blood pressure and stimulate the same stress-reduction hormones triggered by exercise.

4. Simplify. Make a list of your responsibilities, activities, and commitments. Decide which ones you can eliminate, delegate, reduce, or share.

5. Get a good night's sleep. Try to sleep at least seven hours per night. If you can't manage that, try sneaking in a short nap during the day.

6. Surround yourself with the ones you love. This could be making it a point to spend more quality time with your family. Or it could be playing with your favorite furry pet. We love our pets for the calming effect and joy they bring to our lives.

7. Take an occasional mental break. Think about something pleasant, take a quick walk outside to refocus your mind, or take five minutes for a yoga stretch.

8. Start that exercise program! Include strength and flexibility training along with aerobic activity. Teaming up with a personal trainer might be the best way to start.

9. Love your work. If you hate your job, work toward getting a different one.

10. If you are spiritual or religious, begin a regular practice as a means to reflect, relax, and reconnect. Read your scripture, meditate or pray, or join a scripture study group.

How do I know that I am eating according to my Diet Type?

Great question! First, consider your personal health goals. More energy? Weight Loss? Improved mental clarity? Remember that your goals should be reasonable. Losing 10 pounds in two days is not reasonable. But losing 10 pounds in a month may be. We feel the following points best represent a "successful" diet:

- You feel awesome after you eat a meal until the next meal.

- You feel great physical energy all day on most days.

- Your overall health is great.

- For a female, you have a normal regular menstrual cycle with no PMS.

- You are at your ideal weight.

- Your percent body fat is under 20% for females, under 15% for males.

- You have great mental energy with attention to detail and concentration.

If these details describe you, congratulations, it sounds like you are eating according to your Diet Type! You are eating the correct amount of food in the correct proportions. You may have many other signs that you are eating according to your Diet Type, such as a better mood or a remittance of symptoms from a medical condition. Look for these signs to guide you in your food choices. **Remember... when you eat great, you feel great!**

The New You!

We are excited for you! We hope that this book has encouraged you to take the steps toward improving your health. But this book is only a tool and it is up to you to use it. We feel passionate about the Hauser Diet because of the many people, including ourselves, who have been helped by following its principles. We know that not everyone is ready to make these changes. In addition, dietary habits are a difficult area for many people to change. Many of the principles discussed in this book involve thinking outside the box, moving out of the mainstream, and going against the grain. So we expect that some readers will need to take time in order to see how the Hauser Diet can fit into their lives. In this fast-paced age, people are always looking for the magic bullet and the quick fix. But remember, there is no pill, supplement, powder, or shake that can benefit the body like wholesome food. Your health may take longer to turn around than others. But our health is all that matters because without it, we do not have the means to better other areas of our life, or to enrich the lives of those we love. So be patient and understanding, yet diligent with your progress. We hope that you feel the time in your life to take charge is now!

Marion A Hauser, MS, RD

Nicole Baird

The Making of the Hauser Diet

A

B

H

Hauser, Marion, VI, XI, 2, 3, 13-14, 102, 106, 127, 308, 316, 344

Hauser, Ross, VII, 3, 119, 127, 308

Hauser Diet, *See also* Bear Diet Type™; Giraffe Diet Type™; Lion Diet Type™; Monkey Diet Type™; Otter Diet Type™
    development of, 3
    exercise endurance and intensity and, 18-19
    food equivalent chart, 35
    principles for achieving success on, 29-30
    succeeding on, 28-40
    typing of, 326-327

Hauser Diet Quiz, What Animal Are You?, 40

Hauser Diet Wellness Check List, 321-323, 331-334

Heart Check America, 329

Heart rate goals as percentage of maximum heart rate, 311

High-density lipoproteins (HDL) cholesterol levels, *See* cholesterol

Home exercise equipment, 307, 313

Homocysteine levels, 324

Hormones, 317
    cortisol, 11, 22-23, 99, 100, 342
    DHEA, 11, 23, 99-100
    effect of, on blood pH, 9-11
    estrogen, 10-11, 321
    progesterone, 9-11, 99
    rates of, in women, 322
    saliva testing for, 326
    sex, 328
    testosterone, 11, 99
    thyroid, 11

Hot flashes, 11

Hydrogenated fats, 31, 110, 111

Hypoallergenic diet, 23

Hypoglycemia, 11, 20-21, 23, 49, 60
    reactive, 20

Hypoimmunity, 23

I

Insulin, 20-22, 34, 42-43, 54, 73
    levels of, 326
    sensitivity of, 42

Insulin resistance, 21, 42, 54, 326

Irritable bowel syndrome, 23

J

Jams, 103

Juice(s), *See* fruit

Jump rope, 310, 313

L

Lab Tests, *See* Hauser Diet Wellness Check List

Labels. *See* Nutrition labels

Lactate absorption, 4

Legumes, 106, 242
    recipes for, 243-252

Life expectancy, changes in, 333-334

Lion Diet Type™, 3, 4, 42-52
    benefits of proper diet, 42
    beverages for, 45,
    blood pH and, 11, 42
    body building/weight lifting on, 50
    breakfast, 37, 45-49
    carbohydrates in, 43-44
    daily meal plan in, 45-49
    dinner, 45-49
    exercise on, 50
    FAQ myths and, 51
    fats in, 43, 45
    food choices on, 43-45
    Food Pyramid of, 43, 115
    fruits for, 44,
    insulin levels and, 43
    lunch, 45-49
    macronutrient breakdown on, 4, 36, 41, 42
    number of meals on, 51
    nuts for, 103
    obtaining optimal health on, 51-52
    problems in not following, 42-43
    protein for, 43
    recipes, *See* Chapter 9 and view rating scales
    salads, how to make a, 44-45
    soy for, 49-50
    succeeding on, 49-50
    vegetables for, 44
    weight loss on, 50-51

Lipid Profile, 322, 324, 325

Longevity, 334-336

Low-density lipoproteins (LDLs) cholesterol levels, *See* cholesterol

T

Tea, 45, 56, 68, 80, 92,114, 339, 340

Temperature, 13-18

Testicular cancer, 327

Testosterone, 11, 326

Tests, *See* Hauser Diet Wellness Check List

Thyroid, 11

Tofu, 112, 180, 192, 254

Trans-fats, *See* fats

Type II Diabetes, *See* Diabetes

U

Ultrafast CT scan of the heart (Heart Check America), 329, 335

Ultrafast oxidizers, 22-23

V

Vegetable-based meals and sides, 166
 recipes for, 167-179

Vegetables, 105-106
 equivalents, 35
 for Bears, 67
 for Giraffes, 91
 for Lions, 44,
 for Monkeys, 79
 for Otters, 55

Vegetarian/Vegan, 2, 3, 5, 6, 9, 21, 49, 51, 62-64, 78, 83, 87-88, 90, 97, 100, 107, 110

Venous blood pH, *See also* blood pH

Vital signs, 322

W

Walking, 308, 313

Water, 29-30, 114

Weather, blood pH and, 13-17

Weight loss
 for Bears, 73, 74
 for Giraffes, 97-98
 for Lions, 50-51
 for Monkeys, 85-86
 for Otters, 61
 water and, 29-30

Whole grains, 106-107

Women,
 body fat of, 306
 bone density testing for, 328-329
 cancer markers for, 328
 fat utilization by, 5, 6
 hormone rates in, 322
 osteoporosis and, 310
 risk of heart disease, 325

X

Xylitol, 118, 281

My Hauser Diet Notes

My Hauser Diet Notes

My Hauser Diet Notes

Marion A. Hauser, M.S., R.D.

Marion A. Hauser, M.S., R.D., CEO of Caring Medical and Rehabilitation Services, a comprehensive Natural Medicine clinic in Oak Park, IL and owner of Beulah Land Nutritionals, brings a unique approach to diet and nutrition that is scientific, yet practical for everyone. As a busy executive, registered dietitian, food enthusiast and avid athlete, Marion combines her common sense organizational skills with food science, human physiology, and no-nonsense food preparation skills in a unique approach to diet and wellness called *The Hauser Diet™: A Fresh Look at Healthy Living*. This book will really get you thinking, "I can do this—it makes sense."

Nicole M. Baird, C.H.F.P.

Nicole M. Baird is a Certified Holistic Fitness Practitioner, manager of Beulah Land Nutritionals, and Administrative Team Leader of Caring Medical. She combines her extensive knowledge of nutraceuticals, and love for food and exercise with her disdain for the chemical food jungle that we are immersed in to help the reader make wiser food, exercise, and supplement choices. The concepts presented in this book are designed to keep you active for life, while being practical, easy, and fun!

Ross A. Hauser, M.D.

Ross Hauser, M.D. is the Medical Director of Caring Medical and Rehabilitation Services in Oak Park, IL, and renown Prolotherapist and Natural Medicine Specialist, who is responsible for spurring on the concept of Diet Typing and the Hauser Diet principles. Not satisfied with the traditional approach to wellness for his patients, he collaborated with his registered dietitian wife and business partner, Marion, to develop an objective method for determining how each person should eat. You'll find many success stories from the patients at Caring Medical described with this book.

● ● ●

We have all combined our knowledge, skills, and experiences to bring you

The Hauser Diet™: A Fresh Look at Healthy Living.

Happy reading and we hope this book helps you keep active for life!